Ray Tracing in CUDA and DXR

An Introduction

Fabio Suriano

Apress®

Ray Tracing in CUDA and DXR: An Introduction

Fabio Suriano
ROMA, Italy

ISBN-13 (pbk): 979-8-8688-1690-1 ISBN-13 (electronic): 979-8-8688-1691-8
https://doi.org/10.1007/979-8-8688-1691-8

Copyright © 2025 by Fabio Suriano

This work is subject to copyright. All rights are reserved by the Publisher, whether the whole or part of the material is concerned, specifically the rights of translation, reprinting, reuse of illustrations, recitation, broadcasting, reproduction on microfilms or in any other physical way, and transmission or information storage and retrieval, electronic adaptation, computer software, or by similar or dissimilar methodology now known or hereafter developed.

Trademarked names, logos, and images may appear in this book. Rather than use a trademark symbol with every occurrence of a trademarked name, logo, or image we use the names, logos, and images only in an editorial fashion and to the benefit of the trademark owner, with no intention of infringement of the trademark.

The use in this publication of trade names, trademarks, service marks, and similar terms, even if they are not identified as such, is not to be taken as an expression of opinion as to whether or not they are subject to proprietary rights.

While the advice and information in this book are believed to be true and accurate at the date of publication, neither the authors nor the editors nor the publisher can accept any legal responsibility for any errors or omissions that may be made. The publisher makes no warranty, express or implied, with respect to the material contained herein.

    Managing Director, Apress Media LLC: Welmoed Spahr
    Acquisitions Editor: Spandana Chatterjee
    Desk Editor: James Markham
    Editorial Project Manager: Gryffin Winkler

Cover designed by eStudioCalamar

Cover Image by Artur Pawlak from Pixabay

Distributed to the book trade worldwide by Springer Science+Business Media New York, 1 New York Plaza, New York, NY 10004. Phone 1-800-SPRINGER, fax (201) 348-4505, e-mail orders-ny@springer-sbm.com, or visit www.springeronline.com. Apress Media, LLC is a Delaware LLC and the sole member (owner) is Springer Science + Business Media Finance Inc (SSBM Finance Inc). SSBM Finance Inc is a **Delaware** corporation.

For information on translations, please e-mail booktranslations@springernature.com; for reprint, paperback, or audio rights, please e-mail bookpermissions@springernature.com.

Apress titles may be purchased in bulk for academic, corporate, or promotional use. eBook versions and licenses are also available for most titles. For more information, reference our Print and eBook Bulk Sales web page at http://www.apress.com/bulk-sales.

Any source code or other supplementary material referenced by the author in this book is available to readers on GitHub. For more detailed information, please visit https://www.apress.com/gp/services/source-code.

If disposing of this product, please recycle the paper

To my daughter, Lavinia, whose presence brings light and meaning to every page I write.

To Roberta, my companion and love, for her patience and belief in me, and Ginevra, her wonderful daughter, for welcoming me into her life with kindness.

To Maria Grazia, my ex-wife and dear friend, for the kindness, patience, and support that have endured beyond change.

To Ombretta and Olga, Lavinia's beloved dogs and, in every way, mine too, for their quiet company and unconditional affection.

To my parents, who gave me the gift of education.

To all of you, thank you for your patience and understanding. Without it, this book could not have been finished.

Table of Contents

About the Author xi

About the Technical Reviewer xiii

Acknowledgments xv

Chapter 1: Brief History of Modern GPUs 1

    Technical Requirements 2

    GPU Evolution 101 3

    What Is a CUDA Core? 7

    What Happens Internally? 8

    How GPU and CPU Share Resources 8

    Key Analogy 9

    GPU vs. CPU: What's the Difference? 9

    Anatomy of a Modern GPU 13

    How the Hardware Executes a Kernel 20

    The Turing Architecture 22

    Ada Lovelace Architecture (2022: GeForce RTX 40 series) 24

    Hopper Architecture (2022: NVIDIA H100, Datacenter AI GPU) 24

        Blackwell Architecture (2024/2025: Next-Gen AI GPU, e.g., B100/B200) 25

    Big Picture (Ada, Hopper, and Blackwell) 26

    RT Core 26

    Real-Time Ray Tracing Is Finally Here 28

    A Quick Look at Ray Tracing Pipeline 30

    Summary 34

    Questions 35

    Further Reading 36

TABLE OF CONTENTS

Chapter 2: Know Your Hardware: The Streaming Multiprocessor 37

Technical Requirements... 37

How to Find the Code in Visual Studio 38

The Streaming Multiprocessor.. 38

Warp Scheduler and Dispatch Unit 40

Shared Memory, C-Cache, and I-Cache.. 41

    Constants Cache (C-Cache) 47

    Instruction Cache (I-Cache) 48

The Compute Units or Cores 48

Summary... 49

Questions 50

Further Reading 51

Chapter 3: GPGPU Ray Tracing vs. DXR Ray Tracing Approaches 53

Technical Requirements... 53

Ray Tracing in Compute 54

Camera Model Definition... 56

Ray Definition.. 59

Ray-Sphere Intersection 60

Ray Casting in CUDA 64

DXR and the New Shader Stages in Practice.. 67

The TraceRay() New HLSL Function 71

Compute-Based Ray Tracing vs. DXR-Based Ray Tracing... 72

Summary... 73

Questions 74

Further Reading 74

Chapter 4: Enter the Turing Microarchitecture 75

Understanding Turing GPUs... 76

The New RT Cores.. 78

    An In-Depth Analysis of BLAS and TLAS 80

Evolving NVIDIA Architectures and the Future of Real-Time Graphics 83

Summary	83
Questions	84
Further Reading	85

Chapter 5: Ray Tracing Techniques 87

Technical Requirements	88
Sampling Strategies to Reduce Aliasing	88
Understanding Supersampling	89
Supersampling in DXR	95
Understanding Adaptive Supersampling	97
Understanding Stochastic Ray Tracing	101
Understanding Depth of Field	103
Understanding Motion Blur	110
Multi-Hit Ray Tracing for Transparent Objects in DXR	115
Summary	120
Questions	122
Further Reading	122

Chapter 6: Ray and Camera Model Definitions 123

Technical Requirements	124
Defining Math Symbols and Ray Tracing Terminology	124
The Ray-Tracing Camera Model	125
Defining Ray and Basic Lighting	128
Understanding Basic Lighting	130
Understanding Reflection	133
What's Next?	136
Understanding Refraction and Fresnel	137
Understanding Snell's Law	140
Understanding Total Internal Reflection	143
Summary	145
Questions	146
Further Reading	147

TABLE OF CONTENTS

Chapter 7: Basic Ray-Primitive Intersection Techniques 149

Technical Requirements 150
Understanding Ray-Sphere Intersection 150
    Understanding the Analytic Solution 150
    Understanding the Geometric Solution 155
Understanding Ray-Plane Intersection 159
Understanding Ray-Quad Intersection 161
    Understanding the Containment Test 164
Understanding Ray-Triangle Intersection 165
    Understanding Barycentric Coordinates 169
    Understanding Möller-Trumbore Algorithm 177
Floating-Point Precision/Accuracy Issues and How to Account for Them 182
Putting It All Together: A Basic and Simple C++ Interface to Manage Objects 186
Summary 187
Questions 188
Further Reading 189

Chapter 8: The Rendering Equation and Monte Carlo Integration 191

Technical Requirements 192
Understanding the Rendering Equation 193
Understanding the Anatomy of the Rendering Equation 196
Understanding the Most Common BRDFs 198
"Solving" the Rendering Equation 201
Hit-or-Miss Monte Carlo Integration 203
Understanding Monte Carlo Integration (Sample Mean Approach) 208
Understanding Importance Sampling: Variance Reduction 218
A Quick Introduction to Variance 219
Importance Sampling 220
The Inverse Transform Sampling Method 224
Estimating the Rendering Equation 228
Understanding Stratified Sampling 230

Understanding Quasi-Monte Carlo (QMC) Methods 233
Summary 237
Questions 238
Further Reading 238

Chapter 9: DirectX 12 and Real-Time Ray Tracing in DXR 241

Technical Requirements 242
DirectX 12 Setup Under Visual Studio 2022 242
DirectX 12 Boilerplate Initialization Code 247
Initializing the Pipeline 249
Your First Rendering Window and the Swap-Chain 258
Understanding the Frame Resources Creation 262
Understanding DX12 Descriptors Management and Root Signatures 268
Understanding GPU Resources Allocation Strategies in D3D12 272
Understanding Root Signature 275
Understanding CPU-GPU Synchronization and Command Lists 282
DirectX Ray Tracing (DXR) New Structures and Shader Stages 288
Understanding the New Shader Stages and Shader Loading 293
DirectX Ray Tracing (DXR) API Initialization Code 297
Create Ray Tracing Pipeline State Object 297
Create Shader Table 301
    Hit-Group Shader Table Construction 306
Understanding RaySampleFramework Structure 308
    Diagram Description 310
    Creating a Ray_Sample and Why the Abstract Renderer Matters 312
    What a Ray_Sample Is 312
    A Minimal Concrete Sample 312
    Integrating with the Win32 Driver 314
    Picking a Backend (3D Graphics API) (Compile Time or Runtime) 315
    Why an Abstract Renderer Interface Is the Right Design 316

Let's Ray Trace: Whitted Ray Tracing in DXR	317
DirectX Raytracing	319
Proposed Geometry Organization (Whitted Ray Tracing)	325
Why This Layout Works Well for Whitted	327
Summary	328
Questions	328
Further Reading	329

Chapter 10: Path Tracing: Global Illumination 331

Technical Requirements	332
Path Tracing: Global Illumination	332
Path Tracing in CUDA	339
Add Tone Mapping and Gamma Correction to Your Ray Tracer	349
Hybrid Rendering Pipelines	353
Adding Monte Carlo Importance Sampling to Your Path Tracer	354
Choosing the Right PDF	354
Russian Roulette and Unbiased Rendering	356
Performance Tools and Best Practices	356
Summary	358
Questions	358
Further Reading	359

Index 361

About the Author

Fabio Suriano is a senior graphics programmer at LightFury Games, specializing in real-time rendering and low-level graphics systems. His expertise spans advanced rendering techniques, path tracing, and hardware-conscious programming on both CPU and GPU architectures.

Prior to joining LightFury, Fabio worked on Steel Seed at Storm in a Teacup, where he contributed to cutting-edge graphics features. He also represented the studio at Codemotion Rome 2017, delivering a technical talk on realistic FFT-based ocean simulation.

Driven by performance, precision, and visual fidelity, Fabio continues to explore the intersection of rendering algorithms and system-level efficiency in game development.

About the Technical Reviewer

Sultana Begum is a semiconductor product management expert and AI technology enthusiast with more than 12 years of experience at Intel and Accenture. She is a quantum computing enthusiast with a deep understanding of quantum mechanics and physics principles of qubits and quantum dots. She is the lead author of the book *Competitive Semiconductor Product Management*. Sultana has held critical roles in technical product marketing and hardware and software product management to gain broad and deep-rooted expertise in the semiconductor technology industry. With a keen eye for strategic thinking, her expertise spreads widely across semiconductor design development to define and execute a competitive AI product strategy, with hands-on experience in launching multiple software and hardware products.

Sultana holds both bachelor's and master's degrees in electronics, an MBA in product management, and Stanford LEAD Executive Management Education from Stanford University.

Acknowledgments

I am sincerely grateful to my editor for the patience and flexibility that allowed me the time I needed to complete this book. Your understanding and guidance have been invaluable.

CHAPTER 1

Brief History of Modern GPUs

There was a time, in the realm of real-time 3D graphics, where things were going in a slightly different way than what we are used to today. We didn't even have hardware-accelerated graphics. Old, 3D-rendered graphics were pretty much coded in software. Every step that nowadays is performed by the graphics processing unit (GPU) was entirely implemented in C or, worse, in assembly. Geometry was still represented through vertices, and the 3D math-related arithmetic, vectors, and matrices were of course the same. The only difference was that, for example, all the modules that were meant to render and shade the geometry were a mixture of C routines for the screen space mesh projection, lines drawing, polygon filling, and software texture mapping, just to mention a few. Obviously, no hardware Z-buffer was present; therefore, there was something called the *painter algorithm*, which was sorting all the objects in a back-to-front fashion (much like a real painter does when paint on a canvas) before submitting them for rendering. In this way, proper sorting order was achieved, and the scene was rendered correctly. The technique of rendering objects in the 3D world was called *rasterization*. However, rasterization was not the only technique that was possible for rendering a 3D scene. There was another approach called *ray tracing*.

Ray tracing used a *ray* as the main primitive for rendering the scene. A ray represented an actual physical ray of light that was traveling in the scene and that was hitting objects. Every time a ray hit an object, the hit-point on that object surface was rendered, or to be more precise, it was given a color, until all the objects in the scene where rendered. Unfortunately, despite that ray tracing was an elegant and natural way of solving the problem of rendering a 3D scene, it was proven to be expensive.

CHAPTER 1   BRIEF HISTORY OF MODERN GPUS

Ray tracing algorithmic complexity, if we assume a screen resolution of NxN pixels, is a squared complexity O(n2). That complexity doesn't scale well because the resolution of the rendered image keeps growing in size. Not to mention, we might be doing a hell of a lot more computations for each rendered pixel.

It was clear that rasterization was definitely the way to go and that ray tracing was going to be a luxury that only researchers (and, eventually, the movie industry) were actually going to deal with in the years to come.

The following topics will be covered in this chapter:

- Learn how the GPUs evolved through time
- Learn the fundamental differences between a GPU and a CPU
- Learn what a modern GPU looks like in terms of its architecture and how compute-based solutions greatly helped in offloading the CPU
- Learn about the crucial differences in the Turing GPU architecture
- Learn about the possibilities that this new technology offers for the future of computer graphics and real-time rendering engines

Technical Requirements

The following tools are required before we get started:

- Visual Studio 2022 Community
- Cuda Toolkit 13.0.1
- Windows 10 RS5 update

This chapter is for anyone who wants to learn about the evolution of graphics hardware and how it evolved to meet the demand in increasing visual quality for the game industry. It starts by showing the main architectural differences between GPUs and CPUs to better highlight how and why programmers should resort to compute-based solutions to offload the CPU when needed. A ray tracing case study is presented to show how the code for a basic CUDA kernel could be written.

CHAPTER 1 BRIEF HISTORY OF MODERN GPUS

GPU Evolution 101

The first company that truly started the real-time rendering revolution was NVIDIA when it, in October 1999, released the first graphics card featuring hardware transforms and lighting (T&L). This graphics accelerator was the GeForce 256 that, like its predecessor RIVA TNT, was capable of rendering pixel at a fast rate thanks to several pixel pipelines.

With the addition of lighting and a transformation calculation in hardware, it was finally possible to offload the CPU from performing those duties and devote its power to things like realistic physics, frustum culling, and so on. In fact, geometry transformation and lighting were previously handled by the CPU, and you can easily imagine that as soon as the number and geometric complexity of 3D models in a scene grew past a certain point, the workload on the CPU was going to be too high and prohibitive to keep up with that degree of realism. But higher realism meant more geometry with more polygons (and therefore more detail) and obviously nice lighting. So, the lighting calculations were performed per vertex by calculating the point to light vector ($\vec{L}$) (for the diffuse contribution) and the point to camera vector ($\vec{V}$) (for the specular contribution). Those two different vectors were calculated, along with their length, in hardware.

$$\vec{L} = \begin{pmatrix} l_x \\ l_y \\ l_z \end{pmatrix} - \begin{pmatrix} p_x \\ p_y \\ p_z \end{pmatrix}$$

$$\vec{V} = \begin{pmatrix} l_x \\ l_y \\ l_z \end{pmatrix} - \begin{pmatrix} e_x \\ e_y \\ e_z \end{pmatrix}$$

l and **e** represent the light position and the eye (camera) position in a given space (can be world space or view/camera space, depending in what space we want the lighting to be performed).

Figure 1-1 shows the GeForce 256 GPU in all its glory.

CHAPTER 1 BRIEF HISTORY OF MODERN GPUS

Figure 1-1. NVIDIA GeForce 256

The lighting was performed with a simple Blinn-Phong model, which has proven to be very cheap to implement while giving outstanding results for that time.

But 3D games and the game industry itself were evolving so fast that the demand for more realism and visual fidelity was becoming even more important.

At some point, the possibility to have more control on some specific stages of the graphics pipeline became a key factor to create even more realistic graphics. This goal was achieved by giving the programmers the ability to program how the vertices and the pixels (or fragments) were processed. With the addition of vertex shaders and pixel

CHAPTER 1 BRIEF HISTORY OF MODERN GPUS

shaders, a new era was born. The graphics programmers had a lot more control over how the vertices and the pixel were processed.

This was an important milestone because it laid the foundation for modern GPUs (see Figure 1-2).

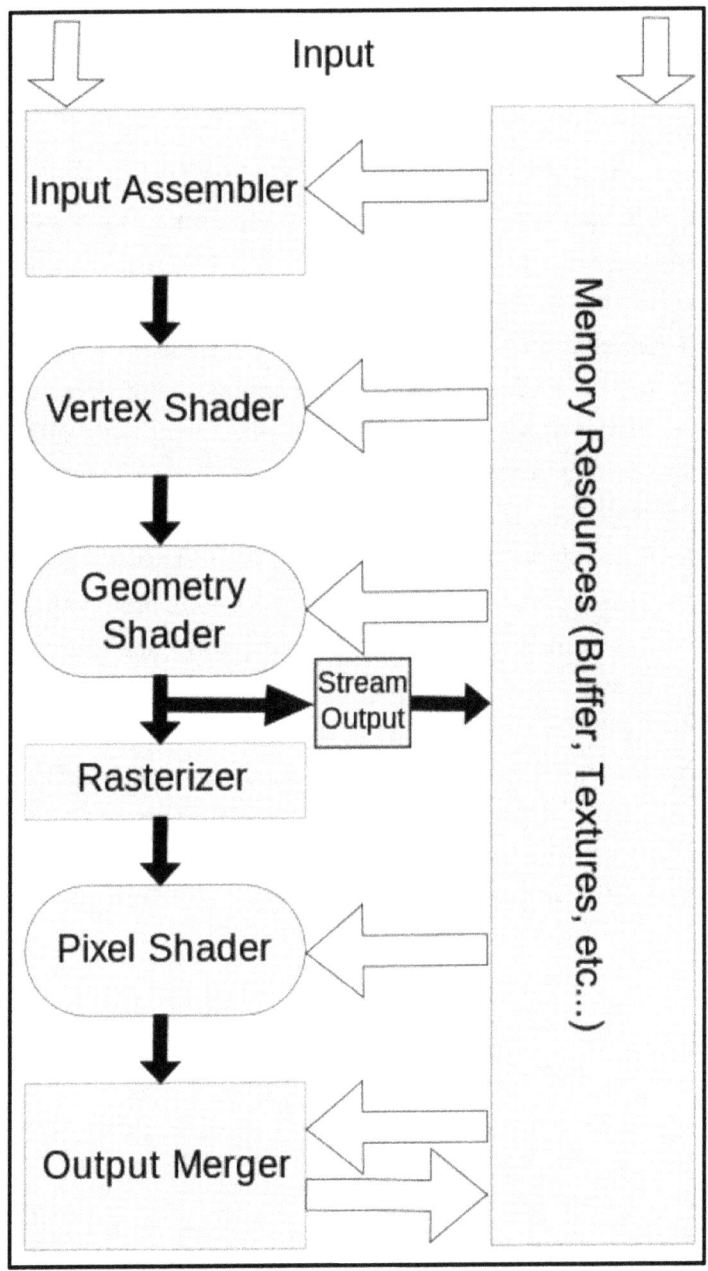

Figure 1-2. D3D graphics pipeline

As shown in Figure 1-2, later in the development additional programmable stages were added, namely, the geometry shader stage and the stream output path, that allowed programming on a per-primitive basis. The geometry shader was running on each triangle, line, and in general polygon after the vertex shader stage. The stream output was added to give the possibility to output on a generic buffer (e.g., a vertex buffer bound to the stream output stage) instead of the main color buffer or a render target. This created the ability to implement techniques like the so-called render to vertex buffer, etc.

The pipeline shown in Figure 1-2 shows how the D3D API was managing each stage. The stages depicted in the rounded boxes are the programmable ones, while the ones in the squared boxes are fixed function stages.

In today's graphics chips, the desktop graphics pipeline and its stages (considering the addition of the tessellation stage too) is still taking a small portion of the die area, while the majority, instead, is dedicated to the streaming multiprocessors (SMs). Modern GPUs are made of clusters of compute units; each compute unit is a small *arithmetic logic unit* (ALU) that is able to perform operations on integers and floating-point numbers. Each SM is an actual cluster of compute units that, for example, are called CUDA cores if we refer to the NVIDIA implementation specifically.

In this book, we will present examples in CUDA, sticking pretty much to NVIDIA hardware because at the time of this writing that is the only hardware architecture that, in later chapters, will allow us to implement real-time ray tracing in hardware. AMD graphics cards will also support DirectX Raytracing (DXR) with the so-called NAVI architecture, but until then we have to stick mostly to the NVIDIA side of things. Moreover, for cross-platform solutions, we have Vulkan and Apple's Metal for MacOS/iOS development.

Figure 1-3 shows what an SM looks like in terms of its architecture.

CHAPTER 1 BRIEF HISTORY OF MODERN GPUS

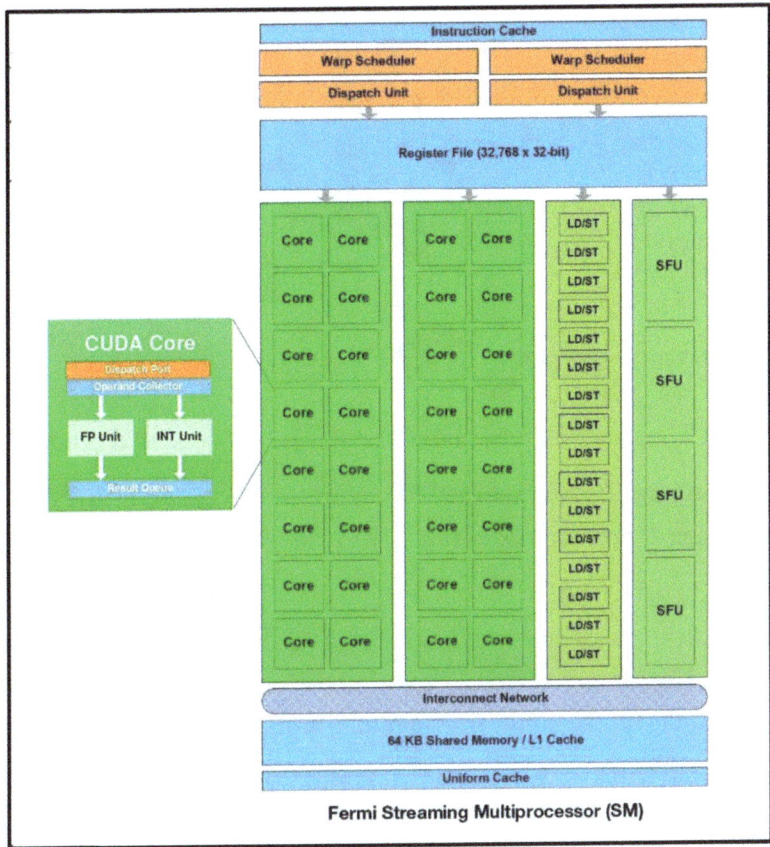

Figure 1-3. *Fermi's streaming multiprocessor*

We are showing the NVIDIA Fermi architecture as an example, but there is not much difference in the way modern GPU are made from vendor to vendor. Let's now take a look at the differences between a GPU and a CPU.

What Is a CUDA Core?

A CUDA core is NVIDIA's term for the basic execution unit inside its GPUs. You can think of it like a CPU core, but much simpler and designed for massively parallel workloads.

- **A CPU core is complex**: It can handle branching, instruction scheduling, caching, and multiple types of operations.

CHAPTER 1   BRIEF HISTORY OF MODERN GPUS

- **A CUDA core is lightweight**: It mainly executes arithmetic and logic operations (e.g., additions, multiplications) very efficiently but relies on the GPU architecture to handle scheduling, memory, and instruction distribution.

So, a single CUDA core is not powerful by itself, but GPUs pack in thousands of them and run them in parallel.

What Happens Internally?

Inside the GPU, CUDA cores are grouped and organized for parallel execution:

- **Streaming multiprocessors**: CUDA cores are bundled into SMs. Each SM may contain dozens of CUDA cores along with shared memory, registers, and control logic.

- **Warps**: Threads are grouped into sets of 32 called *warps*. A warp executes the same instruction simultaneously across different CUDA cores (SIMT model: *single instruction, multiple threads*).

- **Instruction execution**: The GPU scheduler decides which warp to run on which SM. Within an SM, each CUDA core executes one thread of that warp.

This is why GPUs are so efficient at repetitive, parallel tasks like matrix multiplications in deep learning or graphics rendering.

How GPU and CPU Share Resources

The CPU and GPU are distinct processors, but they cooperate:

- **Control vs. execution**:
    - The CPU handles control-heavy, sequential tasks and launches "kernels" (GPU programs).
    - The GPU executes those kernels in parallel across thousands of threads.

- **Memory sharing**:
    - Traditionally, the CPU has its own system memory (RAM) and the GPU has VRAM. Data must be transferred across the PCIe bus, which can be a bottleneck.
    - Modern tech like Unified Memory (CUDA Unified Virtual Addressing) and NVLink reduce this bottleneck by allowing CPU and GPU to share memory more directly.
- **Workload division**:
    - **CPU**: This is good for tasks with lots of branching logic or low parallelism.
    - **GPU**: This is best for tasks that can be split into thousands of independent pieces (linear algebra, physics simulation, image processing).

Key Analogy

Think of it like this:

- The CPU is a manager with a few very skilled workers (cores) who can handle many types of tasks carefully.
- The GPU is a massive factory floor with thousands of simpler workers (CUDA cores), each doing small, repetitive tasks in sync.
- The manager (CPU) tells the factory (GPU) what to do, sends in the raw materials (data), and collects the finished products (results).

GPU vs. CPU: What's the Difference?

What is important to understand now are the main differences between a CPU and a GPU in terms of their architecture. We will not go in great detail, because that is beyond the scope of this book. But we will briefly describe what the main points are in the construction of a CPU and a GPU.

CHAPTER 1   BRIEF HISTORY OF MODERN GPUS

- A central processing unit (CPU) is a chip that is mainly designed for general-purpose tasks that need to be solved quickly. In fact, the main architectural design aspect of a CPU is related to the latency minimization.

- A graphics processing unit (GPU) is a specialized chip that is mainly designed to accomplish graphics task, such as processing a massive number of pixels/tasks in a given amount of time. But that's not the only design aspect behind a modern GPU. In fact, a GPU can handle a massive amount of computation in a given amount of time and those calculations don't have to be strictly graphics tasks.

The main design choice that motivates the architecture of a GPU is throughput. What matters the most, in this case, is how many computations we can get done per second rather than how long it will take to finish a given computation (which is more relevant for a CPU instead). In other words, CPUs are optimized to minimize latency, and GPUs are optimized to maximize throughput.

Now the other question is how a CPU and a GPU can achieve their main design goals? We will start by analyzing the architecture of a typical modern CPU. A modern CPU is comprised of a certain number of physical cores (e.g., up to 32 with AMD Threadripper processors for example and something around 24 cores for the intel solutions). Each core in a modern processor can run two hardware threads, so it's common to talk about logical cores when we consider the threads that each core can manage. So, a n-core processor can handle 2n hardware threads; therefore, it will have 2n logical cores.

So, what is the main problem for what that concern a processor? Well, to perform computation, a CPU needs to have the data ready in its registers. Otherwise, it will be impossible to execute any instruction on them. Data as well as the program that will run on the CPU is normally stored in main RAM, which is actually the slowest memory.

Let's see how this can have an impact on latency:

> *Latency is defined as the time that passes since the data is accessed by issuing, for example, a memory read instruction (typically called load instruction) operation and the time in which that same data it is actually retrieved and ready to be used in the CPU registers. Latency is measured in terms of clock cycles (or, in short, just cycles).*

Any time we ask for a data, being reading that data or writing it, there is a given time that has to pass before that data is available to us and, more precisely, available in the CPU registers. This time, called *latency*, will quickly add up to the total execution time of your program and, in the worst case, will cause your program to perform considerably worse with respect to the optimal case. Of course, we have to profile first to be sure that our program suffers a latency problem and avoid making assumptions with no real data at hand.

To reduce the impact that latency has on a typical program execution time, a hierarchy of memories is added along with the RAM itself. Those memories are smaller and faster than the main RAM and are generally called *caches*. A modern computer will feature up to three cache levels, namely, L1, L2, and L3 caches.

- L1 Cache: First-level cache (smallest size). There is one such memory for each core in a given CPU.
- L2 Cache: Second-level cache (medium size).
- L3 Cache: Third-level cache (larger size).

We can consider the CPU registers to be the fastest "memory" from which we can read. In fact, we can consider the cost to be practically around 0 clock cycles.

To have a better idea of the speed related to the different cache levels in a computer, see Figure 1-4.

CHAPTER 1   BRIEF HISTORY OF MODERN GPUS

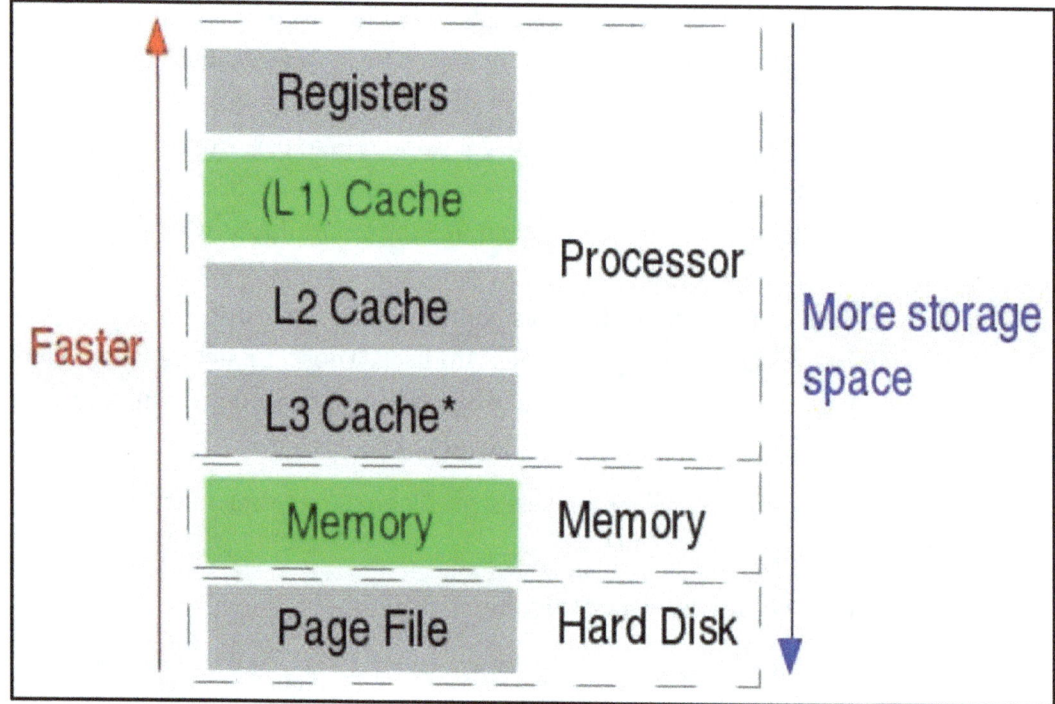

Figure 1-4. *Memory hierarchy. From the physical disk to the processor registers*

The CPU is clearly designed to execute a task in the least amount of time, and it does so by employing a cache hierarchy on top of the main RAM. Every time that data is read from main memory, it gets also cached. Subsequent reads of the same data will happen from cache, and therefore, the data will be retrieved much faster. The number of cycles required to *load* a data from a, for example, L1 cache is going to be around 3/4 clock cycles, which is way faster than RAM, which is about 200/300 clock cycles instead.

However, the aforementioned latency values can change from one architecture to another, but the basic principles stay the same.

Moreover, we will see that in the context of GPU programming, the concepts related to memories and latency are pretty much the same, but with a substantial difference. This difference lies in the context in which we apply them. Now that we understand the difference between a CPU and a GPU, let's dive a little deeper into GPUs to understand their anatomy.

Anatomy of a Modern GPU

We've already mentioned that a GPU is optimized for throughput. But how this is achieved, and what are the needs in this case?

Let's start by saying how we can cope with a problem like this one: we need to process thousands of pixels in a given amount of time. Therefore, in this case we don't care how long it will take to process a single pixel but, rather, how many pixels we can process at once.

The GPU architecture solves this problem by employing several compute units (or in the NVIDIA case CUDA cores) and a scheduler that is able to dispatch and manage thousands and thousands of threads running on those compute units.

Refer to Figure 1-3 to get an idea of how an SM is organized.

The SM warp scheduler will group threads in groups of 32 threads (on NVIDIA cards) called *warps* or 64 threads (on AMD cards) called *wavefronts*. Therefore, a warp/wavefront is the smallest unit of execution at any one time.

Let's get practical now and take a look at the following C code that will go through a grid of pixels with a double for loop:

```c
const int N = 512;
for(int y=0;y<N;++y)
{
   for(int x=0;x<N;++x)
   {
      //do something and produce some color
      //read/modify and store some color
      ColorBuffer[x+y*512] += <some color>;
   }
}
```

CHAPTER 1   BRIEF HISTORY OF MODERN GPUS

See Figure 1-5 for a visual and richer representation of the previous loop.

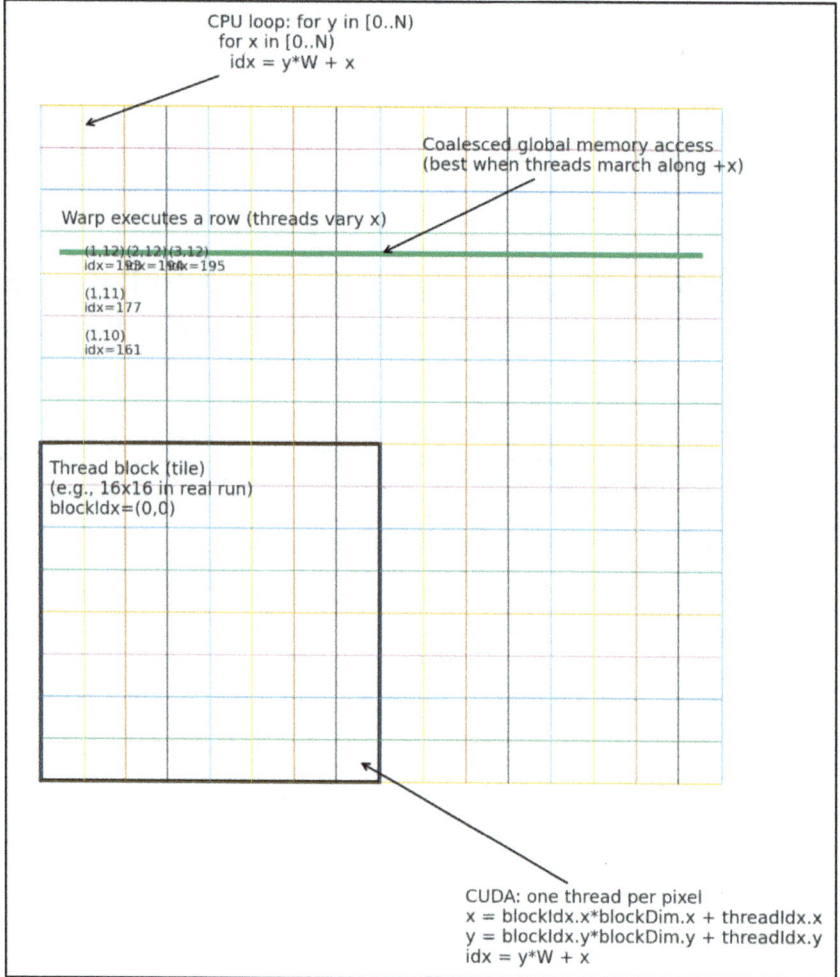

Figure 1-5. A grid of pixels

What are the pros and cons of processing a grid of pixels in this way?
Pros:

- We access the grid in row major fashion. This access pattern is cache friendly and therefore the fastest way to access contiguous memory. This happens because the hardware is designed to speculatively detect linear memory access patterns.

Cons:

- We have to loop through each pixel one at a time in a serial fashion, meaning that for an N*N grid of pixels, if N grows big, we get complexity. We waste a lot of CPU execution time as soon as the loop dimension grows quite significantly.

The hardware is designed to speculatively detect linear memory access patterns. Therefore, linear arrays will always be the preferred choice when it comes to memory latency optimization. (Research coalesced memory access or memory coalescing for an in-depth description.)

Is there a better way to speed up that double for loop? Wouldn't be cool if we could subdivide the computation domain in tiles of a given size and execute several smaller for loops for each tile in parallel? The answer to this question is of course yes! We can achieve this by parallelizing our squared domain, assigning a thread to each pixel contained in each tile.

If we have a color buffer represented by a 2D grid and each element in this grid represents one pixel, we could run a parallel for that will process several tiles in parallel. Or, much better, we could map each and every pixel to a thread! We can achieve this very easily in CUDA, as we will see later in the chapter, and the benefits in terms of gained efficiency will be worth the effort.

See Figure 1-6.

CHAPTER 1   BRIEF HISTORY OF MODERN GPUS

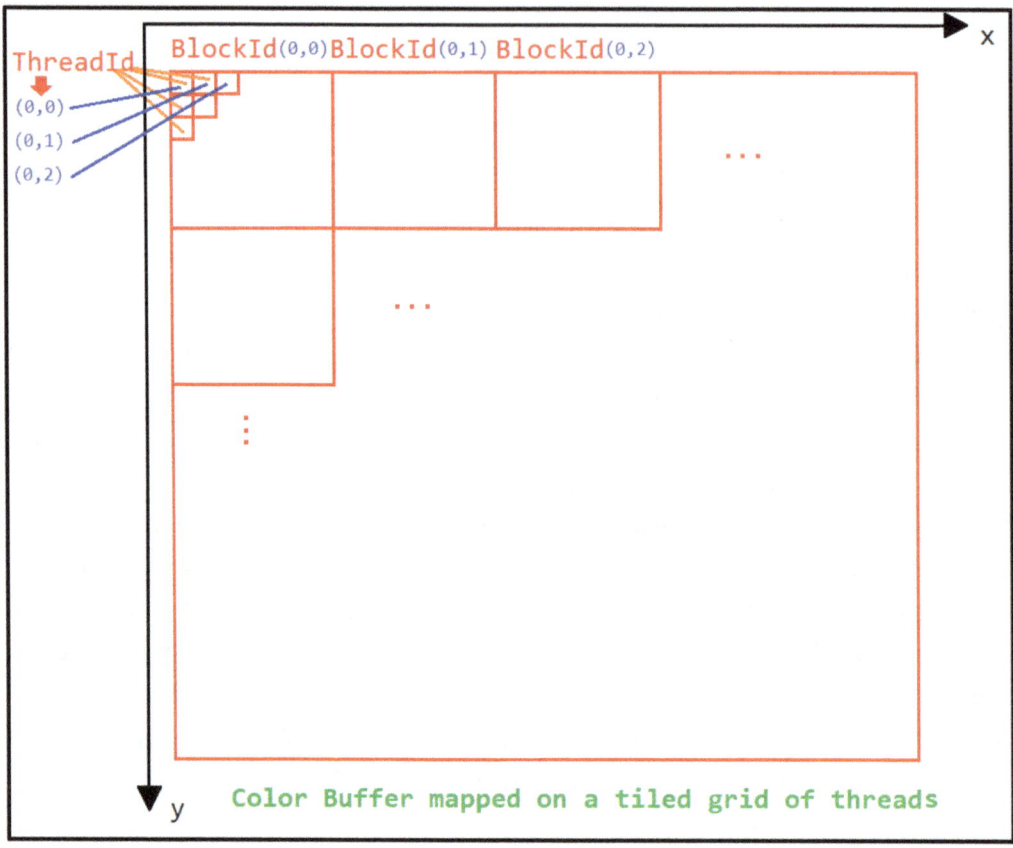

Figure 1-6. *Color buffer represented by a two-dimensional pixel grid subdivided in tiles*

This parallel for loop pattern can be implemented on the CPU by creating as many threads as there are CPU logical cores. Then, let those threads pick tiles from a given queue until the queue is completely empty.

So, a better way is to harness the power of the GPU. But how?

We can write a special program called a *kernel* that will run solely on the GPU. We will launch this kernel from the CPU, and we can tell the GPU exactly how many threads we want to launch given our color buffer size (which is basically our computation domain).

> *All the GPU code, with the exception of the DirectX Ray Tracing (DXR) code, will be presented in CUDA.*

Here is how that same double for loop can be parallelized in CUDA, by completely removing the double for loop:

```
//the keyword __global__ instructs the CUDA compiler that this function is
the entry point of our kernel
__global__ void ParallelFor(const int N,float* ColorBuffer)
{
int x = blockIdx.x*blockDim.x + threadIdx.x;
int y = blockIdx.y*blockDim.y + threadIdx.y;
//checks whether we are inside the color buffer bounds.
//If not, just return
if(x > N || y > N)
{
    return;
}

//We access the linear ColorBuffer storing each color component separately
(we could have a float3 color buffer //for a more compact/cleaner solution)
int offset = (x + y*N)*3;
float3 Color = float3(0.f,0.f,0.f);

//Do some computations here to produce a Color for each pixel (It could
be a lit pixel, or the color resulting from a specific image processing
algorithm etc.) and then store it in our ColorBuffer

//Store the results of your computations
ColorBuffer[offset] = Color.x;
ColorBuffer[offset+1] = Color.y;
ColorBuffer[offset+2] = Color.z;
}
```

Each thread is assigned with a thread ID from the GPU, and each block will represent one of our tiles. To summarize, those are the built-in CUDA types used to identify threads and blocks of threads:

- **threaIdx**: An integer that represents a thread index in a given block (can be *1-2-3 dimensional*). Therefore, if a block is mapped on a 2D computation domain and is 8x8 in size, that means that we will end up having 64 threads in that block and threaIdx will be in [0,8) range in both the **x** and **y** dimension of the block (provided that our domain is a 2D one).

CHAPTER 1   BRIEF HISTORY OF MODERN GPUS

- **blockIdx**: An integer identify a block index (can be 1-2-3 dimensional and is computed as N/blockDim).

- **blockDim**: An integer that represents the size of a given block (can be 1-2-3 dimensional and is determined at kernel launch time depending on how the kernel will perform). Profiling will help in deciding the right block size for your kernel. In the case of a block with 8x8 threads total, BlockDim will be equal to 8 in both the **x** and **y** dimension.

The main advantage here is that we have the luxury to spawn a thread for each and every pixel of our color buffer! Not bad, huh? Plus, all the threads/pixel will be processed in parallel with no synchronization required between them. We can achieve full parallelism due to the intrinsically parallel nature of the problem itself. In fact, *ray tracing* is known to be among the embarrassingly parallel family of problems, because each pixel can be processed with no interdependence.

So, following the previous block of code, we can make a small change to output some more meaningful color values. This output color is part of what we will see as the starting point for a proper ray tracer.

Take a look at the following code:

```
//the keyword __global__ instructs the CUDA compiler that this function is
//the entry point of our kernel
__global__ void RenderScene(const int N,float* ColorBuffer)
{
    int x = blockIdx.x*blockDim.x + threadIdx.x;
    int y = blockIdx.y*blockDim.y + threadIdx.y;
    //checks whether we are inside the color buffer bounds.
    //If not, just return
    if(x > N || y > N)
    {
        return;
    }
    //We access the linear ColorBuffer storing each color component
    //separately (we could have a float3 color buffer for a more
    //compact/cleaner solution)
    int offset = (x + y*N)*3;
```

```
    //Store the results of your computations
    ColorBuffer[offset] = static_cast<float>(x)/static_cast<float>(N);
    ColorBuffer[offset+1] = static_cast<float>(y)/static_cast<float>(N);
    ColorBuffer[offset+2] = 0.0f;
}
```

As you can see, the overall code structure is pretty much the same with the exception that we output the normalized [0,1] coordinates. This, as we'll see in future chapters, is going to be the basic structure for what is needed to construct a ray in world space when it comes time to ray trace a scene.

Figure 1-7 shows the last block of code visually.

Figure 1-7. *Normalized x,y coordinates in [0,1] range. The code structure that produces that output is the starting point for our ray tracer in CUDA*

We can clearly tell that the origins of the x-y axis is positioned in the top-left corner of our 512x512 image (see the blackish corner were the (0,0) origins is supposed to be). Those colors are familiar to every user that is used to work under whatever 3D engine. In fact, they are also the color of the UV texture coordinate space, which we can stumble upon if we ever worked with any node-based material editor (e.g., the Unreal Engine 4 material editor or the Unity 3D engine).

How the Hardware Executes a Kernel

We showed how easy it is to translate a `for` loop that span an entire image grid of pixels in CUDA (or in any general-purpose GPU computing language, like OpenCL, for example). It is so easy and dramatically fast that is also very scalable as soon as the image resolution grows significantly.

Now back to the GPU architecture itself. It is important to notice is how our kernel is executed. Understanding what the hardware does and how threads are mapped to our kernel for the execution of instructions, it is relevant especially when we have to understand where bottlenecks and inefficiencies are happening in code.

Every time a kernel is ready for execution, the GPU warps/wavefronts scheduler starts by assigning them for execution to any of the compute units (or CUDA core if we use the CUDA naming convention). Refer to Figure 1-3.

We've already said that instructions are executed by warps at every clock cycle. Remembering that a warp consists of exactly 32 threads. What is happening is that as soon as this warp is ready to start executing instructions, the memory address of the entry point of the kernel in memory is made available to the warp itself.

Every thread in the warp will have its own program counter. This is necessary so that each one of them can manage the instruction flow control independently. So, one thread can take the first path of a branch in code, for example, another one the second code path, and so on. This is technically referred as *conditional branch divergence*.

Figure 1-8 shows more explicitly what happens when a warp hits a conditional branch.

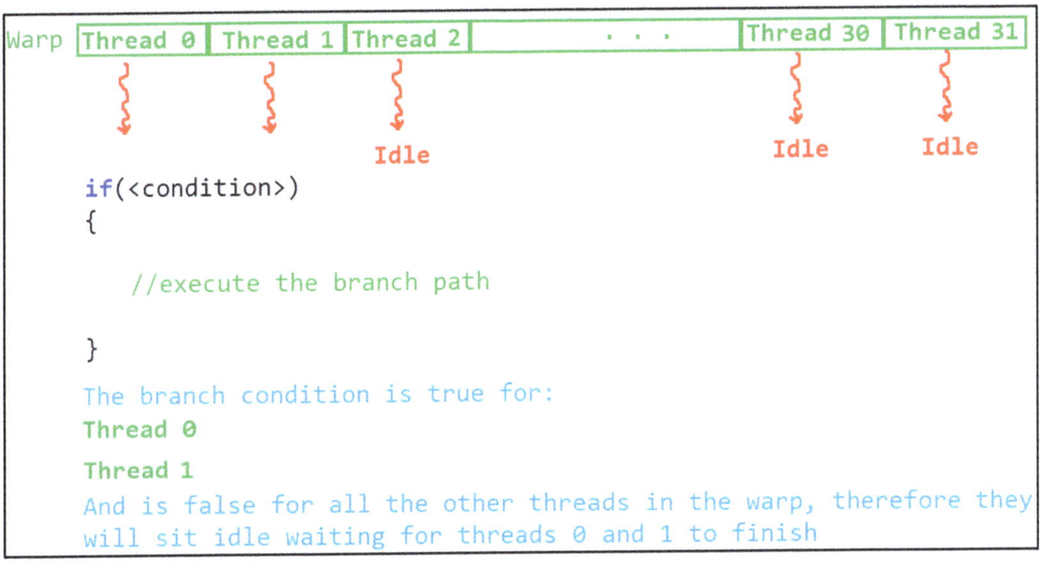

```
Warp  Thread 0  Thread 1  Thread 2        . . .      Thread 30  Thread 31
         ↓         ↓         ↓                           ↓          ↓
                            Idle                        Idle       Idle
    if(<condition>)
    {

        //execute the branch path

    }
    The branch condition is true for:
    Thread 0
    Thread 1
    And is false for all the other threads in the warp, therefore they
    will sit idle waiting for threads 0 and 1 to finish
```

Figure 1-8. *Some threads can take the path of conditional branch; others do not and will sit idle waiting for the others to leave the branch code path*

Therefore, if only five threads in warp will take the branch path, the warp will disable the other threads masking them out as inactive until all the five threads leave the branch path, eventually converging back to the common execution path where the other threads are waiting idle.

We can think of a warp having a 32-bit bitmask, and every bit in this mask can be set to either 1 or 0 to activate (1) or de-activate (0) a specific thread in the warp.

CHAPTER 1 BRIEF HISTORY OF MODERN GPUS

See Figure 1-9.

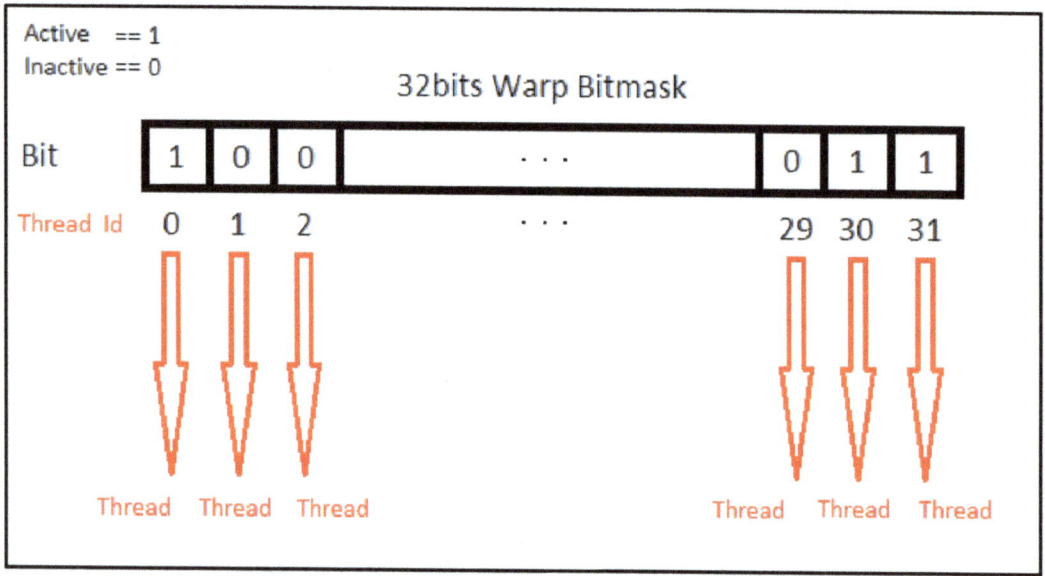

Figure 1-9. *Threads in a warp can be either active (1) or inactive (0). A 32-bit bitmask is used to keep track of the active/inactive threads in a warp*

The fact that when branching other threads might be sitting idle waiting for other thread to finish their work is a waste of resources. It is often one of the problems that will can kill the degree of parallelization of an executing kernel.

The Turing Architecture

The GPU architecture that is definitely to be considered a leap in desktop graphics card technology is the Turing GPU architecture from NVIDIA. It is, in fact, the first GPU that has the capability to perform ray tracing in hardware. This is possible thanks to the addition of the so-called RT Core, a specialized core that accelerates bounding volume hierarchy (BVH) traversal and ray-triangle intersections. Basically, we now have a streaming multiprocessor with the usual CUDA cores but with the addition of RT cores and, of course, tensor cores for deep learning and AI. But despite that we are much more interested in the possibility of having most of the ray tracing techniques in real time, RT cores are not the only important addition to the Turing architecture. In fact, it is now possible to perform floating-point operations and integer operations concurrently, achieving something like an overall 50% boost per core with respect to the previous Pascal architecture.

CHAPTER 1　BRIEF HISTORY OF MODERN GPUS

See Figure 1-10 for a picture of the Pascal SM compared to the new Turing SM.

Figure 1-10. *The Pascal SM and the Turing SM side by side. Notice the new RT Core on the Turing SM*

Volta extends the Pascal architecture by adding tensor cores to the SM and INT32/FP32/FP64 separated cores. Volta is similar to Turing but without the ray tracing core in its SM cluster. If you look at Figure 1-10, you can see that one Turing SM has 16 INT32 and 16 FP32 CUDA cores that can work independently with respect to the Pascal architecture that, instead, it only has the CUDA cores that share the same data path for integer and floating-point instructions. Sharing the same data path means that anytime the GPU is performing integer instructions (or any non-FP instruction), the floating-point instruction execution is idle and the overall throughput will be lower.

23

CHAPTER 1   BRIEF HISTORY OF MODERN GPUS

Ada Lovelace Architecture (2022: GeForce RTX 40 series)

Target: Gaming and creative workloads (consumer GPUs).

- **Main idea**: Built on TSMC's 4N process, it prioritizes *performance-per-watt* and real-time rendering.
- **Key features**:
  - **Third-gen Ray Tracing (RT) cores**: Accelerate BVH traversal and complex ray effects like global illumination.
  - **Fourth-gen Tensor Cores**: Boost DLSS 3 (AI-based frame generation), making games smoother without proportional GPU cost.
  - **Shader Execution Reordering (SER)**: Dynamically reorganizes threads to reduce divergence in ray tracing workloads.
  - **Massive core counts and clocks**: Higher FPS at 4K, strong uplift vs. Ampere (RTX 30).

Hopper Architecture (2022: NVIDIA H100, Datacenter AI GPU)

Target: HPC (High-Performance Computing), AI training/inference at scale.

- **Main idea**: Designed for datacenter workloads where *matrix math + parallelism* dominate.
- **Key features**:
  - **Transformer Engine**: Specialized for deep learning models (especially Transformers, the foundation of modern LLMs). Supports FP8 precision for huge speedups with minimal accuracy loss.
  - **Tensor Memory Accelerator (TMA)**: Efficiently moves blocks of data for compute-heavy AI kernels.

- **NVLink Switch System**: Allows scaling thousands of GPUs together with low latency.
- **Confidential Computing support**: GPU-level security for sensitive workloads.

Hopper represents the "AI-first" architecture, engineered to train trillion-parameter models and power generative AI.

Blackwell Architecture (2024/2025: Next-Gen AI GPU, e.g., B100/B200)

Target: The next leap for AI workloads that includes generative AI, LLMs, scientific computing.

- **Main idea**: Pushes performance, efficiency, and scalability beyond Hopper.
- **Expected/announced features**:
  - **Next-gen Transformer Engine** with even finer-grained mixed precision (beyond FP8).
  - **Chiplet design (multi-die GPUs)**: Improves yields, scalability, and memory bandwidth.
  - **High-bandwidth memory (HBM3e)**: Handles massive datasets efficiently.
  - **NVLink upgrades**: Tighter interconnects for GPU clusters, making "AI supercomputers" more seamless.
  - **Huge performance/watt uplift** (NVIDIA touts ~2× training throughput vs. Hopper).

Blackwell is pitched as the "foundation for trillion+ parameter AI models" and is central to NVIDIA's roadmap for the next generation of datacenter AI.

CHAPTER 1   BRIEF HISTORY OF MODERN GPUS

Big Picture (Ada, Hopper, and Blackwell)

- **Ada Lovelace**: Optimized for gamers and creators. Includes real-time ray tracing, DLSS 3, better rendering pipelines.

- **Hopper**: Optimized for datacenters and AI. Includes transformer acceleration, massive scalability, security.

- **Blackwell** The future of AI. Includes larger-than-Hopper performance, chiplet design, pushing efficiency for LLMs and beyond.

RT Core

What makes real-time ray tracing possible is the RT core. Because in the past real-time ray tracing was already possible, we have to explain what motivates the necessity for a dedicated hardware unit when it comes to Turing. To put it simply, the problem is that BVH traversal along with triangle intersection tests was software emulated in previous hardware generation and, therefore, was running on the SM cores directly requiring thousands of instruction slots per ray. As you can imagine, this is not a problem on a ray tracer that is part of a tool chain dedicated to render only the frames for a Hollywood movie. However, when we talk about games, and in particular AAA games, our frame budget is very diverse, and we have to make sure that every system of our game fits in 33ms/16ms (depending on whether we are targeting 30 or 60 frame per second).

So, we definitely can't waste all our frame just to run our ray tracer. A better solution was required. With RT Core added to the SM, we totally offload the SM itself that is now free to do other work, like compute shading or pixel shading tasks. See Figure 1-11 and Figure 1-12 straight from the NVIDIA documentation for an illustration of what we've already been discussing.

CHAPTER 1 BRIEF HISTORY OF MODERN GPUS

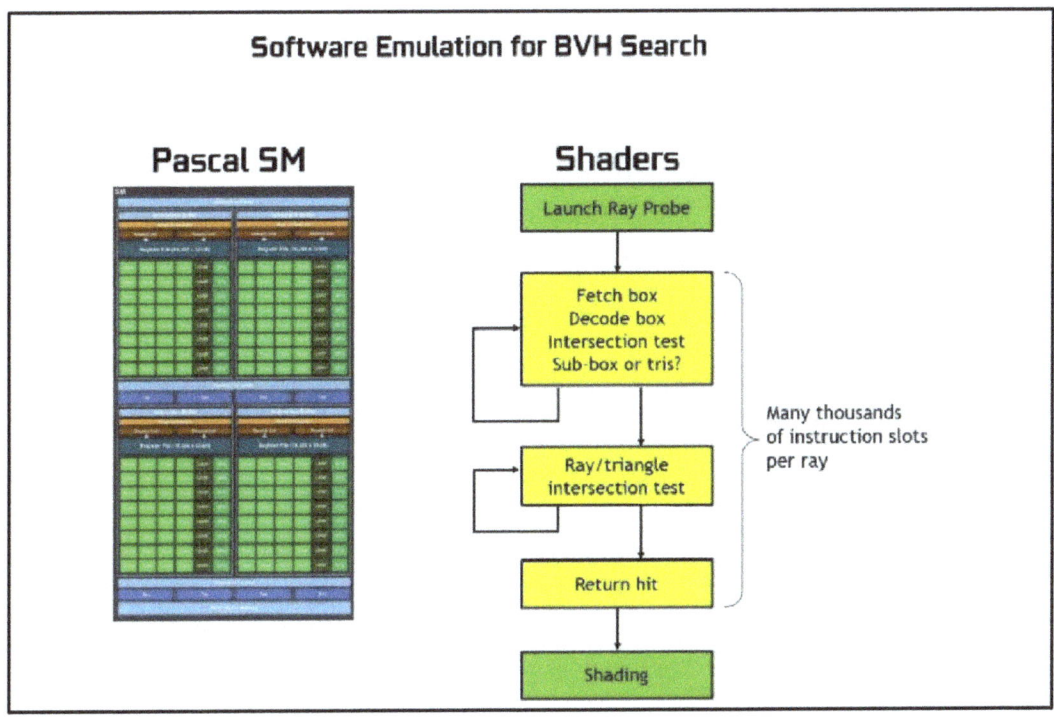

Figure 1-11. *In previous hardware generation, BVH and ray-triangle tests were simulated in software requiring thousands of instruction slots per ray*

CHAPTER 1   BRIEF HISTORY OF MODERN GPUS

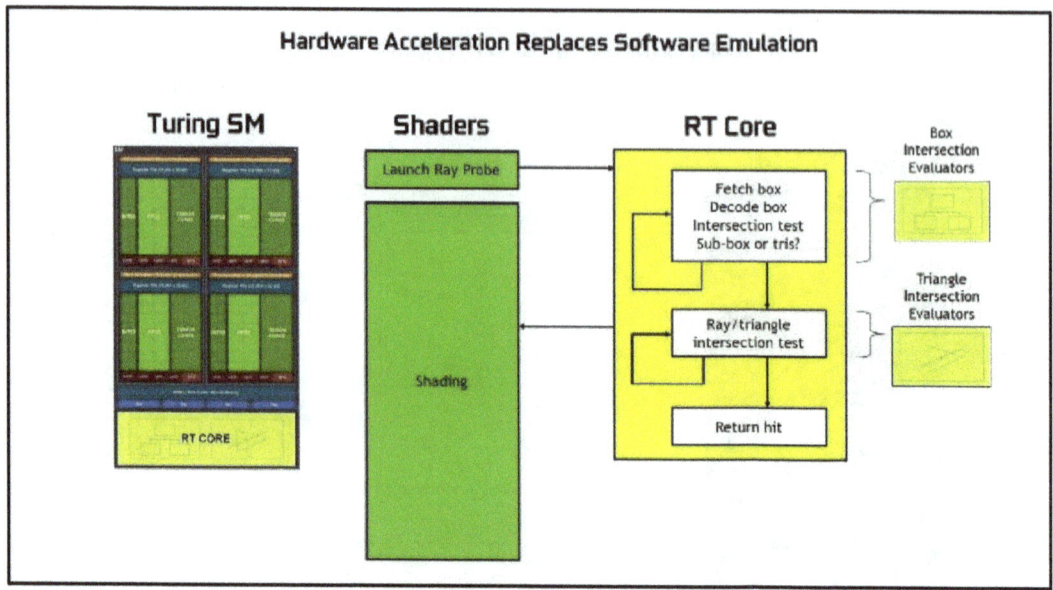

Figure 1-12. *With the new Turing architecture, the BVH and ray-triangle intersection are now handled in hardware, offloading the SM that now can keep working on usual tasks like*

In this book, we will present a C++ project written with DirectX 12 that will employ DXR API to leverage the novel ray-tracing capabilities and a CUDA implementation to compare against. Other APIs exist, like NVIDIA RTX API, but we'll concentrate ourselves mostly on DXR to stick with D3D12. The project will implement a ray tracer that I've called RAY.

See Figure 1-12 for a closer look at the anatomy of RT core.

Real-Time Ray Tracing Is Finally Here

Real-time ray tracing is the holy grail of real-time rendering in games. A bright future for visual quality and lighting accuracy in games will, one day, be possible like it is already possible for movies. We are already experimenting with implementing cheaper ray tracing techniques like reflections, shadows, and refraction in games like *Shadow of the Tomb Raider* or *Battlefield 5*, even though to have real-time global illumination running completely through a path tracer (with no tricks!), we will have to wait at least a couple of hardware generations past this one. Despite this, it is undeniable that games were already looking really good even with just rasterization, and we might expect a further

CHAPTER 1   BRIEF HISTORY OF MODERN GPUS

increase in fidelity with the advent of real-time ray tracing techniques along with the existing raster-based rendering paths.

Ideally, we will start with a hybrid rendering pipeline to end up, one day, to a fully ray-traced pipeline.

The raster-based techniques that will surely be replaced by their ray-traced counterpart in the future are as follows:

- Shadow mapping replaced with ray-traced shadows
- Screen space reflections replaced with ray-traced reflections

These are the limitations of raster-based techniques:

- For screen space reflections (SSR), we can reflect only what is on screen. So, we might expect that SSR artifacts will get fixed in a natural and graceful manner with ray-traced reflections.

- For shadow mapping, we avoid the need of the different render states setup (think about how expensive are point light shadows or the memory needed to store cascades for shadow maps cast by a global directional light) and the additional draw calls overhead needed to render any shadow caster from the light point of view in the shadow map.

Figure 1-13 shows ray-traced shadows in *Shadow of the Tomb Raider*.

CHAPTER 1 BRIEF HISTORY OF MODERN GPUS

Figure 1-13. *Shadow of the Tomb Raider ray-traced shadows. Here we notice the small holes in the shadow cast by the fruit boxes*

A Quick Look at Ray Tracing Pipeline

After having described the Turing architecture, let's shed some light on the ray tracing graphics pipeline itself. This new pipeline model will work along with the traditional rasterization pipeline, simultaneously and cooperatively.

The main steps for the new ray tracing pipeline are the following:

- Ray generation
- Scheduling
- BVH traversal and intersection
- Scheduling
- Shading

For a more explicit view of how the new ray tracing pipeline compares to the traditional rasterization pipeline, see Figure 1-14.

CHAPTER 1   BRIEF HISTORY OF MODERN GPUS

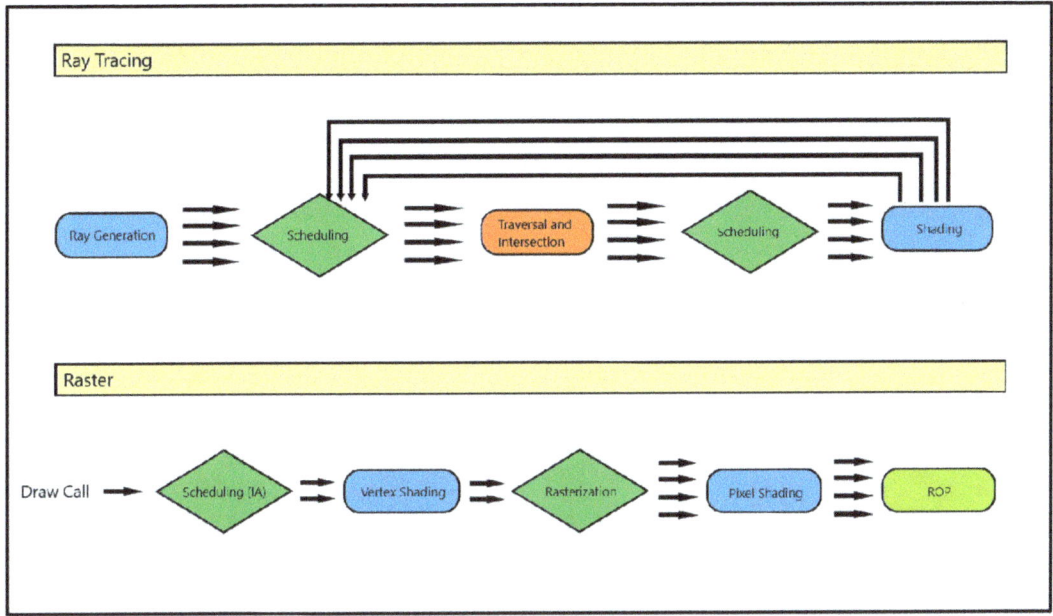

Figure 1-14. *Ray tracing pipeline and traditional raster pipeline works simultaneously and cooperatively to realize hybrid rendering system*

We, as programmers, have the possibility to write a new set of shaders to leverage the power of the new RT cores.

If we are programming with DXR, then we will go with the usual HLSL shading language. Those are the new shaders that we can write to perform our shading through ray tracing:

- **Ray generation shader**:

  The entry point of a ray tracing pass. It runs on the CPU's dispatch command and launches rays into the scene (e.g., primary, shadow, reflection rays). It sets up per-pixel/per-sample work, builds ray payloads, and calls TraceRay.

- **Intersection shader**:

  Custom test for *procedural* geometry (things that aren't built-in triangles—like implicit surfaces, hair, or SDFs). Given a ray and a bounding volume hit, it decides if/where the ray truly intersects the primitive and reports candidate hits to the pipeline.

31

- **Any-hit shader**:

  Invoked for *every* candidate hit along a ray (can be many). It can accept or reject the hit (e.g., alpha-tested geometry, cutouts, masking, transparent leaves) or modify the hit attributes. If it rejects, traversal continues to look for other hits.

- **Miss shader**:

  Runs when traversal finds no geometry hit. Commonly returns an environment color (skybox/IBL), a constant for shadow rays, or other background effects, and finalizes the ray's payload in the "no-hit" case.

- **Closest-hit shader**:

  Runs once for the nearest accepted hit along the ray. This is where you typically compute material shading/lighting (BRDF, textures, normals), spawn secondary rays (reflection/refraction), and write the final contribution to the payload.

- **Mental model**:

  RayGen launches a ray, traverses the acceleration structure to test triangle meshes, and for procedural shapes it invokes the intersection shader to generate hit candidates; any-hit can reject those candidates, closest-hit shades the nearest accepted hit, and if nothing is hit, the miss shader supplies the background.

Along with these new shader types, we will briefly show the basic code structure for each entry point related to any of these new shader types. We will not go too in depth as that is not the goal of this chapter. This is just a taste of what you will be dealing with in the coming chapters.

So, let's throw some simple code in the mix.

Use the following HLSL code to create the entry point for any of the shader types we listed before:

- **Ray generation shader (this is where ray tracing starts)**:

  ```
  //This is the standard HLSL attribute that identifies your shader entry
  //point to be the ray generation shader
  [shader("raygeneration")]
  ```

```
void MyRayGenerationEntryPoint() //you can give whatever name
you want to
//the entry point
{
    //write your code here
}
```

The ray generation shader will start the ray tracing process and will call the TraceRay() function to shoot rays in the scene.

- **Intersection shader**:

```
[shader("intersection")]
void ProcessPrimitiveIntersection()
{
    //write your code here
}
```

- **Any-hit shader**:

```
[shader("anyhit")]
void ProcessMultipleHitPoints(inout UserPayload data, IntersectAttribs
attribs)
{
    //wrtie your code here
}
```

- **Miss shader**:

```
[shader("miss")]
void ProcessIfWeMiss()
{
  //write your code here (typically return the background color/lookup
   //from a global env map etc.
}
```

- **Closest-hit shader**:

  ```
  [shader("closesthit")]
  void ProcessClosestHit(inout UserPayload data, IntersectAttribs
  attribs)
  {
    //write your code here
  }
  ```

Note that any of these entry points can have arbitrary names; I've been verbose just to make the role of each shader type more explicit. `UserPayload` is a user-defined arbitrary named struct that can be used to carry intermediate results during the ray tracing process.

It can contain a color, for example, or more attributes depending on the user needs:

```
struct UserPayload
{
   float3 RayColor;
  //add more fields depending on the algorithm/technique you are
implementing
};
```

`IntersectAttribs` is a built-in type that will hold intersection relevant attributes filled on hits (by the intersection shader).

Summary

In this chapter, you analyzed the history of past GPU architectures and the latest Turing architecture, including how the hardware evolved to meet the ever-growing needs of visual quality. You analyzed the streaming multiprocessor and had a quick look at its architecture, learning about the aspects that were relevant to the graphics programmer. Then we presented the bare minimum skeleton for how to write ray-tracing code in CUDA. Then we gave further details in relation to the Turing architecture, and we presented the new shader types added in the DXR API, showing the actual code in HLSL for every entry point of each shader type.

Questions

Now based on the knowledge that you gained in this chapter, it is your turn to answer some questions:

- How would you go in reimplementing an algorithm in CUDA that multiplies two squared matrices of a given size N?
- What is the main architectural design difference between a CPU and a GPU?
- What is the most efficient way to access memory?
- What are the main reasons behind the creation of a dedicated core like the RT Core?
- In the context of the DXR API, what shader type would you employ to manage translucency between overlapping objects?
- Explain the main differences between the rasterization and ray-tracing techniques for rendering 3D scenes.
- Describe the function of the Bounding Volume Hierarchy (BVH) in ray tracing and why it is important.
- What are the benefits and limitations of using hardware-accelerated ray tracing compared to software-emulated ray tracing?
- How do RT cores in the Turing architecture improve the performance of ray tracing compared to previous GPU architectures?
- What role do tensor cores play in modern GPU architectures, and how do they complement the functionality of RT cores?
- Illustrate how the introduction of programmable stages (like vertex and pixel shaders) transformed the capabilities of GPUs.
- In the context of DXR API, describe the purpose of each shader type (Ray Generation, Intersection, Any-hit, Miss, Closest-hit) and provide a simple example of how one might be used.
- Discuss how the separation of FP32 and INT32 cores in the Turing architecture contributes to improved computational efficiency

CHAPTER 1   BRIEF HISTORY OF MODERN GPUS

Further Reading

The following are few links that you can use to expand your knowledge of this chapter:

- https://www.techspot.com/article/650-history-of-the-gpu/
- https://www.nvidia.com/content/dam/en-zz/Solutions/design-visualization/technologies/turing-architecture/NVIDIA-Turing-Architecture-Whitepaper.pdf
- http://intro-to-dxr.cwyman.org/presentations/IntroDXR_RaytracingShaders.pdf
- https://www.scratchapixel.com/lessons/3d-basic-rendering/rasterization-practical-implementation

CHAPTER 2

Know Your Hardware: The Streaming Multiprocessor

In this chapter, we analyze the anatomy of one of the main components in a GPU: the streaming multiprocessor (SM). This will clarify how threads get scheduled during the processing phase, the importance of memory caches, and how they relate to global memory accesses. We will talk about shared memory, which is among the most important type of memory that the programmer can manage explicitly, to optimize the latency problems that can arise in some situations by accessing global device memory, for example. A practical code sample is provided in which employees shared memory to optimize Gaussian blur.

The following topics will be covered in this chapter:

- The SM
- C-Cache, I-Cache, and shared memory
- The compute units or cores

Technical Requirements

The following tools will be required before we get started:

- Visual Studio 2022 Community
- Cuda Toolkit 13.0.1
- Windows 10 RS5 update

CHAPTER 2 KNOW YOUR HARDWARE: THE STREAMING MULTIPROCESSOR

How to Find the Code in Visual Studio

To access the code for this chapter, open the main Visual Studio solution included with the book's source files. Within the solution, locate the project or folder named `ChapterX`, where X corresponds to the chapter number (for example, the code for this chapter can be found in `Chapter2`).

This convention applies to all chapters that include code samples, so you can use the same approach to find the examples for other chapters.

The Streaming Multiprocessor

As you know, the central component of each modern GPU is the SM. Each GPU generation has improved the previous one by either adding more SM modules or increasing the memory size and the bandwidth. To understand how an SM works and how to take advantage of the architecture to write fast code, we have to start dissecting the relevant parts of the SM and start thinking the same way a GPU does.

The main components of an SM are listed here:

- Warp scheduler/dispatch unit (responsible for organizing and dispatching warps to the compute units/CUDA cores)

  - They are capable of scheduling and dispatching 32 threads/clock cycle.

  - However, in modern GPU architectures, each SM typically contains multiple warp schedulers, allowing several warps to be issued and executed concurrently. This design improves throughput, and the abundance of fast registers ensures that active warps can access their operands without noticeable stalls.

- Register file (registers are the fastest type of memory in a GPU). Their access time is so short that, for practical purposes, it can be considered *zero clock cycles*. Technically, there is still a tiny latency, but it's so small compared to other memory types that it is effectively negligible. They are visible only to a given thread in a given kernel execution.

- Compute units (or CUDA cores if we refer specifically to the CUDA naming convention). They can be considered as many simple ALU able to perform FP and INT operations. While that's broadly accurate, modern GPU architectures go further. In designs such as Volta, Turing, and Ampere, CUDA cores are capable of executing floating-point (FP32, FP64) and integer operations concurrently. This concurrency improves instruction-level parallelism, enabling the scheduler to issue different types of instructions at the same time instead of serializing them.

- This evolution means that CUDA cores are not just simple ALUs; they're highly optimized, versatile processing units designed to maximize throughput across diverse workloads, from graphics shading to general-purpose compute tasks.

- L1 cache and shared memory (it's normally one unique fast on-chip memory). It's normally used as L1 cache as well as shared memory. The amount of L1 or shared memory can be decided by the programmer. To be precise, L1 cache and shared memory share the same physical memory space, even though they are exposed to programmers as distinct entities.

The GPU provides flexibility in how this space is allocated: programmers (or the compiler/runtime) can configure the partitioning between L1 cache and shared memory depending on application needs. For example, on architectures like NVIDIA's Kepler, Maxwell, Pascal, and later generations, a 64KB on-chip pool can be split into 48KB shared memory/16KB L1 cache or inverted as 16KB shared/48KB L1, with other partition options available as well.

This configurability allows developers to tune for workload characteristics:

- More shared memory benefits algorithms with high data reuse and explicit data management (e.g., matrix multiplication tiles).

- More L1 cache benefits workloads with less predictable memory access patterns, improving the automatic caching of global loads.

CHAPTER 2   KNOW YOUR HARDWARE: THE STREAMING MULTIPROCESSOR

Figure 2-1 shows the Fermi SM for reference.

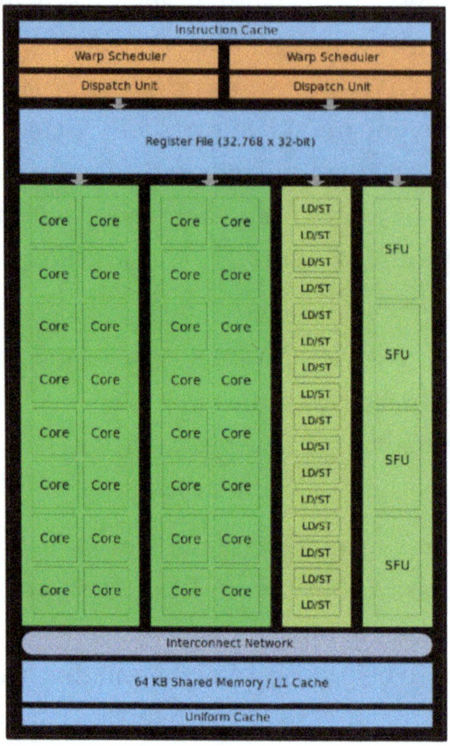

Figure 2-1. *The Fermi SM*

We will briefly go through the description of the previous SM components giving more emphasis to the ones that are most relevant to the programmer. We have seen the main components of the SM. Let's now take a look at its components in detail. We will show code snippets to illustrate clearly why one approach is preferred over another.

Warp Scheduler and Dispatch Unit

Let's start by describing the warp scheduler and the dispatch unit. As already stated, threads are organized in groups of 32, and each group is referred to as a *warp*. The warp scheduler prepares them, and the dispatch unit sends them for execution on the compute unit (or CUDA core).

Because we have two warp scheduler/dispatch units, one SM can issue two warps per clock cycle. All the warp issued are organized in blocks, and, more precisely, blocks of warps are executed on the CUDA cores. Each SM can execute up to a maximum number of blocks (also called *slots*).

Knowing the maximum number of available execution slots is useful to understand how to interpret the performance metrics that the profiler will present to us. *Occupancy*, for instance, is a metric that depends on the number of execution slots currently in use with respect to the maximum number of execution slots available. The number of blocks that we can execute on an SM is limited by the shared memory and number of registers in use. But to understand why there is this limit on the number of blocks that we can execute concurrently, we have to first explain the role of shared memory and registers.

Shared memory is allocated to a given block of threads. This is how threads can share data between them, but it's also a way to optimize the latency of load and store operations on frequently accessed data. In fact, the shared memory is an on-chip fast memory with a throughput of roughly 1+TB/s (depending on the architecture) and a very low latency one.

Shared Memory, C-Cache, and I-Cache

As mentioned, the total amount of fast on-chip memory is subdivided between shared memory and the L1 cache. The programmer is allowed to decide how much shared memory can be allocated with respect to the L1 cache and vice versa, depending on the application/algorithm needs. This is true for the Fermi architecture but is similar in concept even for other architectures. We have a total of 64KB of fast on-chip memory in one of the following configurations:

- 16KB shared and 48KB L1

or

- 48KB shared and 16KB L1

So basically, the way this space is divided depends on the architecture:

- On Fermi GPUs (as mentioned previously), the on-chip pool was 64KB, configurable as 48KB shared/16KB L1 or 16KB shared/48KB L1.

- More recent designs (e.g., Kepler, Maxwell, Pascal, Volta, Turing, Ampere) continued to evolve this flexibility, but with different partition sizes and default allocations. For instance, Volta and later architectures provide larger shared memory capacities per SM (up to 96KB on some configurations) and allow different tuning options.

This is an overview of the chronological order of NVIDIA GPU architectures and their key innovations:

- **Fermi (2010)**: Introduced unified cache/shared memory design, ECC memory support, improved double-precision (FP64) performance.

- **Kepler (2012)**: Energy-efficient design, Hyper-Q for better parallelism, dynamic parallelism, larger register files.

- **Maxwell (2014)**: Enhanced performance per watt, improved shared memory, NVENC/NVDEC hardware video engines.

- **Pascal (2016)**: 16nm FinFET process, HBM2 support (GP100), unified memory improvements, higher memory bandwidth.

- **Volta (2017)**: Introduced Tensor Cores, NVLink 2.0, independent integer/FP32 execution, larger shared memory (up to 96KB).

- **Turing (2018)**: RT cores for real-time ray tracing, second-gen Tensor Cores for AI/ML, concurrent FP/INT execution.

- **Ampere (2020)**: Third-gen Tensor Cores, second-gen RT Cores, improved SM design, sparsity acceleration.

- **Hopper (2022)**: Transformer Engine for AI training/inference, FP8 precision support, NVLink Switch System, massive scaling for datacenters.

This is just to give a taste of how the fast on-chip memory could be partitioned in a given GPU architecture (Fermi architecture is just an example and the previous values might be different for another GPU architecture).

Figure 2-2 shows a block of threads that have access to shared memory.

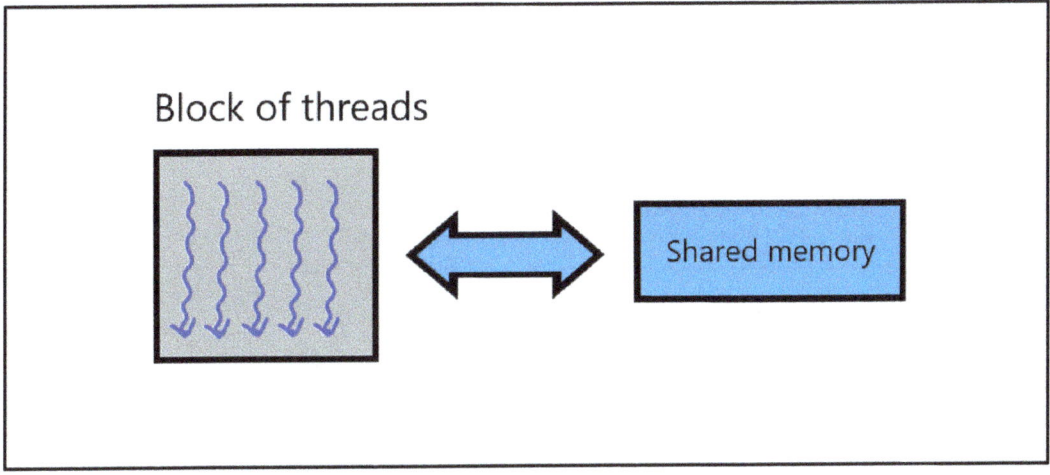

Figure 2-2. *Shared memory is allocated and accessible to all threads in a block*

L2 cache and global device memory are both off-chip and are accessible by all threads in the grid of blocks. L2 cache is a write-back type of cache and any access to global memory, as well as copies to and from CPU host, go through L2 cache. The latency of both types of memory is quite high with the global memory having something around 400 to 800 cycles.

The L2 cache plays a critical role in performance because:

- It reduces the number of direct global memory accesses, allowing frequently used data to be served much faster.

- It helps to amortize memory latency, ensuring that not every load or store has to traverse the high-latency path to DRAM.

- It also improves effective memory bandwidth, since cached data avoids repeated trips to global memory.

In modern architectures, the L2 cache is shared across all SMs, enabling data reuse across threads and blocks running on different multiprocessors. This shared design makes it a vital performance buffer, especially for workloads with irregular or bandwidth-intensive memory access patterns.

CHAPTER 2 KNOW YOUR HARDWARE: THE STREAMING MULTIPROCESSOR

Figure 2-3 shows the GPU memory hierarchy.

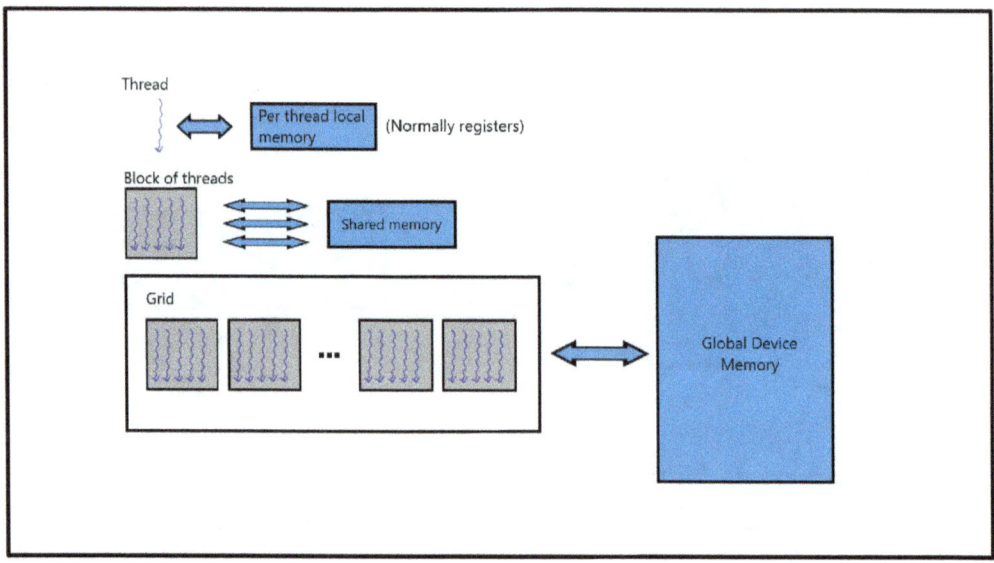

Figure 2-3. *Memory hierarchy*

Now the question is, how and when the programmer can exploit shared memory?

To define a variable in shared memory in CUDA, we use the built-in keyword __shared__. *Other languages like the DirectX HLSL use a different syntax. HLSL, in particular, gives the* groupshared *keyword to the programmer to tell that a variable needs to be allocated in shared memory. Moreover, differently from CUDA, it has to be declared in the global scope of the program. The DirectX subsystem API responsible to manage the compute capability is named Direct Compute, and the shader is normally referred to as compute shader.*

When we use shared memory? When we need to access a given element more than one time from a given thread or from multiple threads in the same block. How we can use it to our advantage?

Let's consider this simple CUDA code snippet that implements image filtering:

```
__global__ void FilterImageKernel(float* ColorBuffer
, const int Width
, const int Height
, float* FilteredColorBuffer)
{
```

```cuda
//shared memory
__shared__ float3 CachedColors[512];
//Compute global x and t coords
int x = blockIdx.x*blockDim.x + threadIdx.x;
int y = blockIdx.y*blockDim.y + threadIdx.y;
//checks whether we are inside the color buffer bounds.
//If not, just return
if (x >= Width || y >= Height)
{
    return;
}
const int ColorBufferOffset = (x + y * Width) * 3;
//Start memory transactions here (copy color from global memory to
shared fast memory)
CachedColors[threadIdx.x].x = ColorBuffer[ColorBufferOffset ];
CachedColors[threadIdx.x].y = ColorBuffer[ColorBufferOffset +1];
CachedColors[threadIdx.x].z = ColorBuffer[ColorBufferOffset +2];
//wait for all the threads in the block to finish their memory
transactions before accessing any value store in CachedColors
__syncthreads();
//Add filter code here
int OffsetThreadId = threadIdx.x - kFilterRadius / 2;
float3 Result = make_float3(0.0f, 0.0f, 0.0f);
for (int x = 0; x < kFilterRadius; ++x)
{
        Result = Result + (CachedColors[Min(Max(0,OffsetThreadId +
        x),Width-1)] * FilterWeights[x]);
}
//write back the filter result in global memory rotating 90° the image
(this is a trick to always have coalesced access pattern on global memory
read)
const int RotatedOffset = (y + x * Width) * 3;
FilteredColorBuffer[RotatedOffset ] = Result.x;
FilteredColorBuffer[RotatedOffset + 1] = Result.y;
FilteredColorBuffer[RotatedOffset + 2] = Result.z;
}
```

In the following code snippet, we've launched a grid of threads from the host (by *host* we mean the code that is running on the CPU and that is responsible for launching our kernel on the GPU) in this way:

```
//Host code
int main()
{
[...]

//Let's suppose that ColorBuffer will contain the results of a previous
render pass and we want              //to blur them
    //Launch the kernel on the GPU
    //Perform horizontal blur pass
    FilterImageKernel << <ThreadBlocks, ThreadsInABlock >> >
    (ColorBuffer,
    ImageWidth, ImageHeight,IntermediateResults);
    //Wait for the GPU to finish before to access results of the
    previous pass
    CHECK_CUDA_ERRORS(cudaGetLastError());
    CHECK_CUDA_ERRORS(cudaDeviceSynchronize());
  //Perform vertical blur pass
    FilterImageKernel << <ThreadBlocks, ThreadsInABlock >> >
    (IntermediateResults, ImageWidth, ImageHeight, ColorBuffer);
    //Wait for the GPU to finish before to access results of the
    final pass
    CHECK_CUDA_ERRORS(cudaGetLastError());
    CHECK_CUDA_ERRORS(cudaDeviceSynchronize());

    [...]
}
```

As usual, we perform a horizontal pass and a vertical pass because a Gaussian blur is linearly separable. Therefore, two simple passes are cheaper than one unique pass that span both the filter dimensions.

In the previous code, we are assuming a fixed dimension of 512×512 pixels for the input image for simplicity, but the code can easily be adapted for arbitrary image dimensions.

You can find the complete code of this sample in the GitHub project under the Chapter2 folder.

But why we want to code a Gaussian blur in CUDA instead of just implement it with a pixel shader? The reason is that as the blur radius get larger, say more than 8/9 texel wide, the pixel shader will start underperforming. The reason is because more texels will start by not fitting in texture cache at all times, while we are filtering the image in the pixel shader. Therefore, many load instructions will hit global memory, which, as we already know, is the one with the highest latency.

If we "touch" each element in an array allocated in global device memory just once, there won't be any advantage in using shared memory in this case. Remember that shared memory should be used only when the same data is accessed multiple times during a given kernel execution.

Constants Cache (C-Cache)

Constants cache C-Cache is a type of memory to which the constant memory (which in general is allocated in global device memory) is cached to.

Variables that are stored in constant memory are cached to the C-Cache. So, they actually reside in global memory, but they exploit the C-Cache for fast subsequent read-only memory accesses.

Any memory that is to be considered constant for a given kernel execution is conveniently created and stored in constant memory that is cached to C-Cache. Storing constant variables in constant memory is generally faster if the accesses of threads in the same half-warp read the same address; otherwise, the accesses are serialized. We could equally store a constant in global memory if we wanted, but the cost would have been higher and in general limited by the higher latency that characterizes this kind of memory (remember, any access to global device memory can cost something like 400/800 cycles).

How we can specify that we want a variable in constant memory?

In CUDA we specify the keyword __constant__ to inform the compiler that the variable has to be allocated in constant device memory and must be defined in the global scope of the program. It will be accessible by all threads.

CHAPTER 2   KNOW YOUR HARDWARE: THE STREAMING MULTIPROCESSOR

The following code snippet defines the radius of the Gaussian kernel:

```
//store this constant in constant device memory
__constant__ const int kFilterRadius = 25
```

On Pascal architecture, C-Cache is generally 64KB big.

So anytime we have a variable or an array of type const that we are sure will not change across kernel executions, we can safely and conveniently define them in constant memory. They will most likely be cached in C-Cache.

Instruction Cache (I-Cache)

Instruction cache (I-Cache) is a read-only cache memory that is responsible for instruction caching. It basically helps during the GPU instruction fetching. Similarly, to the CPU, I-Cache speeds up the execution of recurrent instructions by reducing the accesses to global device memory by the instruction pointer to fetch the next instruction. In the best case, we would expect for an entire, and reasonably small, kernel to fit completely in instruction cache.

We can now continue our journey by taking a brief look at how a CUDA core is organized and works internally.

The Compute Units or Cores

Compute units (CUDA cores), or ALU units, are responsible for processing simple arithmetic operations. In particular, they process integer and floating-point operations. They have a simple architecture internally and are made by a dispatch port, an operand collector, and one integer unit and one floating point unit. The Fermi architecture has 16 cores total per SM (refer to Figure 2-1).

Figure 2-4 visually illustrates all the components that are part of a CUDA core and how they are interconnected.

CHAPTER 2   KNOW YOUR HARDWARE: THE STREAMING MULTIPROCESSOR

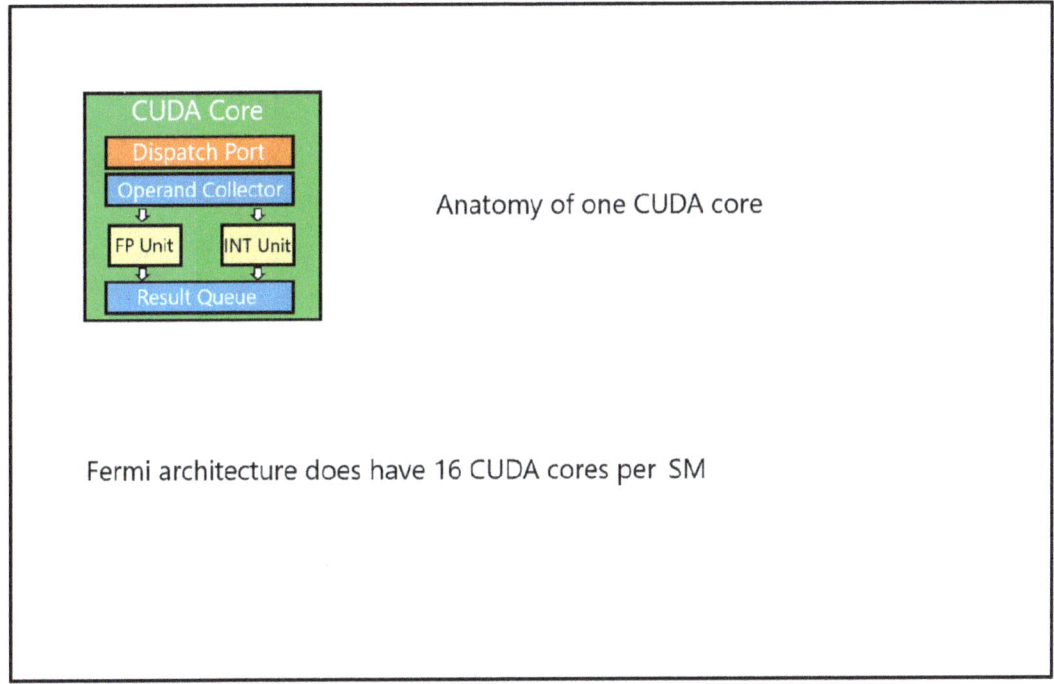

Figure 2-4. One CUDA core is a simple ALU unit that collects the operands of arithmetic operations dispatched from a dispatch port, computing either an FP or an int operation

That's all for a brief explanation of the CUDA core internals.

Summary

In this chapter, you analyzed the streaming multiprocessor closely. The chapter then went through the main components, focusing on the ones that are key to the programmer who wants to understand the hardware and exploit the acquired knowledge to write faster, low-latency compute code. One sample code that performs a simple Gaussian blur was presented. It makes use of the shared memory to optimize the memory latency by preloading image pixels from global memory to shared memory.

The filtering operation was executed by accessing the pixels in shared memory, exploiting the low latency that shared memory provides for fast memory access, and then we stored the results in the resulting filtered buffer in global memory. We then closed the chapter by giving a little more detail about how a CUDA core was architected internally.

CHAPTER 2   KNOW YOUR HARDWARE: THE STREAMING MULTIPROCESSOR

Questions

Based on the knowledge that you gained in this chapter, it is your turn to answer some questions:

- What is the right context in which you want for a variable to be allocated in shared memory?

- What is the right memory access pattern performance-wise?

- Try to write the CUDA code that multiplies two matrices by taking advantage of the shared memory

- What type of memory would you use if you have a variable that won't change during a given kernel execution?

- How does the warp scheduler contribute to the performance of a CUDA kernel?

- Compare and contrast shared memory, constant memory, and global memory in terms of latency and access patterns.

- What are some common strategies to optimize CUDA kernels for better performance on the SM?

- What are bank conflicts in shared memory, and how can they be avoided?

- How do L1 and L2 caches help in reducing memory latency in GPU computations?

- Describe the memory hierarchy in a modern GPU and explain how data moves through this hierarchy during computation.

- What is occupancy in the context of CUDA programming, and why is it important for performance analysis?

- How does conditional branching affect the performance of CUDA kernels, and what techniques can be used to minimize its impact?

- Provide an example of a CUDA kernel that uses shared memory to compute the transpose of a matrix.

- What is the role of the instruction cache (I-Cache) in GPU performance, and how does it differ from the data cache?

Further Reading

The following are few links that you can use to expand your knowledge of the topics in this chapter:

- https://www.paranumal.com/single-post/2018/02/26/Basic-gpu-optimization-strategies
- https://www.microway.com/hpc-tech-tips/gpu-memory-types-performance-comparison/
- http://on-demand.gputechconf.com/gtc/2013/presentations/S3466-Programming-Guidelines-GPU-Architecture.pdf

CHAPTER 3

GPGPU Ray Tracing vs. DXR Ray Tracing Approaches

We will compare GPU compute-based approaches to ray tracing with respect to the novel NVIDIA RTX technology, which, instead, provides dedicated hardware for ray tracing. We will introduce the new shader stages in DXR (Ray Generation Shader, Hit Shader, Miss Shader) as well as bottom-level acceleration structures (BLAS) and top-level acceleration structures (TLAS). We will provide code snippets that will show in practical terms the differences between a CUDA implementation and a DXR one.

By the end of this chapter, it should be clear how to implement a given ray tracing problem with CUDA or DXR. Ray casting is only the beginning, but everything starts from there.

The following topics will be covered in this chapter:

- Ray tracing in compute
- DirectX Ray Tracing (DXR) and the new shader stages
- Compute-based ray tracing vs. DXR-based ray tracing

Technical Requirements

The following tools will be required before we get started:

- Visual Studio 2022 Community
- Cuda Toolkit 13.0.1
- Windows 10 RS5 update

CHAPTER 3   GPGPU RAY TRACING VS. DXR RAY TRACING APPROACHES

Ray Tracing in Compute

We will start this chapter by comparing ray tracing in compute and DXR by providing code snippets that clearly show the differences. The comparison is aligned with how a developer would approach the same ray tracing algorithm in compute with respect to DXR, and vice versa.

We will not address all the possible techniques that can be achieved by using ray tracing. The next chapters will present a few of them to support your learning process.

What we want to render is a bunch of spheres with no lighting, no reflections, no nothing. Just a plain solid color. This is actually the first step in implementing a ray tracer in general. When we talk about rendering the objects with just a plain color, we mean ray casting to be more precise.

Ray casting is the process of shooting the so-called primary rays.

In a typical ray tracer, we have these main steps:

- Shoot primary rays (rays that start at the camera position through each pixel of the screen).

- Shoot any second/third ray. Also known as *reflection* and *refraction* rays, these rays are cast from the point of intersection of the primary rays with the surface. Their direction is determined by the material properties of the surface, specifically the Bidirectional Reflectance Distribution Function (BRDF). The BRDF governs how light is reflected or transmitted, and more details on it will be provided in the following chapters.

- Shoot shadow rays (rays that starts at the point of intersection with a direction that points toward any light source in the scene). Here, any time we find an occluder, we will skip the diffuse/specular term computation, leaving the illumination equation with just the ambient contribution.

The previous bullet points are the main aspects to consider to implement a basic ray tracer. However, we will concentrate mostly on the first bullet point in this chapter, because the other two depend on the first to be defined up front. With the implementation of the first bullet point, we will actually implement ray casting, which in general is nothing new under the sun, and it is also very cheap as it will not involve

CHAPTER 3 GPGPU RAY TRACING VS. DXR RAY TRACING APPROACHES

the processing of further rays in a given scene. We will build our ray caster on top of the small CUDA program that we presented in Chapter 1, which was actually just rendering the buffer with a 0-1 range gradient in both the x- and y-axis. Refer to Chapter 1, if you want to refresh any of the previous concepts.

We will then update the previous CUDA code to incorporate all the previously mentioned points.

So, this was the current state of the CUDA code in Chapter 1:

```
//the keyword __global__ instructs the CUDA compiler that this function is
//the entry point of our kernel
__global__ void RenderScene(const int N,float* ColorBuffer)
{
    int x = blockIdx.x*blockDim.x + threadIdx.x;
    int y = blockIdx.y*blockDim.y + threadIdx.y;
    //checks whether we are inside the color buffer bounds.
    //If not, just return
    if(x > N || y > N)
    {
        return;
    }
    //We access the linear ColorBuffer storing each color component
    //separately (we could have a float3 color buffer for a more
    //compact/cleaner solution)
    int offset = (x + y*N)*3;
    //Store the results of your computations
    ColorBuffer[offset] = static_cast<float>(x)/static_cast<float>(N);
    ColorBuffer[offset+1] = static_cast<float>(y)/static_cast<float>(N);
    ColorBuffer[offset+2] = 0.0f;
}
```

We will start from the above CUDA kernel implementation and build a ray caster on top of it.

Figure 3-1 shows how ray casting works visually.

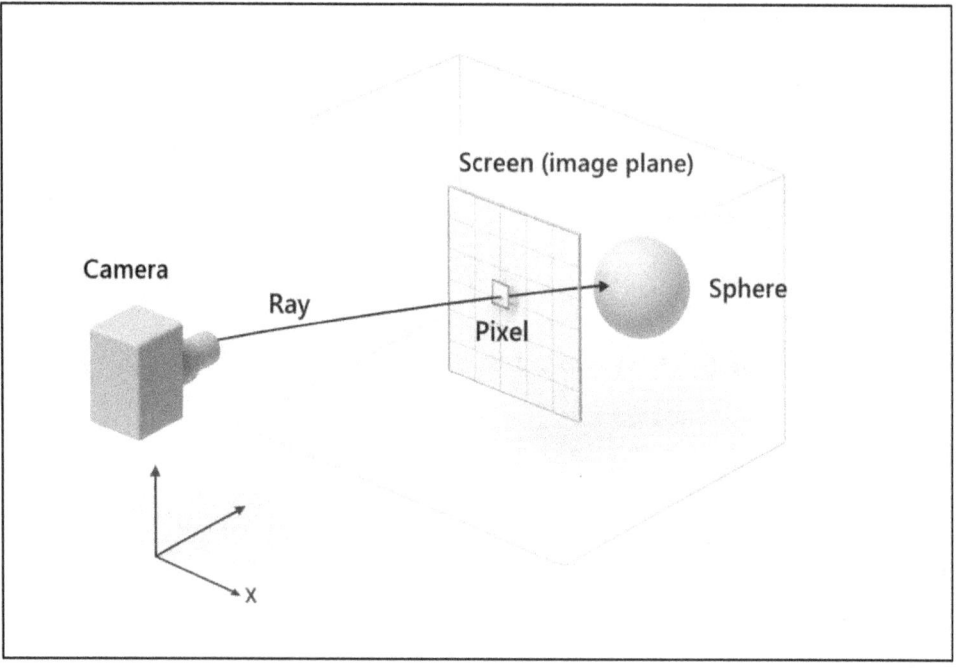

Figure 3-1. *We shoot a ray from the camera position through each pixel calculating the intersection point with each scene object (e.g., a sphere)*

So, what we need them to render is a bunch of spheres in correct depth order with ray casting? Here we list the minimum number of concepts we need in order to implement ray casting:

- We need to define our camera.
- We need to define a ray.
- We want to explain briefly how ray-sphere intersection test works.

Let's see how we can define a camera in practice.

Camera Model Definition

Let's start by defining our camera model theoretically and practically. Our camera is defined by a position, which we can also call the eye; an up vector w; a side vector u; and a forward vector v. The vectors w, u, and v will form the frame of reference of our camera

CHAPTER 3 GPGPU RAY TRACING VS. DXR RAY TRACING APPROACHES

with the eye being the origin. The screen grid, or image plane, will be width pixel wide and height pixel tall. The total number of pixels will be width*height.

With these elements at hand, let's define our camera C++ class:

```
class Camera
{
public:

__device__ Camera(const Vector3& InEye = Vector3(0.f, 0.f, 0.f)
               , const Vector3& InLookAt = Vector3(0.f, 0.f, 50.f)
               , const Vector3& InUp = Vector3(0.f, 1.f, 0.f)
               , float InFov = 60.f
               , float InAspectRatio = 1.f)
    : mEye(InEye)
    , mLookAt(InLookAt)
    , mScaleY(1.f)
    , mScaleX(1.f)
    , mW(0.f,0.f,1.f)
    , mU(1.f,0.f,0.f)
    , mV(0.f,1.f,0.f)
{
    const Vector3& Fwd = InLookAt - InEye;
    mW = Fwd.norm();     // this normalizes the forward vector
    mU = InUp.cross(mW); // This computes the side vector as the cross
                         //            product of the up vector and forward vector
    mV = mW.cross(mU);   // This computes the corrected up vector as the cross
                         //            product of the forward vector and side vector
    mScaleY = tanf(InFov*0.5f);
    mScaleX = mScaleY * InAspectRatio;
}

~Camera() = default;

//We calculate the world space ray direction given the position of the pixel in image space and
//the image plane width and height.
```

```cpp
__device__ Vector3 GetWorldSpaceRayDir(float InPx, float InPy, float InWidth, float InHeight) const
{
    //This transforms pixel coordinates to normalized device coordinates and
    //scales them according to the camera's FOV and aspect ratio
    float Alpha = ((InPx / InWidth)*2.0f - 1.0f)*mScaleX;
    float Beta = ((1.0f - (InPy / InHeight))*2.0f - 1.0f)*mScaleY;
    Vector3 WSRayDir = mU * Alpha + mV * Beta + mW;
    return WSRayDir;
}

__device__ Vector3 GetCameraEye() const { return mEye; }

 //we could add more accessor (getter/setter) if necessary

private:

    //Convenient member variables used to cache the scale along the x and y axis of the
    //camera space
    float mScaleY;
    float mScaleX;

    /**The camera position */
    Vector3 mEye;

    /**The camera forward vector */
    Vector3 mW;

    /**The camera side vector*/
    Vector3 mU;

    /**The camera up vector */
    Vector3 mV;

    /**The camera look at */
    Vector3 mLookAt;

};
```

CHAPTER 3   GPGPU RAY TRACING VS. DXR RAY TRACING APPROACHES

Ray Definition

Now that we've defined our scene camera, we can start by defining a ray. A ray is defined to be a line that starts at an origin, which we will call **o**, and propagates **t** times along its direction **d**. Where **o** is a vector position, **d** is a vector with unit length (i.e., the direction) and **t** a real number. A point **p** along the ray direction **d** is computed as shown in the following formula:

$$p(t) = o + \vec{d} * t$$

Figure 3-2 gives a visual representation of a ray to better clarify the concept.

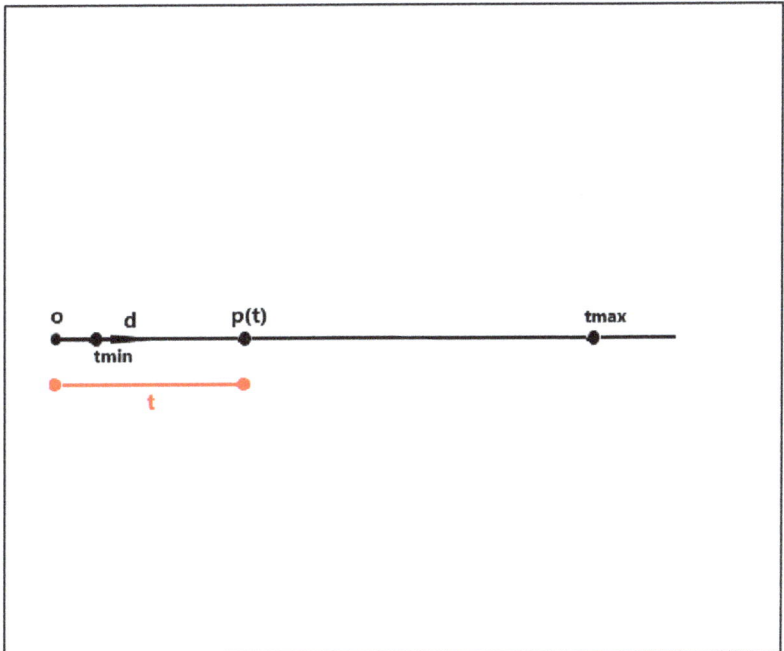

Figure 3-2. *Point p(t) is t times distant from o and between tmin and tmax*

We will also define two additional useful parameters for our ray. These are tmin and tmax, and we will use them to define the interval in which a given intersection is valid. We will see the advantage of defining such an interval later. Now, as we've done for the camera class, we define a simple ray C++ class:

```
//Simple ray class
class Ray
{
public:
```

Chapter 3 GPGPU Ray Tracing vs. DXR Ray Tracing Approaches

```
    /** Ctor */
    __device__ Ray(const Vector3& InOrigin = Vector3(0, 0, 0), const
    Vector3& InDirection = Vector3(0, 0, 1), float InTmin = 0.01f, float
    InTmax = 100000.0f) : mOrigin(InOrigin),mDirection(InDirection),mTmin(
    InTmin),mTmax(InTmax) {}
    /** Copy Ctor */
    __device__ Ray(const Ray& InRay) : mOrigin(InRay.mOrigin),
    mDirection(InRay.mDirection) { }

    //Method used to compute position at parameter t
    __device__ Vector3 PositionAtT(float t) const
    {
    return mOrigin + mDirection * t;
    }
    Vector3 mOrigin;
    Vector3 mDirection;
    float mTmin;
    float mTmax;
};
```

In the next section, you will see how to perform one of the simplest intersection tests: Ray-sphere intersection.

Ray-Sphere Intersection

Last but not least, we will discuss ray-sphere intersection. There are two different approaches that we can follow to compute it. One is a vector-like approach, and another one is more analytic. We will go for the analytic one, as it's the most straightforward for the theory and to implement.

Figure 3-3 shows the different solutions for the resulting quadratic polynomial equation.

CHAPTER 3   GPGPU RAY TRACING VS. DXR RAY TRACING APPROACHES

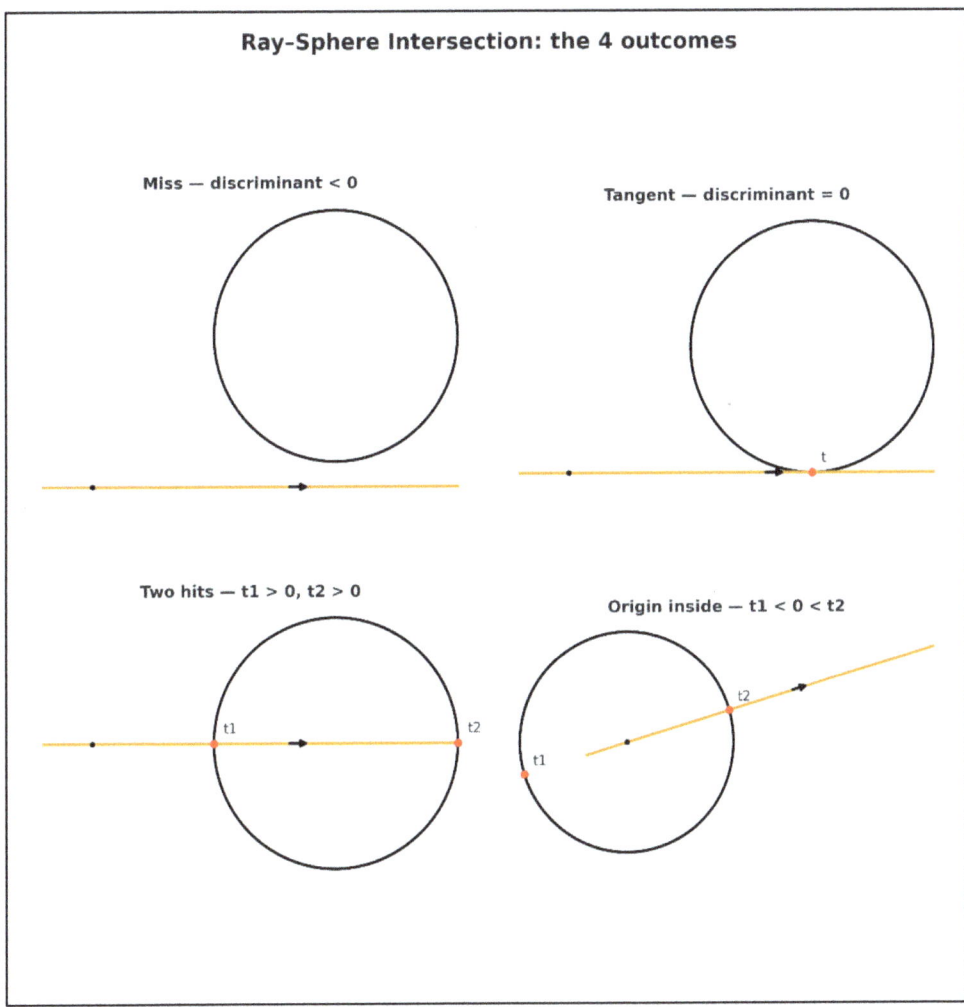

Figure 3-3. *Ray-sphere intersection outcomes. What happens with different discriminant values*

We now define the C++ class to describe a sphere that has a method to compute the intersection with a ray:

```
//Simple sphere class
class Sphere
{
private:

  /** The center of the sphere */
  Vector3 mCenter;
```

61

CHAPTER 3   GPGPU RAY TRACING VS. DXR RAY TRACING APPROACHES

```cpp
  /** The radius of the sphere */
  float mRadius;

public:

  /** Ctor */
  __device__ Sphere(const Vector3& InCenter = Vector3(0, 0, 0), float InRadius = 1) : mCenter(InCenter), mRadius(InRadius) { }

  /** Copy Ctor */
  __device__ Sphere(const Sphere& InSphere) : mCenter(InSphere.mCenter), mRadius(InSphere.mRadius) { }

//Compute the ray-sphere intersection using the analitic solution approach
__device__ bool Intersect(const Ray& InRay, float InTMin, float InTMax, HitData& OutHitData)
{
    const Vector3& oc = (InRay.mOrigin - mCenter);
    const float a = InRay.mDirection.dot(InRay.mDirection);
    const float b = oc.dot(InRay.mDirection);
    const float c = oc.dot(oc) - mRadius * mRadius;
    const float Disc = b * b - a * c;

    if (Disc < 0.0f)
    {
       return false; // no real roots
    }
    // Small epsilon to treat near-tangent hits as a single root.
    // If you truly want exact "== 0" handling, replace the fabsf check
    // with (disc == 0.0f).
    constexpr float kEps = 1e-8f;

    auto try_commit = [&](float t) -> bool
    {
      if (t > inTMin && t < inTMax)
      {
         OutHitData.t = t;
         OutHitData.mHitPos = inRay.PositionAtT(t);
```

CHAPTER 3 GPGPU RAY TRACING VS. DXR RAY TRACING APPROACHES

```
         // already unit-length
         OutHitData.mNormal = (OutHitData.mHitPos - mCenter) / mRadius;
         return true;
      }
      return false;
   };

   if (fabsf(Disc) <= kEps)
   {
      // Single root (tangent)
      const float t = (-b) / a;
      return try_commit(t);
   }

   // Two roots - check the nearer one first
   const float SqrtDisc = sqrtf(Disc);
   float t = (-b - SqrtDisc) / a;
   if (try_commit(t)) return true;

   t = (-b + SqrtDisc) / a;
   return try_commit(t);
}
};
```

As you can see, we are getting a `HitData` object in the output, which will hold all the relevant information that we'll use later to shade our sphere.

The `HitData` data structure looks as follows:

```
//Simple struct used to collect post hit data (i.e. hit position,
normal and t)
struct HitData
{
   /** Ctor */
   __device__ HitData() : mHitPos(0.f,0.f,0.f), mNormal(0.f,1.f,0.f) { }

   //The position at the intersection
   Vector3 mHitPos;

   //The normal at the intersected position
```

63

```
    Vector3 mNormal;

    //The distance at the intersection
    float t = 0.0f;
};
```

In the next section, we will put together all the previous concepts and build a ray caster in CUDA.

Ray Casting in CUDA

If we put together all the previously explained concepts, we can start casting rays in world space from our camera via our ray struct and sphere class. So, the CUDA kernel from Chapter 1 will turn into this:

```
__global__ void RenderScene(const int N, float* ColorBuffer)
{
    int x = blockIdx.x*blockDim.x + threadIdx.x;
    int y = blockIdx.y*blockDim.y + threadIdx.y;
    //checks whether we are inside the color buffer bounds.
    //If not, just return
    if (x >= N || y >= N)
    {
        return;
    }
    //Create a simple sphere 10 units away from the world origin
    Sphere sphere(Vector3(0.0f,0.0f,3.0f),2.5f);
    //Prepare two color
    Vector3 Black(0.0f, 0.0f, 0.0f); //Black background if we miss a
    primitive
    Vector3 Green(0.0f, 1.0f, 0.0f); //Red color if we hit a primitive (in
    //our case a sphere, but can be any type of primitive)
    //Create a camera
    Camera camera(Vector3(0.0f,0.0f,-10.0f));
    //Cast a ray in world space from the camera
    //Compute the world space ray direction
```

```
auto WSDir = camera.GetWorldSpaceRayDir(x,y,N,N);
//Construct a ray in world space that originates from the camera
Ray WSRay(camera.GetCameraEye(), WSDir);
//Compute intersection and set a color
HitData OutHitData;
Vector3 ColorResult = sphere.Intersect(WSRay,0.0f,FLT_MAX,OutHitData) ?
Green : Black;
//We access the linear ColorBuffer storing each color component
//separately (we could have a float3 color buffer for a more
//compact/cleaner solution)
int offset = (x + y * N) * 3;
//Store the results of your computations
ColorBuffer[offset] = ColorResult.X();
ColorBuffer[offset + 1] = ColorResult.Y();
ColorBuffer[offset + 2] = ColorResult.Z();
}
```

Figure 3-4 shows the output of this kernel.

CHAPTER 3 GPGPU RAY TRACING VS. DXR RAY TRACING APPROACHES

Figure 3-4. *Ray casting against a sphere in world space (the sphere is at the center of the image plane and 3 units away from the world origin). Rendered with CUDA*

If we hit something (in this case our sphere), we return a green color as a result and otherwise a black color (you can also change the code if you want and output different colors for the sphere as well as for the background).

I presented the approach that you can take in CUDA to implement a simple ray caster. But I did not tell you the whole story, and that is that we normally won't render analytic surfaces (e.g., a sphere, a plane, etc.) in a real-world scenario, but real triangle meshes.

Therefore, one of the most important routines is represented by the ray-triangle intersection. This will take us to evaluating the following code to render the triangles that belong to a given mesh:

```
for(int py=0;py<ScreenHeight;++py)
  for(int px=0;px<ScreenWidth;++px)
    for(int i=0;i<NumOfTriangles;++i)
      Triangles[i].Intersect(Ray(px,py),i)
```

We can clearly see that for a mesh of 200,000 triangles and a resolution of 1024×1024, we have to evaluate 200,000 * 1024* 1024 = 209 billion of ray-triangle intersection tests. That is not definitely viable for an offline ray tracer, not to mention if that ray tracer is supposed to run in real time.

Fortunately, there is a solution. We can use an acceleration data structure to detect quickly whether a ray intersects a given triangle or group of them.

By employing a spatial data structure, we can quickly perform a query to know if a given ray will hit or not a bunch of triangles. This will prevent us in iterating the whole set of triangles, which is normally what happens if we do not have any spatial relationship telling us how triangles are grouped in space.

There has been plenty of research over the years concerning the topic of spatial data structures (or acceleration structures) applied to ray tracing acceleration.

These data structures are KD-Tree, BVH, and Octrees. The new NVIDIA Turing architecture implements BVH traversal with intersection tests in hardware in the RT cores. The BVH choice is mainly related to the fact that ray-box test is very computationally efficient and can be implemented with no `if` statements, making it a good choice for massive parallel execution.

In the next section, you will see how DXR will handle the ray casting process and then compare it to the previous CUDA compute solution.

DXR and the New Shader Stages in Practice

DirectX Ray Tracing (DXR) is the new interface that Microsoft added to the D3D12 graphics API; it allows developers to exploit the new real-time ray tracing capabilities of the new NVIDIA Turing GPUs. Ray tracing is supported in hardware on all the NVIDIA RTX series graphics cards and is emulated in software by the graphics driver from the NVIDIA GeForce GTX 1060 and up. Every graphics card below that will not support any DXR feature.

DXR will allow us to create two types of acceleration data structures:

- Bottom-level acceleration structure (BLAS). BLAS is mainly used to store real geometry inside a BVH.

- Top-level acceleration structure (TLAS). TLAS is used to implement geometry instancing.

CHAPTER 3   GPGPU RAY TRACING VS. DXR RAY TRACING APPROACHES

In fact, each TLAS will reference an underlying BLAS (which will contain our actual mesh geometry), together with a transformation matrix and an instance ID.

We will not go in detail with respect to how any D3D12 ray tracing resources are created as this will be discussed in more detail in Chapter 9. Rather, we will show just the shader that realizes the same ray casting process.

To start casting rays, we have to create the so-called ray generation shader. The following HLSL code shows the implementation:

```
// Hold the acceleration data structure (built from the application)
RaytracingAccelerationStructure Scene : register(t0, space0);
// Alias for the triangle intersection attributes
typedef BuiltInTriangleIntersectionAttributes IntersectionAttributes;
// UAV used to store the ray tracing results
RWTexture2D<float4> RenderTarget : register(u0);
// User defined struct
struct RayPayload
{
    float4 color;
};
// PI
static const float kPI = 3.1415927f;
// Helper function used to convert from Degree to radians
float DegToRad(float Deg)
{
    return (Deg * kPI / 180.0f);
}

[shader("raygeneration")]
void RayCastingShader()
{
    float2 NormCoords = (float2)DispatchRaysIndex() /
    (float2)DispatchRaysDimensions();
    float2 ScreenSize = (float2)DispatchRaysDimensions();
    // Re-normalize to -1,1 range
    NormCoords.x = NormCoords.x*2.0f - 1.0f;
    NormCoords.y = NormCoords.y*2.0f - 1.0f;
```

```hlsl
// Construct the ray in world space with a perspective projection
// The projection data and camera data are normally passed from the
application through a CBuffer, but
// we hardcode them for illustration purposes.
    const float InFov = DegToRad(60.0f);
    const float HFov = InFov * 0.5f;
    const float AspectRatio = (ScreenSize.x / ScreenSize.y);
    const float ScaleY = tan(HFov);
    const float ScaleX = ScaleY * AspectRatio;
// Camera is positioned one unit away from the origin along Z
    const float3 CameraEye = float3(0.0f,0.0f,-2.5f);
    // We assume a fixed camera looking down positive Z
    // The up axis in our case is Y
    float3 u = float3(1, 0, 0);
    float3 v = float3(0, 1, 0);
    float3 w = float3(0, 0, 1);
    // Let's suppose this is our look at position (target)
    float3 LookAt = float3(0.0f,0.0f,5.0f);
    w = normalize(LookAt - CameraEye);
    u = cross(w,float3(0.0f,1.0f,0.0f));
    v = cross(u, w);
    // Here we construct a world space ray starting from the perspective
    camera position
    float3 rayDir = u * ScaleX * NormCoords.x + v * ScaleY * NormCoords.y + w;
    float3 origin = CameraEye;
    // Here we start tracing rays
    // RayDesc is a built in HLSL struct
    RayDesc ray;
    ray.Origin = origin;
    ray.Direction = rayDir;
    // Remember tmin and tmax? We set them here as well to account for
    certain precision issues
    ray.TMin = 0.001;
    ray.TMax = 10000.0;
```

CHAPTER 3 GPGPU RAY TRACING VS. DXR RAY TRACING APPROACHES

```
    // RayPayload is user defined struct in which we can return the return
    result of the TraceRay call
    RayPayload payload = { float4(0, 0, 0, 0) };
    // TraceRay is the new HLSL intrinsic that starts the ray
    tracing process
    TraceRay(Scene, RAY_FLAG_CULL_BACK_FACING_TRIANGLES, ~0, 0, 1, 0, ray,
    payload);
    // If we hit an object we return its color
    RenderTarget[DispatchRaysIndex().xy] = payload.color;
}
```

Figure 3-5 shows the output of the previous ray generation shader.

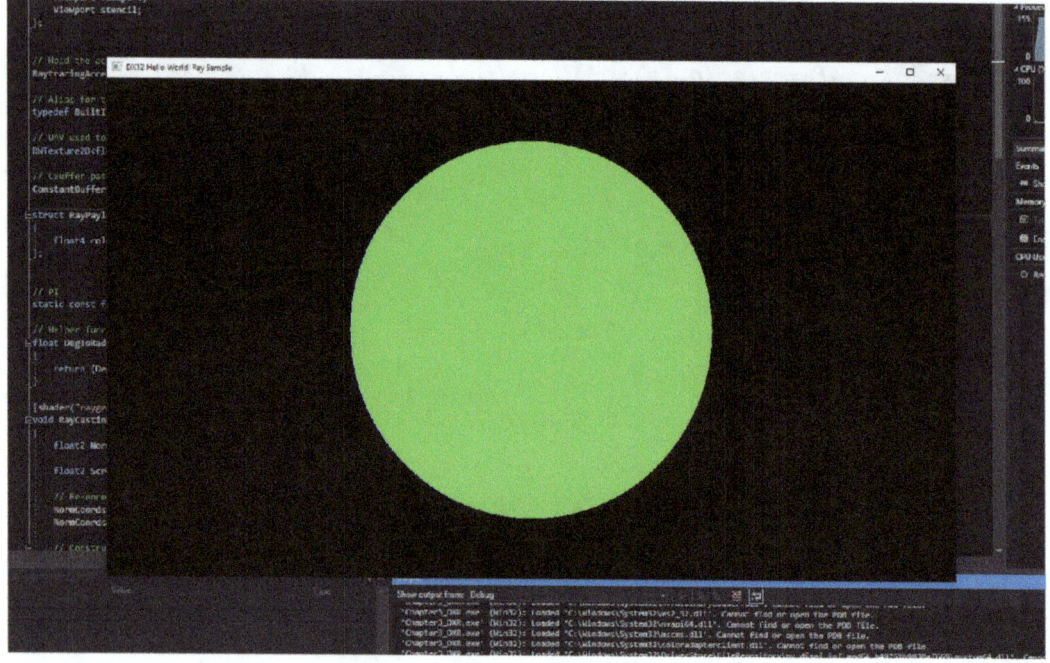

Figure 3-5. *Ray casting against a sphere in world space (the sphere is at the center of the image plane and 3 units away from the world origin). Rendered with the new DirectX Ray Tracing API*

The TraceRay() New HLSL Function

A ray is traced by calling the TraceRay() intrinsic HLSL function. The process is repeated for each pixel, and when an intersection is found, we are interested in the closest one because we want the objects correctly sorted with respect to their depth from the camera.

Let's take a look at some of the most relevant parameters of the TraceRay() function:

- The first parameter is the top-level scene acceleration structure that is traversed during the ray-intersection process.

- The second parameter is a flag (also called RayFlags). In this case we want to cull back-facing triangles.

- The third parameter an unsigned integer, the bottom 8 bits of which are used to include or reject geometry instances based on the InstanceMask in each instance.

- The parameter before the last one is the ray to be traced.

- The last parameter is a user-defined struct that can be accessed both for both input and output by shaders invoked during raytracing.

I've addressed only a subset of the total number of parameters accepted by the TraceRay() function. For a complete and more precise description of all the parameters accepted by the TraceRay() function, I suggest you look at the Microsoft online documentation as a reference.

To account for the closest intersection (or closest hit), we have to implement the so-called closest hit shader.

The HLSL code is straightforward and is shown here:

```
[shader("closesthit")]
void RayCastingClosestHit(inout RayPayload Payload, in
IntersectionAttributes Attr)
{
    // We could compute the barycentric coordinates and output them as a
    color to check form correctness
    // float3 barycentrics = float3(1 - Attr.barycentrics.x -
    Attr.barycentrics.y, Attr.barycentrics.x, Attr.barycentrics.y);
```

```
    // Payload.color = float4(barycentrics, 1);
    // We return green to be consistent with the previous example
    Pauload.color = float4(0.0f,1.0f,0.0f,1.0f);
}
```

When we hit a primitive and that hit is the closest one, the previous shader is called. This is the typical place to account for the shading of the primitive or, like in our simple example, just return the barycentric coordinates of the triangle we just hit. We could also return just the green color if we wanted. That will be consistent with the same code sample we did in our first CUDA example at the beginning of this chapter. Or we could call TraceRay() again if we are implementing ray traced reflections/refractions or a path tracer.

In fact, TraceRay() can be called in the ray generation shader as well as in the closest-hit. If we don't hit any primitive in the scene, we call the miss-shader, and that typically means we "hit" the background.

Again, in our specific example, here is the code for our miss shader:

```
[shader("miss")]
void RayCastingMiss(inout RayPayload payload)
{
    payload.color = float4(0.0f, 0.0f, 0.0f, 1.0f);
}
```

Very simple in this case. We just return black as a background color or any color, or we could look up our color from a cubemap! We presented two ways of performing ray casting in this chapter.

In the next section, we will briefly discuss the main practical differences of using one or the other way of casting rays.

Compute-Based Ray Tracing vs. DXR-Based Ray Tracing

The first difference that we can notice is that the intersection process as well as the tracing itself are both handled automatically under DXR. In fact, as we will see in the next chapter, the RT cores in the Turing GPUs are responsible for performing the ray tracing as well as the TLAS traversal in hardware. This is an important advantage of the new Turing hardware because the main CUDA cores (or compute units to stay general) are now completely offloaded from the ray tracing. Prior to the Turing generation, ray tracing was running completely on the compute units of the GPU, which were also responsible for performing rasterization and general compute tasks.

In a scenario where we need to render the scene of a game, the problem of sharing that power between the ray tracing process and the rasterization, for example, was going to be surely a problem when shooting rays was not the only task running.

In fact, many of the ray tracing implementations that were previously leveraging the GPU were employed solely on scenarios where the GPU itself was used just to render the scene and nothing more. One such scenario is, for example, offline rendering in CGI-based movies.

In a typical game we don't have just rendering. We have AI, physics, sound, etc. Therefore, we cannot allocate all the GPU compute resources just for ray tracing. The solution with the new ray tracing capable hardware is to give dedicated cores (called RT cores) just for ray tracing.

Summary

In this chapter, you analyzed the ray casting implementation in CUDA (purely compute based) and in DXR.

You saw a simple example made by a ray-traced sphere placed at the center of the screen. The simplest intersection routine that we briefly showed, just to serve our code sample, is the ray-sphere intersection. We explained what a ray is mathematically and how it could be visualized on a piece of paper (Figure 3-2).

The chapter presented a C++ implementation for each class that was involved in the ray casting process (e.g., camera class, ray class, etc.)

In the DXR part, we started using practically the new shaders introduced with the ray tracing support in D3D12. Finally, a comparison has been made to show the main differences in going from a purely compute CUDA solution with respect to a D3D12 DXR-based one. In this way, we have been able to understand what it takes structurally and practically to implement a given ray tracing-based algorithm in CUDA as well as in DXR. Of course, this is a bare-bones introduction but still important to understand some of the practical differences in both approaches. Bear with me because there is more to come in the next chapters.

That's all for this chapter.

In the next one, we will shift our attention on the Turing hardware to understand how RT cores work. We of course cannot know the internals of those cores as that is not released publicly. However, we can for sure look at their role in the ray tracing process and how they relate to the rest of the standard CUDA cores.

Questions

Based on the knowledge that you gained in this chapter, it is your turn to answer some questions:

- How you would implement a ray-plane intersection routine?
- How you would compute the normal of a sphere?
- How are called the rays that have their origin at the camera position?
- Based on what decision you would implement ray tracing under DXR other than CUDA?
- Why do you want the closest-hit when we trace a ray?
- Why do you want to consider more than one hit for a given ray?
- What is the main difference between a BLAS and a TLAS, and how do they relate to each other?

Further Reading

The following are few links that you can use to expand your knowledge of the topics in this chapter:

- `https://developer.nvidia.com/rtx/raytracing/dxr/dx12-raytracing-tutorial-part-1`
- `http://robbinmarcus.blogspot.com/2015/10/real-time-raytracing-part-1.html`
- `https://learn.microsoft.com/en-us/windows/win32/direct3d12/directx-12-programming-guide`
- `https://devblogs.nvidia.com/introduction-nvidia-rtx-directx-raytracing/`

CHAPTER 4

Enter the Turing Microarchitecture

At the time of writing this book, the Turing GPUs are considered the state of the art in current GPU technology. This cutting-edge technology is the first that is capable of rendering real-time ray-traced scenes at interactive rates provided that the scene and the materials are organized and tuned in the right way. The new RT cores (ray tracing cores) are the main component we are interested in here.

In this chapter, you will learn what changed in terms of GPU architecture when it comes to managing a ray tracing engine in hardware. This is important because we don't want to write DXR code without knowing what is happening at the hardware level, especially when it comes time to profile our ray-traced frame.

Moreover, it's an important milestone for real-time computer graphics, much like what happened when the programmable pixel/vertex shader was introduced a long time ago.

The following topics will be covered in this chapter:

- GPU Turing micro-architecture, a major step toward real-time photorealistic rendering
- The new RT cores
- BLAS and TLAS explained in detail
- Evolving NVIDIA architectures and the future of real-time graphics

© Fabio Suriano 2025
F. Suriano, *Ray Tracing in CUDA and DXR*, https://doi.org/10.1007/979-8-8688-1691-8_4

CHAPTER 4   ENTER THE TURING MICROARCHITECTURE

Understanding Turing GPUs

This first step toward real-time ray tracing has been taken by NVIDIA with its Turing GPUs.

What we will show in this chapter will be related solely to this new architecture, with a lot of emphasis on the new RT core engines.

What was needed was a new way to offload the *streaming multiprocessor* (SM) from dealing with *bounding volume hierarchy* traversal and intersections, leaving it with more computing power to handle pixel shader, vertex shader, and compute-related tasks.

A **bounding volume hierarchy (BVH)** is a tree structure used to accelerate ray tracing by organizing scene geometry into nested bounding volumes, usually boxes. Each parent node encloses its child nodes, and leaf nodes contain the actual primitives (like triangles). When a ray is cast, the traversal process quickly discards large portions of the scene by testing intersections with bounding volumes first, checking detailed geometry only when necessary.

This hierarchical approach significantly reduces the number of intersection tests compared to brute-force methods, making BVH traversal one of the most critical optimizations in real-time ray tracing. Modern GPUs use dedicated RT cores and specialized hardware logic to speed up BVH traversal, ensuring efficient handling of complex scenes while keeping frame times manageable.

> *The scene traversal is one of the steps of the ray tracing process that is central in speedily determining the ray-mesh/triangle intersection. It allows us to skip large portions of the scene that will not be intersected by a given ray up front. The brute-force approach was to scan all the meshes in the scene and all their triangles while testing them for intersection (very bad performance-wise).*

Moreover, the possibility to have the scene traversal managed completely in hardware is going to save a lot of resource slots (i.e., registers, constants, structured buffers, and so on...).

All of these resources were necessary when we were dealing with BVH data structures on the software side of things, and if we were dealing with them on the GPU compute side of things, we were using tons of GPU resources to keep all the data related to the scene bounding volume data. Figure 4-1 shows what the Turing GPU SM looks like, with RT cores our main focus for this chapter.

CHAPTER 4   ENTER THE TURING MICROARCHITECTURE

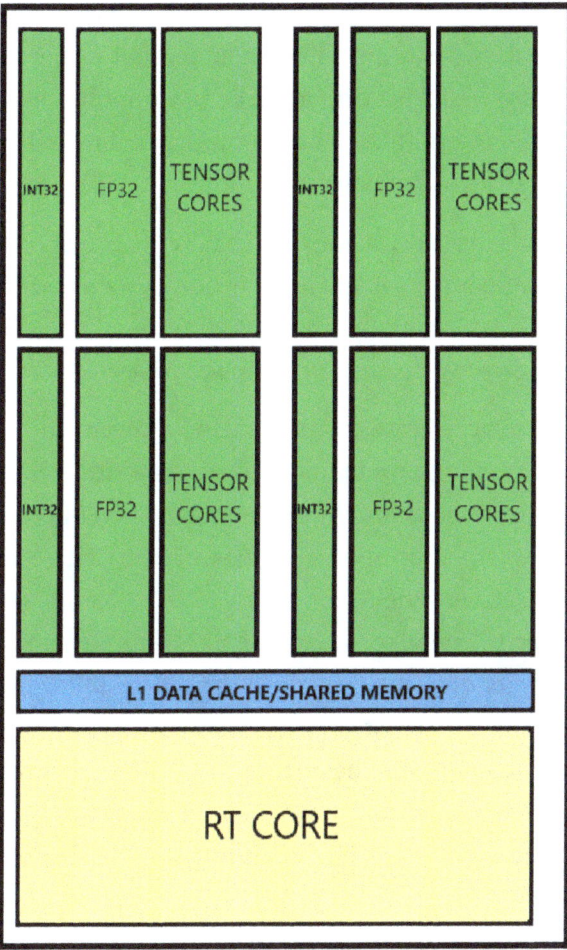

Figure 4-1. *NVIDIA Turing SM and RT cores*

In Figure 4-1 we can see the following main blocks:

- **INT32**: Integer arithmetic logic unit (ALU).
- **FP32**: Floating-point ALU.
- **Tensor Cores**: Tensor cores are able to perform complex matrix math (here we refer to big matrices). They are normally used in the context of deep learning to accelerate algorithms based on neural networks.

- **L1 Data Cache/Shared Memory**: Data cache is a fast cache that is used to cache data coming from global GPU memory, for fast subsequent access. It is a portion of memory that is shared with the shared memory, which is normally used in compute shaders by the programmer to optimize the reading and writing of frequently accessed data in a given shader execution.

- **RT Core**: Stands for "ray tracing core." This core is responsible for performing scene traversal and intersection by using a BVH to subdivide the scene spatially. This was considered one of the main slowdowns in any ray tracing engine in the past.

The RT core is there to accelerate this process in hardware and, more importantly, to separate the workload of managing a memory heavy data structure, like the BVH is, by using the traditional registers slots and by offloading the CUDA cores from the duty of computing the scene traversal themselves. In this way, the CUDA cores can be used for other operations in parallel with the RT Core.

Anytime there will be the need to update the BVH data structure to reflect the changes in the geometry it holds, the driver will handle the refitting and building process by itself. The application, instead, will be responsible for performing shading by employing the new shader types. The next section will explain the RT cores in more detail by introducing them in a typical usage scenario. By seeing a utilization context for RT cores, you will be able to better understand the role of this hardware unit.

The New RT Cores

We do not know the internals of the new RT core as they are not publicly available. But we can describe what they do from a more high-level view:

- Traverse the scene by constructing a tree

- Perform BVH traversal by computing ray-box intersection

To construct the bounding volume hierarchy, we pass our index and vertex buffer from the application, and a specific API call will be responsible for constructing the BVH.

At the root of the BVH tree data structure that subdivides the scene spatially, a box encloses all the scene geometry. As we go down the hierarchy levels, we encounter smaller AABB that subdivides the space even further until we eventually reach a leaf that will contain actual geometry (in our case triangles).

CHAPTER 4   ENTER THE TURING MICROARCHITECTURE

Figure 4-2 shows a top-level schematic view of what an RT core does.

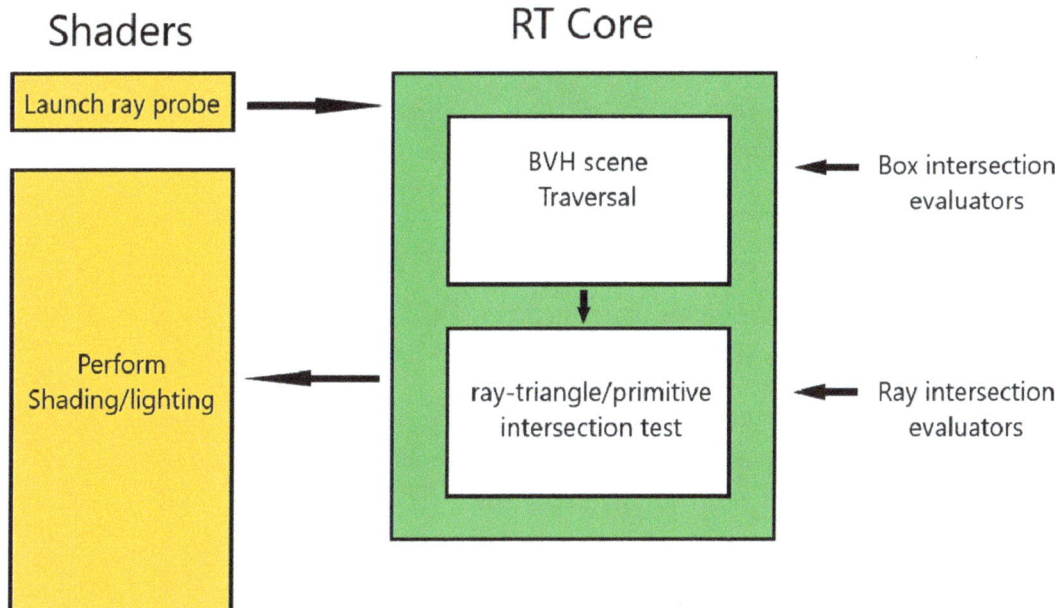

Figure 4-2. *RT core and application shaders interaction*

Let's try to explain each block from Figure 4-2 in more detail:

- The user launches a ray probe (a yellow small box on the left of the block diagram) typically by invoking TraceRay() from the ray generation shader, which as we've seen in Chapter 3 is the entry point of the ray generation shader defined by DXR API specification.

- The RT core will take in the scene acceleration structure (BVH) and perform BVH traversal to determine which subportion of the scene (and then which mesh precisely) needs to be tested for intersection with a given ray.

- Box intersection evaluators (rightmost part of the block diagram in Figure 4-2) are responsible for testing the ray-box intersection to decide on the subportion of the tree data structure.

- Ray intersection evaluators will perform the actual ray-primitive intersection.

- After the intersection with a given primitive (typically a triangle) has been found, the data that will be given in output will be used to perform lighting and shading operations.

DXR is a new interface that Microsoft added to DrectX12. It allows the user to program ray tracing on the GPUs that have that hardware support.

The DXR Microsoft API provides two concepts to manage the geometry representation, as we've already discussed in the previous chapter:

- The bottom-level acceleration structure (BLAS) stores real geometry in a BVH data structure.

- The top-level acceleration structure (TLAS) stores one or more references to BLAS and an index to the shader table in order to give the possibility to implement instancing.

We can consider a given BLAS and the geometry it holds, like having the granularity of a draw-call. In Chapter 9, we will talk about DX12 initialization for ray tracing by going into more detail in relation to TLAS and BLAS. We will look at the real C++ code that will fill the gaps between theory and practical side of things.

In the next section, we will give more detail than we did in the previous chapter in relation to both data structures.

An In-Depth Analysis of BLAS and TLAS

The top-level acceleration structure, as mentioned in the previous section, has been made to implement geometry instancing. It does so by holding references to the bottom-level acceleration structures, a transformation matrix, and a shader binding table (SBT) table offset that directly maps to an SBT record. SBT will realize the connection between the shader to be executed and the resources that are necessary during the execution of that shader.

See Figure 4-3 for an illustration of BLAS and TLAS and how they relate to each other.

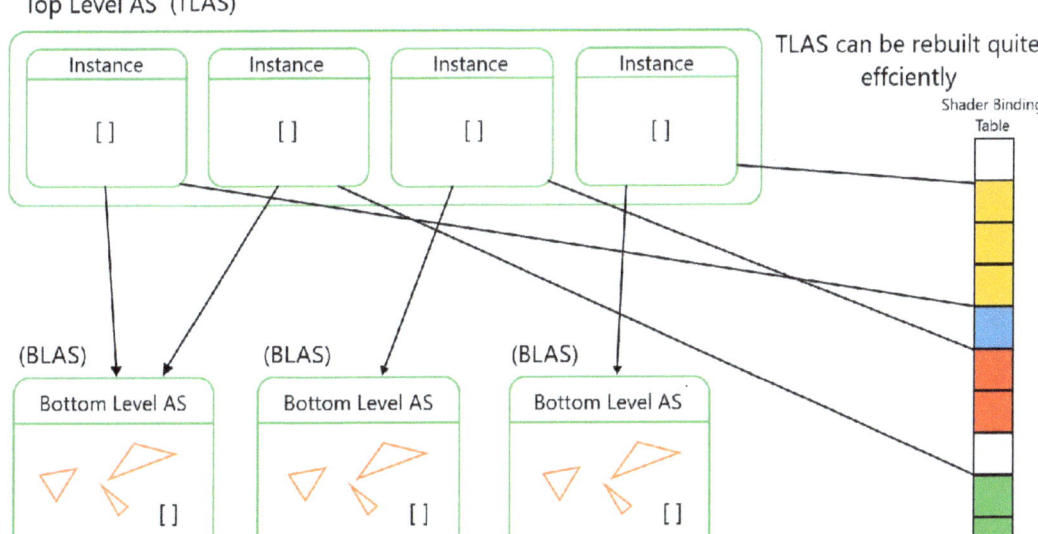

Figure 4-3. *BLAS and TLAS*

Each TLAS instance is referring to a BLAS and the related SBT offset. This can be considered similar to a draw call with its shaders and index and vertex buffers, but with a big difference: all the shaders of the scene objects must be available at any time and not just the shader related to the mesh that is being drawn. The reason for this is because we could hit pretty much anything anywhere in the scene. We cannot know in advance the shaders of a given triangle unless we associate a shader table offset that maps to an SBT record. The aforementioned table will contain all the scene shaders. Moreover, the TLAS must be available to the shaders during the ray tracing process because it's actually an integral part of it.

Figure 4-4 shows the anatomy of the shader table record.

CHAPTER 4   ENTER THE TURING MICROARCHITECTURE

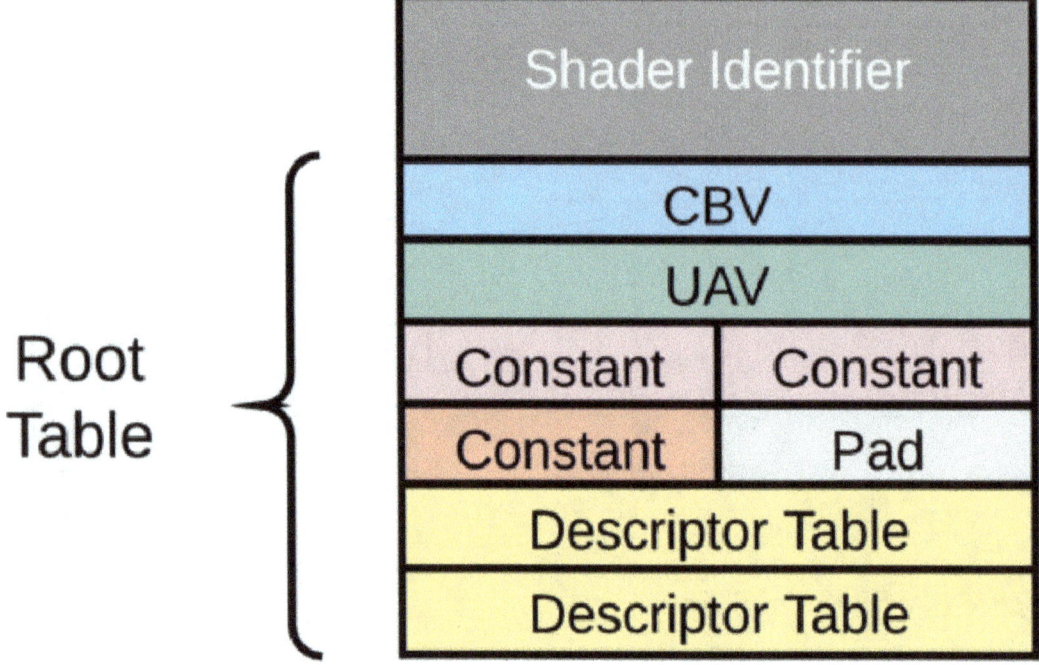

Figure 4-4. *Shader table record*

Let's go through each field of the block diagram of Figure 4-4:

- *Shader Identifier:* This is an integer opaque identifier that uniquely identifies a shader (or a hit group).

- *CBV:* This is a constant buffer view (a buffer that will hold shader uniform constants). This buffer is constructed and its field are filled by the user from the C++ application. More on this on Chapter 9.

- *UAV:* Unordered access view (basically read/write buffers).

- One or more constant (constants that don't go directly in the CBV and that are set directly by the user from the C++ application). More on this on Chapter 9.

- One or more descriptor tables. More on this on Chapter 9.

All the previous resources are part of the root table, as you can see in Figure 4-4, and the shader identifier is the header of the SBT record. In relation to the RT core, we will not add further pieces of information. This is all that you need to know for the programming side of things.

During the DXR object's creation, we will deal with BLAS and TLAS creation. Knowing what they are and how they work will help a lot in understanding all the parameters during their creation in code.

Evolving NVIDIA Architectures and the Future of Real-Time Graphics

Recent NVIDIA GPU architectures such as Ada Lovelace, Hopper, and the upcoming Blackwell family continue to push the boundaries of computer graphics, particularly in the domains of DirectX (DX) and real-time ray tracing (RT). Ada Lovelace introduced third-generation RT Cores and fourth-generation Tensor Cores, significantly enhancing real-time path tracing and AI-based rendering techniques. Hopper, while designed primarily for data centers, introduced innovations like the Transformer Engine, which indirectly benefits graphics research by accelerating neural rendering and real-time denoising methods. Looking ahead, Blackwell is expected to further refine RT performance, improve efficiency in hybrid rasterization + ray tracing pipelines, and provide a deeper integration of AI into the graphics pipeline. Together, these architectures illustrate the convergence of traditional graphics APIs (like DX12 Ultimate) with AI-driven acceleration, shaping the future of interactive and cinematic-quality rendering in games and professional visualization.

Summary

This was a more in-depth description of what the RT core actually does and how it does it. Moreover, the chapter introduced how the shaders in DXR are mapped to their respective TLASs and how they relate to scene rendering. We also mentioned that there is a global table where the SBT is responsible for holding each shader and its respective pieces of information. Those pieces of information are represented by the shader inputs, in most cases, like constant, constant buffer objects, unordered access view (UAV) (which are basically read/write buffers), and one or more descriptor tables.

We have all the main pieces of the puzzle in place for a useful schematic view of what we will deal with in the coming chapters.

Ray tracing with the new DXR API is very straightforward when it comes to the shader's implementation. The initialization of the main components in the C++ part of DXR, instead, is more involved in terms of code complexity.

The RayFramework, which is the C++ wrapper on which this book examples will be based, is thought to minimize the impact of all the main steps required to get a DXR sample up and running. It tries to do so by modularizing as much as possible, separating the concepts in classes. In this way, it should be simpler for to construct a mental map of the main components involved in the initialization process without getting lost in the verbosity of the initialization boilerplate C++ code.

In the next chapter, you will learn about some of the most common and basic ray-tracing techniques, which will serve as a gentle introduction of what we can actually implement with a ray-tracing setup.

Questions

Based on the knowledge that you gained in this chapter it is your turn to answer some questions:

- What are the main duties of a RT core in the Turing SM?
  - *Guiding note:* RT cores accelerate BVH traversal and ray–triangle intersection tests, freeing CUDA cores for shading and other computations.
- Why we need to define two acceleration structures (TLAS and BLAS)?
  - *Guiding note:* TLAS organizes instances of objects, while the BLAS stores the actual geometry. This separation allows efficient reuse of geometry data when objects are repeated or transformed.
- Why we need to have a SBT containing pretty much all the shaders of the scene?
  - *Guiding note:* The SBT acts as a lookup table that maps geometry to the correct shaders (e.g., closest-hit, miss, any-hit). It ensures that the ray tracer knows which shader to execute when a ray interacts with an object.

- What is a BVH and why it is important?

  - *Guiding note:* A BVH is a tree structure of bounding boxes used to accelerate ray tracing. It reduces the number of intersection tests by quickly discarding large portions of the scene, making traversal much more efficient.

Further Reading

The following are a few links you can use to expand your knowledge of the topics in this chapter:

- `https://devblogs.nvidia.com/introduction-nvidia-rtx-directx-raytracing/`

- `https://devblogs.nvidia.com/practical-real-time-ray-tracing-rtx/#part1`

- `https://www.nvidia.com/content/dam/en-zz/Solutions/designvisualization/technologies/turing-architecture/NVIDIA-Turing-Architecture-Whitepaper.pdf`

CHAPTER 5

Ray Tracing Techniques

In this chapter, we will talk about some of the most common techniques that can be implemented on top of an existing ray tracing engine. Some of these techniques can boost the image quality, but they come at some performance cost.

By the end of this chapter, you will understand the main problem affecting image quality. In addition, we will cover aliasing, providing different approaches to tackle the problem and the related solutions.

Other techniques, like depth of field and motion blur, will help to give a more realistic camera implementation from a practical standpoint. The pinhole camera model (more on this in the next chapter) is a crude simplification of what a real camera is. These effects are in fact part of any post-processing rendering pipeline nowadays, so we show how easy it is to implement them in a ray-tracing context compared to their rasterization counterpart.

Finally, we jump in the DXR realm and show how to address transparent objects rendering in a modern way through ray tracing. We all know that transparent objects rendering has been a crucial part of every rasterization-based engine regarding performance.

The following topics will be covered in this chapter:

- Sampling strategies to reduce aliasing
- Depth of field
- Motion blur
- Multi-hit ray tracing in DXR
- Ray tracing for high-quality scientific visualization

CHAPTER 5   RAY TRACING TECHNIQUES

Technical Requirements

The following tools will be required before we get started:

- Visual Studio 2022 Community
- Cuda Toolkit 13.0.1
- Windows 10 RS5 update

Minimum hardware requirements:

- GeForce RTX 2k series

Recommended hardware requirements:

- GeForce RTX 3k series and up

Sampling Strategies to Reduce Aliasing

Aliasing, and in our particular case spatial aliasing to be more precise, is the result of a poor reconstruction of the signal (in our case represented by the stream of samples of a rendered image) that causes two signals (or images) to be indistinguishable. In other words, they *alias* each other.

Such reconstruction is directly dependent upon the sampling strategy we adopt to reconstruct an image. We will show a few sampling strategies during the first part of this chapter all devoted to solving, or maybe it is better to say reducing, the aliasing of a rendered image.

So, it's clear that aliasing is surely one of the hot problems when it comes to ray tracing and ultimately image quality. The inherent nature of discrete point sampling in ray tracing causes continuous phenomena to be represented with discrete samples. Aliasing shows up as *jaggies* at the edges of the objects. When it comes to signal reconstruction, we have two types of aliasing:

- **Spatial aliasing**: This type of aliasing occurs in spatially sampled signals (e.g., *moiré* patterns in digital images).

- **Temporal aliasing**: This type of aliasing occurs in signals sampled in time (e.g., digital audio or series of image frames that are part of a rendered animation).

In this section, we will concentrate mostly on spatial aliasing, not to be confused with temporal aliasing, which shows up, instead, during the representation of animated frames.

In this section, we will use the term ray *or* sample *to mean pretty much the same thing. So, they will be used in an interchangeable way.*

Those techniques will be applicable to solve problems even in other areas, like for example in motion blur or texture filtering to mention a few.

We will talk about:

- Supersampling
- Supersampling in DXR
- Adaptive supersampling
- Stochastic ray tracing
- Statistical supersampling

Understanding Supersampling

One way to approach the aliasing problem is by tracing more rays across the pixel area and take their average. This technique is called *supersampling*.

This approach will not eliminate the aliasing problem, but, instead, will only reduce it. By shooting more rays, we will basically "fill" a part of the gaps that were generated because of rays missing the object.

In fact, the discrete nature of the pixel grid of the image plane is such that shooting one ray (or one sample) per pixel is not enough to cover an object completely. This is especially true if the object is very small or very far, where in that case the chance to miss that object will be higher.

See Figure 5-1 for a better visual description of what we've just explained.

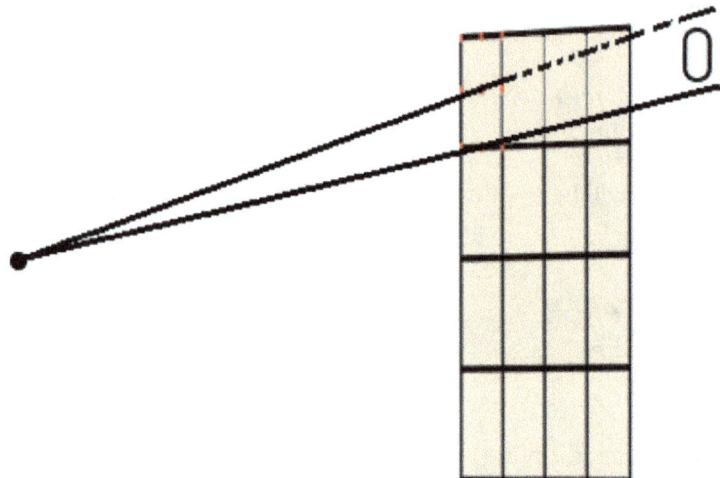

Figure 5-1. *Two rays are shot from the camera*

> *Shooting more rays per pixel will not solve the aliasing problem; it will only reduce it.*

So, for instance, we could pick nine samples per pixel. That will translate in using basically a 3x3 sample pattern for each pixel and then average the results for each ray that we shoot for each sample.

We will show a CUDA code snippet for this approach to illustrate how it can be implemented practically and show the usual screenshot of the rendered frame with the actual output. We will compare the supersampled results with the one ray/sample per pixel ones.

But before we do that, let's take a look at some C-like pseudocode just to give a quick idea of how supersampling works in principle:

```
int i = 0;
int j = 0;
Color Result = (0,0,0); // this is a 3D vector representing a color
Color PixelBuffer[Width*Height];
for each y < Height
for each x < Width
{
    for each j < 3
```

```
    for each i < 3
    {
        int index_x = i / 2;
        int index_y = j / 2;
        Result += SampleImage(x + index_x,y + index_y);
    }
// Average the result dividing by the total number of samples (in this case
9 //samples
    PixelBuffer[x+y*Width] = Result / 9.0f;
}
```

In Figure 5-2 we have a representation of a grid that is 4x4 pixels. Each cell in the grid represents a pixel. The red points are the samples that we pick on a given pixel. A 3x3 regular sample/rays pattern is taken.

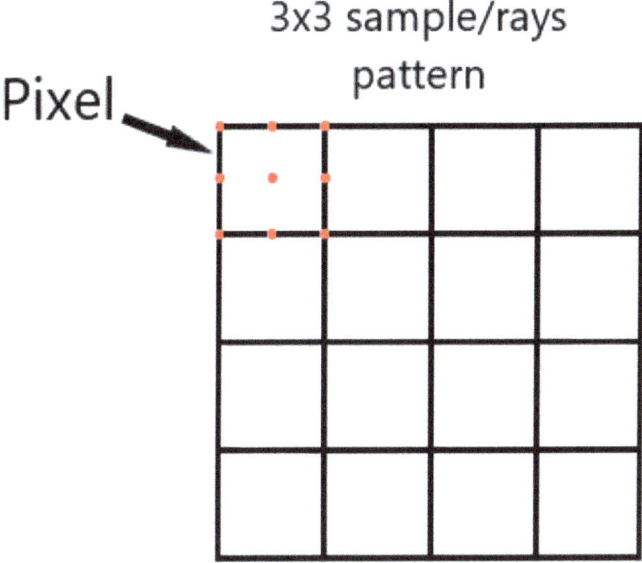

Figure 5-2. *We take nine samples in a regular grid pattern inside a given pixel and then we average them*

Now let's compare the same sphere we rendered in the previous chapter in CUDA/DXR with and without supersampling. Figure 5-3 shows a rendered scene without supersampling.

CHAPTER 5   RAY TRACING TECHNIQUES

***Figure* 5-3.** *Spheres rendered without supersampling applied (one sample and anti-aliasing disabled basically)*

Figure 5-4 shows the same scene with supersampling applied. Notice how the aliasing is dramatically reduced.

CHAPTER 5   RAY TRACING TECHNIQUES

Figure 5-4. Sphere rendered with supersampling applied (1024 samples and anti-aliasing active)

As you can see, aliasing has been reduced though it is not completely eliminated if you look really close to the silhouette of the spheres (you have to be really close). This confirms what we've just said. Now let's take a look at the following two code snippets. The first implements supersampling for the CUDA version, and the second will account for the same but for the DXR version. This is the code snippet for supersampling implemented in CUDA.

The first part of this snippet will compute a gradient `GradientInterp` just to fill the background and convenient constant `InvSamples` used to average the result at the end:

```
float GradientInterp = (static_cast<float>(y)/static_cast<float>(ScreenHeight));
Vector3 BkgColor = Lerp(Vector3(0.671f,0.875f,0.973f),
Vector3(0.992f,0.941f,0.918f),GradientInterp);
const float InvSamples = 1.f / (3.0f * 3.0f);
```

93

We are ready to pick our nine samples by implementing a double for loop of three iteration each. We shoot 3x3 samples, and we sample each pixel regularly. What we obtain at the end of this process is antialiasing by supersampling:

```
for(u32 j = 0;j < 3;++j)
    for (u32 i = 0; i < 3; ++i)
    {
        #if AA_ENABLED
            float rx = static_cast<float>(i) * 0.5f;
            float ry = static_cast<float>(j) * 0.5f;
            auto WSDir = camera.GetWorldSpaceRayDir(((float)x) + rx,
            ((float)y)
            + ry , ScreenWidth, ScreenHeight);
        #else
            auto WSDir = camera.GetWorldSpaceRayDir(((float)x), ((float)y),
            ScreenWidth, ScreenHeight);
        #endif
```

Then we construct a world space ray from the camera position given the sampled direction, and we create a DOFRay (if DOF is required/enabled). This is not necessary for the purpose of antialiasing, though. We get the closest-hit result, and if there is a hit, we accumulate the color of the object and otherwise the background color. Finally, we average the result represented by the variable ColorResult:

```
    Ray WSRay(camera.GetCameraEye(), WSDir);
    Ray DOFRay = GetDOFRay(WSRay, ApertureSize, FocalLength, &Seed0,
    &Seed1);
    HitData OutHitData;
    bool Hit = GetClosestHit(DOFRay, 0.001f, FLT_MAX,
    OutHitData,SphereList,kNumSpheres);
    ColorResult += (Hit ? SphereList[OutHitData.mObjId].mColor : BkgColor);
}
ColorResult *= InvSamples;
```

Now a small subsection will be devoted to the DXR implementation of supersampling. So, without anything further to add, let's take a look at the next subsection.

Supersampling in DXR

In the following code we show how we implement supersampling in DXR. The first part of the code will show a common camera setup, and the next part will show the actual sampling loop that, by shooting 3x3 rays for each pixel, will produce the filtered result.

The function RayCastingShader is the entry point of our ray generation shader. We can tell this because we have the annotation [shader("raygeneration")] just above the function name itself.

First, we compute [0,1] normalized coordinates starting from the ray index DispatchRaysIndex() and the screen size and get the screen size DispatchRaysDimensions().

```
[shader("raygeneration")]
void RayCastingShader()
{
    float2 NormCoords = (float2)DispatchRaysIndex()/(float2)
    DispatchRaysDimensions();
    float2 ScreenSize = (float2)DispatchRaysDimensions();
```

Construct the ray in world space with a perspective projection. The projection data and camera data are normally passed from the application through a CBuffer (constant buffer in DirectX 12 naming convention), but we've hardcoded them in the shader for illustration purposes:

```
    const float InFov = DegToRad(60.0f);
    const float HFov = InFov * 0.5f;
    const float AspectRatio = (ScreenSize.x / ScreenSize.y);
    const float ScaleY = tan(HFov);
    const float ScaleX = ScaleY * AspectRatio;
    // Camera is positioned 2.5 unit away from the origin along Z
    const float3 CameraEye = float3(0.0f,0.0f,-2.5f);
```

Construct then the frame of reference for our camera. We assume a fixed camera looking down positive Z, and the up-axis in our case is Y. By keeping this in mind, we construct a frame of reference starting with our LookAt and CameraEye vectors (just a pretty standard camera construction code).

The code continues by showing the 3x3 loop that actually realizes supersampling by sampling in a 3x3 regular sample pattern. RayDesc is a built-in HLSL struct that represents a ray. It has an origin, a direction, and tmin and tmax data members. We also construct the world space ray direction and origin. The origin will be the camera position itself, as well as the direction a vector that starts from the camera origin and passes through the image plane.

```
for(int j=0;j<3;++j)
  for(int i=0;i<3;++i)
  {
      NormCoords.x += (HalfPixelSize*i);
      NormCoords.y += (HalfPixelSize*j);
      // Re-normalize to -1,1 range
      NormCoords.x = NormCoords.x*2.0f - 1.0f;
      NormCoords.y = NormCoords.y*2.0f - 1.0f;
      // Here we construct a world space ray starting from the
      perspective camera position
      float3 rayDir = u * ScaleX * NormCoords.x + v * ScaleY * NormCoords.y + w;
      float3 origin = CameraEye;
      RayDesc ray;
      ray.Origin = origin;
      ray.Direction = rayDir;
```

We fill the tmin and tmax members of the ray structure, inizialize the payload (which in our case contains just the color), and then start tracing rays by calling the HLSL intrinsic TraceRay. Accumulate the color returned in the payload struct as a result of a hit or miss (in that case the background color will be returned).

```
      ray.TMin = 0.001;
      ray.TMax = 10000.0;
      RayPayload payload = { float4(0, 0, 0, 0) };
      TraceRay(Scene, RAY_FLAG_CULL_BACK_FACING_TRIANGLES, ~0, 0, 1, 0,
      ray, payload);
      FinalColor += payload.color;
  }
  FinalColor *= InvSamples;

  RenderTarget[DispatchRaysIndex().xy] = FinalColor;
}
```

We finally divide by the inverse of the total number of samples taken and store the final filtered color in our RenderTarget unordered access view (UAV) buffer.

That is it for the DXR supersampling approach. In the next section, we will focus on a different sampling strategy that, by looking at the neighbor color similarities, will adapt the sampling strategy until the colors are similar enough that they can be averaged.

Understanding Adaptive Supersampling

The idea behind a*daptive supersampling* is to shoot more rays only where it is needed the most. The key idea is to send more rays where there is enough color variation and fewer rays where the colors are pretty much uniform.

One way to go about this is to start by sending five rays per pixel: four rays at the corners and one at the center of the pixel itself.

Figure 5-5 image shows the five rays per pixel process.

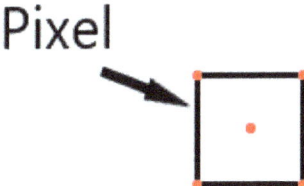

Figure 5-5. *We take five samples to start the process*

After we took our five samples, the process goes like this:

1. If the five colors are about the same color, we can assume that they all hit the same object, and we will just use their average color.

2. If the five colors are different, then we will subdivide the pixel into smaller regions.

3. If the five colors in the subdivided region are about the same color, go to step 1; otherwise, go to step 2.

See Figure 5-6.

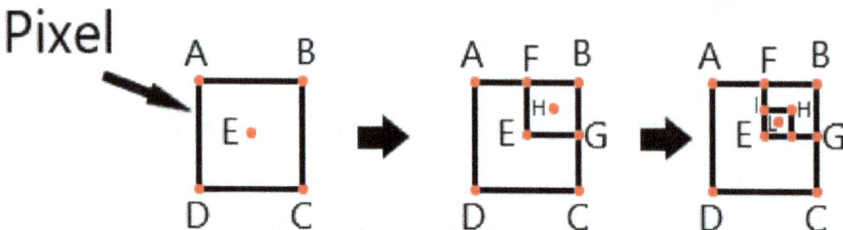

Figure 5-6. *The process of adaptive supersampling subdivides the pixel further and further and shoot rays where the most color variation is present*

Here is the pseudocode that implements the adaptive supersampling technique we've just described.

In the following pseudocode, we will assume to have a definition for a color and a 2D point position in code. For the color, we might imagine having a C-like struct like this one:

```
struct Color
{
  float red;
  float green;
  float blue;
};
```

And for the 2D point something like this:

```
struct Vec2
{
  float x;
  float y;
};
```

All the arithmetic operations on Color and Vec2 are assumed to be implemented.

First, we define the recursive function that is responsible for handling the nested subdivisions:

```
Color RecurseSubdivide(Vec2 posA,Vec2 posB,Vec2 posC,Vec2 posD,Vec2 posE)
{
    Color A = SampleImage(posA.x + 0,posA.y + 0);
    Color B = SampleImage(posB.x + 1,posB.y + 0);
```

```cpp
Color C = SampleImage(posC.x + 1,posC.y + 1);
Color D = SampleImage(posD.x + 0,posD.y + 1);
Color E = SampleImage(posE.x + 0.5,posE.y + 0.5);

Vec2 pDpC = (posD+posC) * 0.5;
Vec2 pApD = (posA+posD) * 0.5;
Vec2 pApB = (posA+posB) * 0.5;
Vec2 pBpC = (posB+posC) * 0.5;

constexpr float kEpsilonColor = 1e-4f;

// We assume that Color is not in HDR format but normalized between [0,1]
auto AlmostEqual = [](float a, float b, float epsilon = kEpsilonColor) {
    return std::fabs(a - b) <= kEpsilonColor;
};

if(AlmostEqual(A, B))
{
    if(AlmostEqual(B, C))
    {
      if(AlmostEqual(C, D))
      {
        if(AlmostEqual(D, E))
        {
          return (A + B + C + D + E) / 5;
        }
        // Bottom left subquad
        return RecurseSubdivide(pApD, posE , pDpC, posD,
        (posE+posD)*0.5);
      }
      // Bottom right subquad
      return RecurseSubdivide(posE , pBpC,posC, pDpC,(posE+posC)*0.5);
    }
    // Top right subquad
    return RecurseSubdivide(pApB,posB, pBpC,posE,(posE+posB)*0.5);
}
```

CHAPTER 5 RAY TRACING TECHNIQUES

```
   // Top left subquad
   return RecurseSubdivide( posA , pApB , posE , pApD,(posA+posE)*0.5);
}
```

Then in our main loop, we go through each pixel of our rendered image/frame by calling the previous function on each pixel:

```
Color Result;
for each y < Height
  for each x < Width
  {
    Vec2 posA = Vec2(x + 0,y + 0);
    Vec2 posB = Vec2(x + 1,y + 0);
    Vec2 posC = Vec2(x + 1,y + 1);
    Vec2 posD = Vec2(x + 0,y + 1);
    Vec2 posE = Vec2(x + 0.5,y + 0.5);
    Result = RecurseSubdivide(posA,posB,posC,posD,posE);
    PixelBuffer[x+y*Width] = Result;
  }
```

As you can see in the previous pseudocode, for each pixel we compute its corner sample positions represented by the variables posA, posB, posC, posD, and posE. We pass those sample positions to the function RecurseSubdivide. Because the technique we've just explained in this section is recursive, the function RecurseSubdivide is a recursive function.

What RecurseSubdivide does is outlined in the following steps:

- Sample the image frame by picking the five samples as outlined in Figure 5-5.

- Check each couple of colors relative to every couple of positions.

- If any of the ifs fail, the function will call itself by actually further subdividing the initial samples. And the cases are:

    - A is not equal to B: Recurse on top left quad.

    - B is not equal to C: Recurse on top right quad.

- C is not equal to D: Recurse on bottom right quad.
- D is not equal to E: Recurse on bottom left quad.
- If all the four `ifs` will be true, we will then return the average of the five colors (A+B+C+D+E) / 5.

Obviously, in a real implementation, we would consider a tolerance when we compare the five colors pair-wise (don't forget that the red, green, and blue components are using a floating-point representation and cannot be compared like we did in the previous pseudocode). Moreover, we should consider converting the `RecurseSubdivide` function from recursive to iterative. The reason is because if we would like to implement this technique in a compute shader either with CUDA or DirectCompute, we will not have support for recursion on all GPU architectures. Plus, in terms of efficiency, an iterative version of the same function is always better, considering that each thread will have to do recursion. The next section will go through another approach to solve the aliasing problem. The problem will be considered from a different perspective. In fact, stochastic ray tracing is the technique that will be presented, and the perspective is different because this approach will take advantage of random numbers to pick the samples in a given pixel.

Understanding Stochastic Ray Tracing

The previous two methods were able to reduce some of the aliasing problems. However, the fact that we were covering our pixels with a regular grid pattern will still cause edges that pop at the edge of our rendered polygons. Not to mention, the same edges will exhibit a staircase pattern.

So, what we do then? We break the pattern! Pure and simple.

Randomness is our friend; in this case, nature is random. Our brain is very good at noticing regularities and repetitions; therefore, randomness has always been a good solution to let us believe that what we were seeing was actually real.

In the ray-tracing case, distributing rays evenly across the pixel with a stochastic distribution will basically produce a random varying pattern in each pixel.

Figure 5-7 shows this.

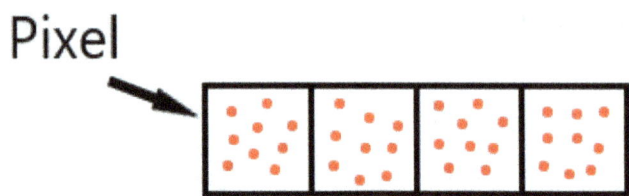

Figure 5-7. *We shoot the same nine rays but give them a stochastic distribution. In this way, we generate different random patterns in each pixel*

This different and random sample distribution will get rid of the regular aliasing artifacts that were part of the regular grid that we employed in the previous techniques.

As we have already done for the previous two methods, we will show code snippets for this method too. We will not go in-depth in relation to which sample distribution to use or not use, even if that is still important.

Because the sampling distribution is one important aspect, this approach is also named *distributed ray tracing*.

The following code snippet shows how we can achieve this sampling strategy:

```
// For a given number of samples N execute the following code:
// Pick a random sample in 0-1 range
float rx = GetRandom01(&Seed0, &Seed1);
float ry = GetRandom01(&Seed0, &Seed1);
//Compute the world space ray direction for each jittered sample and then
average the results
auto WSDir = camera.GetWorldSpaceRayDir(((float)x) + rx, ((float)y) + ry ,
ScreenWidth, ScreenHeight);

// Shoot this ray into the scene to find an intersection
```

Finally, we've presented some of the most used and popular approaches to reducing the image aliasing. In most cases, the stochastic approach is the way to go, because it doesn't exhibit itself as a visually detectable sampling pattern like the other methods do. The human eyes are very sensitive when it comes to visual repetitions.

Sampling randomly and, therefore, irregularly is the key to eliminating regular patterns that are easily detectable by the observer.

CHAPTER 5 RAY TRACING TECHNIQUES

As a side note, we have to remember that, in the ray tracing context, when we talk about samples and rays that are fired from the camera, we mean the same thing, as the result of a ray intersection will always produce a sample.

In the next sections, we'll see how to use the samples to produce interesting camera effects.

Understanding Depth of Field

One typical effect that belongs to the category of effects applied to the camera is the depth of field (DOF).

DOF represents which objects are in focus and which are out of focus. To implement that in our path tracer, we need to add two new data members to our camera class:

- **Focal length**: Used to describe how far an object must be from the camera to be considered in focus

- **Aperture size**: Used to measure the level of blurriness of objects that are considered out of focus

The previous two variables are needed to control the DOF effect. The focal length identifies the distance of the so-called focal plane, as in Figure 5-8.

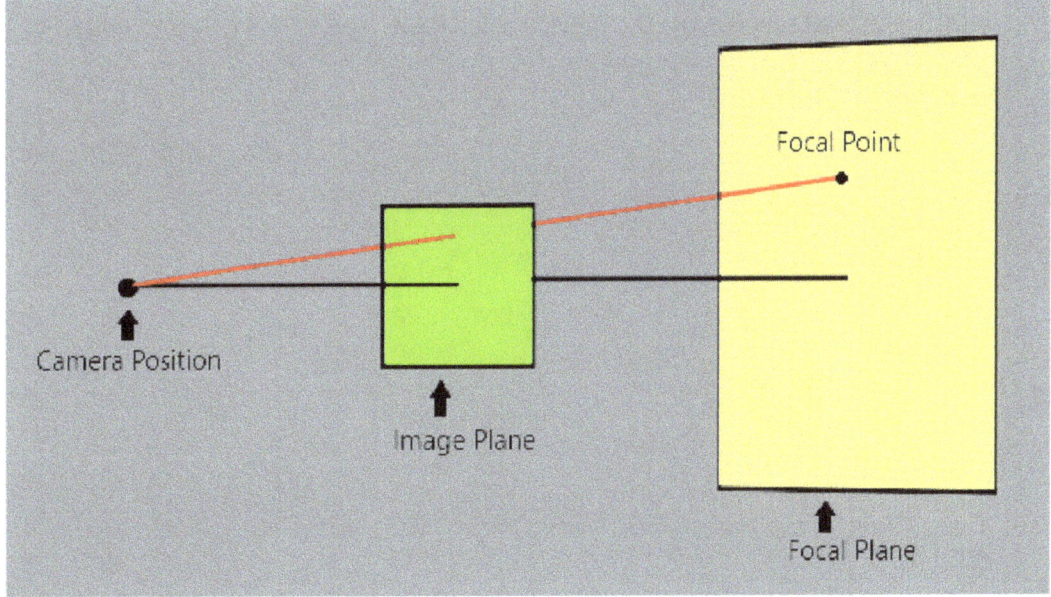

Figure 5-8. *Depth of field parameters*

So, what are the main steps to implement DOF in a path tracer? Here are the main points that represent the main steps:

1. Calculate the focal point p_f starting from:
    - Ray origin
    - Ray direction
    - Focal length
2. To get the focal point p_f we need to multiply the focal length by the ray direction.
3. Then we have to generate a random number in the range -0.5 and 0.5 and create a vector out of them. We will call it a random vector $\vec{r}$.
4. We then multiply R by the aperture size and the result to the ray origin, and we get the new ray origin o_{new}.
5. Finally, with the new shifted origin, we re-calculate the new ray direction considering the focal point p_f.

$$d_{new} = o_{new} - p_f$$

Figure 5-9 should clarify what the new rays will look like if represented visually.

CHAPTER 5   RAY TRACING TECHNIQUES

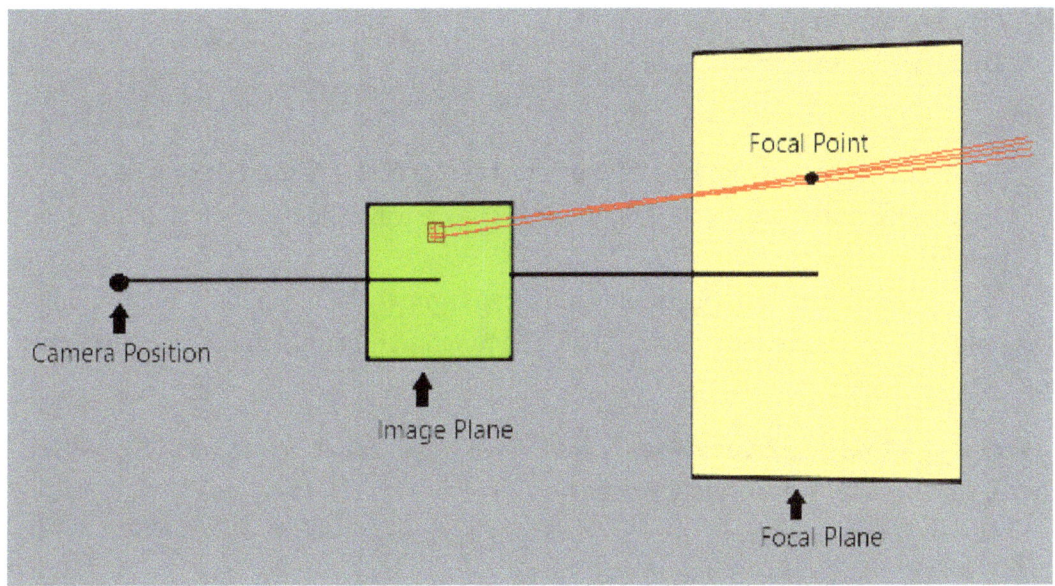

Figure 5-9. *Camera rays are re-created based on the new randomly shifted origin and the new direction computed out of the focal point p_f and the newly shifted random origin o_{new}*

We show a code snippet representing a portion of the camera class and the newly added data member variables that we've just described.

So, let's take a look at the following code block to better understand what we've just said:

```
class Camera
{
public:
// We omitted most of the code of the camera that is not relevant for
   DOF explanation
//...
__device__ float GetFocalLength() const { return mFocalLength; }
__device__ float GetApertureSize() const { return mApertureSize; }
private:
    // Newly added data member to give the camera class the support for DOF
    /**Focal length */
    float mFocalLength = 0.0f;
```

105

CHAPTER 5 RAY TRACING TECHNIQUES

```cpp
    /**Aperture Size */
    float mApertureSize = 0.0f;
};
```

The last two data members in the previous camera class are used during DOF parameter calculation. Their role will be clearer as we will explain how a DOF ray is computed.

Here's another code snippet, representing this time the computation involved in determining the new camera rays for DOF. The function that implements the DOF ray computation is called GetDOFRay.

```cpp
__device__ static Ray GetDOFRay(const Ray& ray, float ApertureSize, float FocalLength, u32* Seed0, u32* Seed1)
{
    // This is the focal point for a given primary camera ray (Dir is unit
    //length
    auto P = ray.mOrigin + ray.mDirection * FocalLength;
    // Get two random number in -0.5-0.5 range for each component
    float u1 = GetRandom01(Seed0, Seed1);
    float u2 = GetRandom01(Seed0, Seed1);
    float r1 = 2.0f * M_PI * u1;
    float r2 = u2;
    auto RandVec = Vector3(cosf(r1)*r2, sinf(r1)*r2, 0.0f) * ApertureSize;
    // This is the new ray origin
    auto NewRayOrigin = ray.mOrigin + RandVec;
    // New ray direction
    auto NewRayDir = (P - NewRayOrigin).norm();
    return Ray(NewRayOrigin, NewRayDir);
}
```

This is the focal point for a given primary camera ray (Dir is unit length):

```cpp
auto P = ray.mOrigin + ray.mDirection * FocalLength;
```

We get two random number in the -0.5-0.5 range for each component:

```cpp
float u1 = GetRandom01(Seed0, Seed1);
float u2 = GetRandom01(Seed0, Seed1);
```

CHAPTER 5 RAY TRACING TECHNIQUES

```
float r1 = 2.0f * M_PI * u1;
float r2 = u2;
auto RandVec = Vector3(cosf(r1)*r2, sinf(r1)*r2, 0.0f) * ApertureSize;
```

This is the new ray origin. Take a look at this line of code:

```
auto NewRayOrigin = ray.mOrigin + RandVec;
```

Finally, we can compute the new ray direction:

```
auto NewRayDir = (P - NewRayOrigin).norm();
```

When we have both ray origin and direction, we return the new DOF ray. Then later in code we have the actual DOFRay computation by a call to the function GetDOFRay we've just presented in the previous code block:

```
Ray WSRay(camera.GetCameraEye(), WSDir);
Ray DOFRay = GetDOFRay(WSRay, ApertureSize, FocalLength, &Seed0, &Seed1);
HitData OutHitData;
bool Hit = GetClosestHit(DOFRay, 0.001f, FLT_MAX,
OutHitData,SphereList,kNumSpheres);
ColorResult += (Hit ? SphereList[OutHitData.mObjId].mColor : BkgColor);
```

We construct a ray in world space that originates from the camera:

```
Ray WSRay(camera.GetCameraEye(), WSDir);
```

Then we create a ray based on the DOF parameters (please refer to the function GetDOFRay to understand how it's implemented):

```
Ray DOFRay = GetDOFRay(WSRay, ApertureSize, FocalLength, &Seed0, &Seed1);
```

Compute the closest-hit intersection by making a call to the function GetClosestHit:

Then return the color for a given sample and accumulate the result:

```
ColorResult += (Hit ? SphereList[OutHitData.mObjId].mColor : BkgColor);

/Compute intersection and set a color
HitData OutHitData;
bool Hit = GetClosestHit(DOFRay, 0.001f, FLT_MAX,
OutHitData,SphereList,kNumSpheres);
```

CHAPTER 5 RAY TRACING TECHNIQUES

This is how we can add a DOF effect in our path tracer. It's easy and straightforward, probably easier than the one implemented in the rasterization-based 3D engines.

Figure 5-10 shows more depth in the scene when DOF is applied.

Figure 5-10. *Depth of field effect in action. Notice how the blue and green spheres are more defined as they lie on the focal plane*

Figure 5-11 shows how the scene depth perception drastically changes when we disable DOF.

CHAPTER 5   RAY TRACING TECHNIQUES

Figure 5-11. *Same scene but without the depth of field*

DOF is surely the standard for any post-processing pipeline nowadays. It is an essential component in game cinematics scenes but also in in-game gameplay action. By using DOF, the player will have a more immersive feeling during gameplay. However, we cannot end this presentation without introducing motion blur. The next section will talk about motion blur and how is possible to implement it with a ray tracing setup. So, without anything further to say, let's get to the next section.

109

CHAPTER 5   RAY TRACING TECHNIQUES

Understanding Motion Blur

The next effect that we would like to include is motion blur. It's a pretty simple effect to include at this stage. In fact, once we have our basic ray tracer architecture in place, the addition of subsequent effects is quite simple in most cases.

Motion blur is a blur effect that we experience when a fast-moving object is passing by a camera with a longer exposure time than usual. This blur effect is often used in racing games to give the player the feeling of speed.

The things that we need for motion blur to take place are listed here:

- We need to store the time at which a given ray exists.

- We need to modify the camera to keep track of two points in time (t0–t1) and let it generate rays at random time values between t0-t1.

- We have to add the fact that also the objects have to move in time, so, for example, the sphere class needs to be movable and, therefore, we will have to define two-position/centers for it. The center0 is at time t0, and the center1 is at time t1. Basically, the center of the sphere will be a function of the frame time.

That is pretty much it.

We now want to add the necessary additions that we just listed and see what the outcome will be. Let's start by adding a time variable to our ray struct (note that we have omitted most of the Ray methods and member variables that are not relevant for this explanation. However, you can find the complete implementation in the source code that comes with this chapter).

```
//Simple ray class
class Ray
{
public:
    __device__ Ray(const Vector3& InOrigin = Vector3(0, 0, 0), const Vector3&
    InDirection = Vector3(0, 0, 1)) : mOrigin(InOrigin),
    mDirection(InDirection) {}
    // ... code omitted for simplicity
    float mTime = 0.0f;
};
```

CHAPTER 5 RAY TRACING TECHNIQUES

As you can see in the previous code snippet, we've just added a data member called mTime to keep track of the time at which the ray was created.

Now we need to modify the camera and the sphere too. Basically, we need to consider a movable sphere and not a static one as we did before.

This means that:

- For the sphere, we need two centers: one at time0 and another at time1. We create a time interval in which we suppose the sphere is moving. And when we need to read what the center is at any given time, we add a specific method in the sphere class that will interpolate based on the time between the center at time0 and the center at time1. More on this soon.

- For the camera class, we add time0 and time1 that will represent the time at which the shutter was open and the time at which was closed, respectively.

For the sphere struct, we have the following changes in the code (even in the sphere class we omitted code not relevant for this explanation):

```
//Simple sphere class
struct Sphere
{
    // We also need for the sphere to move to account for motion blur
    /** The center of the sphere at time 0*/
    Vector3 mCenter0;
    /** The center of the sphere at time 1*/
    Vector3 mCenter1;
    /** Time at which the sphere started moving (coincides with camera
    shutter open) */
    float mTime0 = 0.0f;
    /** Time at which the sphere ended up being (coincides with camera
    shutter closed) */
    float mTime1 = 1.0f;
    // As we just pointed out we interpolate between mTime0 and mTime1
    __device__ Vector3 GetCenterAtTime(float Time) const noexcept
```

```
    {
        return mCenter0 + (mCenter1 - mCenter0)*((Time - mTime0) / (mTime1
          - mTime0));
    }
    // ... code omitted for simplicity
};
```

We have the following code for the camera class:

```
class Camera
{
public:
    __device__ Camera(const Vector3& InEye = Vector3(0.f, 0.f, 0.f)
      , const Vector3& InLookAt = Vector3(0.f, 0.f, 50.f)
      , const Vector3& InUp = Vector3(0.f, 1.f, 0.f)
      , float InFov = 60.f
      , float InAspectRatio = 1.f
      , float InTime0 = 0.0f
      , float InTime1 = 1.0f) : mEye(InEye),
    mLookAt(InLookAt),mTime0(InTime0),mTime1(InTime1)
    {
        //...
    }
    // Motion blur variables
    // Time at which the shutter was open
    float mTime0;
    // Time at which the shutter is closed
    float mTime1;
};
```

Most of the code in the camera class implementation has been omitted here in order to show just the one that is relevant to motion blur. You can find a complete working implementation in the source code that comes with this chapter.

CHAPTER 5   RAY TRACING TECHNIQUES

Finally, when we have to shoot a ray, what we actually do is to shoot N samples in a given pixel. The following code does this:

```
for (u32 i = 0; i < SAMPLES; ++i)
{
    // Pick a random sample in 0-1 range
    #if AA_ENABLED
    float rx = GetRandom01(&Seed0, &Seed1);
    float ry = GetRandom01(&Seed0, &Seed1);
    //Compute the world space ray direction for each sample and then
    average the results
    auto WSDir = camera.GetWorldSpaceRayDir(((float)x) + rx, ((float)y)
    + ry , ScreenWidth, ScreenHeight);
    #else
    auto WSDir = camera.GetWorldSpaceRayDir(((float)x), ((float)y),
    ScreenWidth, ScreenHeight);
    #endif
    //Construct a ray in world space that originates from the camera
    Ray WSRay(camera.GetCameraEye(), WSDir);
    // Get Random time interval between 0-1
    WSRay.mTime = GetRandom01(&Seed0, &Seed1);
    // Compute intersection and set a color
    HitData OutHitData;
    // Get the closest hit
    bool Hit = GetClosestHit(WSRay, 0.001f, FLT_MAX, OutHitData,
    SphereList, kNumSpheres);
    // Return the color for a given sample and accumulate the result
    ColorResult += (Hit ? SphereList[OutHitData.mObjId].mColor :
    BkgColor);
}
// Average the results
ColorResult *= InvSamples;
```

We set a random time interval in the 0-1 range in the ray time variable, and we get Figure 5-12.

113

CHAPTER 5 RAY TRACING TECHNIQUES

Figure 5-12. *Motion blur applied on just two spheres of the five that we see here (the green and yellow sphere)*

The next section will be related to a special shader that belongs to the family of DXR shaders: *any-hit* shader. We've already presented this kind of shader while we were describing the new set of DXR shaders, but we will show its practical usage in a more specific context: efficient rendering of transparent objects.

Multi-Hit Ray Tracing for Transparent Objects in DXR

We all know the cost and the issues when it comes to rendering transparent objects in a game. It turns out that instead of traditional rasterization, we can, thanks to any*hit shaders in DXR, implement *multi-hit ray tracing*.

> *With "Niq" we want to set the maximum number of intersections queries we want to process. It is necessary to define an upper bound in this case, because we could potentially allow a ray to intersect an infinite number of objects.*

Multi-hit ray tracing is a class of techniques that are normally used to account for multiple intersections along a given ray. In this context, any-hit shaders will be employed to detect any possible intersection along a ray. Our duty will be to collect each intersection hit-record in a 3D buffer (Width x Height x Niq) and a 2D buffer (Width x Height) that will hold the intersections count for each ray. Niq represents the maximum number of intersection queries. We stop at no more than Niq because potentially we could go forever. In this way, we have also control on the depth that we want for our intersections.

Figure 5-13 shows a conceptual view of how logical the hit-record looks.

CHAPTER 5 RAY TRACING TECHNIQUES

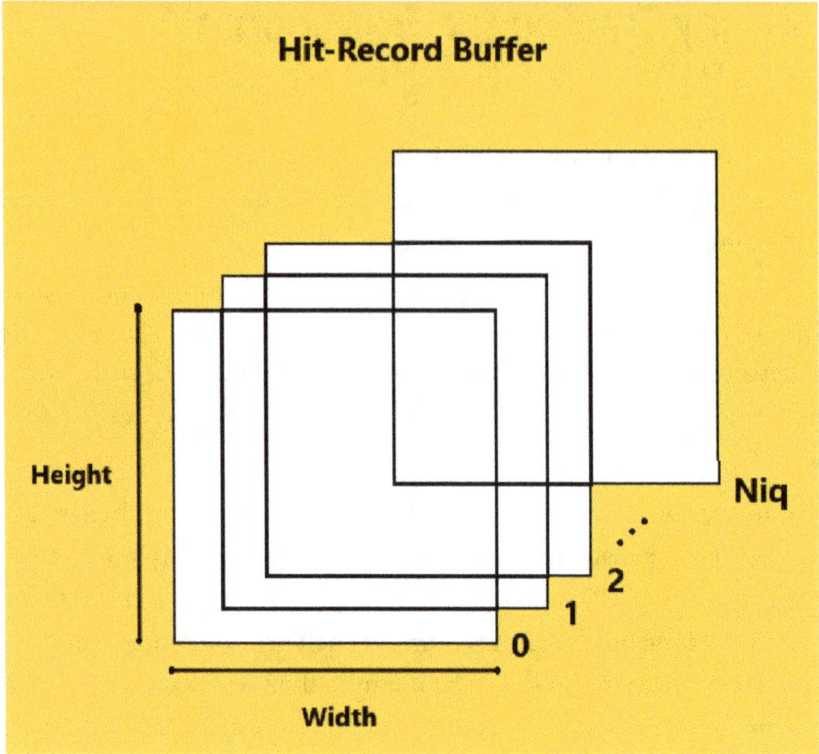

Figure 5-13. *Hit-record buffer is made up of Niq layers. Each layer holds the correct value of t for a given intersection. Each t in each buffer layer is sorted*

For the hit-count buffer we have the representation shown in Figure 5-14.

CHAPTER 5   RAY TRACING TECHNIQUES

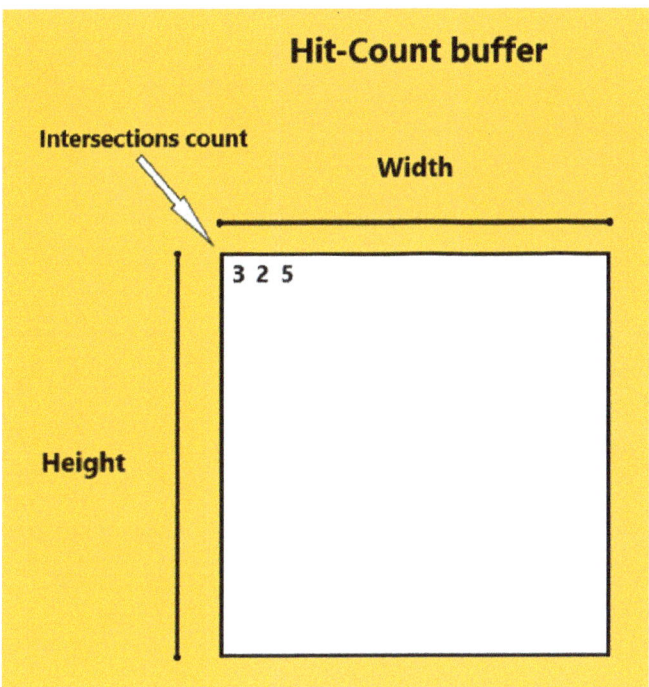

Figure 5-14. *Hit-count buffer is a simple 2D buffer that stores the number of hits for each ray*

Other use cases for any-hit shaders will comprise the following:

- Ambient occlusion
- Shadows

So, we basically create a layer to store the intersection distance for each ray. In this case, Niq equals the max number of layers.

Another constraint that we want is that the intersections need to be sorted back to front for correct transparency blending to happen. We start by collecting all valid intersections we encounter along the ray path. These intersections will be looked in the ray interval $[t_{min}, t_{max}]$.

We collect intersections along the ray path. We want for them to be sorted by their distance with respect to the ray origin, as shown in Figure 5-15.

117

CHAPTER 5   RAY TRACING TECHNIQUES

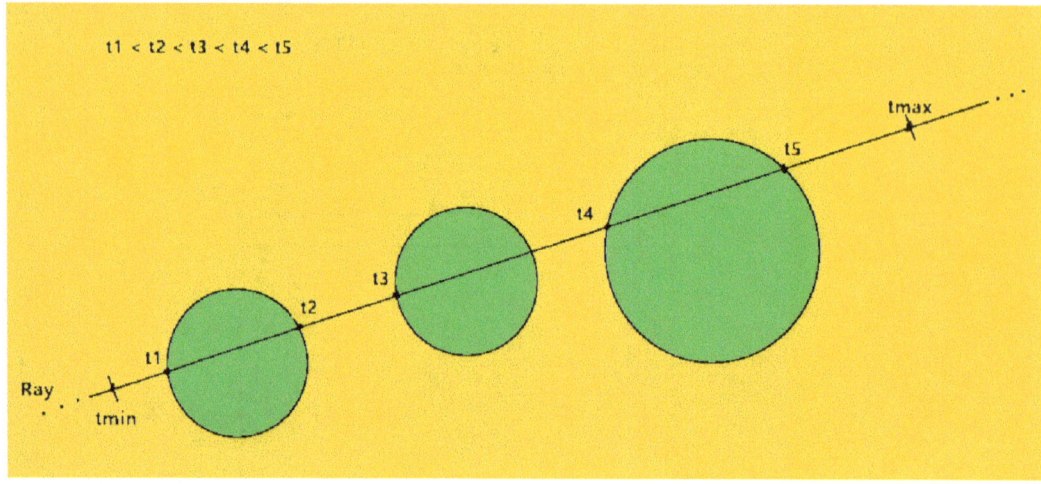

Figure 5-15. We have three objects (spheres for simplicity) intersected by a given ray

Any-hit shader will be called any time there is an intersection. Referring to Figure 5-13 we have multiple intersections for three simple spheres. Unfortunately, multiple intersections are invoked in arbitrary order; therefore, it is our responsibility to make sure they are sorted.

In the any-hit shader implementation, as we collect intersections, we also test them with their existing neighbors to see if they are sorted correctly; if not, we swap them to keep them sorted.

So, to recap, we need the following:

Hit-record buffer (Figure 5-13)

Hit-count buffer (Figure 5-14)

But we still don't know what fields will be part of the hit-record. These are the fields that we need in order to correctly blend the objects during the transparent object blending phase. Let's just assume for now that we will not shade transparent objects for simplicity. Therefore, we will need just two parameters the hit distance t and the diffuse color.

See the following code:

```
struct HitRecord
{
    // The diffuse color of the object we've just hit
```

```
    float3 DiffuseColor;
    // The hit distance
    float t;
};
```

This struct will represent an element of the Hit-Record buffer. As for the Hit-Count buffer, we will obviously have just an integer as the only element. The following is the code for the any-hit shader implementation that performs multi-hit:

```
[shader = ("anyhit")]
void MultiHit(inout MultiHitPayload
multiHitPayload,BuiltinIntersectionAttribs attribs)
{
    // TODO: add anyhit shader code here
    IgnoreHit();
}
```

The ray payload struct will hold the number of hits for a given ray and will return to the ray generation shader already filled with the number of hits for that ray. Then in the ray generation shader we just store the total number of hits in the hit-count buffer given the ray index.

Basically, we have this:

- Any-hit shader will make sure to store hit-record information in a sorted way.
- The ray generation shader will take the payload struct after any-hit has been executed storing the number of hits in the hit-count at ray index.

The ray generation shader should look roughly like this:

```
// Hold the acceleration data structure (built from the application)
RaytracingAccelerationStructure Scene : register(t0, space0);
Buffer<uint> HitCountBuffer : register(u0);

// User defined payload struct
struct MultiHitPayload
{
    uint hitcount;
};
```

```
[shader=("raygeneration")]
void RayGenMultiHit()
{
    uint2 RayIndex = DispatchRaysIndex();
    // We initialize our payload struct here
    MultiHitPayload multiHitPayload;
    multiHitPayload.hitcount = 0;
    // Code to generate and construct a ray is omitted. Refer to
       the code on
    the book github repo
    // Start tracing rays in the scene
    TraceRay(Scene, RAY_FLAG_NON_OPAQUE, ~0, 0, 1, 0, ray,multHitPayload);
    // We return from tthe TraceRay function. We store the number of hit we
    collected after shooting that ray
    HitCountBuffer[RayIndex] = multiHitPayload.hitcount;
}
```

This approach to multi-hit ray tracing is not the most efficient, because we have to trace the whole tree hierarchy even if we established that we might want to accept Niq number of queries out of the total possible ones.

These are all interesting techniques we can implement with a ray tracing setup. But this is just the beginning of our journey to what is possible to achieve with ray tracing.

Summary

In this chapter, you saw a few simple and interesting techniques. But this is just a small taste of what you can do with a ray tracing setup. These techniques are also very simple compared to their respective traditional rasterization versions. But simple in this case means also expensive.

In fact, you will see that ray tracing tends to be inherently expensive despite its simplicity, and even though CUDA/DXR will help a lot in letting us render very quickly, we will still have to be careful about performance in general.

There are techniques to optimize various areas of ray tracing. The idea is that at some point you should be able to render something like in Figure 5-16 (rendered with a simple path tracer that I've implemented for this book in CUDA).

CHAPTER 5   RAY TRACING TECHNIQUES

Figure 5-16. *A classic Cornell Box rendered with 10,000 samples per pixel at 1024x1024 resolution and 15 bounces!*

Pretty cool, huh? But that image is static and not real time! If it's not real time, it's not fun. But as a first attempt, it's a good point to start from and build upon. You can see a reflective sphere on the left and the refractive sphere on the right with caustics too! In the next chapter, you will see some of the basics concepts that will be necessary to build a ray tracer. We encountered a few of them in previous chapters, but we did not go into too much in detail about them.

This is the beauty of global illumination.

CHAPTER 5   RAY TRACING TECHNIQUES

Questions

Based on the knowledge that you gained in this chapter, it is your turn to answer some questions:

- What is the reason of aliasing?
- How can you solve the aliasing problem?
- How many techniques do you know to mitigate aliasing in your ray traced images?
- What are the main parameters involved in the DOF computation?
- What are the relevant parameters for motion blur?
- What is the main purpose that led us in using motion blur in our pictures?
- In which order the intersection queries are executed, when it comes to any-hit shader invocations?

Further Reading

The following are few resources that you can use to expand the horizon of your knowledge on this chapter:

- `https://medium.com/@elope139/depth-of-field-in-path-tracinge61180417027`
- `https://www.realtimerendering.com/raytracing/Ray%20Tracing_%20The%20Next%20Week.pdf`
- Gribble, (2019). 'Multi-Hit Ray Tracing in DXR', in Haines, A. Möller (ed.) *Ray Tracing Gems.* Apress Open, pp. 111-133.

CHAPTER 6

Ray and Camera Model Definitions

This chapter will introduce you to the basics of mathematical concepts when it comes to ray tracing.

This is the bare-bones foundation needed to understand all the upcoming concepts and techniques introduced throughout this and the coming chapters of this part of the book.

We have presented some of these topics in previous chapters, but the goal of this chapter, in particular, is to bridge the gap between the practical applications of these concepts and the theory behind them.

Specifically, the chapter will cover reflection, refraction, and Fresnel to mention a few. By the end of this chapter, you will have an understanding of the basics concepts needed to fully understand ray tracing. You will also understand the basic Phong/Lambert lighting model and how it is different from more accurate approaches for specular reflection computation. Finally, proper physically correct specular reflection and refraction will be presented and compared against the approximated specular Phong reflection. The following topics will be covered in this chapter:

- Defining math symbols and ray tracing terminology
- The ray-tracing camera model
- Definition of a ray and basic lighting
- Reflection
- Refraction, Snell's law, and Fresnel

CHAPTER 6 RAY AND CAMERA MODEL DEFINITIONS

Technical Requirements

For the code related to this chapter, refer to the "How to Find the Code in Visual Studio" section in Chapter2.

Defining Math Symbols and Ray Tracing Terminology

You can return to this section anytime if the role of a symbol or term is not clear.

The following are the math symbols and letters that we will refer to during the math formula presentation:

- Incoming ray direction
  - I: Light intensity
  - N: Surface normal
  - R: Reflected ray direction
  - T: Transmitted ray direction
  - o: Ray origin
  - d: Ray direction
  - t: A real scalar parameter
- The set of real numbers
  - r(t): A position along the ray direction at distance t from the ray origin
- Index of refraction
  - TIR: Total internal reflection
- Light vector (point to light source vector)
- View vector (point to camera vector)
- Reflected vector
  - IOR: Index of refraction

Now that we are familiar with the symbols and terminologies, let's see how a ray-tracing model works in the next section.

CHAPTER 6 RAY AND CAMERA MODEL DEFINITIONS

The Ray-Tracing Camera Model

When we talk about the ray tracing camera model, we are mostly referring to what is known to be the pinhole camera model. In this representation, the camera is conceptually constructed by taking a box, piercing a hole on one of its faces with a pin, and covering the hole with a piece of opaque tape. Inside this box, opposite to where the hole is, we place the film with a special chemical emulsion on the surface.

Figure 6-1 shows this camera model.

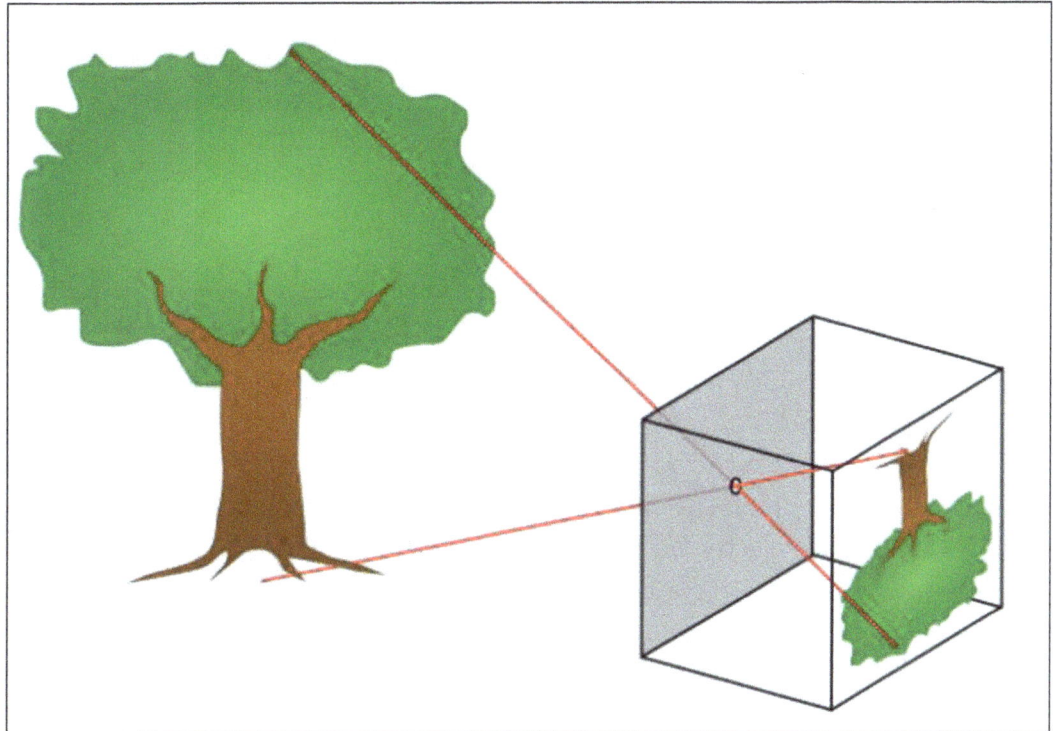

Figure 6-1. *Pinhole camera model*

The idea is that thanks to the small hole, only a specific portion of the scene light will enter the box and hit the film. If we were just removing the box face completely, the surface where the film was lying would be hit uniformly by the light coming from the scene. The film would end up completely saturated in color, becoming completely white (or in better terms over-exposed).

So, the idea is to keep the hole and remove the opaque tape for a short amount of time and then place it back. During that "short" time period, the film will get hit by correctly focused light rays coming from the hole.

CHAPTER 6 RAY AND CAMERA MODEL DEFINITIONS

Figure 6-2 shows how the rays hitting an object are passing through the hole and how the image of the object will look like on film.

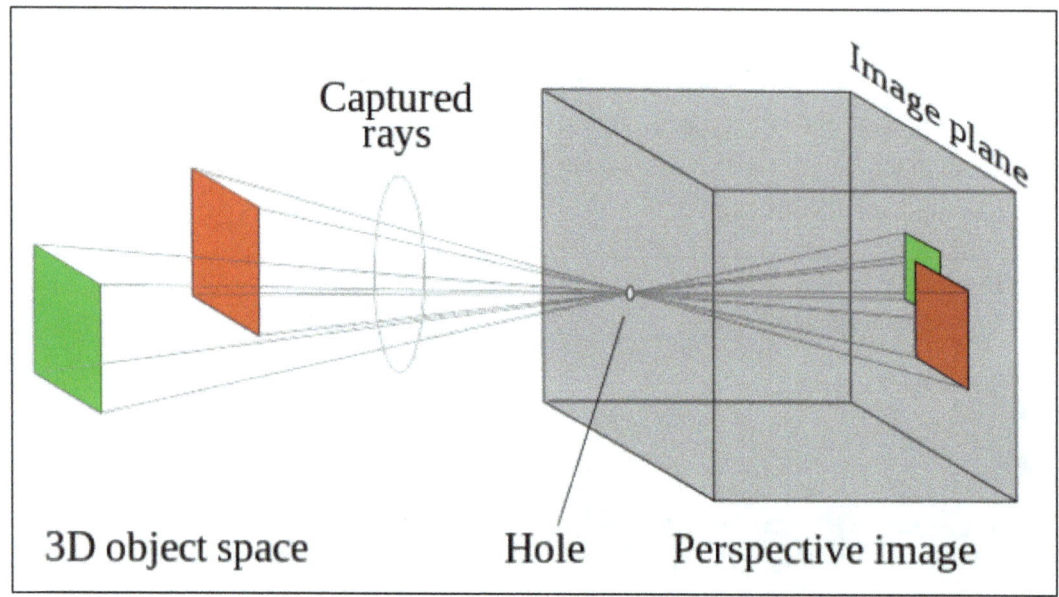

Figure 6-2. *Rays hitting an object in the scene passing through the hole*

The pinhole camera model is simple yet very effective and used even today in modern computer graphics. The differences from the conceptual model that we presented are that the hole is replaced by the so-called *eye* (which is basically the camera position) and the film with the so-called *image plane*.

If we connect the eye with the corners of the image plane and we extend those connection lines endlessly, we get what we call a *frustum* (a pyramid without its top part). This is often referred to as *camera frustum*. The idea is that everything that is in front of the image plane is visible to the eye.

Figure 6-3 shows the computer graphics camera model.

CHAPTER 6 RAY AND CAMERA MODEL DEFINITIONS

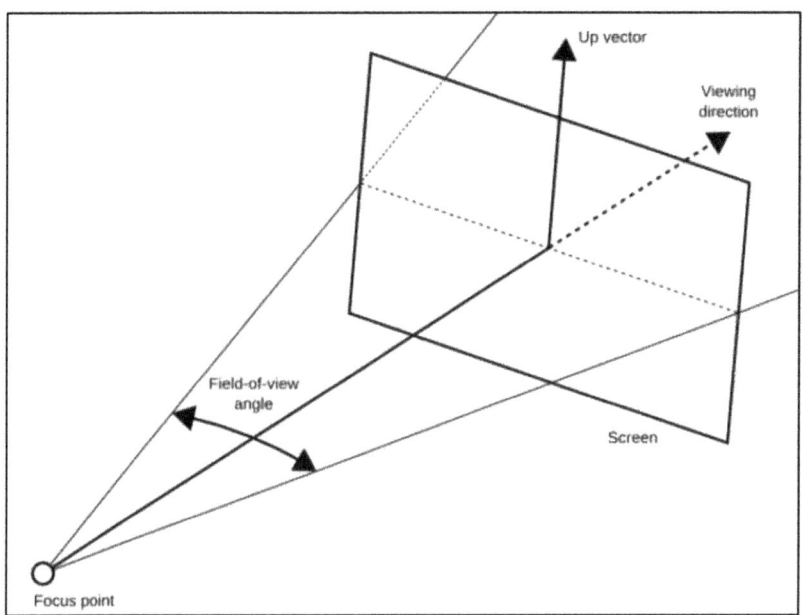

Figure 6-3. *The computer graphics camera model*

We show a simple code snippet for a potential camera implementation (we've just encountered this camera class in previous chapters, and therefore we will show only a simple skeleton). For more implementation details, refer to the previous chapters and to the GitHub code repository.

```
// A very simple pinhole camera implementation
// Note that in this case we assume that the hole is like a point in space
(therefore its radius is 0)
class Camera
{
private:
    // The camera position (the hole in the case of the conceptual pinhole
    camera representation)
    Vector3 mEye;
    // Camera frame of reference vectors
    Vector3 mUp;
    Vector3 mSide;
    Vector3 mForward;
    // Camera field of view
```

```
    float mFov;
    // Camera aspect ratio
    float mAspectRatio;
public:
    // Camera ctor
    // Fov is in degrees
    Camera(const Vector3& InEye,const Vector3& InLookAt,const Vector3&
    InWorldUp,float InFov = 60.0f,float InAspectRatio = 1.0f) :
    mFov(InFov),mAspectRatio(InAspectRatio)
    {
    }
};
```

Nevertheless, we have to say that to mimic real-world cameras, we do have parameters to represent *aperture* and *focal plane distance* (as we've just discussed during the depth of field explanation in Chapter 5). In this case, we are outlining a bare-bones basic pinhole camera representation for illustration purposes. Extending it with more functionalities is then trivial.

In the next section, we will define a ray and how to implement some basic lighting.

Defining Ray and Basic Lighting

To connect the conceptual vision of a ray of light entering a hole hitting a film, we need to define what is a ray mathematically. A ray **r(t)** is defined to be a line with an origin **o** and a direction **d**.

In its parametric-mathematical form, we have this:

$$r(t) = o + \hat{d} * t$$

and $t \in R$.

So, that is how we represent our ray of light. We can quickly realize that if we let **t** grow to infinity, our ray will start at **o** and extend to infinity. Obviously, in our case and in practical terms, our infinity will be just a big enough number! How big will become clear further in this chapter, so keep reading!

So, when we start processing rays, we have to account for the fact that they will hit anything they encounter along their path, but sometimes we are just interested in intersections happening within a given range; therefore, we will add a specified range to our ray formulation.

To this purpose, we define **minT** and **maxT** to be the minimum and maximum value of **t** and impose a constraint that, if an intersection returns a value of **t** that is within **minT**/**maxT** range, then it will be accepted otherwise rejected.

The following code snippet shows a basic ray definition:

```
struct Ray
{
    // Ray origin
    Vector3 mOrigin;
    // Ray direction
    Vector3 mDirection;
    // Min t value for an intersection to be accepted
    float mMinT;
    // Max t value for an intersection to be accepted
    float mMaxT;
};
```

As you can see, we've added the range bounds. Why do we want to limit the set of valid intersections in a given range? The reason behind this choice is related to precision in floating-point calculations. To give a practical example, let's just imagine that the camera is very close to an object that is almost touching it, then chances are that the intersection point, in that case, will almost match the camera eye. But in real-world applications, we know that we have to deal with the limited numerical precision. In fact, when it comes to floating-point computations, we have a limit to how small or how big a number can be represented. This "how small/how big" depends on the number of bits that we use to represent a given floating-point number.

To solve the problem when there is the risk for a number to get too small, almost close to zero, we normally use a threshold, like an epsilon, to mean "almost zero."

Something like 0.001.

By checking against a number that is small enough but not too small, we can prevent a given intersection value of **t** from getting too small and, therefore, incurring underflow issues.

CHAPTER 6   RAY AND CAMERA MODEL DEFINITIONS

So, in this specific case, when we create a ray, we would do something like this:

```
// We construct a ray, just before shooting it in the scene (so this normally might happen in the main
// shooting loop or if we rebounce a given ray based on a given BRDF
Ray myRay;
// some origin
mRay.mOrigin = ...
// some direction
mRay.mDirection = ...
// Specify an epsilon
mRay.mMinT = 0.001f;
// The biggest number we can represent
mRay.mMaxT = FLT_MAX;
// ...
```

For the **maxT**, we obviously want to know what the biggest number we can represent is. In this case, we have a predefined value that is platform-dependent and is defined, in our case, to be FLT_MAX (or FLT_MIN if we want to refer to the minimum float representable value).

So, by accepting intersections only from 0.001 to infinity (FLT_MAX), we prevent intersections very close to the camera to give unexpected results. In the next section, we will see how we can implement basic lighting given an incoming ray that hits a point on a surface.

Understanding Basic Lighting

When it comes to implementing a basic lighting calculation, there is an approximation that we have to do. This approximation will get us to what is called the *illumination equation*. The illumination equation is expressed like this:

$$I = k_a I_a + \sum_{k=0}^{n-1} I_{i,k}(k_d(\vec{L}_k \cdot \vec{N}) + k_s(\vec{V} \cdot \vec{R})^n)$$

This equation accounts only for the direct lighting of the light sources.

This is a crude approximation of the *rendering equation* that, instead, as we will see in the next chapters, is able to describe the complete light propagation in a given scene.

The illumination equation approximates the rendering equation locally, and it has been used for years to light games because it's very cheap to evaluate, yet the visual results are quite convincing.

By approximating locally, we mean it doesn't take into account the light coming across the whole hemisphere but, instead, considers just the direct lighting. In fact, the only direction that is plugged in the illumination equation is **L**, which is the light to point the direction, and the view vector **V**, which is the point to eye vector for the specular part. Both are used to compute the direct diffuse and specular contributions. But what about the light coming from all the other directions to a given point? We decide to ignore it.

BRDF stands for bidirectional reflectance distribution function. It is a probability distribution function that describes how the light is reflected/absorbed by a given material.

We will now explain every term of the illumination equation separately.

The intensity **I** at a given point **x** is the result of the sum of these three terms:

Ambient BRDF (simplified version):

$$I = k_a I_a$$

- k_a is the ambient coefficient of an object.
- I_a is the ambient light intensity (normally used to simulate the indirect lighting effect).

Then we sum the contribution of the specular part and diffuse part of each of the n lights present in the scene (see the sum in the illumination equation).

Diffuse Lambert BRDF (simplified version):

$$I = k_d (\vec{L} \cdot \vec{N})$$

- k_d diffuse coefficient of an object or an approximation of the **Lambert** diffuse **BRDF** (the light of a given wavelength that is reflected from the object uniformly across the hemisphere). Basically, it is the **RGB** color of the object.
- $\vec{L}$ point to light vector.
- $\vec{N}$ surface normal.

Specular Phong BRDF (simplified version):

$$I = k_s(\vec{V} \cdot \vec{R})^n$$

- k_s specular coefficient of an object
- $\vec{V}$ vector pointing to the camera eye
- $\vec{R}$ reflected light direction with respect to the surface normal $\vec{N}$
- $(.)^n$ shininess factor (used to approximate the surface glossiness)

Alternate Specular BRDF (Blinn formulation):

$$I = k_s(\vec{N} \cdot \vec{H})^n$$

- $\vec{H}$ is the half vector and is defined to be:

$$\vec{H} = \frac{\vec{L} + \vec{V}}{||\vec{L} + \vec{V}||}$$

All the other parameters for the Blinn formulation remain the same.

- I_i the color intensity of the incoming k-th light.

The indirect illumination is ignored, and the ambient BRDF helps to reinject some of the lost energy into the system.

Figure 6-4 shows how the surface and light interact with the previously presented terms of the illumination equation.

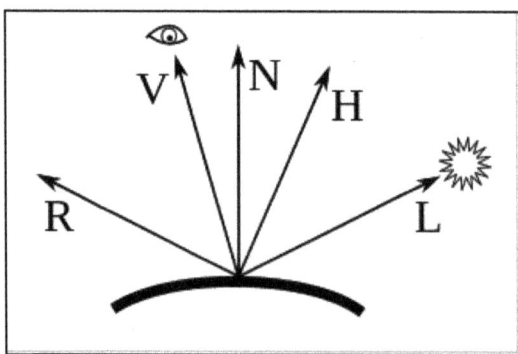

Figure 6-4. *Light/surface interaction according to the illumination equation terms*

Oftentimes the Blinn formulation for the specular BRDF is used in place of the usual Phong one. The Blinn formulation is much better because with the introduction of the half-vector H is able to guarantee that the specular highlight is visible even at a very steep angle. In fact, if we simply use the Phong specular BRDF, we notice that when the angle between the reflected vector R and the surface normal N approach 90 degrees, the cosine drops to zero showing no specular at all. We don't want this to happen when, for example, we are looking at the specular reflection on a wet road in the distance (where the angle is likely to approach 90 degrees). If we use the Phong model in the wet road case, we see that the specular "tail" will disappear in the distance. Too bad!

The implementation of this lighting model is very simple, and we can find it in any old-school pixel shader. Therefore, we will not provide any implementation for it. We will assume that you are already aware of it. We introduced it anyway in this section because it's going to be useful when we present the correct way of describing light propagation through the *rendering equation*.

Moreover, most of the 3D engines out there feature a physically based BRDF for their material system, which is much closer to how the light interacts with the surface material of an object. Most of these are specular BRDFs and are a variant of some microfacet lighting model. See Disney BRDF as an example or the Unreal Engine 4 GGX.

You should now be familiar with what is involved in the context of basic lighting and shading, particularly the illumination equation and its role in the context of how cheap and approximated lighting was done in the past. In the next two sections, we will have a closer look at reflection and refraction.

Understanding Reflection

When a ray hits a specular surface, it gets reflected. That type of reflection is called *specular reflection*. In the *illumination equation* we were approximating the specular reflection effect with the term:

$$I = k_s (\vec{V} \cdot \vec{R})^n$$

While it is acceptable to some degree and together with an environment map will do quite well visually, it's not the correct physical way of dealing with specular reflection. In this way, we just get the specular highlights, but we neglect the surrounding scene if we don't consider other bounces, and that is not acceptable.

CHAPTER 6 RAY AND CAMERA MODEL DEFINITIONS

But first, let's define what a specular lobe is. The specular lobe represents the set of scattered directions toward which the light is going to be reflected. In our case, we proposed the Phong BRDF for the specular reflection in the previous section.

To be more precise, we were mimicking visually how the effect of many directions getting reflected with respect to the perfect mirror direction looked. The specular term coming from the Phong reflection model represents just the specular highlight of the light source. We can call it *direct specular reflection*. What we dropped in the Phong model is the indirect specular reflection coming from everywhere else but the light source.

Figure 6-5 shows a schematic illustration of the specular cosine lobe.

Figure 6-5. *Specular lobe*

The problem is that we don't take into account any bounce, but, instead, we simulate a supposed specular reflection by showing just the results of the specular cosine lobe on top of the surface of an object. By changing the value of the shininess exponent, we can spread or concentrate the specular reflection lobe to approximate the glossiness look of the surface. Figure 6-6 depicts a specular Phong reflection.

CHAPTER 6 RAY AND CAMERA MODEL DEFINITIONS

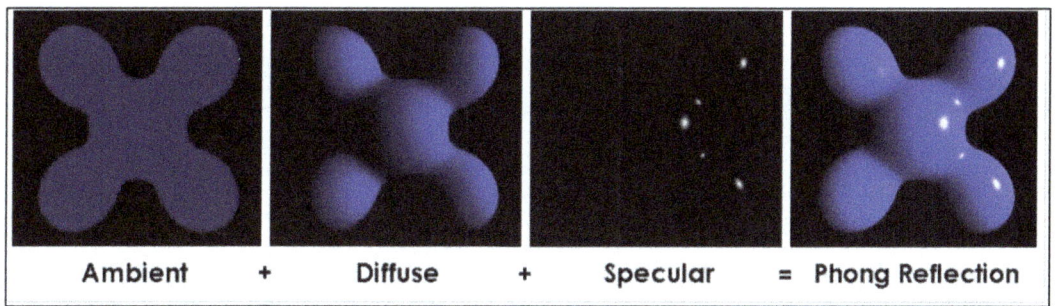

Figure 6-6. *Specular Phong reflection*

In this section, we will consider the simple case of perfect mirror reflection, meaning that an incoming ray is reflected perfectly like when a ball rebounds from a pool table cushion with an angle equal to the angle of incidence (see Figure 6-7).

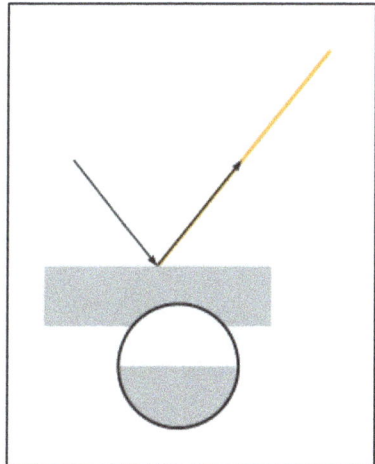

Figure 6-7. *Perfect mirror reflection*

Having said that, given an incoming ray **I** incident, at a point **x** on a surface with normal **N** is reflected toward the direction R following this equation:

$$\vec{R} = 2\vec{N}(\vec{I} \cdot \vec{N}) - \vec{I}$$

That's pretty simple and straightforward. What we then do is to trace a ray along **R** to get to the next potential surface bounce.

The visual result will basically show the surrounding environment reflected across any object that is supposed to have a specular material.

CHAPTER 6   RAY AND CAMERA MODEL DEFINITIONS

But the story is a little bit more complicated than how we have presented it here because we do not have only perfect mirror specular materials in the real world. In fact, most of them have a glossy surface reflection, which is common to most surface metal materials.

But, as we will see, to account for glossy specular surfaces, we have to employ a different type of specular BRDF.

Such a BRDF is among the ones that have their foundation on microfacet models. As we've already mentioned, GGX or Cook-Torrance specular BRDFs are able to model the surface accounting for the microsurface imperfections. These micro imperfections represent the irregularities of the surface at a small scale.

Basically, any ray of light that would interact with specular surfaces that have such a property will be scattered in a different direction than the perfect mirror one, causing the reflection to appear somewhat blurred. Such a blurry look gives the impression of a glossy surface.

Figure 6-8 shows what a glossy specular reflection looks like.

Figure 6-8. *Specular glossy reflection. Glossiness grows from the rightmost to the leftmost sphere*

What's Next?

We've analyzed the illumination equation and provided a detailed explanation of the pros and cons of using that kind of lighting setup. Now we want to understand what happens when the light doesn't get just reflected but passes through a transparent object.

In the next section, we will explain exactly that through the introduction of refraction, Fresnel, and Snell's law.

Understanding Refraction and Fresnel

First we'll introduce Fresnel law and Snell's law. In particular, we want to talk about the probability for a ray to be reflected (and refracted).

Let's also define what the index of refraction (**IOR**) is. When light travels in a vacuum its speed is **c** (the speed of light), but when the light travels through a different medium, its speed decreases. By denoting the speed of light in this medium as **v**, we define the index of refraction to be the ratio of **c** over **v**:

$$\eta = \frac{c}{v}$$

Fresnel law is defined to express the probability of reflection, and in its complete formulation, it is expressed by this equation for vertically polarized or s-polarized light reflectivity R_s (**s** stands for *senkrecht* that in German means perpendicular/vertical):

$$R_s = \left| \frac{\eta_1 \cos\theta_i - \eta_2 \sqrt{1 - (\frac{\eta_1}{\eta_2} \sin\theta_i)^2}}{\eta_1 \cos\theta_i + \eta_2 \sqrt{1 - (\frac{\eta_1}{\eta_2} \sin\theta_i)^2}} \right|^2$$

For p-polarized (parallel polarized light) R_p it is as follows:

$$R_p = \left| \frac{\eta_1 \sqrt{1 - (\frac{\eta_1}{\eta_2} \sin\theta_i)^2} - \eta_2 \cos\theta_i}{\eta_1 \sqrt{1 - (\frac{\eta_1}{\eta_2} \sin\theta_i)^2} + \eta_2 \cos\theta_i} \right|^2$$

Conversely, for the law of conservation of energy, we have the expressions for the transmitted power for **s** and **p** polarized components, respectively:

$$T_s = 1 - R_s$$

and

$$T_p = 1 - R_p$$

CHAPTER 6 RAY AND CAMERA MODEL DEFINITIONS

Considering that we are dealing with "natural light," we can consider it as *unpolarized*. This means there is an equal amount of power for s and p polarization. Therefore, the effective reflectivity can be computed as the average of the two: $R_{eff} = \dfrac{(R_s + R_p)}{2}$

The index of refraction η is simply the ratio of c over v.

Where η_1 and η_2 represent the indices of refraction (IOR) and θ_i is the angle of incidence. However, most of the time, in computer graphics applications, where numerical precision is not as important as in the scientific field, we use an approximation for the Fresnel term that works quite well in practice. It is called the Schlick Fresnel approximation.

The Schlick Fresnel equation for a reflectivity (or probability of reflection) $R(\theta_i)$ at an incident angle θ_i is defined here:

$$R(\theta_i) = R_0 + (1 - R_0)(1 - cos\theta)^5$$

where:

$$R_0 = \left(\dfrac{\eta_1 - \eta_2}{\eta_1 + \eta_2}\right)^2$$

η_1, η_2 are the indices of refraction of the two media. R_0 is the probability (reflectivity) of reflection at normal incidence, aka given $\theta_i = 0$.

Let's take a look at Figure 6-9 to have a better understanding of what is actually happening at the interface between two media; see Figure 6-9.

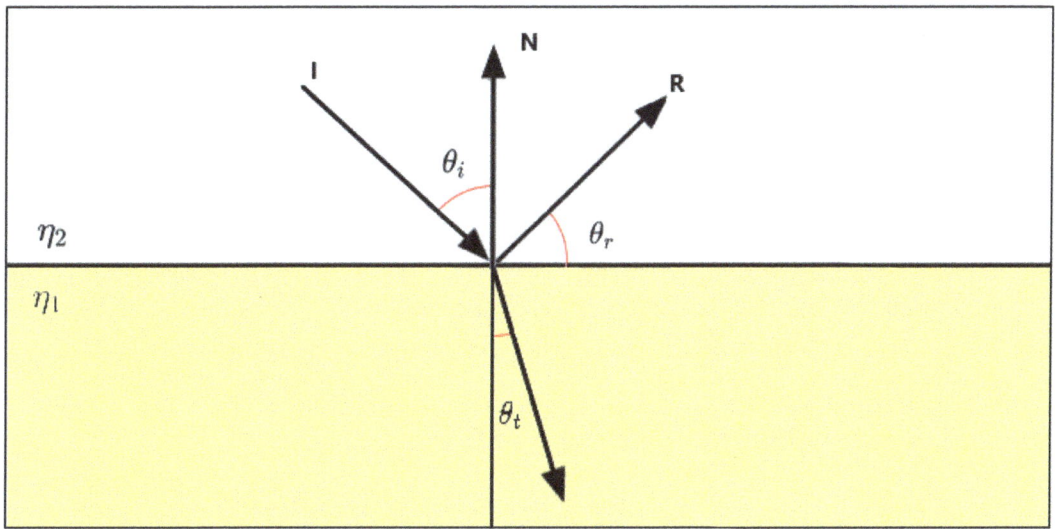

Figure 6-9. Light that arrives at an incident angle at the interface of two media

I is the incident ray direction, **N** the surface normal, **R** the reflected ray direction, and **T** the transmitted/refracted direction.

> *As you can see, the Schlick approximation is way simpler and cheaper to compute than the two previous expressions. In fact, it has only a cosine function to compute, and the rest of it is just standard sum and multiplications. Moreover, the fifth power applied to the cosine expression can be optimized away by multiplying the expression five times by itself. In this way, we can avoid a costly pow(,) function.*

If we just consider air-medium interactions, we know that the index of refraction for air is $\eta_2 = 1$, and therefore, we have the following:

$$R_0 = \left(\frac{\eta_1 - 1}{\eta_1 + 1}\right)^2$$

Here, η_1 is the index of refraction of the other denser medium.

The next subsection will be devoted to the introduction of Snell's law, which is crucial to understand refraction, and TIR.

Understanding Snell's Law

Up until now, we've been talking about the probability for a ray to be reflected given an angle of incidence. Now we want to address another point, and the question that we will ask to ourselves is: "OK fine, we know how to compute the probability for a ray to be reflected/refracted, but what is the angle of the refracted/transmitted direction in which refracted rays will continue their path?"

While the reflected direction is very straightforward to compute (see the previous section on how to compute it), the same thing doesn't go for the refracted direction.

We need some relation that will help us in computing the transmitted angle (and therefore the transmitted direction from it).

The equation that we are looking for is the one that expresses the Snell's law. This equation states:

$$\eta_1 \sin\theta_i = \eta_2 \sin\theta_t$$

where, as you can see, refraction indices, incidence angle θ_i and transmitted angle θ_t are present. Now we have a clear equation that tells us how the incidence angle and the transmitted angle are related to each other. We can rewrite the previous relation as:

$$\sin\theta_t = \frac{\eta_1}{\eta_2} \sin\theta_i$$

But this relation is valid only if a condition holds:

$$\sin\theta_t = \frac{\eta_1}{\eta_2} \sin\theta_i \Leftrightarrow \sin\theta_t \leq \frac{\eta_2}{\eta_1}$$

If that condition is not satisfied, then we will have a total internal reflection (TIR). We will talk about TIR in the remainder of this chapter. We will assume that the previous condition is satisfied during our transmission derivation.

Let's first try to derive the transmission direction **T**. Note that when we say transmitted or refracted direction, we mean the same thing. Therefore, we will freely use one or the other. To better understand how we get to derive **T**, let's take a look at Figure 6-10.

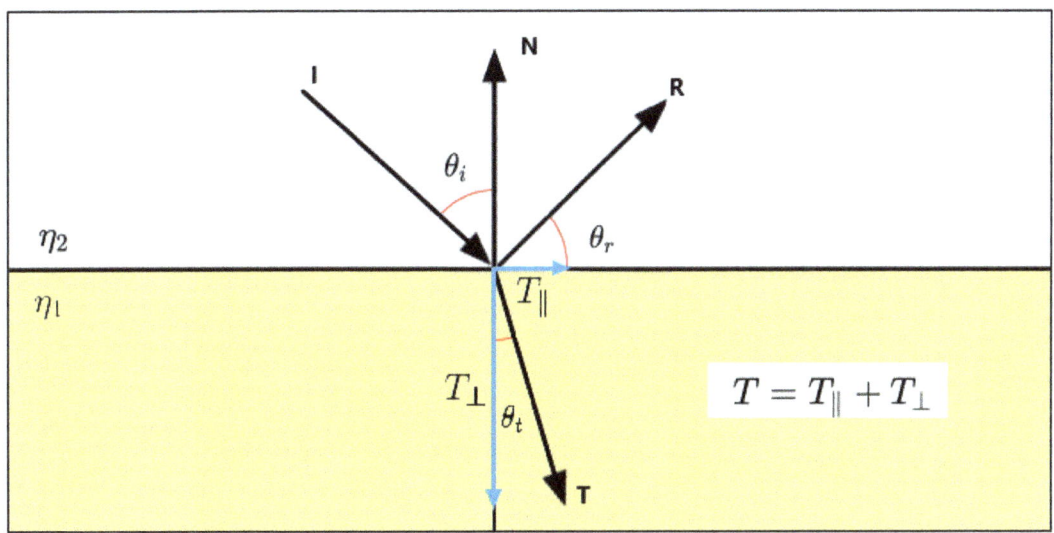

Figure 6-10. Transmission direction T derivation

By looking at Figure 6-10, we see the following:

$$T = T_\| + T_\perp$$

where is the parallel component or tangent part and is the perpendicular component of **T**.

Here is the preliminary formula for **T**. We need to substitute for the sin term, and we'll get to the final form for **T**:

$$T = \frac{\eta_1}{\eta_2}I + (\frac{\eta_1}{\eta_2}cos\theta_i - \sqrt{1 - sin^2\theta_t})N$$

Because of Snell's law, we can find $sin^2\theta_t$:

$$sin^2\theta_t = (\frac{\eta_1}{\eta_2})^2 sin^2\theta_i = (\frac{\eta_1}{\eta_2})^2(1 - cos^2\theta_i)$$

We now can rewrite the formula for **T** by substituting $sin^2\theta_t$, and we get the following:

$$T = \frac{\eta_1}{\eta_2}I + (\frac{\eta_1}{\eta_2}cos\theta_i - \sqrt{1 - [(\frac{\eta_1}{\eta_2})^2(1 - cos^2\theta_i)]})N$$

The previous equation is the final expression for **T**. Having it expressed in terms of cosines is much better as we can compute them easily by the dot product of the related vectors, where **I** is the incident ray direction and **N** is the surface normal.

Here is the C/C++ code snippet that we use to compute the refracted direction **T** as in the previous formula:

```
__device__ static Vector3 refract(const Vector3& I, const Vector3& N,
float IOR)
{
    // refraction indices
    float nc = 1.f;
    float nt = IOR;

    // This is the cosine of the incident angle theta given by the dot
        product between I and N
    // We assume for I and N to be normalized
    float dot_dn = I.dot(N);
    // Are we entering or exiting the denser medium?
    bool RayIsEntering = dot_dn < 0.0f;
```

Now that we know whether a ray is entering or exiting the medium, we can take appropriate actions in the second part of this function:

```
// If we are exiting the denser medium we must flip the normal
auto nl = RayIsEntering ? N : -N;
// We have to know whether we are entering or exting the medium
const float nnt = RayIsEntering ? nc / nt : nt / nc;
const float ddn = RayIsEntering ? dot_dn : -dot_dn;
// We compute the square root term upfront
const float cos2t = 1 - nnt * nnt*(1 - ddn * ddn);
// T.I.R. - Total internal reflection
if (cos2t <= 0.0001f)
{
    // We just reflect the direction
    return reflect(I, nl);
}
```

```
else // We finally compute the refracted/transmitted direction
{
    // Transmission direction
    Vector3 tdir = (I*nnt - nl * (ddn*nnt + sqrtf(cos2t))).norm();
    return tdir;
    }
}
```

However, in the previous code, we are not considering the Fresnel term to keep things simple, but we concentrated just on the refracted direction computation.

Understanding Total Internal Reflection

If we take a closer look at the transmission equation, we notice that it is valid until the term under the square root is greater or equal than zero.

What happens if it is negative? The answer to this question is *total internal reflection* (TIR). How can we handle TIR then?

In the C/C++ implementation for **T** that we've just shown, we can notice that there is a check that we have to do. We basically check the square root argument up front and, if it is negative, we simply reflect the ray otherwise we compute the refracted direction **T**.

But there is a specific incoming angle at which TIR happens, and that is defined as the critical angle. We denote it with the letter θ_c. If we apply the Snell's law, we can easily calculate the critical angle θ_c:

$$\theta_c = \arcsin(\frac{\eta_2}{\eta_1}) \Leftrightarrow \eta_1 > \eta_2$$

Something really important to notice here is that the previous expression is valid if and only if we are traveling from a denser medium (index of refraction η_1) at the interface with a medium with a lower density (index of refraction η_2).

The inequality $\eta_1 > \eta_2$ clearly states what we've just said. See Figure 6-11.

> *We can notice the TIR effect in real life if we are, for example, underwater and we look up above our head at the interface with the air. The reason why we are not able to see through the water interface is due to the total internal reflection. Actually, because the water surface is not static, the perceived effect is variable because of the critical angle variates as the water moves.*

Figure 6-11. *Transmission direction T derivation*

In Figure 6-12 (a picture taken by my wife during summer), we more clearly define the boundaries at which TIR happens. You will notice even isolated areas on the surface where refraction is happening due to the movement of the liquid surface that has the power of changing the critical angle continuously and not homogeneously.

CHAPTER 6   RAY AND CAMERA MODEL DEFINITIONS

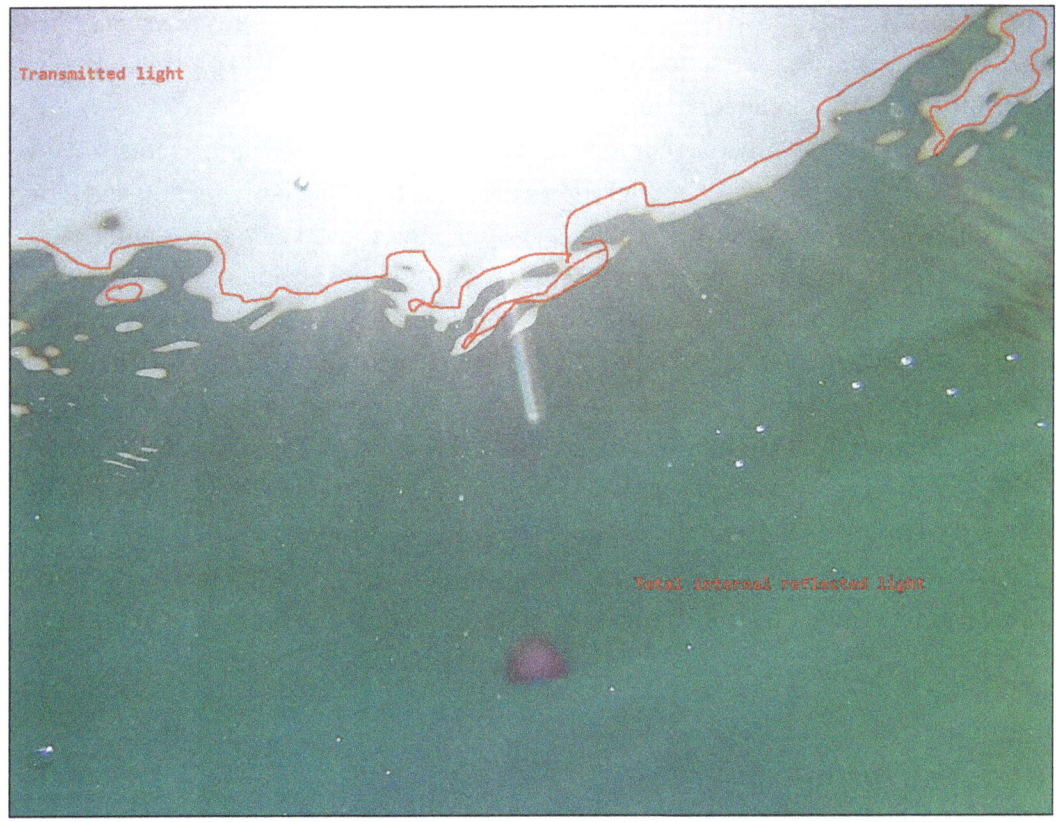

Figure 6-12. *Total internal reflection. Boundaries are highlighted more clearly in red*

The end of this section is also the conclusion of this chapter. In the next chapter, we will go through different categories of ray tracing implementations to illustrate how ray tracing approaches evolved over time to solve the limitations of any previous implementation. We will also introduce the basic ray-primitive intersection approaches. We will start with the so-called Whitted ray tracing, and we will present improvements made on it to get to distributed ray tracing and path tracing.

Summary

In this chapter, we presented the foundations you must be aware of when diving for the first time in the ray tracing realm. Those are the bare minimum concepts that are needed to build any basic ray tracer with a minimum of basic lighting and shading, not to mention good reflection and refraction. You should now understand how to implement diffuse, specular, and transparent materials. We still did not present any physically based BRDF model, because as we stated at the beginning, we were going to present only a basic, approximated model for lighting: the Phong model.

What we did, instead, was to compare the Phong specular reflection against a proper physically correct way of computing perfect mirror specular reflection and glossy reflection. We also covered refraction, Fresnel, and Snell's law, which represent the foundation for transparent object rendering. We gave a basic introduction, but we still did not connect the refraction part with the Fresnel part. Every material has a Fresnel that influences the percentage of reflection over-refraction, and vice versa. In the next chapter, this connection will happen, and the results will be shown. You should now be familiar with what the illumination equation is and what its limitations and advantages are. This will be crucial when we introduce physically correct BRDF models because we will often compare them against the illumination equation.

Moreover, by having a foundation on how transparent objects behave, you should be quite comfortable when more advanced shading models are introduced in the next chapters.

Questions

Based on the knowledge that you gained in this chapter, it is your turn to answer some questions:

- Why is the pinhole camera model still used in the computer graphics world?
- How is the pinhole camera model converted to be used practically as a 3D graphics camera?
- Why do we add a **minT** and a **maxT** in the ray struct definition?
- What is the illumination equation?
- What are the main terms of the illumination equation?
- What are the limitations of using the illumination equation?
- What happens when we get past the critical angle? Reply and explain why.

- How Fresnel is defined, and why it is important?
- What is TIR? Why does it happen?
- Provide a real-world example of TIR.
- What is the index of refraction?

Further Reading

The following are a few resources you can use to expand the horizon of your knowledge on this chapter:

- https://graphics.stanford.edu/courses/cs148-10-summer/docs/2006--degreve--reflection_refraction.pdf
- http://www.huevaluechroma.com/021.php
- https://www.scratchapixel.com/lessons/3d-basic-rendering/introductionto-shading/reflection-refraction-fresnel
- https://en.wikipedia.org/wiki/Phong_reflection_model

CHAPTER 7

Basic Ray-Primitive Intersection Techniques

The foundation of any ray tracer is represented by the intersection techniques that are employed to actually render primitives. There are different ray-primitive intersections depending on which primitive we are targeting.

In this chapter, we first present some of the most relevant techniques, and then we try to propose a simple C/C++ implementation that will show a basic way to approach the problem. This implementation will still be part of our CUDA ray tracer, and it will bridge the knowledge gap between the ray-primitive intersection that you met in the code of the previous chapters.

The most common primitives that we will account for are spheres, planes, quads, and last but not least triangles! Of course, there are many more basic primitives we could consider like cones or cylinders, but here we will show just the most widely used and simple to implement.

Yes, triangles, too! They are important because meshes are made by triangles, and in real-world applications, we will mostly deal with triangle meshes.

During the presentation of each intersection routine, we will keep an eye on optimizations. So, it is important to produce not only a correct solution to the intersection problem but also a performant and numerically stable one.

Floating-point numerical stability will also be discussed to justify some of the choices made in the intersection routines themselves. This needs to be taken into account mainly for a matter of numerical stability.

By the end of this chapter, you will have gained a solid grasp of the most common intersection techniques and be able to create a basic C/C++ implementation that will build on the concepts presented throughout the chapter.

Chapter 7 Basic Ray-Primitive Intersection Techniques

The following topics will be covered in this chapter:

- Understanding ray-sphere intersection
- Understanding ray-plane intersection
- Understanding ray-quad intersection
- Understanding ray-triangle intersection
- Floating-point precision issues and how to account for them
- Putting all together: a basic and simple C++ interface to manage objects

Technical Requirements

The following tools will be required before we get started:

- Visual Studio 2022 Community
- Cuda Toolkit 13.0.1
- Windows 10 RS5 update

Minimum hardware requirements:

- GeForce RTX 2k series

Understanding Ray-Sphere Intersection

The simplest and widely used primitive is surely the sphere. It is present in pretty much any basic ray tracer implementation because it is simple and quick to implement.
We will present two potential solutions to find a ray-sphere intersection. The first one is the analytic solution, and the second one is known to be a geometric solution. We present both of them and will discuss the pros and cons of adopting one or the other approach.

Understanding the Analytic Solution

Let's start by first defining how a sphere is defined mathematically:

$$\|p-c\|^2 = r^2$$

where **p** is a point on the sphere surface, **c** is the sphere center, and **r** is its radius. What the previous equation states is simple: a sphere is defined by the set of points whose distance from its center **c** is exactly equal to the radius **r**.

A sphere is the set of points that are equidistant from the sphere center c. The distance of any of those points is equal to the radius r.

If we let:

$$p = \begin{bmatrix} x_1 \\ x_2 \\ x_3 \end{bmatrix}$$

and

$$c = \begin{bmatrix} c_1 \\ c_2 \\ c_3 \end{bmatrix}$$

we could also rewrite the equation like this:

$$(x_1 - c_1)^2 + (x_2 - c_2)^2 + (x_3 - c_3)^2 = r^2$$

This component-wise expansion of the sphere equation is another way of looking at the original equation. However, it is not the form that we will use to show our analytic solution to the ray-sphere intersection problem. We will still keep it in compact form for the sake of simplicity and because it's much more compact during the calculation.

Now we know that the equation of a ray is as follows:

$$r(t) = o + \hat{d}t$$

Note that we are assuming that the ray direction $\hat{d}$ is normalized, but bear in mind that it might not be always the case.

CHAPTER 7   BASIC RAY-PRIMITIVE INTERSECTION TECHNIQUES

Then if we want to find the intersection point between a ray and a sphere, we have to construct this linear system:

$$\begin{cases} \|p - c\|^2 = r^2 \\ r(t) = o + \hat{d} * t \end{cases}$$

So, if **r(t) = p**, then we can substitute for **p** in the sphere equation and solve for **t**. We get the following:

$$\|o + \hat{d} * t - c\|^2 - r^2 = 0$$

If we develop the previous equation, we get the following:

$$\hat{d}^2 t^2 + 2\hat{d}(o - c)t + (o - c)^2 - r^2 = 0$$

Now to solve for t, we notice that this is a second-degree polynomial equation of the form $ax^2 + bx + c = 0$. And we surely know how to solve it. See Figure 7-1.

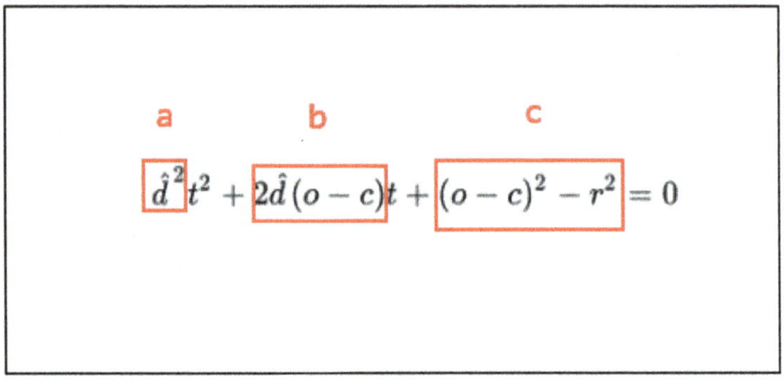

Figure 7-1. a, b, and c coefficients marked in red on top of the related parts of our equation

So, because our equation is known to be a quadratic equation, there is a very well-known formula to solve it:

$$t = \frac{-b \pm \sqrt{b^2 - 4ac}}{2a}$$

$$\Delta = b^2 - 4ac$$

CHAPTER 7   BASIC RAY-PRIMITIVE INTERSECTION TECHNIQUES

Δ is known to be the **discriminant**.

*We know from math that if the **b** coefficient of a quadratic equation is even (and in our case it is), we can use a slightly simplified version of the previous equation. In particular, what changes is the discriminant and the denominator. For the discriminant we have that:*

$$\Delta = b^2 - 4ac$$

becomes:

$$\Delta = b^2 - ac$$

*and the denominator **2a** will become just **a**.*

If we rewrite the previous equation, we then have the following:

$$t = \frac{-b \pm \sqrt{b^2 - ac}}{a}$$

This last form of the equation is the one we will use to practically implement our intersection routine for the analytic solution.

Now we know where our coefficients a, b, and c need to be plugged to solve for **t**. Being a quadratic equation means that we will have two, one, or zero solutions. We can understand how many solutions we get by checking the sign of the **discriminant** Δ.

Figure 7-2 shows all the cases we have to consider once we've calculated our t_0 and t_1.

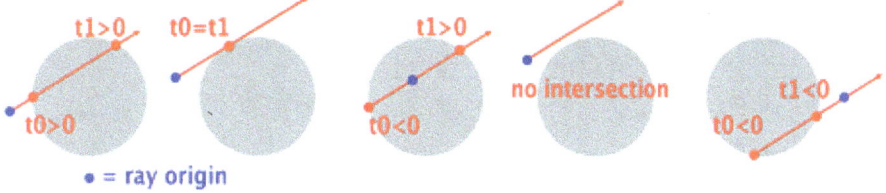

Figure 7-2. *These are all the cases we have to consider for t_0 and t_1.*

153

CHAPTER 7   BASIC RAY-PRIMITIVE INTERSECTION TECHNIQUES

> $\Delta > 0$ We will have two solutions (i.e. the ray intersect the sphere in two points)
> $\Delta = 0$ We will have one solution (i.e. the ray is tangent to the sphere)
> $\Delta < 0$ We will have no solutions (i.e. the ray doesn't intersect the sphere)

We denote the sphere center to be c_s instead of just c, to distinguish it from the quadratic equation coefficient c.

So, in our case we let:

$$a = \hat{d}^2$$
$$b = 2\hat{d}(o - c_s)$$
$$c = (o - c_s)^2 - r^2$$

We plug them into the previous equation, check the sign of the discriminant, and then take appropriate actions based on whichever of the three previous cases we are dealing with.

Once we get the value of **t**, we can plug it back into the ray equation to get the intersection point we've been looking for. Finally!

This following code snippet shows the implementation for the analytic solution:

```
//Compute the ray-sphere intersection using analytic solution
__device__ virtual bool Intersect(const Ray& InRay, float InTMin, float InTMax, float& t) noexcept override
{
// Analytic solution (less efficent)
    const Vector3& oc = (InRay.mOrigin - mCenter); //
    const float a = InRay.mDirection.dot(InRay.mDirection); //
    const float b = oc.dot(InRay.mDirection); //
    const float c = oc.dot(oc) - mRadius * mRadius; //
    const float Disc = b * b - a * c; //
    if (Disc > 0.0001f) // Now let's check the discriminant sign
    {
        float SqrtDisc = sqrt(Disc);
        float temp = (-b - SqrtDisc) / a;
        if (temp < InTMax && temp > InTMin)
        {
```

```
            t = temp;
            return true;
        }
        temp = (-b + SqrtDisc) / a;

        if (temp < InTMax && temp > InTMin)
        {
            t = temp;
            return true;
        }
    }
    return false;
}
```

As you can see in the previous code, we first check for the discriminant to be positive before computing its square root. That is a good way to compute it only if it's needed, saving a few precious CPU cycles.

But there is another way to approach the ray-sphere intersection problem. This will consist of the application of the Pythagorean theorem and some vector algebra. The next subsection will provide a solution for the so-called geometric solution.

Understanding the Geometric Solution

What you've seen in the previous section is the analytic approach, where we consider a linear system of equations and we solve for **t** in perfect algebraic style! However, there is another way to approach the problem that considers a more geometric approach so to speak. Basically, we can work out the same solution, reasoning just on vectors and their lengths. Let's see how.

We can summarize the approach with these steps (see Figure 7-3):

- Geometry
- Trigonometry
- Pythagorean theorem

CHAPTER 7   BASIC RAY-PRIMITIVE INTERSECTION TECHNIQUES

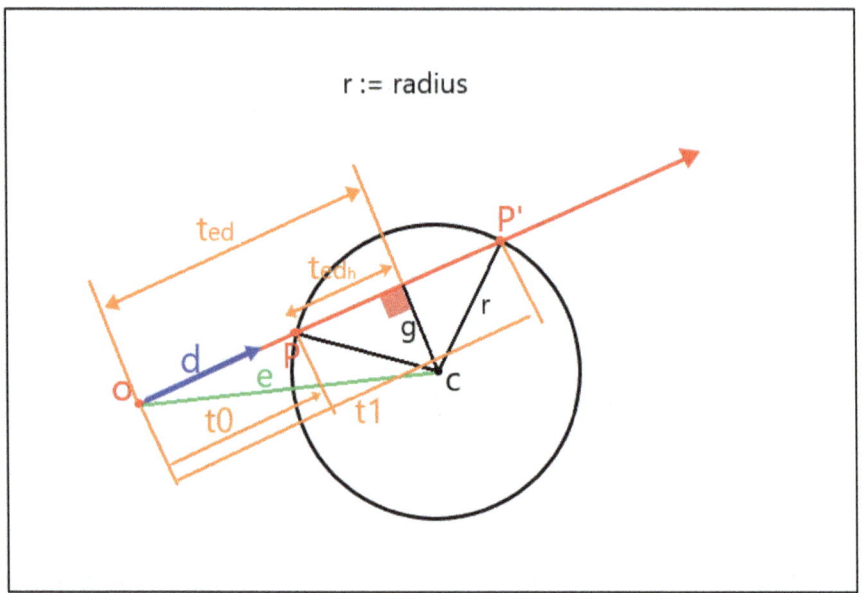

Figure 7-3. *The geometric solution is based on the use of vectors and their lengths*

We need to find t_0 and t_1, which are the distances from the ray origin allowing us to also compute the two intersection points for a given ray.

So, as you can tell from Figure 7-3, we start by computing this data first:

$$\vec{e} = c - o$$

$$t_{ed} = \vec{e} \cdot \hat{d}$$

$$if(t_{ed} < 0)\ return\ false$$

To find **g**, we apply the Pythagorean theorem:

$$g^2 + t_{ed}^2 = ||\vec{e}||^2 \text{ then } g = \sqrt{e^2 - t_{ed}^2}$$

$$if(g > r)\ return\ false$$

If **g** is greater than the radius **r**, then the ray misses the sphere. With this check, we can reject the ray and get out early from the function, as we will know for sure that the ray will never hit the sphere.

CHAPTER 7 BASIC RAY-PRIMITIVE INTERSECTION TECHNIQUES

It's very simple and straightforward. Now we are ready to finally calculate t_{ed_h}.
As we can see, there is another right triangle made by **g**,**r** (the sphere radius) and t_{ed_h}.
Then we apply **Pythagoras** again and we get this:

$$r^2 = g^2 + t_{ed_h}^2 \text{ then } t_{ed_h} = \sqrt{r^2 - g^2}$$

Then finally we have our two solutions:

$$t_0 = t_{ed} - t_{ed_h}$$
$$t_1 = t_{ed} + t_{ed_h}$$

After we've computed t_0 and t_1, if we want the closer intersection (which is normally what we are after), we just pick the min between them and check that it is actually greater than zero too.

Something like this:

$$t_i = min(t_0, t_1)$$

and $t_i >= 0$ (if it's equal to zero, that means the intersection point and the ray origin are the same).

So, we will get the closest intersection point p_c by plugging the previously computed t_i value into the ray equation:

$$p_c = o + t_i * \hat{d}$$

Because we actually use g^2 in our calculation for t_{ed_h} and never g, when we test against the radius, we can make this kind of check:

$$if(g^2 > r^2) \; return \; false$$

In this way, we save one square root!

A common trick to avoid computing the square root is to compare the squared distances instead.

OK, what's left? Of course, we have to check the values of t_0 and t_1 because what we are looking for is actually the closest point and whether we actually are in one of the cases outlined in Figure 7-2.

CHAPTER 7   BASIC RAY-PRIMITIVE INTERSECTION TECHNIQUES

Here is the code for the geometric solution to the ray-sphere intersection:

```
//Compute the ray-sphere intersection using the geometric solution
__device__ virtual bool Intersect(const Ray& InRay, float InTMin, float
InTMax, float& t) noexcept override
{
   // Vector that points from the ray origin to the sphere center
   const Vector3& e = (mCenter - InRay.mOrigin);
   // Projection of e onto d
   float ted = e.dot(InRay.mDirection);
   // Pythagora
   float gsq = e.dot(e) - ted*ted;
   // Squared radius
   float RadiusSq = mRadius*mRadius;
   // The ray overshoot/misses the sphere
   if (gsq > RadiusSq)
   {
      return false;
   }
// From the other right smaller right triangle let's calculate tedh
// Pythagoras Theorem again
   float tedh = sqrtf(RadiusSq-gsq);
```

Now that we've applied Pythagorean theorem to find the lengths for t_{ed} and t_{ed_h}, we can compute the value for t_0 and t_1 and go straight to the second part of this function:

```
// Now let's calculate t0, t1 finally
   float t0 = ted - tedh;
   float t1 = ted + tedh;
// Here we check the sign of t0,t1 to see in which case we fall into
// Let's keep in mind that we accept only the closest intersection,
therefore we assume that t0
// will represent the closest intersection for us.
   if(t0 > t1)
   {
      std::swap(t0,t1);
```

158

CHAPTER 7 BASIC RAY-PRIMITIVE INTERSECTION TECHNIQUES

```
// The sphere is behind the ray origin
    if(t0 < 0)
    {
       return false;
    }
 }
// Since we've added a specific range in which we can or not accept an intersection let's add
// a final check.
    if(t0 >= InTMin && t0 < InTMax)
    {
       return false;
    }

    return true;
}
```

That's all for the ray-sphere intersection theory and implementation. Now you should be familiar with how to implement your routine. If you find yourself in trouble, you can always refer to the provided source code and find your way in there. This will get us to the next section in which we will face another type of ray-primitive intersection, which is a ray-plane intersection. This technique is at the heart of other intersection techniques like, for example, the ray-triangle intersection. It will basically be an important intermediate step for the aforementioned technique. Let's get straight into it.

Understanding Ray-Plane Intersection

The intersection between a ray and a plane is way simpler than you might imagine. In fact, and I would say, fortunately, there is just one approach to account for. Learning the ray-plane intersection technique is important to understand the remainder of this chapter because this method is present during the ray-triangle intersection as well as the ray-quad intersection.

We will then present the one and only method to calculate this kind of intersection. Take a look at Figure 7-4.

CHAPTER 7   BASIC RAY-PRIMITIVE INTERSECTION TECHNIQUES

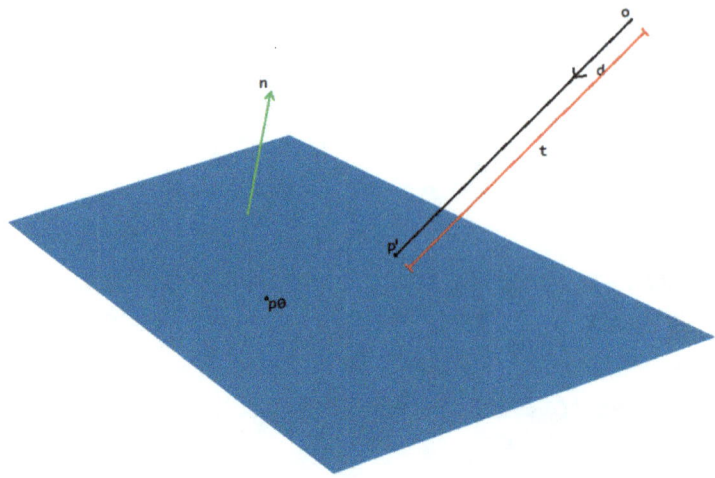

Figure 7-4. Ray-plane intersection

But let's define first a plane mathematically, as shown by the following formula:

$$(p - p_0) \cdot \hat{n} + d = 0$$

p_0 is a point belonging to the plane.

$\hat{n}$ is the plane normal, and d is the distance of the plane along the plane normal from the world space origin.

Having said that, we need just to test whether a point p belongs to a plane or not. For this purpose, the previous plane equation needs to be satisfied once we have plugged any point p into it.

Knowing the equation of a ray, we get this equation of a ray:

$$r(t) = o + \hat{d}\,t$$

So, if we plug that into the plane equation, we get this:

$$(o + \hat{d}\,t - p_0) \cdot \hat{n} + d = 0$$

If we solve for *t*, we get this:

$$(o \cdot \hat{n} + \hat{d}\,t \cdot \hat{n} - p_0 \cdot \hat{n}) = 0$$

Finally, we isolate for t:

$$t = \frac{(p_0 - o) \cdot n}{\hat{d} \cdot \hat{n}}$$

Here's the code:

```
//Compute the ray-plane intersection using analitic solution
__device__ virtual float Intersect(const Ray& InRay) override
{
   // assuming vectors are all normalized
   float Den = dot(mNormal, InRay.mDirection);
   float t = -1.0f;
   if (Den > 1e-6)
   {
      float3 pOlO = mPoint - InRay.mOrigin;
      t = dot(pOlO, mNormal) / Den;
      return t;
   }
   return t;
}
```

If the denominator Den is close to zero or negative, the ray misses the plane. In particular:

- If $\hat{d} \cdot \hat{n} \simeq 0$ or $\hat{d} \cdot \hat{n} < 0$, then the ray is parallel to the plane or pointing away from it.

As you can see, we check for the denominator in the code up front to account for the missing outcome. If we have a miss, we return a negative *t* in both cases.

Now we are ready for the next in the list: the ray-quad intersection. So, let's get straight to the next section and see how the ray-plane intersection technique will be useful for the quad intersection technique and, as we will see, in the section related to a ray-triangle intersection.

Understanding Ray-Quad Intersection

To account for the ray-quad intersection, we need two pieces of information:

CHAPTER 7   BASIC RAY-PRIMITIVE INTERSECTION TECHNIQUES

1. To determine the ray-plane intersection

2. To determine whether a point is in front of a plane or not

Everything else will flow from there. How? Keep reading! Determining whether a point is in front or behind a plane means computing the signed distance of that point. If that distance is positive, the point is in front of the plane; otherwise, it is behind it.

In particular, if we have a point p and a plane, what we need to do is to just plug the point p into the plane equation and check the sign of the result.

If $p \cdot \hat{n} + d \geq 0$, then the point is in front of or lying on the plane surface; otherwise, it is behind it. So, to find the ray-quad intersection, the only thing we need to do is to first find the ray plane intersection and then test that the intersection point is in front of the four planes all together that pass through the quad edges.

Figure 7-5 shows a quad, a ray, and the four bounding planes normal.

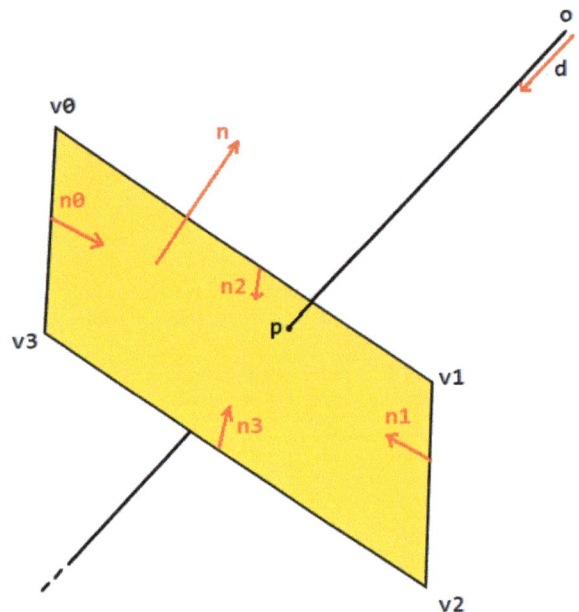

Figure 7-5. Ray-quad intersection

n_0, n_1, n_2, n_3 represents the normal of each of the four planes that pass through each quad edge ($\overline{v_0 v_3}$, $\overline{v_0 v_1}$, $\overline{v_1 v_2}$, $\overline{v_3 v_2}$), and n is the normal of the quad.

> Here we are not considering a quad as made by two right triangles. In fact, another way is to compute the intersection with each one of the two right triangles.

CHAPTER 7 BASIC RAY-PRIMITIVE INTERSECTION TECHNIQUES

Computing the normal of each one of the four planes is easy. What we need to do is to just compute two of them (say n_0 and n_2 for example) and observe that we can retrieve the remaining ones by just inverting n_0 and n_2 like so:

$$n_1 = -n_0$$
$$n_3 = -n_2$$

Pretty straightforward!

Let's see how to practically compute the normal n_0 and n_2 first. You can always refer to Figure 7-5 during the upcoming explanation to understand the role of each variable/symbol throughout.

Let's compute the vector that points from to using the formula given here:

$$\hat{c}_0 = \frac{v_2 - v_1}{||v_2 - v_1||}$$

The compute the vector that points from to using the formula given here:

$$\hat{c}_1 = \frac{v_3 - v_2}{||v_3 - v_2||}$$

By performing the cross product with $\hat{c}_0$ and the plane normal n, we get n_1, which is denoted as follows:

$$n_1 = \hat{c}_0 \times n$$

With the cross product between $\hat{c}_1$ and, again, the plane normal n, we obtain n_3:

$$n_3 = \hat{c}_1 \times n$$

Finally finding n_2 and n_0 is just a matter of flipping the normal vectors n_1 and n_3:

$$n_2 = -n_3$$
$$n_0 = -n_1$$

Now that we have n_0, n_1, n_2, n_3, we can easily compute whether the intersection point p is contained within the quad boundaries defined by its edges by just computing the dot product between the point and n_0, n_1, n_2, n_3 of the planes. In this case, obviously we also need to compute the ***d*** value for each of the four bounding planes (so basically four different d values).

Those planes will look like this:

$$n_0 \cdot p + d_0 = 0$$
$$n_1 \cdot p + d_1 = 0$$
$$n_2 \cdot p + d_2 = 0$$
$$n_3 \cdot p + d_3 = 0$$

So, the containment test, given that ***p*** is our intersection point with the quad plane, will look like this:

$$if((n_0 \cdot p + d_0 \geq 0)\ and\ (n_1 \cdot p + d_1 \geq 0)\ and\ (n_2 \cdot p + d_2 \geq 0)\ and\ (n_3 \cdot p + d_3 \geq 0))$$

If the previous statement is true, the point ***p*** is contained in the positive half-space defined by the previous four planes.

Let's get straight to the next subsection to see how the ray-quad intersection is implemented in code.

Understanding the Containment Test

Once we have computed the previous four normal and the intersection of the ray with the quad plane, we need to verify that the actual intersection point is contained in the quad boundaries.

We already know how to determine whether a point is in front of a plane or not; therefore, to know if a point is contained inside a quad, everything that we need to do is to just verify that the point is in front of the four planes defined by the four normals. Refer to Figure 7-5 to keep track of each variable involved.

Let's see how to do it in practice with some C-like pseudocode:

```
bool RayQuadIntersect(Ray ray, float& t)
{
    // Do we have an intersection with the quad plane?
    if( !PlaneIntersect(Ray,t) )
```

```
    {
      return false;
    }
    // Intersection point (this point is lying on the quad-plane)
    p = ray.o + ray.dir * t;
    // Verify that p is actually contained inside the quad boundaries
    return PointPlaneTest(p,plane0) == IN_FRONT && PointPlaneTest(p,plane1)
    == IN_FRONT && PointPlane  Test(p,plane2) == IN_FRONT &&
    PointPlaneTest(p,plane3) == IN_FRONT;
}
```

And that's it. It's pretty straightforward.

This will let us compute the ray-quad intersection. But, as we will see, the most general way to compute any intersection is to consider a triangular mesh (with the exception of very basic primitives of course). If we consider the quad as made by two triangles, we will still be able to find the intersection point, but we will also be able to find the intersections with more complex meshes. That is what ultimately we want to end up with at some point and what pretty much any modern renderer does nowadays.

So, the next section will be devoted to exactly this: ray-triangle intersection. This technique is important because most of the 3D models that are rendered by any real-world ray tracer are actually triangle meshes.

Understanding Ray-Triangle Intersection

So, for the ray-triangle intersection, we have now to define our triangle. A triangle is obviously defined by three vertices and a normal.

Let's name the vertices: v_0, v_1, v_2. If we consider the vertex winding order as counterclockwise, the normal will point up with respect to the triangle surface plane.

Figure 7-6 shows how our triangle looks.

CHAPTER 7   BASIC RAY-PRIMITIVE INTERSECTION TECHNIQUES

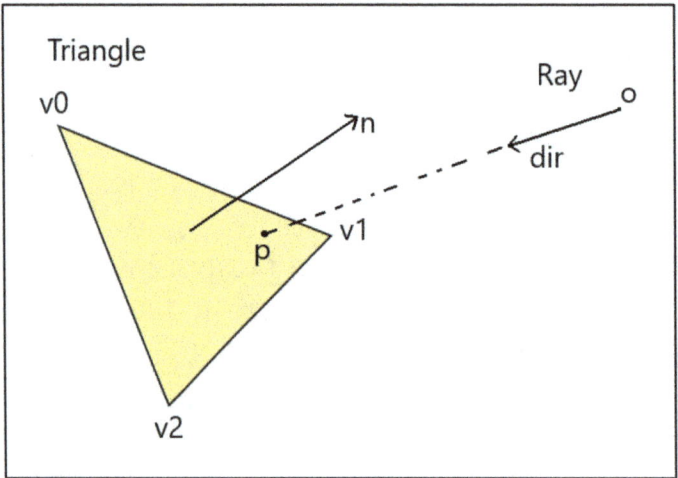

Figure 7-6. *This is a triangle with normal η and vertices v_0, v_1, v_2 with a ray that intersects the triangle at the point **p***

Figure 7-6 shows a triangle with its normal. We shoot a ray against it, and then we make a containment test, pretty similar to the ray-quad intersection.

So, to summarize:

1. Shoot a ray against a triangle.

2. Test whether the ray is parallel to the triangle plane or not (in that case we have a miss).

3. Test whether the ray is pointing away from the triangle with its direction (another miss).

4. Compute ray-plane intersection with respect to a plane defined by the triangle normal **n** and the **d** of that plane. Find a point of intersection **p**.

5. Make a containment test to verify whether the previously computed point is inside the triangle or not.

The code will look like this:

```
bool RayTriangleIntersect(Ray ray,const Vector3& v0,const Vector3& v1,const Vector3& v2,float& t)
{
// Ray origin and direction
```

```
   auto dir = ray.mDirection;
   auto o = ray.mOrigin;
// Let's compute the triangle normal
   auto c0 = v1 - v2;
   auto c1 = v0 - v2;
   auto n = c0.cross(c1);
   float area = n.length();
// Check whether the ray is parallel with respect to the triangle plane
   float nDotDir = n.dot(dir);
   if(nDotDir < 0.0001f)
   {
      return false;
   }
// Compute the d of the plane
   float d = n.dot(v0);
// Ready to compute t
   t = (n.dot(o) + d) / nDotDir;
// Check whether the triangle is behind the ray
   if(t < 0.0f)
   {
      return false;
   }
// Compute the intersection point
   auto p = o + t*dir;
```

The code continues with the containment test:

```
// Containment test
// We need to compute the vector perpendicular to the triangle's plane
   Vector3 h; // perpendicular vector
// Considering that we assumed counter-clockwise vertex winding order we
```

CHAPTER 7 BASIC RAY-PRIMITIVE INTERSECTION TECHNIQUES

```
// will take that into account during vector edge computation that will be
// used for containment test
// First edge
   auto v0v1 = v1 - v0;
   auto v0p = p - v0;
   h = v0p.cross(v0v1);
   if(n.dot(h) < 0.0f)
   {
      return false;
   }
// Second edge
   auto v2v1 = v2 - v1;
   auto v1p = p - v1;
   h = v1p.cross(v2v1);
   if(n.dot(h) < 0.0f)
   {
      return false;
   }
// Third edge
   auto v2v0 = v0 - v2;
   auto v2p = p - v2;
   h = v2p.cross(v2v0);
   if(n.dot(h) < 0.0f)
   {
      return false;
   }

   return true;

}
```

Now, the previous code will compute the ray-triangle intersection using a geometric solution. However, there is one more bit of information that we need. This is represented by barycentric coordinates.

The next subsection will briefly explain what barycentric coordinates represent and how they can be used in the context of rendering.

Understanding Barycentric Coordinates

At some point, we might need to interpolate vertex attributes (e.g., vertex color, vertex normal, texture coordinates, etc.) when it comes to the time of shading a triangle. That is why barycentric coordinates are important to us.

Let's take a look at the previous triangle, as shown in Figure 7-5.

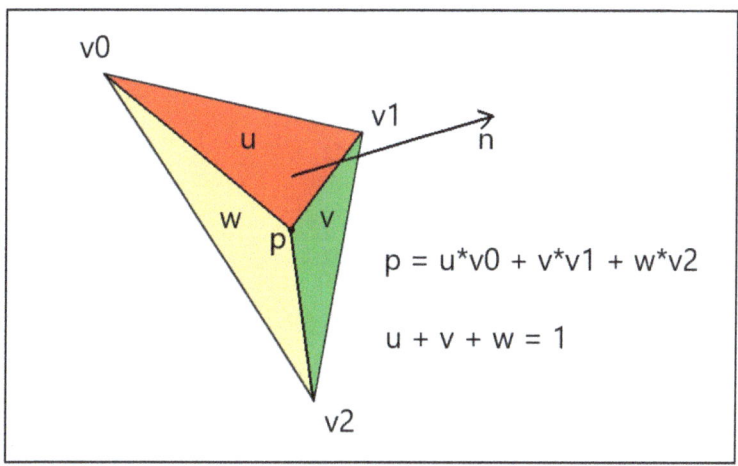

Figure 7-7. *Barycentric coordinates and their relation with the intersection point **p***

u,v,w are the barycentric coordinates, and the intersection point **p** can be defined with respect to them thanks to this relation:

$$p = u * v_0 + v * v_1 + w * v_2$$

and

$$u + v + w = 1$$

p is inside the triangle or on any of the three edges if and only if:

$$0 \leq u, v, w \leq 1$$

We can spot three subtriangles in Figure 7-7:

- Subtriangle $v_0 p v_2$

CHAPTER 7 BASIC RAY-PRIMITIVE INTERSECTION TECHNIQUES

- Subtriangle $v_0 p v_1$
- Subtriangle $v_1 p v_2$

Barycentric coordinates are the ratio of the area of any of the three subtriangles and the area of the triangle.

We can compute the barycentric coordinates by taking into account their ratio with respect to the area of the triangle $v_0 v_1 v_2$.

$$u = \frac{v_0 p v_1{}_{area}}{v_0 v_1 v_2{}_{area}}$$

$$v = \frac{v_1 p v_2{}_{area}}{v_0 v_1 v_2{}_{area}}$$

$$w = \frac{v_0 p v_2{}_{area}}{v_0 v_1 v_2{}_{area}}$$

Now all that we need to know is how to calculate the area of each subtriangle and the area of the triangle $v_0 v_1 v_2$. This is pretty straightforward because we know that the magnitude of the cross product is equal to the area of the parallelogram defined by the two coplanar vectors. Therefore, the area of one of the subtriangles is the magnitude of the cross product between the coplanar vectors divided by 2.

So basically, we have for the main triangle area:

$$v_0 v_1 v_2{}_{area} = \frac{||(v_1 - v_2) \times (v_0 - v_2)||}{2}$$

For the three subtriangle areas, we have the following three formulas:

$$v_0 p v_1{}_{area} = \frac{||(p - v_0) \times (v_1 - v_0)||}{2}$$

$$v_1 p v_2{}_{area} = \frac{||(p - v_1) \times (v_2 - v_1)||}{2}$$

$$v_0 p v_2{}_{area} = \frac{||(p - v_2) \times (v_0 - v_2)||}{2}$$

Knowing that each one of the barycentric coordinates is the ratio between each subtriangle area and the main triangle area we have:

$$u = \frac{\frac{||(p-v_0) \times (v_1-v_0)||}{2}}{\frac{||(v_1-v_2) \times (v_0-v_2)||}{2}} = \frac{||(p-v_0) \times (v_1-v_0)||}{||(v_1-v_2) \times (v_0-v_2)||}$$

$$v = \frac{\frac{||(p-v_1) \times (v_2-v_1)||}{2}}{\frac{||(v_1-v_2) \times (v_0-v_2)||}{2}} = \frac{||(p-v_1) \times (v_2-v_1)||}{||(v_1-v_2) \times (v_0-v_2)||}$$

Note that the triangle normal n is computed as follows:

$$n = (v_1 - v_2) \times (v_0 - v_2)$$

By knowing that:

$$u + v + w = 1$$

we can easily retrieve w without too much effort knowing u and v, because:

$$w = 1 - u - v$$

That's it! It's pretty straightforward.

The code for the ray-triangle intersection will now include the barycentric coordinates result as output. See the following code:

```
bool RayTriangleIntersect(Ray ray,const Vector3& v0,const Vector3& v1,const Vector3& v2,float& t,float& u,float& v)
{
// Ray origin and direction
   auto dir = ray.mDirection;
   auto o = ray.mOrigin;
// Let's compute the triangle normal
   auto c0 = v1 - v2;
   auto c1 = v0 - v2;
   auto n = c0.cross(c1);
   float area = n.length();
// Check whether the ray is parallel with respect to the triangle plane
```

CHAPTER 7 BASIC RAY-PRIMITIVE INTERSECTION TECHNIQUES

```
    float nDotDir = n.dot(dir);
    if(nDotDir < 0.0001f)
    {
        return false;
    }
// Compute the d of the plane
    float d = n.dot(v0);
// Ready to compute t
    t = (n.dot(o) + d) / nDotDir;
// Check whether the triangle is behind the ray
    if (t < 0.0f)
    {
        return false;
    }
// Compute the intersection point
    auto p = o + t*dir;
```

Then look at the containment test:

```
// Containment test
// We need to compute the vector perpendicular to the triangle's plane
    Vector3 h; // perpendicular vector
// Considering that we assumed counter-clockwise vertex winding order
// we will take that into account during vector edge computation that will
be used for containment test
// First edge
    auto v0v1 = v1 - v0;
    auto v0p = p - v0;
    h = v0p.cross(v0v1);
// Barycentric coord u
    u = h.length() / area;
    if(n.dot(h) < 0.0f)
    {
        return false;
    }
// Second edge
```

```
    auto v2v1 = v2 - v1;
    auto v1p = p - v1;
    h = v1p.cross(v2v1);
// Barycentric coord v
    v = h.length() / area;
    if(n.dot(h) < 0.0f)
    {
        return false;
    }
// Third edge
    auto v2v0 = v0 - v2;
    auto v2p = p - v2;
    h = v2p.cross(v2v0);
    if(n.dot(h) < 0.0f)
    {
        return false;
    }

    return true;
}
```

We now have our barycentric coordinates, and we can use them to interpolate any vertex attribute we want.

So, for example if we have vertex colors c_0, c_1, c_2, we can use them to retrieve the interpolated color c_p at the intersection point p by interpolating this:

$$c_p = u * c_0 + v * c_1 + w * c_2$$

The same process can be applied to interpolate vertex normal and texture coordinates so that we will be able to gather any shading relevant data by interpolation.

Let's compute the barycentric coordinates by applying the knowledge related to the fact that the magnitude of the cross product is the area of the parallelogram defined by the vector for which we are computing the cross product itself. Let's start by computing the ratio between the areas of each subtriangle and the area of the whole triangle (refer

CHAPTER 7 BASIC RAY-PRIMITIVE INTERSECTION TECHNIQUES

to Figure 7-7 to have a clear idea of how every subtriangle area is defined in terms of its vertices):

$$n = (v_1 - v_2) \times (v_0 - v_2)$$

then:

$$||n|| = ||(v_1 - v_2) \times (v_0 - v_2)||$$

and

$$u = \frac{||(p - v_0) \times (v_1 - v_0)||}{||n||}$$

$$v = \frac{||(p - v_1) \times (v_2 - v_1)||}{||n||}$$

By observing that we've already computed some terms in the previous code for the containment test, we can make some clever changes to the previous *u* and *v* formulation such that we can reuse as man terms as we can saving ourselves additional computation steps.

For the containment tests we've already computed:

$$(p - v_0) \times (v_1 - v_0) \cdot n$$

and

$$(p - v_1) \times (v_2 - v_1) \cdot n$$

Therefore, we rewrite the expression for u and v like this:

$$u = \frac{(p - v_0) \times (v_1 - v_0) \cdot n}{n \cdot n}$$

$$v = \frac{(p - v_1) \times (v_2 - v_1) \cdot n}{n \cdot n}$$

So, the code for the ray-triangle intersection with the new simplified/cheaper expressions for *u* and *v* will be:

```
bool RayTriangleIntersect(Ray ray,const Vector3& v0,const Vector3& v1,const
Vector3& v2,float& t,float& u,float& v)
{
  // Ray origin and direction
    auto dir = ray.mDirection;
    auto o = ray.mOrigin;

// Let's compute the triangle normal
    auto c0 = v1 - v2;
    auto c1 = v0 - v2;
    auto n = c0.cross(c1);

// The denominator as in the simplified expression is the normal dotted
with itself
    float den = n.dot(n);

// Check whether the ray is parallel with respect to the triangle plane
    float nDotDir = n.dot(dir);
    if(nDotDir < 0.0001f)
    {
      return false;
    }
// Compute the d of the plane
    float d = n.dot(v0);
// Ready to compute t
    t = (n.dot(o) + d) / nDotDir;
// Check whether the triangle is behind the ray
    if(t < 0.0f)
    {
      return false;
    }
// Compute the intersection point
    auto p = o + t*dir;
```

CHAPTER 7   BASIC RAY-PRIMITIVE INTERSECTION TECHNIQUES

Then for the containment test, we have:

```
// Containment test
// We need to compute the vector perpendicular to the triangle's plane
   Vector3 h; // perpendicular vector

// Considering that we assumed counter-clockwise vertex winding order
// we will take that into account during vector edge computation
that will be
// used for containment test

// First edge
   auto v0v1 = v1 - v0;
   auto v0p = p - v0;
   h = v0p.cross(v0v1);
   u = n.dot(h);

   if (u < 0.0f)
   {
       return false;
   }

   // Second edge
   auto v2v1 = v2 - v1;
   auto v1p = p - v1;
   h = v1p.cross(v2v1);
   v = n.dot(h);

   if (v < 0.0f)
   {
       return false;
   }
   // Third edge
   auto v2v0 = v0 - v2;
   auto v2p = p - v2;
   h = v2p.cross(v2v0);
   if(n.dot(h) < 0.0f)
   {
```

```
        return false;
    }
    // Compute the barycentric coordinates for this triangle by dividing
    be ndotn
    u /= den;
    v /= den;
    return true;
}
```

So, this finally concludes the ray-triangle intersection and the computation of the barycentric coordinates. This section is quite important as it represents the basis for the mesh rendering of any ray tracing-based renderer.

Understanding Möller-Trumbore Algorithm

The last ray-triangle intersection technique that we want to explain is also among the fastest ones. This method takes its name from Tomas Möller and Ben Trumbore who discussed it in the paper titled "Fast, Minimum Storage Ray/Triangle Intersection" for the first time.

After this last technique, we should have a quite complete set of different approaches/techniques to add to our arsenal when it comes time to compute a ray triangle intersection.

This algorithm will exploit the fact that the intersection point p contained in a given triangle can be expressed as a linear combination between the triangle barycentric coordinates (i.e., u, v, w) and its vertices (i.e., v_0, v_1, v_2):

$$p = u * v_0 + v * v_1 + w * v_2$$

As already stated, the relation must hold:

$$u + v + w = 1$$

Also, the point p can be expressed in terms of the ray equation like this:

$$p = o + t * d$$

CHAPTER 7 BASIC RAY-PRIMITIVE INTERSECTION TECHNIQUES

where t is the distance of intersection point p from the ray origin o.
We can then rewrite the first expression in this way:

$$o + t * d = u * v_0 + v * v_1 + w * v_2$$

We also know that:

$$u + v + w = 1 \Leftrightarrow w = 1 - u - v$$

Therefore, substituting for ω we get:

$$o + t * d = u * v_0 + v * v_1 + (1 - u - v) * v_2$$

If we develop this equation further, we should get to a better form for it:

$$-td + u(v_0 - v_2) + v(v_1 - v_2) = o - v_2$$

Then we can rewrite the previous in matrix form and we get this:

$$\begin{pmatrix} -d & (v_0 - v_2) & (v_1 - v_2) \end{pmatrix} \begin{bmatrix} t \\ u \\ v \end{bmatrix} = o - v_2$$

Now, Möller and Trumbore consider the idea that our triangle is basically translated in a local system thanks to the term that is on the right side of the previous equation (i.e., $o - v_2$). This will actually translate our triangle in a reference system that has its origin in the v_2 vertex of the triangle.

We also know that our barycentric coordinates are u and v, so the following must be true:

$$u + v \leq 1$$

So, they are in the **[0,1]** range.

Since we know that our intersection point can be expressed also in terms of barycentric coordinates and that they are invariant with respect to the translation/rotation/scaling applied to the triangle (i.e., they won't change even after we've transformed the triangle), we can safely express our triangle with respect to the vector basis $\begin{pmatrix} t & u & v \end{pmatrix}$.

CHAPTER 7 BASIC RAY-PRIMITIVE INTERSECTION TECHNIQUES

This will actually express the triangle vertices, previously defined in the coordinate system, in the $(t\ u\ v)$ coordinate system.

In this space, the triangle coordinates will have these values: $(0, 0), (1, 0), (0, 1)$. See Figure 7-8 to have a better understanding of what is actually happening.

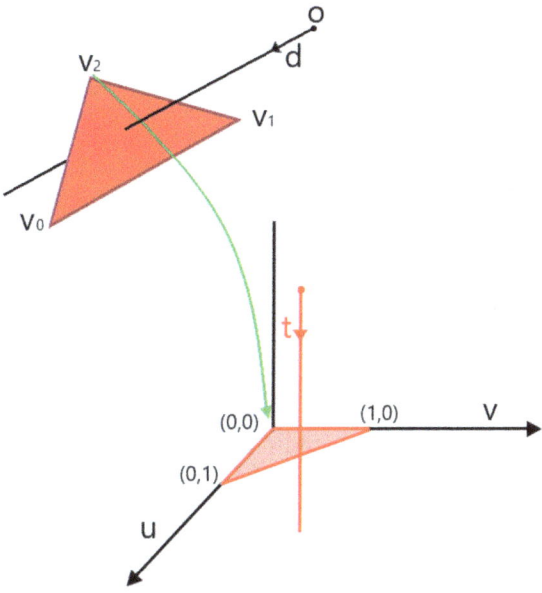

Figure 7-8. *Translating the triangle from **x, y, z** coordinate system to express its coordinates in the coordinate system defined by **(t u v)***

What we have to do now is to solve for t, u, and v.

*In this case, we know what **v** and **u** are, but what about **t**? t is still the distance of our intersection point. Therefore, our intersection point position is defined completely by three variables. The barycentric coordinates u and v and its distance from the ray origin **t**.*

To solve such a linear system, Möller and Trumbore, apply the *Cramer's rule*. We will not show how the Cramer's rule works here, but you can easily find it in the references at the end of this chapter (see the reference at the end of this chapter related to Möller and Trumbore).

For our purposes, we will just show the code, as it's very short, compact, and faster compared to the previous ray-triangle intersection methods.

CHAPTER 7 BASIC RAY-PRIMITIVE INTERSECTION TECHNIQUES

See the following code:

```
bool RayTriangleIntersect(Ray ray,const Vector3& v0,const Vector3& v1,const Vector3& v2,float& t,float& u,float& v)
{
   // Ray origin and direction
   auto dir = ray.mDirection;
   auto o = ray.mOrigin;
   auto c0 = v1-v2;
   auto c1 = v0-v2;
   auto dCrossc1 = dir.cross(c1);
   // Compute the determinant of our matrix (Cramer's rule use this determinant as the denominator)
   auto det = c0.dot(dCrossc1);
   // Check if we want backface culling or not or if we are missing the triangle
#if CULL_BACKFACE
   // if the determinant is close to 0 we are missing the triangle
   // if the determinant is negative the triangle is backfacing
   if (det < kEpsilon)
   {
      return false;
   }
#else
// if the determinant is close to 0 the ray direction and triangle plane are parallel
   if(fabs(det) < kEpsilon)
   {
      return false;
   }
#endif
```

The next part of the code will compute the determinant of the matrix related to our equation, and it will solve for *t*, *u*, and *v* by computing the determinant for *u*, the one for *v*, and finally for *t* (overall three determinants).

```
// Defined for convenience
float invDet = 1.0f / det;
auto transVec = o - v2;
// Cramer's rule determinant of the matrix to solve for u divided the
determinant of the intial matrix
u = transVec.dot(dCrossc1) * invDet;
// Check that u is in the correct range
if(u < 0 || u > 1)
{
   return false;
}
// Cramer's rule determinant of the matrix to solve for v divided the
determinant of the intial matrix
auto transVecCrossc0 = transVec.cross(c0);
v = dir.dot(transVecCrossc0) * invDet;
if(v < 0 || (u+v) > 1)
{
   return false;
}
// Compute t here
// Again Cramer's rule to compute the last unknown t
t = c1.dot(transVecCrossc0) * invDet;
return true;
}
```

You can see that the previous code, if you remove the comments and so on, is much more compact than any other method shown before. It also heavily reuses previously computed terms. This algorithm is actually the faster one that we have presented in this paragraph, and just as any other previous method, it gives us what we want:

- The barycentric coordinates *u* and *v*
- The distance *t* of the intersection point from the ray origin *o*

CHAPTER 7   BASIC RAY-PRIMITIVE INTERSECTION TECHNIQUES

In the next section, we will spend some time covering floating-point precision accuracy and any related issue and how to account for it. It's quite useful to know a little bit about how floating-point numbers work and how they are represented in memory.

In fact, when we deal with intersection routines and we test floating-point values very close to one another or near zero, we want to understand why we tackle the test in a certain way.

Floating-Point Precision/Accuracy Issues and How to Account for Them

In the context of intersection tests/collision detection, the cases in which we have to deal with floating-point precision issues are usually always specific to some very well-defined operations. Like the comparison of one value against/near zero and, in general, in any case where the floating-point value can get really small (or in some cases really big).

One key point to remember here is that we are dealing with a numerical machine representation of real numbers; therefore, the arithmetic is consequently subject to the limitation of the machine representation itself.

We know about two typical representations for real numbers:

- Fixed-point numbers

- Floating-point numbers

We will mostly deal with the second type of numbers. What we have to keep in mind at all times while we write code is that the floating-point arithmetic is not completely exact as the real numbers' math.

The standard that established how a floating-point number had to be represented is the IEEE-754. Based on this standard, any real number can be represented as 32 bits or 64 bits in memory; this leads us to two possibilities in relation with the precision:

- Single precision (i.e., 32 bits)

- Double precision (i.e., 64 bits)

For single-precision we have that the value V on IEEE-754 is of the form:

$$V = (-1)^s * (1.F) * 2^{E-127}$$

CHAPTER 7 BASIC RAY-PRIMITIVE INTERSECTION TECHNIQUES

See Figure 7-9 for an in-memory representation of the single-precision floating-point.

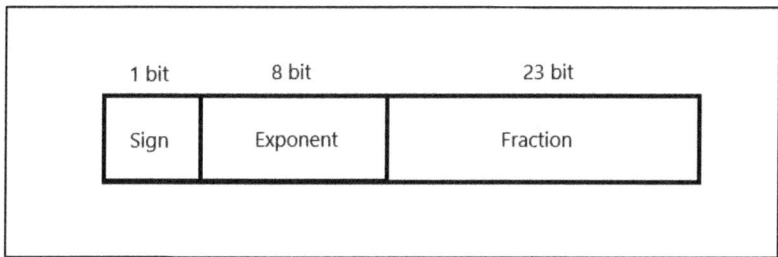

Figure 7-9. *Single precision 32 bits IEEE-754 in-memory representation*

Here, from left to right, we have this:

- A sign bit
- The so-called mantissa
- An exponent

The leading bit before the mantissa is not stored because it is always one, actually giving to the fractional part of the mantissa one extra bit that adds up to the precision of the number itself.

For double-precision, we have that the value V on IEEE-754 is of the following form:

$$V = (-1)^s * (1.F) * 2^{E-1023}$$

Figure 7-10 shows the double-precision in-memory representation.

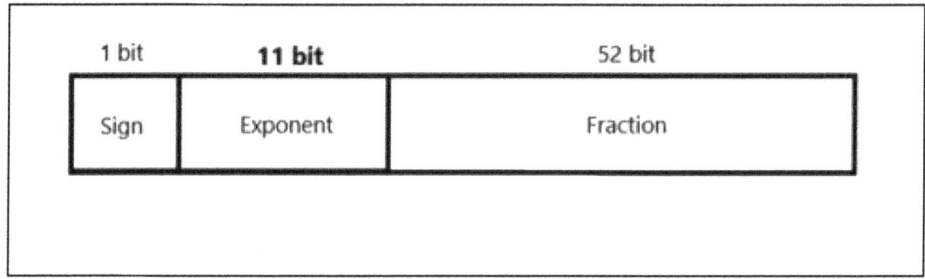

Figure 7-10. *Double-precision 64 bits IEEE-754 in-memory representation*

183

CHAPTER 7   BASIC RAY-PRIMITIVE INTERSECTION TECHNIQUES

One observation that we have to do is in relation to the representation of special values like 0. In that special case, we can indicate that special cases with the exponent field to be 0 or 255 (i.e., in binary you will have 00000000 or 11111111).

The value V is represented in a normalized form as shown previously. What we are interested in is how we can make floating-point numbers robust. They obviously are not robust at all because they are subject to roundoff errors, cancellation errors, division by zero, etc. All of those types of errors can affect the precision and accuracy and can be a problem in the implementation of collision detection/intersection algorithms if not tackled accordingly.

We can make floating-point numbers robust in two main ways:

- Using tolerances
- Sharing common subexpressions between the calculations

So, the first source of problems is when we try to compare floating-point numbers in expressions.

Something like, for example, this `if` statement:

```
if (x == 0.0f)
{

}
```

It seems perfectly normal, but, in fact, it's not! Remember that we've said that due to accumulation errors and so on, **x** might never be exactly equal to **0.0f**; therefore that **if**-statement might fail in most cases.

The solution here is to use tolerance and consider x to be zero only when within some small range of values-centered around zero.

So, the test then becomes the following:

```
if(fabs(x) <= kEpsilon)
{

}
```

Here **kEpsilon** is chosen based on the range of values that **x** can get and the type of computation performed. Take as an example the ray-plane intersection, and you can see that we apply this same approach when we have to test whether the dot product between the plane normal and the ray direction is close to zero enough to be actually considered zero. In fact, in that case, we use a tolerance of like 10^{-6}. That epsilon is obviously chosen by assuming some kind of potential range for **x** but might change in cases where the range for **x** might be wider (e.g., the scene scale is bigger).

The other situation we might encounter is when we have the generalized form. Compare **x** against another value, say, **y**:

```
if(fabs(x-y) <= kEpsilon)
{
}
```

This kind of way of performing the test is referred to as *absolute tolerance comparison*. Even this method is not free from problems. As already stated, a solid knowledge of the input values, their ranges, and the specific problem we are trying to solve in general is what will determine how we will choose our epsilon/tolerance.

There is always the chance that x and y will grow big enough that their difference will be either smaller or bigger than the chosen epsilon. So, the test in those cases will fail, which is what we don't want to happen.

> *As x and y grow big, the absolute test requires that more and more digits agree. So, the tolerance should be changed to be consistent with that.*

That is all for what concerns floating-point precision issues. There should be more to add and talk in relation to the **IEEE-754** format and its limitation, but this is not the main scope of the book. However, you can find a good reference if want to go more in-depth in the "Further Reading" section.

The next section will give you a glimpse of a potential architecture to manage objects that need to be rendered from a hypothetical ray-traced renderer. It is not to be intended as a production-ready design/implementation, but just as a way to scratch the surface and understand how to start facing the problem of managing multiple types of objects during rendering.

Putting It All Together: A Basic and Simple C++ Interface to Manage Objects

In this section, we will describe a potential way to organize your geometric objects in order to be rendered gracefully by your ray tracer. Take a look at Figure 7-11 for a class diagram illustrating our bare-bones architecture.

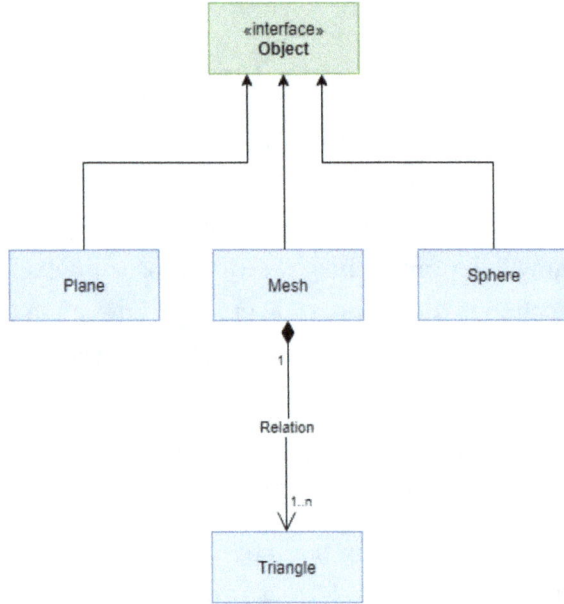

Figure 7-11. *A simple class diagram showing our basic object architecture*

As you can see, a base class represents the interface. Then we have implemented the interface for a plane, a sphere, and a mesh. The interface will have a virtual method called *intersect,* for example, that will be reimplemented specifically by each one of the three subclasses (or any class that will be added later).

To translate that in code, we would have something like this:

```
// Interface
class IObject
{
public:
    // ...
    virtual bool Intersect(Ray& ray,float& t) = 0;
```

```
    // ...
};

// For the plane for example
class Plane : public IObject
{
public:
    // ...
    virtual bool Intersect(Ray& ray,float& t) override
    {
    // handle ray-plane intersection here, return true if an intersection
    exists otherwise false
    }
    // ...
};

// Same goes for the other sub-classes
```

With this architecture in mind, it's elementary to create a flat array of pointers to IObject and loop through them and call Intersect() to find their intersection with a given ray, compare their t value, and get the smaller one (remember we are interested in the closest intersected object).

As for meshes, as you can tell by the class diagram in Figure 7-11, they own one or more triangles and eventually a BVH data structure (to be added).

Just to remind you, this is by no means a complete architecture. We might want to add a material to manage the appearance of each object and, for meshes, a tree acceleration structure like a bounding volume hierarchy (BVH) to get fast ray-object/ray-triangle intersection response. Otherwise, in the worst case, we need to loop over all the scene objects for each ray and, once found the object, loop again through all its triangles to find the intersected one.

Summary

This chapter has definitely set a milestone for this book. In fact, the intersection algorithms explained are at the heart of any ray-traced renderer. The reader now should have a comprehensive understanding of the main ray-primitive intersection algorithms. Among these are the ray-triangle intersection algorithm and the computation of the barycentric coordinates, which are two key algorithms to know, since most of the geometry in a scene is made by a triangle, and the interpolation of the vertex attributes implies that the barycentric coordinates are given.

Next, we explained the floating-point IEEE-754 standard with an emphasis on the precision and accuracy limitations of representing real numbers in this way. This was necessary to give you a way to understand robustness and how to achieve it through the use of tolerances/epsilon when needed. Intersection tests are still part of that group of algorithms that belongs to the collision detection realm.

You should have now a better understanding of the limitations of the floating-point numbers.

In the next chapter, we will go through the rendering equation, and we will get closer to global illumination. We will dissect the equation, explaining every term in order to shed some light on its, apparently cryptic, expression.

The rendering equation is the key to photorealism.

Questions

Based on the knowledge that you gained in this chapter, it is your turn to answer some questions:

- How do you know if a ray misses a sphere completely?
- Why you would want to use the geometric approach instead of the analytical one for the ray-sphere intersection test?
- How many cases do we have for a ray-sphere intersection test in general?
- Explain how the containment test works, either in the context of ray-quad intersection or in ray-triangle intersection.
- Why are barycentric coordinates useful?
- Explain the geometric meaning of barycentric coordinates.
- Why do we need to introduce tolerances during floating-point calculations?
- Is there a general way to define a tolerance/epsilon value?

Further Reading

You can use the following to expand the horizon of your knowledge on this chapter:

- https://www.scratchapixel.com/lessons/3d-basic-rendering/minimal-raytracer-rendering- simple- shapes/ray-sphere-intersection
- https://www.scratchapixel.com/lessons/3d- basic- rendering/ray-tracingrendering-triangle/barycentric- coordinates
- https://www.scratchapixel.com/lessons/3d-basic-rendering/minimal-raytracer-renderin-simple-shapes/ray-plane-and-ray-disk-intersection
- https://www.scratchapixel.com/lessons/3d-basic-rendering/ray-tracingrendering-triangle/moller-trumbore-ray-triangle-intersection
- Ericson, CRC Press (2004). 'Numerical Robustness', in Ericson, *Real-time collision detection,* pp. 427-443.

CHAPTER 8

The Rendering Equation and Monte Carlo Integration

Ray tracing theory is still important in order to understand algorithms like Whitted ray tracing or path tracing when it comes to global illumination. An important role is played by the theory behind the lighting and shading of surfaces, and the rendering equation is central when it comes to light transport and shading. In this chapter, you will learn how the propagation of light is fully described by the aforementioned equation.

The global illumination (GI) problem is what we are trying to solve here. Monte Carlo (MC) integration techniques will be presented as well, as they represent an invaluable tool to solve infinite-dimensional integrals like the rendering equation. Then we will talk about importance sampling and, in the end, different approaches to draw our samples.

Among those we have *stratified sampling* techniques and Quasi-Monte-Carlo methods, the latter based on *low-discrepancy* quasi-random sequences.

After discussing MC integration, we will dive into how to solve the rendering equation to get a solution that can be used practically in our implementation.

We will understand that ray tracing is a very general term. In fact, depending on the context, it can be applied to solve the light propagation problem completely or borrow just a subset of the light propagation effects (i.e., reflections, shadows, or ambient occlusion only).

This chapter will create the foundations that are the key to understanding the practical implementation of path tracing that we will present and, also, the subset of effects that come with it.

By the end of this chapter, you should have all the tools needed to understand the theory behind the global illumination problem, path tracing, and Whitted ray tracing.

CHAPTER 8   THE RENDERING EQUATION AND MONTE CARLO INTEGRATION

The following topics will be covered in this chapter:

- The rendering equation
- Anatomy of the rendering equation
- "Solving" the rendering equation in order to get pretty pictures
- Monte Carlo integration
- Inverse sampling method
- Importance sampling: variance reduction
- Stratified sampling
- Quasi-Monte Carlo methods (QMC)

Technical Requirements

The following tools will be required before we get started:

- Visual Studio 2022 Community
- FreeGLUT
- Cuda Toolkit 13.0.1
- Windows 10 RS5 update

Minimum hardware requirements:

- GeForce RTX 2k series

Sources:

- π estimate with Monte Carlo
- Quasi-random sequences

CHAPTER 8   THE RENDERING EQUATION AND MONTE CARLO INTEGRATION

Understanding the Rendering Equation

The rendering equation has been introduced for the first time by James Kajiya in 1986. This equation states that the reflected radiance at a point along an outgoing direction is the sum of the emitted radiance at that point and the reflected radiance.

The reflected radiance is defined to be the sum of the incoming radiance $L_i(x,\omega_i)$, coming from all the directions across the hemisphere and multiplied by the BRDF of the surface material and the cosine of the incident angle with respect to the surface normal n of the point where the reflection occurs.

At the heart of the rendering equation, there is the law of conservation of energy. In practical terms, this means that no more radiance can be reflected than the sum of the absorbed and reflected one at the material interface.

$$Light_{incoming} \approx (Light_{reflected} + Light_{absorbed})$$

Here is the complete expression for the rendering equation:

$$L(x, \omega_o) = L_e(x, \omega_o) + \int_\Omega L_i(x, \omega_i) f_r(\omega_i, x, \omega_o) \cos\theta_i d\omega$$

In this chapter, we will use either radiance or light interchangeably, and we will denote it with the letter **L**.

Let's spend a few words on this equation. First, we notice the presence of a term, which basically represents the emitted light and, as we know, a body that emits light is definitely to be considered a light source. In reality, this could be either a proper light bulb, a ceiling lamp, or, why not, a body so hot that will emit light.

Then we have the integral over the hemisphere. It basically means we are summing the contribution of the reflected light in each and every outgoing direction across the hemisphere centered at the point with the surface normal **n**.

Figure 8-1 shows the hemisphere and the incoming direction and the outgoing one at point **x**.

CHAPTER 8   THE RENDERING EQUATION AND MONTE CARLO INTEGRATION

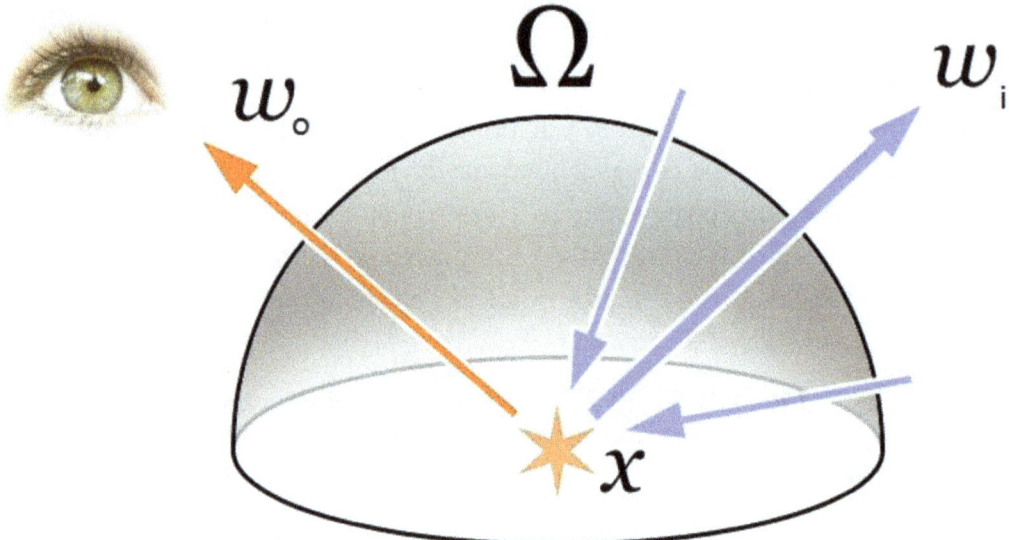

Figure 8-1. *Incoming light and reflected light with respect to incoming and outgoing directions, respectively*

There is something quite important to note. In Chapter 6, we talked about the illumination equation as a means to approximate, in a crude way, the shading of a given surface point.

Let's now explain with a little more detail what this means. When we consider the light direction, the normal and view vector at a given surface point, we are actually approximating the lighting locally. The reason behind this is simple: we are not considering the "surrounding" of the point. When we say "surrounding," we mean the incoming radiance that comes from all the other directions across the hemisphere around the point (refer to Figure 8-1).

The rendering equation will address this by introducing the integral sum of the incoming radiance across the unit hemisphere centered around the point **x**.

Because the rendering equation is considering also the incoming radiance from every other direction across the hemisphere and the illumination equation just the local light vector and the view vector, we can say that the rendering equation solves the light propagation problem in a scene globally. Hence, we can talk about global illumination (GI).

Here you can see both the illumination equation and the rendering equation next to one another, highlighting the relevant missing/added terms to show the differences:

194

Rendering equation

$$L(x, w_o) = L_e(x, w_o) + \int_\Omega \boxed{L_i(x, w_i)} f_r(w_i, x, w_o) \cos\theta \, dw$$

Illumination equation

$$I_p = k_a i_a + \sum_{m \,\in\, \text{lights}} (k_d (\hat{L}_m \cdot \hat{N}) i_{m,d} + k_s (\hat{R}_m \cdot \hat{V})^\alpha i_{m,s})$$

The term in the rendering equation inside the red box is the incoming reflected radiance at point x coming from all the surroundings of the scene. That is the term that is missing from the illumination equation that, instead, is just approximating the direct illumination coming from each of the "m" light sources (i.e., the summation for "m" light sources in the illumination equation). If we want to model light transport completely, we need to also consider indirect radiance and not just the direct one. The illumination equation compensates for the missing incoming reflected radiance by adding a term called *ambient term* (i.e., term in the illumination equation), but that is a poor and crude approximation for what is the real deal!

- **Direct radiance/light**: Light contribution coming straight from a given light source

- **Indirect radiance/light**: Incoming light contribution coming from the surrounding of the scene across the hemisphere of a given point x

The illumination equation has been employed for many years by real-time rendering engines (e.g., particularly through the use of shading models like the Phong/Blinn for specular reflection) because it is very cheap to compute. However, it is far from being physically correct and, therefore, realistic.

Nowadays pretty much all the rendering engines feature a physically based rendering pipeline. For example, Unreal Engine 4 (UE4) and Unity are among them. However, real-time indirect lighting, the real holy grail, is still something that has to be dealt with separately. The problem, in this case, is related to the number of rays/samples that need to be processed per pixel and for each bounce. That is what quickly kills the performance. In fact, most of the time, we precompute just the indirect diffuse contribution of the light, and we bake it into a lightmap. For example, UE4 does exactly this for lightmaps by employing a radiosity processor (i.e., a specific offline rendering engine that is able to precompute diffuse lighting bounces) to account for just the diffuse indirect light bounces. The radiosity processor has been around since Unreal Engine 3 and is called *Lightmass*.

Luckily, things got a little bit better with the advent of hardware ray tracing in the mass market. However, we have still to be careful of how many rays we shoot. In fact, most of the time, one or four rays or samples per pixel and a denoiser are the way to go as of today.

Let's try to understand a little bit more in-depth every "piece" of the rendering equation.

The next section will be devoted to exactly this and, as we will see, one of the more interesting terms that is the *bidirectional reflectance distribution function* (BRDF). By using different types of BRDFs, we can model and create a wide variety of materials like purely diffuse to mirror-like surfaces, glossy surfaces, and, last but not least, glass-like surfaces.

Understanding the Anatomy of the Rendering Equation

In this section, you will learn about each term of the rendering equation and the role that this equation plays in the context of global illumination.

Let's rewrite the rendering equation expression:

$$L(x, \omega_o) = L_e(x, \omega_o) + \int_\Omega L_i(x, \omega_i) f_r(\omega_i, x, \omega_o) \cos \theta_i d\omega$$

Here is the meaning of each term in the expression:

- **$L(x, \omega_o)$**: The total reflected light/radiance leaving point along the outgoing direction.

- **$L_e(x, \omega_o)$**: The emitted radiance leaving point along the outgoing direction (a light source or a hot body).

- **$L_i(x, \omega_i)$**: The incident incoming radiance reaching point along the incident/incoming direction.

- **$f_i(x, \omega_i)$**: The BSDF, which is a probability distribution function introduced to model how light is scattered by a surface.

- ***cos θ$_i$***: The cosine attenuation factor, because the light flux might be smeared on a surface area that is larger than the projected area perpendicular to the incoming light ray. The angle is the angle between the incoming direction and the surface normal at point. We can obviously rewrite provided that both are normalized.

Now let's go for the real thing. What we are interested in the most is BSDF, as that is the way in which we can model how light interacts with surface material. A BSDF is basically a superset that includes both the BRDF and the BTDF, and it represents the most general way to refer to BxDF functions (where x can be any type of function that models how light is scattered from the surface material upon interaction).

To be more precise:

$$BSDF = BRDF \cup BTDF$$

and:

- **BRDF:** Bidirectional reflectance distribution function
- **BTDF**: Bidirectional transmittance distribution function

Of course, they both are probability distribution functions. They describe how the radiance is probabilistically scattered given the physical properties of a given material. This is why we refer to them as *distribution functions*.

BSDFs functions have these important properties:

- **Rotational symmetry**: The surface appearance doesn't change when it is rotated about the normal. This is because BSDFs are a function of the incoming and outgoing directions only.
- **Helmholtz reciprocity**: The surface appearance doesn't change when incoming and outgoing directions are swapped.

Without anything further to say, we will continue talking about the three basic types of BRDFs, i.e., Diffuse, Specular, and Glossy. To start understanding more about them.

The next section will address the three basic BRDFs. There are more complex types of BRDFs with more or less accurate visual results. The BRDFs that we will discuss in the subsection are the most common ones and are easy to understand. Moreover, they are also easy to implement, as we will see.

CHAPTER 8   THE RENDERING EQUATION AND MONTE CARLO INTEGRATION

Understanding the Most Common BRDFs

We will present here the most common and simple types of BRDFs. They represent the easiest ones to implement in code and are listed here:

- **Diffuse BRDF (also known as Lambertian BRDF)**: This describes purely diffuse surfaces. If we shoot a ray in, every outgoing direction on the hemisphere has the same probability.

- **Specular BRDF**: This describes mirror-like surfaces. Meaning that an incoming direction can only exit in one direction. It assumes for a material to be highly polished and we know that perfect polished object doesn't exist in reality, but it can still be a good and easy starting point to model pretty mirror-like surfaces.

- **Glossy BRDF**: This describes glossy-like surfaces. It can be thought to be something in between a diffuse and specular BRDF. There are many types of glossy BRDFs we will present one in particular here, just to outline the basic idea. These types of BRDFs are taking into account the fact that surfaces are not perfectly smooth. In fact, they present micro imperfections at the microscopic surface level. These BRDFs models are also named microfacet BRDFs models, and they model the micro-imperfections with what is referred to *roughness*. The light rays will be scattered in a lobe that will be more or less wide as the roughness of the surface is more or less high (normally the roughness is in the [0,1] range; 0 for no roughness and 1 for a fully rough surface).

Let's take a look at their expressions:

$$f_r(\omega_i, x, \omega_o) = \frac{1}{\pi}$$

For the diffuse BRDF, we have (see Figure 8-2).

CHAPTER 8   THE RENDERING EQUATION AND MONTE CARLO INTEGRATION

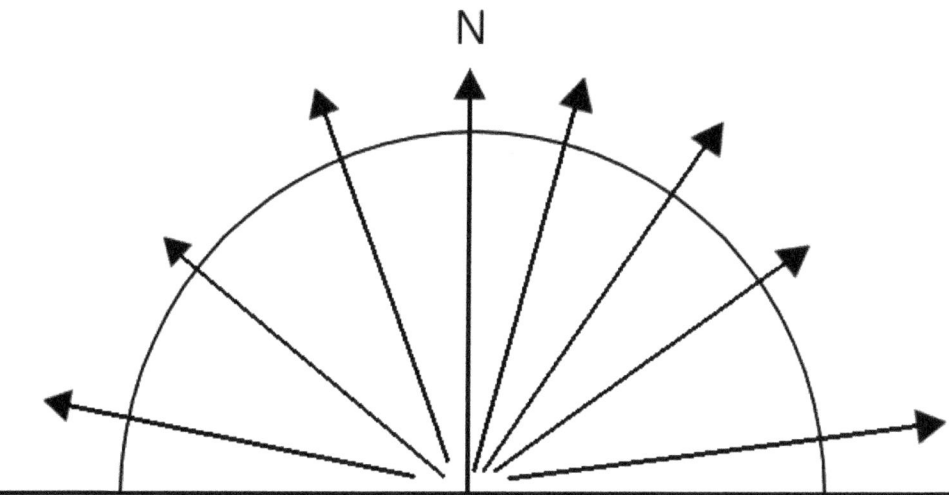

Figure 8-2. *Diffuse BRDF*

There is the probability for the radiance to be reflected in a given outgoing direction, but we don't need to reflect all the incoming radiance, so we can introduce the so-called *albedo* of the material surface.

Albedo is defined to be a property of the material surface and represents how the material reflects the radiance with a very specific wavelength. We denote it with the Greek letter (rho).

To keep the things simple from the previous very theoretical definition, we can say that it is just the pure color of the object surface when no light is applied to it. It might come from a texture, or it could just be a simple constant RGB color depending on the material.

So, having said that, we can just "weigh" the previous definition of diffuse BRDF by the albedo of the material surface, and we get the following expression:

$$f_r(\omega_i, x, \omega_o) = \frac{\rho}{\pi} \quad \rho \in (0, 1)$$

ρ is the albedo of a diffuse object surface material, and it's practically represented by either a constant RGB color or a color coming from a texture. In the last case, we refer to the texture as albedo texture or albedo map.

For the **specular BRDF**, we have the following expression, and it can be depicted by Figure 8-3.

CHAPTER 8 THE RENDERING EQUATION AND MONTE CARLO INTEGRATION

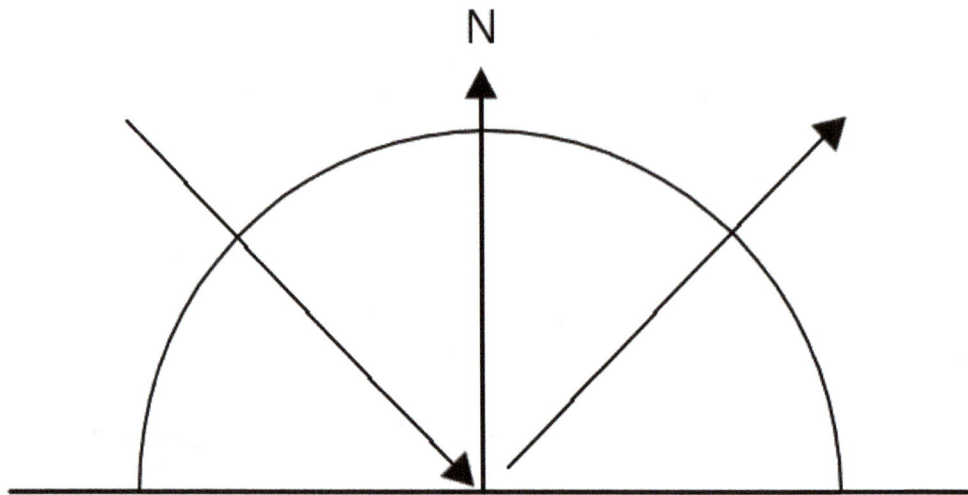

Figure 8-3. *Specular BRDF*

That means it takes a value of 1 for the reflected direction and 0 everywhere else. For the glossy BRDF we have Figure 8-4.

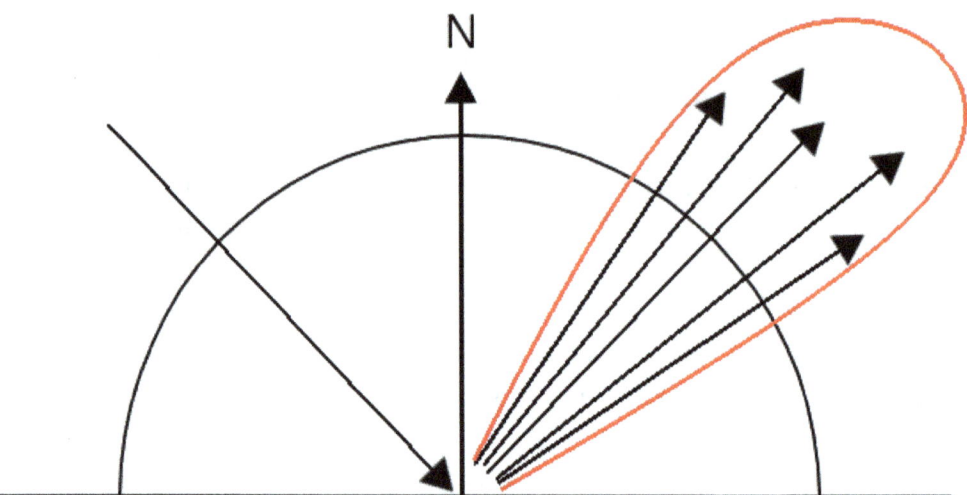

Figure 8-4. *Glossy BRDF*

Notice how the incoming light ray direction is scattered due to the surface roughness into many directions in a lobe (the curve line containing the scattered/reflected directions). That lobe will get wider and wider as the roughness of the surface approaches 1. If the roughness has a value of 0, we will fall back in the case of the perfectly specular surface (i.e., see Figure 8-3 for the perfect mirror direction).

One last question is, what is the dimension of the integral in the rendering equation?

Well, the answer to this question is simple: it is recursively infinite because we could bounce at any surface point of a scene forever. In fact, the incoming radiance that is present inside the integral and can be considered like another nested rendering equation and so on recursively.

This is bad news because the rendering equation integral cannot be solved in closed form. The rendering equation integral is infinite-dimensional. Moreover, we can't even try to use Riemann sums to solve it, because they become increasingly expensive in the number of dimensions. We need a clever way to find our solution or, as we will see, to estimate our solution. Monte Carlo integration is the answer, and the next sections will introduce you to the foundations behind MC integration.

"Solving" the Rendering Equation

We would better off saying we are finding a different way to solve an integral than the classic Riemann method. If we can find an approximated solution to solve any integral, we would then be able to apply the same method to the rendering equation integral too.

Now for the good news: approximated solutions exist and are based on numerical integration methods. One of the most popular and easy to implement integration is *Monte Carlo (MC) integration*.

Let's suppose we have an impossible-to-solve integral that is defined like this:

$$\int_a^b f(x)dx$$

We need to find a way to start sampling the integration domain and find a numerical solution to at least approximate it.

> *When we talk about "impossible integral," we mean an integral that cannot be solved in closed form (i.e., by just computing the primitive of the integrand and substituting the interval values to find the actual value).*

The idea behind MC is that we have, for example, a complex integral that cannot be solved in closed form, but there is one thing we can do: we can sample the function.

CHAPTER 8 THE RENDERING EQUATION AND MONTE CARLO INTEGRATION

We know about two approaches for MC:

- Hit or miss
- Sample mean

We will use the sample mean approach 99% of the time, but, just to visualize the intuition, we will start by introducing the hit or miss approach.

This hit-or-miss method will consider the function, and it will enclose it inside a unit cube, so basically every point will fall inside an interval defined to be where are the domain dimensions.

To keep the things simple, we will consider a 2D domain (i.e., s == 2). To sample the function, we will start by generating pseudorandom samples in this domain with a uniform distribution to be sure to cover the domain uniformly.

Each point will be denoted by *(x,y)* and:

$$(x, y) \in [0, 1] \times [0, 1]$$

A uniform pseudorandom 2D distribution over the previous domain will look like the one shown in Figure 8-5.

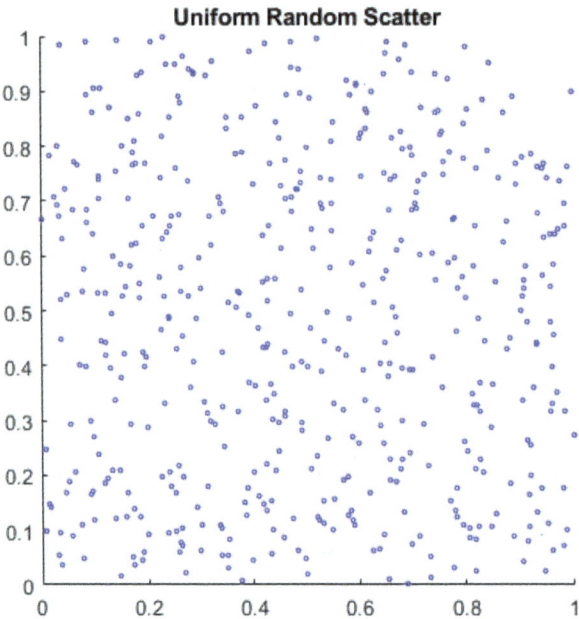

Figure 8-5. *Uniform pseudorandom distribution in $[0,1]^2$*

The key points to understand here are related to that we are literally "throwing" samples to a given domain. Moreover, it will also be important how we distribute these samples in the aforementioned domain.

Let's get straight into the problem by looking at the first MC integration approach: hit or miss. The next subsection will show exactly how to apply this to compute the value of π.

Hit-or-Miss Monte Carlo Integration

The following is basically the receipt for hit-or-miss (or rejection sampling) Monte Carlo integration:

- Draw a function on a paper.
- Enclose it in a square of known size B.
- Shoot in lots of points onto the paper.
- For each point determine if it's below (hit) or above (miss) the function (if we get a hit we take the sample, if we get a miss we "reject" it).

After that we've thrown a high enough number of points/samples that we get the integral of the function by using the following formula:

$$\int_a^b f(x)dx / B \approx \frac{hits}{hits + misses}$$

For the hit or miss, we will try to estimate the value of π. We will achieve this by computing the proportion of samples or points that fall inside the unit circle (hit), with respect to the total number of samples that we've generated in the given domain.

In Figure 8-6 we can see more explicitly how the whole process will look.

CHAPTER 8   THE RENDERING EQUATION AND MONTE CARLO INTEGRATION

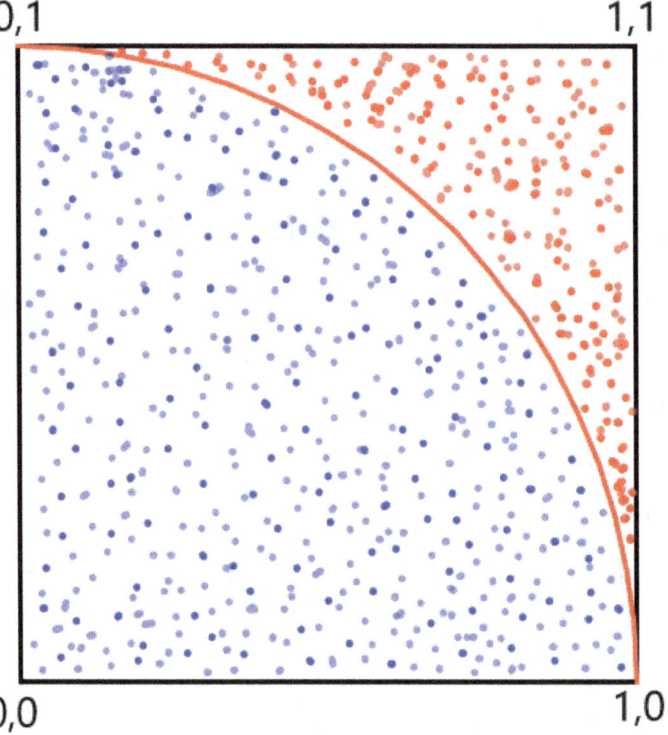

Figure 8-6. *We estimate the value of π by computing a proportion between the number of hits and the total area of the square (in this case Area = 1)*

Every time that a point falls inside the unit circle, we will have a hit (dots below the quarter of a unit circle in Figure 8-6), and vice versa. If it will fall outside the unit circle (dots above the quarter of a unit circle in Figure 8-6), we will have a miss.

So basically, our estimate (in general terms) will be something like this:

$$\pi \approx \frac{hits}{hits + misses}$$

But, to compute the value in practical terms, we need to translate the previous concept to real math. Let's apply the receipt we showed at the beginning of this section:

- Draw a unit square of size B=1.

- Draw a quarter of unit circle inside it, r=1.

204

CHAPTER 8　THE RENDERING EQUATION AND MONTE CARLO INTEGRATION

- Start shooting in points.
- Compute:

$$\frac{hits}{(hits + misses)}$$

- Multiply the result by 4 in order to get this
:

$$\int_a^b f(x)/B = \frac{\pi r^2}{4}/1 = \frac{\pi}{4}$$

This is a quarter of the unit area for our unit circle. If we want the total area, we have to just multiply the previous result by 4, and we get π.

That's it! Easy enough!

Now we can show practically how to implement hit-or-miss MC in code. The following code snippet is showing exactly how to implement the method we just explained:

```cpp
double HitOrMissMonteCarlo_EstimatePI(int N)
{
   std::random_device device;
   std::mt19937 generator(device());
   std::uniform_real_distribution<> distribution;
   int hits = 0;
   for (int i = 0; i < N; ++i)
   {
      double x = distribution(generator);
      double y = distribution(generator);
      if (sqrt(x * x + y * y) <= 1.0)
      {
         ++hits;
      }
   }
   return (static_cast<double>(hits) / static_cast<double>(N)) * 4.0;
}
```

CHAPTER 8   THE RENDERING EQUATION AND MONTE CARLO INTEGRATION

We start by preparing the random number generator:

```
double HitOrMissMonteCarlo_EstimatePI(int N)
{
    std::random_device device;
    std::mt19937 generator(device());
    std::uniform_real_distribution<> distribution;
```

Then we start generating N random samples:

```
    int hits = 0;
    for (int i = 0; i < N; ++i)
    {
        double x = distribution(generator);
        double y = distribution(generator);
```

For each sample, we check whether there is a hit. If the test succeeds, we increment the hit counter variable; otherwise, we don't do anything:

```
        if (sqrt(x * x + y * y) <= 1.0)
        {
            ++hits;
        }
    }
```

Finally, we divide the number of hits by the total number of samples N. We then multiply by 4 because our computation domain is a quarter of a unit circle, and we need the total area:

```
    return (static_cast<double>(hits) / static_cast<double>(N)) * 4.0;
}
```

As you can see for the hit-or-miss method, we just count the number of hits and divide the result by the total number of samples (, as we've already mentioned, in this case it is equivalent to the sum of hits and misses). We then multiply by 4 because we are considering a quarter of unit circle enclosed in a box of unit size.

In this case, the edge of the unit box matches the circle's radius! If we run the previous code for a variable number of samples, we note that, as we increase them, the result gets more and more accurate.

CHAPTER 8   THE RENDERING EQUATION AND MONTE CARLO INTEGRATION

In Figures 8-7, 8-8, and 8-9, we performed three runs, for 100, 1000, 1000000000 samples. The output of the program is the estimate of PI and the error of our estimation (i.e., how far we are from the real value of PI; the smaller the error the better).

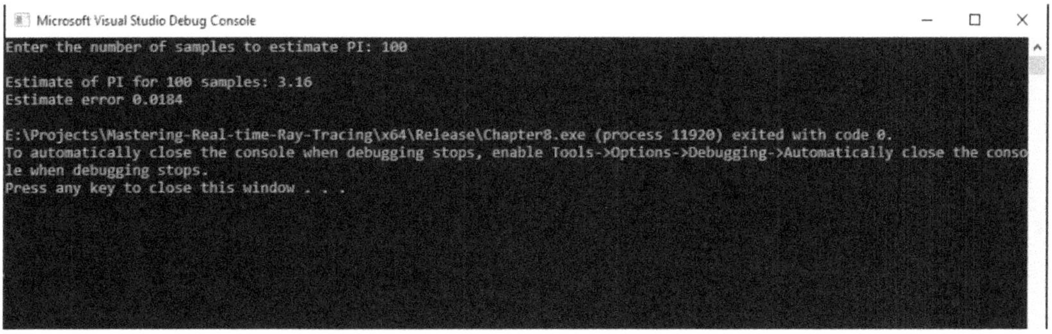

Figure 8-7. Hit or miss with 100 samples

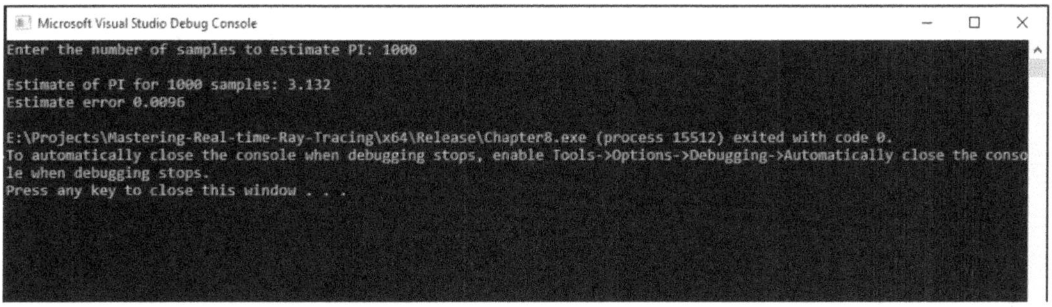

Figure 8-8. Hit or miss with 1,000 samples

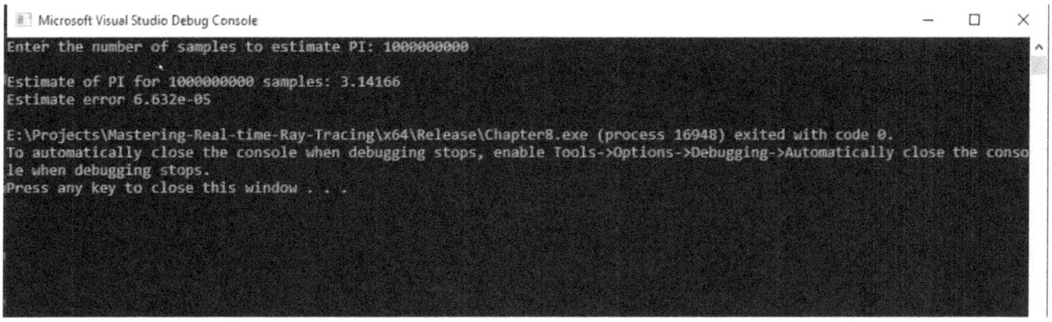

Figure 8-9. Hit or miss with 1,000,000,000 samples

CHAPTER 8   THE RENDERING EQUATION AND MONTE CARLO INTEGRATION

Now as you can see, the last output is definitely damn close to the estimate of PI, and the error is also very small. After that, we discussed the hit-or-miss MC method (also called *rejection sampling method*). We want to show another way to estimate the integral with MC. The second approach is the MC integration, and it considers the sample mean. The sample mean approach will be the topic of the next section.

Understanding Monte Carlo Integration (Sample Mean Approach)

The second MC method we can employ to estimate the value of a function is known as the *sample mean approach*. The idea is still the same: we don't know the integral of our function, and this time, we try to get the missing information from the function by sampling it.

We still have our integral and integrand functions that we have to integrate. Let's rewrite it for completeness; after rewriting, it will look like the following equation:

$$I = \int_a^b f(x)dx$$

What we do in this case is basically take samples of the function, sum them up, and average them.

Let's take, as an example, the integral of a simple function and see what we can get out of it:

$$\int_0^1 x \, dx$$

So, this can be obviously solved by finding the primitive function, which is very straightforward in this case.

$$\int_0^1 x \, dx = \left[\frac{x^2}{2}\right]_0^1 = \frac{1}{2}$$

But let's suppose that we cannot easily determine the primitive of the function due to the highly complex, if not impossible to solve, integrand function *f(x)*. What do we do?

For illustrative purposes, we assume we were not able to find the primitive. Therefore, based on the sample mean approach for MC integration, what we do is to sample the function *f(x)* by picking the samples in the integration interval [0,1].

Let's suppose that the aforementioned *f(x)* is defined like this:

$$f(x) = x$$

Figure 8-10 shows that all that we are looking to compute is the area of the right triangle having edge size equal to one.

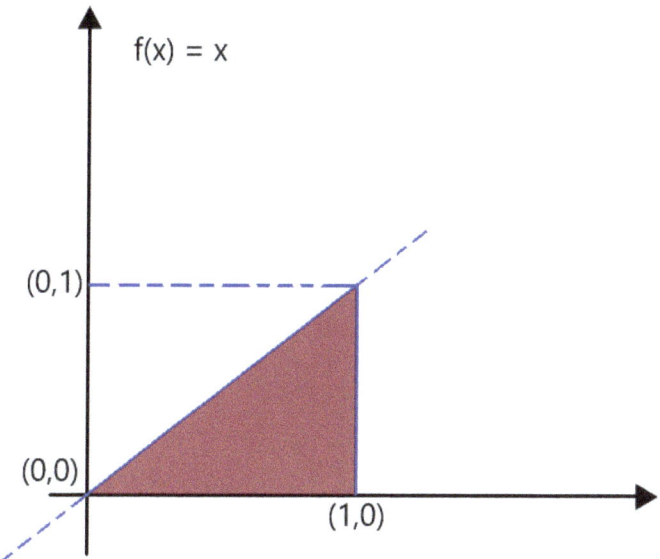

Figure 8-10. *We want to integrate the function f(x)=x in [0,1] interval*

Let's sample the function f(x) = x picking the samples in [0,1] interval and then sum them up and average the result (in this case we've chosen to pick a total of four samples), as shown here:

$$\frac{f(0.2) + f(0.5) + f(0.6) + f(0.75)}{4} = \frac{0.2 + 0.5 + 0.6 + 0.75}{4} = 0.5125$$

This is pretty close as an estimation of the real value of the previous integral. The estimate to our solution will be closer to the real solution, as the number of samples we pick grows! This basically translates to the fact that the error gets smaller and smaller as we keep adding samples.

CHAPTER 8 THE RENDERING EQUATION AND MONTE CARLO INTEGRATION

If we start computing the value of the integral for an increasing number of samples and print it every n sample, we will observe a sequence of underestimation and overestimation until we will get, eventually, to the right solution.

The value 0.5125 was an overestimation to the real value 0.5 because it is greater than the real result. Conversely, if it was coming out smaller, like for example 0.47, it was to be considered an underestimation.

This kind of up and down in the result as the number of samples that we throw to the mean grows is called *stochastic convergence*.

As we will show, if we let the number of samples go to infinity, the sample mean will be exactly the value of the integral. The previous example was simple, but it illustrated the whole process quite clearly.

Now let's try to clarify what we actually did to get to where we are. What we tried to compute was the value of the integral by considering the relation with the expected value of our function.

In the previous example, the probability to pick any of the samples in the interval [0,1] was 1.

But, we can generalize the process for a generic [a,b] interval. So, if we have a function and we want to compute its expected value, we have from the probability theory that:

$$E[f(x)] = \int_a^b f(x)p(x)dx$$

where:

$$p(x) = \frac{1}{b-a}$$

is the probability to pick any of the values in the given interval, and it is basically a uniform distribution on [a,b].

Having said that we can rewrite the integral like the following:

$$E[f(x)] = \int_a^b f(x)p(x)dx = \int_a^b f(x)\frac{1}{b-a}dx$$

What we are interested in is the value of the integral, so with some math tricks, we can show that the value of the integral is equivalent to the expected value of the estimator $E[F_N]$.

$$F_N = \frac{b-a}{N} \sum_{i=1}^{N} f(X_i)$$

If we apply the definition for the expected value and we try to compute the expected value of our F_N, we get this:

$$E[F_N] = \left[\frac{b-a}{N} \sum_{i=1}^{N} f(X_i)\right] = \frac{b-a}{N} \sum_{i=1}^{\infty} E[f(X_i)] = \frac{b-a}{N} \sum_{i=1}^{\infty} \int_a^b f(x)p(x)dx =$$

For there on it's just a matter of following the computation until we get that the expected value E is equal to the integral I. This is expressed in the continuation of the previous computations:

$$= \frac{b-a}{N} \sum_{i=1}^{\infty} \int_a^b f(x) \frac{1}{(b-a)} dx = \frac{1}{N} \sum_{i=1}^{\infty} \int_a^b f(x)dx = \int_a^b f(x)dx = I$$

hence:

$$E[F_N] = I$$

This is perfect because if the expected value of our estimator is equivalent to the integral I that we want to calculate, then we are guaranteed that we can reliably use the estimator to approximate our integral I.

$F_N[f(X_i)]$ is the expected value of the function after **N** samples.

In the previous section, we said that as the number of samples grow, we get closer to the correct solution. Better, we get a better estimate for our solution. And what happens if our growing number of samples is infinite?

We simply get that the value of the integral is exactly equivalent to the value of the estimator after an infinite number of samples N. This is expressed very clearly by the following expression:

$$E[f(x)] = \int_a^b f(x)p(x)dx = \lim_{N \to \infty} \frac{(b-a)}{N} \sum_{i=1}^{N} f(X_i)$$

CHAPTER 8   THE RENDERING EQUATION AND MONTE CARLO INTEGRATION

Notice that the approximation symbol has been replaced by the equality because we are considering an infinite number of samples for N. Therefore, we converge to the correct solution for the integral.

This is ensured from *the law of large numbers* that states the following:

$$\lim_{N \to \infty} F_N = I$$

where *I* is the value of the integral itself, which is what we are looking for.

This is the Monte Carlo estimator for a number of uniformly distributed samples on Ω, which is also known as the naive estimator:

$$I \approx F_N \equiv \frac{(b-a)}{N} \sum_{i=1}^{N} f(X_i)$$

As you can see, this is just the average of the samples multiplied by their respective probability to be chosen. For this estimator, the probability density function (PDF) is uniform and is equal to the following:

$$p(x) = \frac{1}{b-a}$$

Let's try now to give an estimate of PI by using the sample average method for N given samples as we did previously for the hit-or-miss case.

Let's start with the code as usual, and then we will give a further explanation of what it does.

The code for the equation of a unit circle is given here:

```
double f(double x)
{
    return sqrt(1.0 - x*x);
}

double SampleMeanMonteCarlo_EstimatePI(int N)
{
    std::random_device device;
    std::mt19937 generator(device());
    std::uniform_real_distribution<> distribution;
```

```cpp
    double a = 0.0;
    double b = 1.0;
    double sum = 0.0;
    for (int i = 0; i < N; ++i)
    {
        double x = distribution(generator);
        sum += f(x);
    }
    double En = (sum * (b - a) / static_cast<double>(N)) * 4.0;

    return En;
}
```

First, we have the equation of a unit circle, implemented with this simple function:

```cpp
double f(double x)
{
    return sqrt(1.0 - x*x);
}
```

Then we have the actual function that implements the PI estimate through MC integration.

We start by preparing the random number generator:

```cpp
double SampleMeanMonteCarlo_EstimatePI(int N)
{
    std::random_device device;
    std::mt19937 generator(device());
    std::uniform_real_distribution<> distribution;
```

next comes the definition of the integration interval:

```cpp
    double a = 0.0;
    double b = 1.0;
```

CHAPTER 8   THE RENDERING EQUATION AND MONTE CARLO INTEGRATION

We then start throwing N random samples and evaluating the integral of the function f(x):

```
double sum = 0.0;
for (int i = 0; i < N; ++i)
{
    double x = distribution(generator);
    sum += f(x);
}
```

Once we are out of the loop, we can average the result by applying simple Monte Carlo estimator (we also multiply by 4 because we are still evaluating a quarter of a unit circle):

```
    double En = (sum * (b - a) / static_cast<double>(N)) * 4.0;
    return En;
}
```

What we need to evaluate is the integral of the function that defines our unit circle. This is pretty easy because we know that for a unit circle it must hold that:

$$x^2 + y^2 = 1$$

If we express **y** as a function of **x** like this:

$$y = \sqrt{1 - x^2}$$

Then we get a handier expression for our function, and we can actually try to estimate our integral. So, by relying on the fact that

$$I \approx F_N \equiv \frac{(b-a)}{N} \sum_{i=1}^{N} f(X_i)$$

and that our area will be equal to PI for a unit circle, we can write this:

$$F_N = \frac{4(1-0)}{N} \sum_{i=1}^{N} \sqrt{1-x^2} = \frac{4}{N} \sum_{i=1}^{N} \sqrt{1-x^2}$$

CHAPTER 8   THE RENDERING EQUATION AND MONTE CARLO INTEGRATION

Remember that our integration interval is **[a,b] = [0,1]** and that we are estimating a quarter of the unit circle; that's the reason for the multiplication by 4. So, the last expression in the previous formula is the one we are actually using to compute an estimation for the value of PI.

It can happen to see either F_N as well as E_N throughout this chapter. They actually mean the same thing (i.e., the expected value after N samples). This doesn't have to be confused with an expected value of a given population, which instead is denoted as E[x].

Then again as we did for the hit-or-miss MC method we've also run the program for the three sets of samples (100; 1000; 1,000,000,000 samples).

Figure 8-11 shows the MC sample mean after 100 samples.

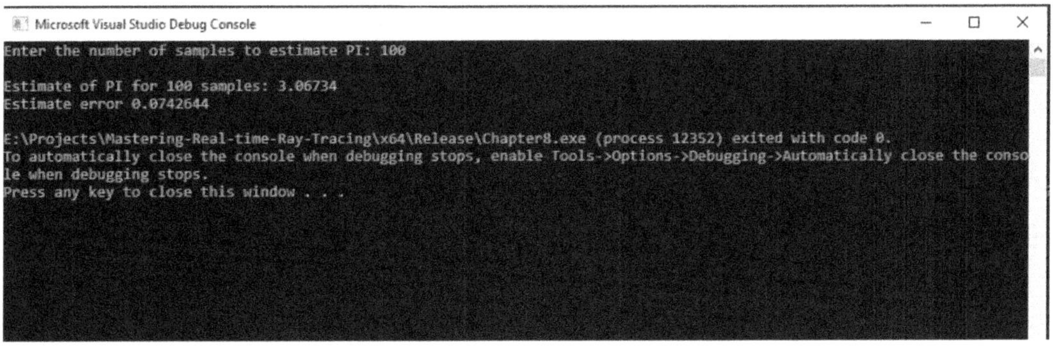

Figure 8-11. *Sample mean with 100 samples*

Figure 8-12 shows the MC sample mean after 1,000 samples.

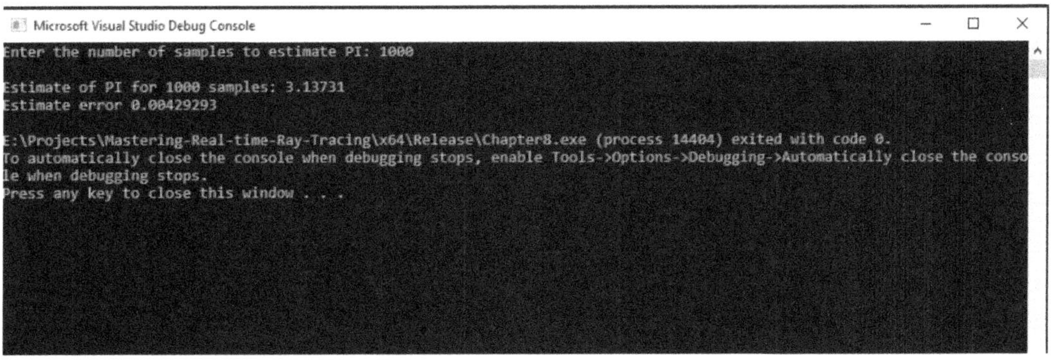

Figure 8-12. *Sample mean with 1,000 samples*

Figure 8-13 shows the MC sample mean after 1,000,000,000 samples.

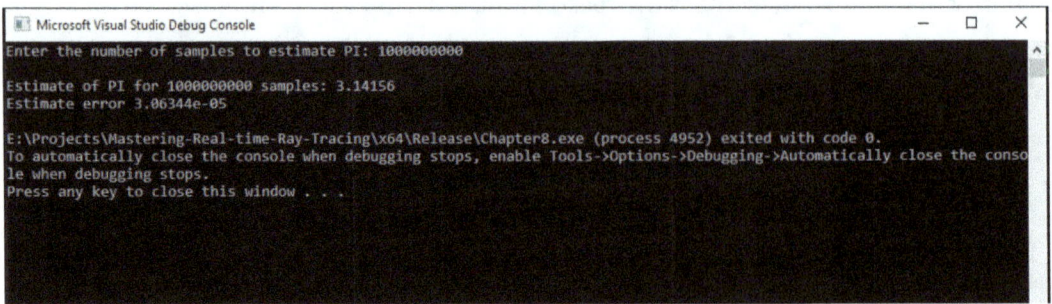

Figure 8-13. *Sample mean with 1,000,000,000 samples*

This concludes this section for what concerns the naïve MC estimator.

There is just one missing point: we haven't explained why we refer to this estimator with the word *naïve*. The reason is that a uniform distribution might not be the better choice when we have to deal with something called variance. We still haven't introduced the concept of variance (more on this in the remainder of this chapter), but suffice to say that in most cases (if not all) a uniform PDF is not the best choice to reduce the estimator variance. The variance, as we will see, is what "slows" down the convergence rate of our MC estimator, and it shows up as noise (when it comes to rendering images, it is the noise we see on the rendered frame). This is pretty bad, and we want to find a better probability distribution function (PDF) from which we want to throw our samples, and in most cases, this is not a uniform PDF.

In Figure 8-14, we can see that by applying the basic MC estimator we get to the solution, but we also note that every time that we approximate the area of our function, there are a lot of portions of the function itself that are left out. This is what causes the result to produce a series of underestimations and overestimations that will converge to the right solution as we keep throwing more and more samples.

$$I \approx F_N \equiv \frac{(b-a)}{N} \sum_{i=1}^{N} f(X_i)$$

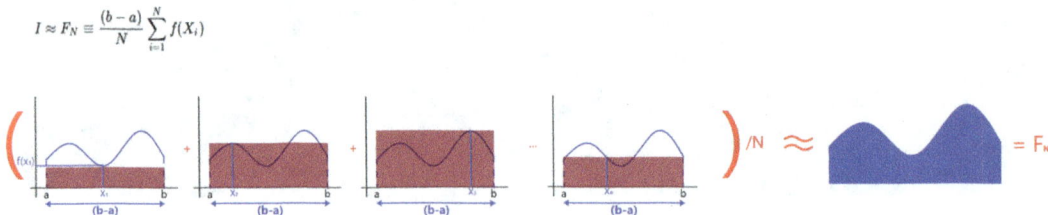

Figure 8-14. *Using a uniform distribution to draw samples is shown visually for a given f(x)*

CHAPTER 8   THE RENDERING EQUATION AND MONTE CARLO INTEGRATION

Summarizing the meaning of this oscillating behavior is represented by:

- Underestimation (means we sample below the function area)
- Overestimation (means we sample above the function area)

We can observe this behavior by running the program that comes with this chapter with different values for the number of samples N (i.e., PI estimate with Monte Carlo under the technical section of this chapter).

What we can see is that, as N grows big, the estimate will converge in probability to the expected value (the average area of our function).

After having observed visually what happens in Figure 8-14 when we use a uniform PDF, we have to ask ourselves: can we do better than that? This translates to: can we draw samples nonuniformly to closely match the function as much as possible?

Bonus tip: For the rendering equation integral, we will converge to the average reflected radiance L for a given number of samples N.

Finally, the other question that we could think about is: why do we have to use Monte Carlo integration and not other methods like Riemann sum to estimate the value of an integral?

The reason is that in MC integration the number of samples N can be chosen regardless of the dimension of the integrand. While, for example, this is not true for deterministic quadrature techniques (e.g., Riemann sum) where the dimensionality of the integrand grows, the number of samples N required is exponential in the dimension.

The following are the MC estimator pros and cons:

- Pros
  - **Simplicity**: It's perfect for multidimensional integrals. In fact, the number of samples chosen is independent on the dimensionality of the integrand function.
  - **Unbiased**: The difference of the expected value of the estimate and the ground truth is zero. Or, in other words, the estimate and the mean of the population are exactly equivalent.
  - **Consistent**: It is consistent because it follows the *law of large numbers*; therefore, consistency is verified.

- **Rate of convergence**: This is $O(\sqrt{N})$ and is independent of the dimensionality of the integrand function, while for Riemann sums, for example, it gets worse as the dimensionality of the integral increases.
- Cons
  - It does have a slow rate of convergence (in the order of $O(\sqrt{N})$ in the number of samples N).

Even if the rate of convergence is slow for the MC methods, it's independent of the dimensionality of the integral. Because of this, it is still the only viable choice with respect to deterministic quadrature techniques. In fact, they exhibit a faster rate of convergence for one-dimensional integrals (faster than $O(\sqrt{N})$), but their performance becomes exponentially worse as the dimension of the integrand increases. So, they are not viable in all cases.

Hence, there are no doubts that MC methods are the only convenient numerical integration choice for multidimensional integrals. Moreover, if we can manage to find a PDF that closely matches the shape of the function we have to sample, we will be able to sample our f(x) where it is more "important." This will have an impact even on the variance that in this case will be reduced, and, therefore, our estimator will converge faster to the expected value given the same number of samples. This will be the topic of the next section, which will introduce to a variance reduction method called *importance sampling* and another key method called *inverse transform sampling*.

Understanding Importance Sampling: Variance Reduction

As we've already stated, the variance is the primary concern when it comes to the rate of convergence of an MC estimator. The smaller the variance, the faster the estimate will converge in probability to the expected value or to the population mean.

> *When it comes to rendering, variance exhibits itself as noise on the rendered frame, meaning that for that amount of N samples, the estimate was not "fast" enough in converging to an acceptable solution. Of course, we could think to raise the number of samples N and eventually reduce the noise, but considering that the speed is in the order of $O(\sqrt{N})$ we would need four times more samples to halve the variance from the previous number of samples.*

In probability theory, there is a difference when it comes to *mean* or expected value and *sample mean*. They indicate two subtly different concepts even if they are both, in fact, a mean. The key difference is that the sample mean is a *statistic*, computed considering a subset of samples of the real population of which we'd like to compute the mean. The population mean, instead, which is denoted with the Greek letter **μ**, represents a *parameter*, that is, the mean computed on the whole population (so not just a subset as in the case of the sample mean).

What we've just described is the difference between a *statistic* and a *parameter*.

> *A parameter describes an entire population a statistic subset (i.e., samples) of that population.*

Our goal in this section is to outline a way to get a faster convergence rate given for a fixed amount of samples N. This means we need a way to reduce the variance of our estimate.

We first need to give a quick introduction of what variance is, and then we will introduce the concept of importance sampling as a way to reduce the variance of a given estimate.

Last, we will introduce a method to draw random samples from an arbitrary PDF, which is at the heart of importance sampling. The method we will adopt to achieve our goal is the *inverse transform sampling*.

A Quick Introduction to Variance

Let's start by introducing the variance of a random variable X, which states that the variance of a random variable X is equal to the summation of the squared distance of each x_i (i.e., outcome) weighted by its probability p_i. In simple terms, this is the average distance of the samples from the expected value $E[X]$.

The smaller this distance, the quicker the estimate will get closer to the mean. In the context of rendering, this means that we will get faster to the average estimated radiance L of a given pixel, given the same number of samples N.

> *Our goal is to reduce the variance of our estimator to get a faster convergence out of it.*

We've seen that, by using a uniform distribution, we were eventually able to approximate our function. The basic MC estimator was doing exactly that. What we

CHAPTER 8   THE RENDERING EQUATION AND MONTE CARLO INTEGRATION

didn't say, though, was how fast we were converging to the solution, which is what we are interested in this section.

Well, the informal answer to the previous sentence is: Not very fast as you can tell by looking at Figure 8-14.

The formal answer is to the previous sentence is: we were converging to the expected value with possibly high variance.

It's clear that the rectangular area that is the result of a uniform distribution is a poor approximation for what the real area of that function is. Yes, it will converge to the solution eventually, but after how many samples? We don't have all our life to wait for the function to converge; therefore, it would be good if we could keep the sample count low. This can be obtained by refining how we draw the samples that need to approximate the function area.

> *The higher the variance of an estimator, the slower it will converge to the expected value. To rephrase this: the higher the average squared distance is from the expected value, the further we are from it! Our aim is to reduce this squared distance because we want to be close to the average as much as possible. After all, in rendering, we aim to estimate the average radiance L, and what we want is to be as close as possible to real estimate.*

Wouldn't it be better to have an area that closely matches the function of which we want to estimate the integral? Of course, yes!

But that is possible only by picking our samples by importance, which keeps us to the topic of Importance sampling in the next subsection.

Importance Sampling

Importance sampling is the process of drawing samples with a nonuniform probability distribution. The goal is to sample the function that we want to approximate, where it is more "important." When we say "where," we actually want to mean exactly where on the curve of a given function we pick the samples.

The MC estimator defined for a generic nonuniform probability distribution function (**PDF**) is defined here:

$$F_N = \frac{1}{N} \sum_{i=0}^{N-1} \frac{f(X_i)}{pdf(X_i)}$$

This states that the expected value after **N** samples is the summation of the ratio between the function $f(X_i)$ and a **PDF**, divided by the total number of samples **N**.

The point is that we can choose any **PDF** and it will still work! But not all the **PDFs** are good **PDFs**. This means not all of them will weigh our sampling process in such a way that our area estimate will be closer to one of the real function $f(X_i)$. Therefore, choosing the right **PDF** is an art and can make a difference in how successfully we reduced the variance in our estimate.

Let's take a look at Figure 8-15 to better understand what we mean by "good PDF."

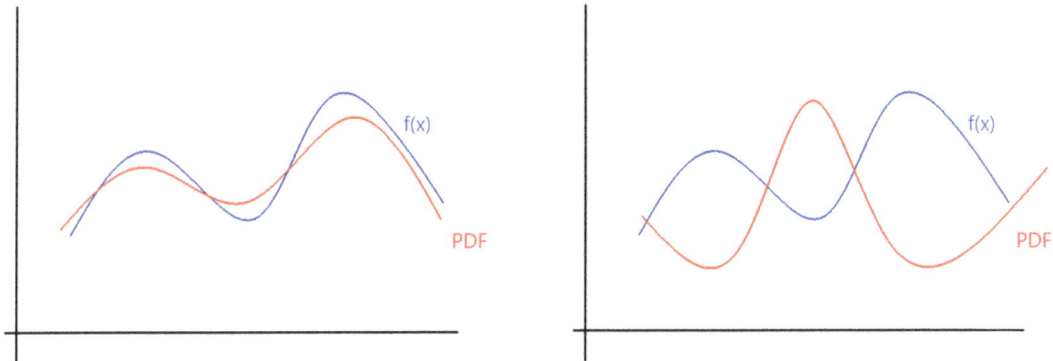

Figure 8-15. *Good PDF left, bad PDF right*

As you can tell from Figure 8-15, the PDF (in red) on the left of the picture is much closer in shape compared to the one on the right of the diagram.

We are not saying that the one on the right (Figure 8-15) will not work once we stick it into the MC estimator. We want to draw our attention to the fact that it is just a poor way of sampling the function, not the wrong one. Bad PDF means poor estimate, which in turn means high variance and ultimately more noise in our rendered frame.

Hence, the choice of a good **PDF** is crucial to reduce variance and get a better estimate of our integral. But there is one thing we still don't know to account for and that is, how we can draw samples from our **PDF** given that a **PDF** will just map a given outcome to its probability? There should be a way to find a function that, given a uniformly distributed random sample ξ (or to be more general a random sample), will map that sample to the one that closely matches our function.

This is necessary because most of the time when we write a rendering program, what we have in our random library is just a uniform random number generator. So, finding a function that maps a uniform random sample to another nonuniform random sample is crucial!

The process looks like Figure 8-16.

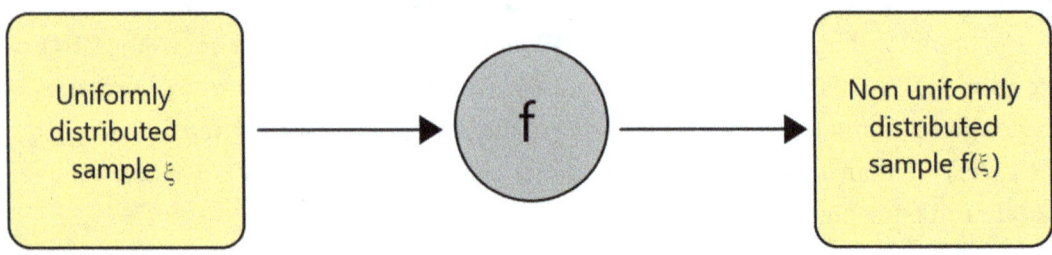

Figure 8-16. *Uniform random sample ξ in input and nonuniform random sample in output f(ξ)*

Now the missing bit is the function that will allow us to draw nonuniform random samples (i.e., the *f* in the gray circle of Figure 8-16).

We can draw uniformly distributed samples by using any of the C++ functions defined in the random standard C++ library.

If you refer to the code that we presented when we discussed how to estimate the value of π, you will see a use case of one of the standard functions that is part of the random C++ library (you need to include <random> at the beginning of your source file to use the standard random library).

The following snippet shows more clearly how to declare and use the random C++ library:

```
#include <random>

std::random_device device;
std::mt19937 generator(device());
std::uniform_real_distribution<float> distribution;
int main()
{
    float r = distribution(generator);
    float rn = SomeNonUniformSamplingFunction( r );
    // Use rn as the new sample in the MC estimator
}
```

Let's go through the previous code snippet and explain briefly what each line does.

CHAPTER 8   THE RENDERING EQUATION AND MONTE CARLO INTEGRATION

First, we need to declare the C++ standard random header file:

```
#include <random>
```

Then we need to instantiate three main objects. First, we need to declare an object that represents our random device:

```
std::random_device device;
```

Then we can pick a random generator of our choice given the previously declared device (in this case we've chosen a Mersenne-Twister 19937).

```
std::mt19937 generator(device());
```

Then we instantiate an object that will represent a uniform real distribution of floats (the samples will be drawn from the [0,1) interval):

```
std::uniform_real_distribution<float> distribution;
```

In the main entry point of the program, we are then ready to draw or first uniform random float like so:

```
float r = distribution(generator);
```

Then we can pass the uniform random sample r to any nonuniform sampling function. The result we will get back will be still a random sample rn but drawn according to a nonuniform distribution function:

```
float rn = SomeNonUniformSamplingFunction( r );
```

Finally, we could the sample rn to sample an MC estimator according to a PDF of our choice (and rn will be drawn from a function proportional to the PDF).

As you can see in the previous code snippet, drawing uniform random samples is very straightforward, but we need a way to find our float SomeNonUniformSamplingFunction(float r) because what we ultimately need is to map our uniform sample to a nonuniform one according to our PDF. The PDF, in turn, has been chosen to match our integrand function as much as possible.

The function SomeNonUniformSamplingFunction, as we will see in a bit, will be computed out of our chosen PDF.

To know how to find our nonuniform random sampling function, we need to introduce the concept of *cumulative distribution function* (CDF).

CHAPTER 8   THE RENDERING EQUATION AND MONTE CARLO INTEGRATION

This will take us to the next subsection where we will show how the CDF can be exploited to find the aforementioned function.

The Inverse Transform Sampling Method

Before to get straight to the inverse sampling method, we need to introduce one more concept. The cumulative distribution function (CDF) of a random variable X. The CDF is at the heart of this method and is directly related to the PDF (in fact the PDF is the integrand function itself!).

The CDF is defined like this:

$$CDF(X) = P(X \le t) = \int_{-\infty}^{t} pdf(x)dx$$

The CDF is basically the probability for the random variable X to get values less than or equal than a given outcome t. This is the integral of the PDF in the interval $(-\infty, t]$.

Figure 8-17 shows a discrete PDF.

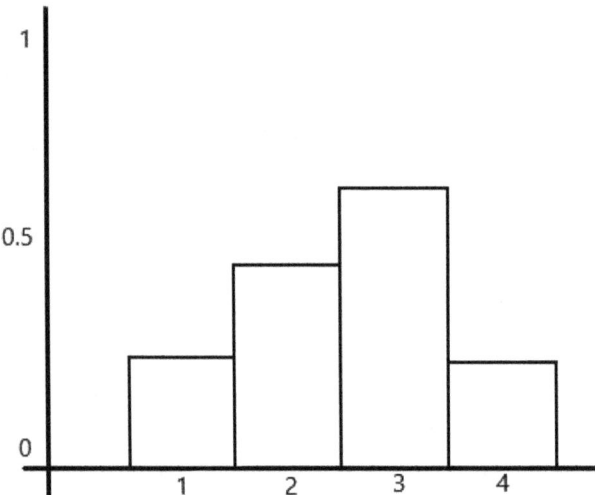

Figure 8-17. *A discrete PDF given a total of four outcomes and their corresponding probability (i.e., the height of each column) on the vertical axis*

The corresponding discrete CDF computed from the PDF of Figure 8-17 is plotted in Figure 8-18.

CHAPTER 8 THE RENDERING EQUATION AND MONTE CARLO INTEGRATION

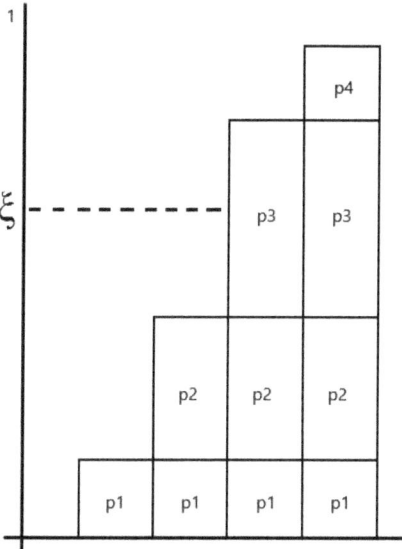

Figure 8-18. CDF computed from a given probability distribution function. We can see that ξ represents the random sample that we throw on the vertical axis that intersects the column of the third outcome with probability p_3

As you can see from Figure 8-18, if we invert the CDF, we will be able to draw a random sample ξ and get the outcome of a given probability distribution according to the PDF. The key here is that there is a relation between the PDF and the CDF; that is why the inverted CDF will be able to draw the sample according to the PDF.

So, given the definition for the CDF, we formalize also what we've already stated up to now in relation to the PDF.

That is, the PDF must be chosen to be proportional to ensure that it matches the integrand function as much as possible.

Let's translate this concept in math:

$$pdf(X_i) \propto f(X_i)$$

This means the **pdf(X_i)** is proportional to the integrand function *f(X_i)*.

The inverse sampling method states that if we compute the CDF from the PDF we've just chosen, we can then invert the CDF and draw nonuniform random samples straight from it.

The inverse of the CDF is our `SomeNonUniformSamplingFunction` that we were referring to in the previous code snippet.

225

CHAPTER 8   THE RENDERING EQUATION AND MONTE CARLO INTEGRATION

Now let's see a practical example of how to compute the **CDF^{-1}**.

Let's suppose we want to draw samples from an exponential distribution:

$$pdf(x) \propto e^{-kx}$$

The PDF for the exponential distribution is defined like so: $pdf(x) = ce^{-kx}$

The constant **c** is there to normalize the PDF.

Now in the information box we've summarized the process (in the form of a receipt) to compute the inverse of the CDF.

Inverse sampling method receipt:

- Find a PDF that is proportional to $f(X_i)$.

- Compute its cumulative distribution function (CDF).

- Invert the CDF to draw random samples according to the previous PDF.

Now we compute the CDF. By the probability theory, we know that the PDF must integrate to one:

$$\int_0^\infty pdf(x)dx = \int_0^\infty ce^{-kx}dx = 1$$

By solving the previous integral, we will be able to find the normalization constant c and, therefore, our final PDF.

The previous integral is pretty simple to solve, so let's solve it then:

$$-\frac{1}{k}\int_0^\infty cke^{-kx}dx = -\frac{1}{k}c[e^{-kx}]_0^\infty = \frac{c}{k} = 1 \iff c = k$$

So, we've found that c = k. Therefore, our final PDF is as follows:

$$pdf(x) = ke^{-kx}$$

Now that we have our PDF, we can compute the corresponding CDF, invert it, and we are done.

$$CDF(x) = \int_0^t ke^{-kx}dx = -\int_0^t -ke^{-kx}dx = -[e^{-kx}]_0^t = 1 - e^{-kt}$$

CHAPTER 8 THE RENDERING EQUATION AND MONTE CARLO INTEGRATION

The CDF is then as follows:

$$CDF(x) = 1 - e^{-kt}$$

Now we need to compute the inverse function of the **CDF(x)**. We will refer to it like **CDF(x)$^{-1}$**.

The function that we have to invert is (we renamed t as x just for a commodity):

$$1 - e^{-kx} = y \iff e^{-kx} = 1 - y \iff \ln(e^{-kx}) = \ln(1-y) \iff -kx = \ln(1-y) \iff x = \frac{\ln(1-y)}{k}$$

Therefore, our **CDF(x)$^{-1}$** is as follows:

$$CDF(x)^{-1} = \frac{\ln(1-y)}{k}$$

More formally, we would say that we can draw a nonuniform random sample *X* given a uniform random sample *ξ*, drawn by uniform random distribution, by rewriting the previous equation like this:

$$X = \frac{\ln(1-\xi)}{k}$$

The previous equation is the final form for our nonuniform random generation function. It is also the one that we would use in code when we need to sample any BRDF function.

Obviously, the exponential function is one among many of the PDFs that we can use to draw a sample from. For what concerns the rendering equation, we might need to choose a different PDF for a given BRDF. The exponential function was just taken into account for illustration purposes in this section.

> *The inverted CDF will map a uniform random sample to its corresponding nonuniform counterpart. This is possible thanks to the inverse transform sampling method we've just presented in this section.*
>
> *The samples generated by the function we've just computed will follow the PDF shape that, in turn, we've chosen to be proportional to our integrand function.*

CHAPTER 8   THE RENDERING EQUATION AND MONTE CARLO INTEGRATION

With all that said, we should be in good shape to start analyzing how we can estimate the rendering equation integral. Moreover, we will find a good PDF for our estimator too.

As we will see, we will not go through the whole process of determining the PDF for an infinite-dimensional integral like the rendering equation is. The process is a little bit more involved in that case, and because we want to keep this book as practical as possible, we will limit ourselves to providing straight solutions.

But considering that the theory we provided in this chapter should be enough to give a general understanding of the process, it should not be a problem to pick the underlying concept. The next section will show how to estimate the rendering equation with MC integration, given a diffuse BRDF. So, let's jump straight to it.

Estimating the Rendering Equation

Estimating the rendering equation is what finally we were aiming for. This is what we were expecting after all this probability and statistics theory. The concepts introduced in this chapter constitute the foundations in understanding how to estimate the rendering equation and, ultimately, the average reflected radiance of a given pixel after N samples.

So, for the rendering equation, we consider the integrand function only, and we try to plug it into the MC estimator.

Here is the rendering equation:

$$L(x, \omega_o) = L_e(x, \omega_o) + \int_\Omega L_i(x, \omega_i) f_r(\omega_i, x, \omega_o) \cos\theta d\omega$$

Here is the MC estimator applied to the integrand function:

$$F_N = \frac{1}{N} \sum_{i=0}^{N-1} \frac{L_i(x, \omega_i) f_r(\omega_i, x, \omega_o) \cos\theta}{pdf(\omega_i)}$$

Our *f(X_i)* in this case is exactly the integrand function of the rendering equation integral. If we try to sample the diffuse BRDF, we should rewrite the previous formula as follows.

The diffuse BRDF is as follows:

$$\frac{\rho}{\pi}$$

where ρ is the albedo of the material. Therefore, we have the following:

$$F_N = \frac{1}{N} \sum_{i=0}^{N-1} \frac{L_i(x, \omega_i)\rho/\pi \cos\theta}{pdf(\omega_i)}$$

The missing bit, as you can see, is the PDF! So, how we choose the PDF in this case? Well, we know it now, because we went through all this process in the previous sections of this chapter.

Of course, the PDF should be proportional to the integrand function, and, in our case, the only function we can spot there is the term **cosθ**.

So basically, the following expression:

$$pdf \propto \cos\theta$$

and the final PDF for a diffuse BRDF is equal to the following:

$$pdf = \frac{\cos\theta}{\pi}$$

We will not show how to derive the final PDF, but know that this is the best PDF we can use to sample diffuse BRDFs.

So, if we plug that PDF in the estimator, we get this:

$$F_N = \frac{1}{N} \sum_{i=0}^{N-1} \frac{L_i(x, \omega_i)\rho/\pi \cos\theta}{\frac{\cos\theta}{\pi}}$$

Finally, the expression will look like the following:

$$F_N = \frac{1}{N} \sum_{i=0}^{N-1} L_i(x, \omega_i)\rho$$

It is pretty simple I would say. What we've just done is applying the theory that we've just introduced in this chapter to estimate the light transport integral (i.e., rendering equation) in the context of the interaction of the light with a diffuse material (diffuse BRDF).

CHAPTER 8   THE RENDERING EQUATION AND MONTE CARLO INTEGRATION

So, for a diffuse material, we just need to collect the incoming-reflected radiance in a given randomly sampled direction weighted by the albedo/reflectance of our diffuse material. We need to generate as many directions on the hemisphere as the number of samples N, sum all them up, and average them (see again the previous equation).

In Chapter 10, you will see how the previous formula will be used in practice to compute the reflected radiance of a diffuse material.

But let's see what happens when we sample our directions with a random sequence. In fact, drawing samples following a random distribution is not the best choice, for many reasons that we will see in the next sections. It still works, but we will see that the choice of the "random" samples counts if we want to reduce variance in our estimator.

To summarize, we have two ways now to reduce variance:

- Importance sampling

- Choosing a clever "random" sequence from which drawing our samples from

The next section will address the second bullet point: choosing an almost or, we should better say, a *quasi*, "random" sequence.

We will go through the *stratified sampling strategies* and, in the end, land in the world of *quasi-random low discrepancy sequences*.

Understanding Stratified Sampling

The problem with standard MC integration and importance sampling is that, because they rely on random sample distributions, they will suffer from sample overlaps and gaps in the distribution space. This problem is endemic in the random distributions themselves. Figure 8-19 shows a 1D random distribution of 10 samples (the ideal case would be that each sample should fall in exactly each grid cell).

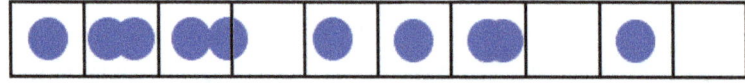

Figure 8-19. *A random 1D sample distribution presents gaps and overlaps in the sample space*

This will obviously cause the MC estimator to converge slower. This slow convergence will manifest itself in terms of higher variance; hence, there is noise in the rendered frame. Ideally what we'd like to have is a well-distributed set of samples, not necessarily uniform; otherwise, we will fall back to the uniform distribution case.

Saying that the samples are well distributed doesn't necessarily have to imply that they follow a uniform distribution.

We could be tempted to use Riemann sum, as it is a deterministic method, and it works for sure. But the problem is that as the dimensionality of the integral grows, the computational complexity of Riemann sum grows in turn. So, this method doesn't scale well. MC integration is independent of the dimension of the integral and is therefore perfectly suitable for our purposes.

The visual problems that we can face by using either MC integration or Riemann sum are as follows:

- For MC integration noise in the image
- For Riemann sum aliasing in the image

One other approach that can be used to address the problems present in the MC integration that uses standard random distribution is called *stratified sampling* or *jittered sampling*. The method works by subdividing the sample space into regular subintervals of the same size and then generating a random sample within each subinterval. In this way, it will be possible to constrain each sample in its own interval, and the resulting distribution will have no gaps nor overlapping samples, yet it will still be well distributed. Each subinterval or cell is also called *strata*.

Figure 8-20 shows a clearer view of how samples will fall into each subinterval.

Figure 8-20. *Stratified sampling will generate random samples within subintervals or strata of size ω*

CHAPTER 8   THE RENDERING EQUATION AND MONTE CARLO INTEGRATION

We proceed by placing samples on the leftmost border of each stratum, and we will then offset them by $\xi * \omega$. Where ξ. is a random distribution defined in the interval [and is the width of a given subinterval [0,1).

The formula for stratified sampling is defined like this:

$$F_N = \frac{(b-a)}{N} \sum_{i=1}^{N} f(a + \left(\frac{i+\xi}{N}\right)(a-b))$$

The difference, as you can see, is that we generate the i-th sample in the i-th cell and divide by the total number of samples N to obtain a normalized value in *[0,1]*, which will actually be used to interpolate between the extreme "a" and "b" of the integration domain. This process will be repeated for each term of the sum.

By using stratified sampling, we can reduce the variance linearly in the number of samples N. Therefore, if we denote the variance as σ, we will have the following:

$$\sigma \propto \frac{1}{N}$$

The variance is proportional to one over the number of samples N. This shows clearly the superiority of stratified sampling with respect to standard random sampling, which, if you remember, is proportional to one over the square root of the number of samples N instead.

We will not add more information in relation to stratified sampling, because it is a very math dense topic, and what we are interested in here is to just give a general idea yet give a practical view of the method. We will follow this pragmatic approach in the next section on Quasi-Monte Carlo methods too.

We will see that Quasi-Monte Carlo is very similar in spirit to stratified sampling but with a very subtle difference. The idea is still the same: trying to distribute the samples in a way such that we can avoid the limitations of standard random sampling yet maintain a good distribution over the sample space.

When we talk about path tracing, we will see how all the theories we've just presented throughout this chapter will come together in code.

Let's get now to the previous section of this chapter. This section will briefly scratch the surface of the Quasi-Monte Carlo (QMC) methods while providing a general overview of what is out there. It has to be intended as a guide just in case we decide to employ better strategies to sample our functions.

Understanding Quasi-Monte Carlo (QMC) Methods

The idea behind QMC methods is similar to the stratified sampling one. The only difference is that a quasi-random sequence presents a periodic pattern. This repeating pattern is what will guarantee that all the samples are surely and deterministically well distributed in the sample space.

Examples of such sequences are represented from:

- Halton, Van der Corput, Hammersley, Faure sequences (built out of coprime numbers as a basis)

- Sobol sequences (built out of primitive polynomials as a basis)

- Kronecker/Weyl or Richtmyer sequences (irrational fractions, no basis required!).

We can refer to them as sequences for short, where d is the number of dimensions (meaning 1D, 2D... sequence, etc.)

- Niederreiter sequences (built out of irreducible polynomials as a basis)

Figure 8-21 shows a direct visual comparison of most of the previous sequences. All of the graphs that you see in the remainder of this section have been generated with a simple OpenGL C program that has been written for this section. The sample uses FreeGLUT to have access to OpenGL for quick 2D renderings of points and lines. If you don't know about OpenGL, it doesn't matter; what you should concentrate on are the functions that generate the sequences.

CHAPTER 8   THE RENDERING EQUATION AND MONTE CARLO INTEGRATION

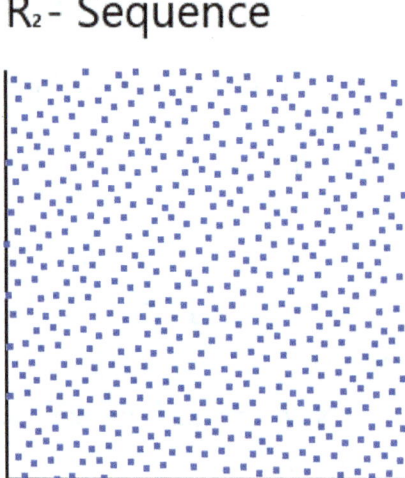

Figure 8-21. *Quasi-random **R**$_2$ 2D point sequence that follows Kronecker irrational fractions. Notice no sample clumps nor large empty areas*

So going back to where we left the basic idea is that most of the time, we expect a random sequence to not be truly random but, rather, to cover the sampling space in a well distributed way with no gaps or samples that clump together.

In Figure 8-21 samples are nicely distributed, and they cover the sample space efficiently and effectively. They don't clump together, and the empty areas are really small and constant across the sample space.

Truly random point sequences clump together in contrast, and they present themselves with large and empty areas in the sample space (i.e., no samples will fall in those areas at all).

We also refer to this situation as *white noise*.

See Figure 8-22 for a direct comparison to Figure 8-21.

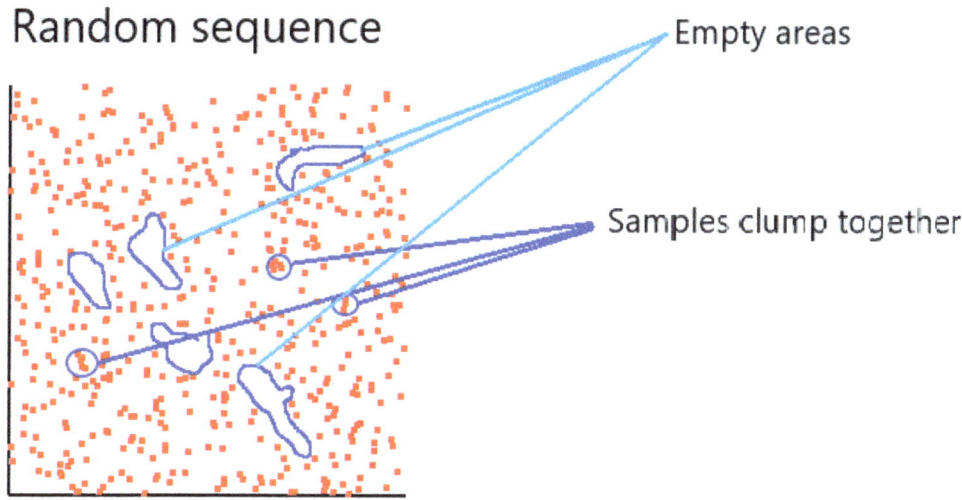

Figure 8-22. *Truly random 2D point sequence*

> *QMC sequences cover the sampling space more efficiently with no point clustering or gaps. They are not truly random, but they act as if they are. QMC integration converges faster than standard MC integration, which is based, instead, on truly random sequences.*

In the context of QMC, we talk about *discrepancy* and *variance* in the context of standard MC integration.

The discrepancy is defined as the distance between each point in a quasi-random sequence and the uniformly distributed counterpart of these same points. The smaller this distance, the closer the quasi-random sequence is to a uniform one. In fact, quasi-random sequences are also referred to as *low-discrepancy* sequences. Yes **low**, but not zero! This is important; otherwise, we would fall back to the uniform distribution case, which is what we were trying to avoid in the first place.

Figure 8-23 shows a direct comparison from left to right between quasi-random sequences and a random sequence (red dots).

CHAPTER 8   THE RENDERING EQUATION AND MONTE CARLO INTEGRATION

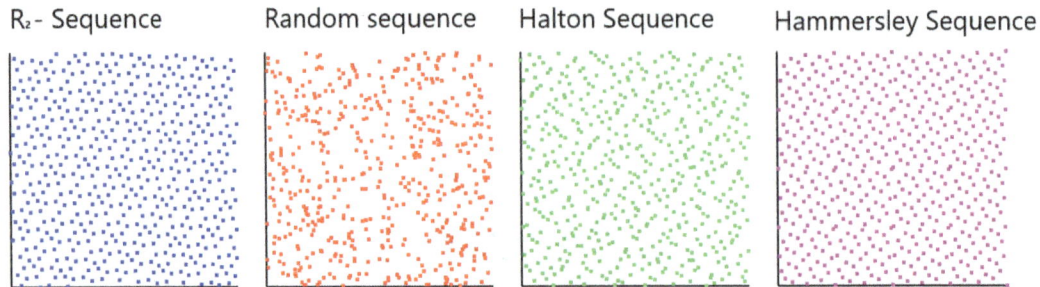

Figure 8-23. *The random sequence and all the other quasi-random sequences (R_2, Halton and Hammersley sequence)*

> *If you want more insight on how I've been able to generate the quasi-random sequences of this section, you can find few links in the "Further Reading" section at the end of this chapter and also take a look at the GitHub link where you can see the implementation that produce the sequences in Figure 8-23. Each sequence is generated for a total of 512 samples, but you can modify the code to reduce or raise the number of samples and see how each 2D distribution changes.*

QMC sequences can, sometimes, suffer from aliasing artifacts due to their periodic repeating pattern. There are strategies to also reduce the chance to have such aliasing artifacts. These strategies are based on the jittering or scrambling of the quasi-random samples by basically offsetting each sample in the sequence by a small random amount (i.e., very similar to what we normally did with stratified sampling). This will actually break the pattern and will re-introduce a bit of randomness in the sequence.

This concludes our trip through quasi-random sequences, and it actually concludes this chapter. The topics that we discussed here are going to be the foundations for what we will learn in the next set of chapters. Path tracing is one of those algorithms that will rely a lot on what we've just presented here, and every sampling strategy is based on the concept that we introduced. So, be sure to be confident about them before proceeding to the next set of chapters. Moreover, there is more from the math side of things concerning the argumentations that have been presented in this chapter. However, the goal was to condense and keep the focus on the practical side of things, and, therefore, many mathematical derivations have been omitted in favor of the end results and their application in code.

Summary

You should now have a solid grasp of what Monte Carlo integration is, how it will be used to estimate the rendering equation, and what the meaning of the rendering equation is when it comes to light transport.

The math can seem a bit involved, but, as you will see, you will use just the relevant formulations to compute the light transport when it comes to path tracing. Of course, we could write an entire book on MC integration, but that is beyond the scope of this chapter that was devoted to giving enough background so you can understand how to compute light transport with path tracing in the next chapter. You should understand what a BRDF is, what variance is in relation to rendering, and how to reduce it through the employment of importance sampling techniques. Noise reduction techniques are crucial to obtain noise-free rendered frames. Modern 3D engines and offline renderers use advanced denoising techniques that are not just plain blur filters but more complex filtering algorithms that make use of deep learning to reconstruct/filter the rendered frame in real time like never before. This is possible thanks to the tensor core acceleration of the new NVIDIA graphics cards. By using denoiser, we can keep the number of the sample very low (like one to two samples per pixel max) while getting a clear and smooth-looking image thanks to the aforementioned filtering technique. This is what modern ray tracing is at the time of this writing.

The code provided in this chapter gave you a glimpse into what is possible with MC integration as well as MC hit-or-miss approach. You should now know how to apply the MC estimator by relying on the simple examples presented.

Moreover, you will learn how to use it to solve the rendering equation when we talk about path tracing in the context of light transport in the next chapter.

The next chapter will introduce the DirectX Ray Tracing (DXR) API, which is built on top of DirectX 12 (DX12). It will show how to set up DXR setup Visual Studio 2019 and the bare minimum boilerplate initialization code needed to get a DX12 application up and running.

Then, given that setup, we will start tracing rays the modern way!

CHAPTER 8   THE RENDERING EQUATION AND MONTE CARLO INTEGRATION

Questions

Based on the knowledge that you gained in this chapter, it is your turn to answer some questions:

- What part of the rendering equation will be involved in the modeling of light-medium interaction?
- How can we solve the rendering equation integral?
- According to the law of conservation of energy, what relation is there between the incident and the reflected/absorbed light?
- Why do we sometimes use BSDF instead of BRDF or BTDF?
- What is the difference between light and radiance?
- What is the Monte Carlo integration method?
- What is the difference between MC integration and the MC hit-or-miss approach?
- What techniques can we employ to reduce the variance of our estimator?
- What mean by low discrepancy when it comes to QMC methods?
- Why random sequences are not the best choice to generate samples for MC estimator?

Further Reading

The following are a few links that you can use to expand the horizon of your knowledge on this chapter:

- Kajiya, James T. (1986), "The rendering equation" (PDF), Siggraph 1986: 143–150
- J.H. Halton, *On the efficiency of certain quasi-random sequences of points in evaluating multi-dimensional integrals*, Numerische Mathematik, Volume 2, 1960, pages 84-90.

- https://www.scratchapixel.com/lessons/mathematics-physics-forcomputer-graphics/monte-carlo-methods-in-practice/monte-carlosimulation

- Pharr M., Humphreys G. (2016), "Physically Based Rendering: From Theory to Implementation"

- http://extremelearning.com.au/unreasonable-effectiveness-ofquasirandom-sequences/

CHAPTER 9

DirectX 12 and Real-Time Ray Tracing in DXR

In this chapter, we will go through the DirectX 12 (DX12) setup and initialization under Visual Studio 2022. The DX12 initialization and sample creation is part of the RaySampleFramework (see the GitHub link). The aforementioned framework has been created for this book and is organized in such a way that the user can derive its own sample (similarly to the `DXSample` class that comes with the standard DirectX Graphics set of samples).

The DX12 component that we will concentrate our attention is represented by Direct3D 12 (D3D12).

You will be guided through a basic D3D12 initialization, going through the main parts required to define a bare-bones DX12 application.

We will also have a rendering window and a swap-chain (more on this later) associated with it. After we've got a rendering window going, we will have all that is required to render stuff. We could rasterize or trace rays! In our case, we will go for the second of the two options.

The last sections will be devoted to the introduction of the relevant DirectX Ray Tracing API (DXR). Here, functions, interfaces, and C++ structures will be explained to give you the tools that are necessary to build a very basic DXR-capable application.

In the last section, we will reconnect with the ray tracing world and present a basic form of ray tracing: *Whitted ray tracing*. Whitted ray tracing will be implemented in DXR to better illustrate the API usage.

The D3D12 presentation that will be given in this chapter doesn't have to be considered exhaustive. The goal of this chapter is to introduce you to D3D12 initialization so you can start tracing rays with DXR.

CHAPTER 9   DIRECTX 12 AND REAL-TIME RAY TRACING IN DXR

The following topics will be covered in this chapter:

- DirectX 12 setup under Visual Studio 2022
- DirectX 12 boilerplate initialization code
- Your first rendering window and the swap-chain
- DXR new structures and shader stages
- DXR API initialization code
- Understanding the `RaySampleFramework` structure
- Whitted ray tracing in DXR

Technical Requirements

The following tools will be required before we get started:

- Visual Studio 2022 Community (Visual Studio 2015 is the minimum supported dev environment and it will include the D3D12 graphics debugging tools)
- Windows 10 RS5 update
- Windows 10 SDK

Minimum hardware requirements:

- GeForce RTX 2k series

DirectX 12 Setup Under Visual Studio 2022

This section will provide the necessary information needed to set up DirectX 12 (DX12) under the Visual Studio 2022 (VS2022) development environment.

The first thing you should install (if you already haven't done so) is the Windows 10 SDK. In fact, D3D12 headers and libraries come with the Windows 10 SDK installation. You don't need to install them separately like you had to do in the past with D3D11.

CHAPTER 9   DIRECTX 12 AND REAL-TIME RAY TRACING IN DXR

The following are the headers and libraries that you need to include to use D3D12:

- `D3d12.h`
- `D3d12.lib`
- `D3d12.dll` (you can use the DLL to get the entry point for each API function straightaway if you like)
- `dxgi1_6.h` (necessary for the DXGI interfaces; they are necessary to get access to adapter interfaces, and they represent a display subsystem)

There are also (as it is tradition since older versions of D3D) helper libraries. To use them in code, you need to include the following:

- `D3dx12.h` (the code contained in this header file is open source, and it can be modified freely)

The `RaySampleFramework` will wrap most of the initialization code, and it will therefore include any necessary DX12 header. It is a good starting point to understand how to begin coding with D3D12.

Most of the headers we just mentioned are included in a precompiled header, included by our framework, named:

- `RayPCH.h`

The `D3D12.lib` library file is added as part of any project that will derive a sample from the `RaySample` class that is part of our framework.

Figure 9-1 shows the **VS2022** solution explorer with the project tree.

CHAPTER 9   DIRECTX 12 AND REAL-TIME RAY TRACING IN DXR

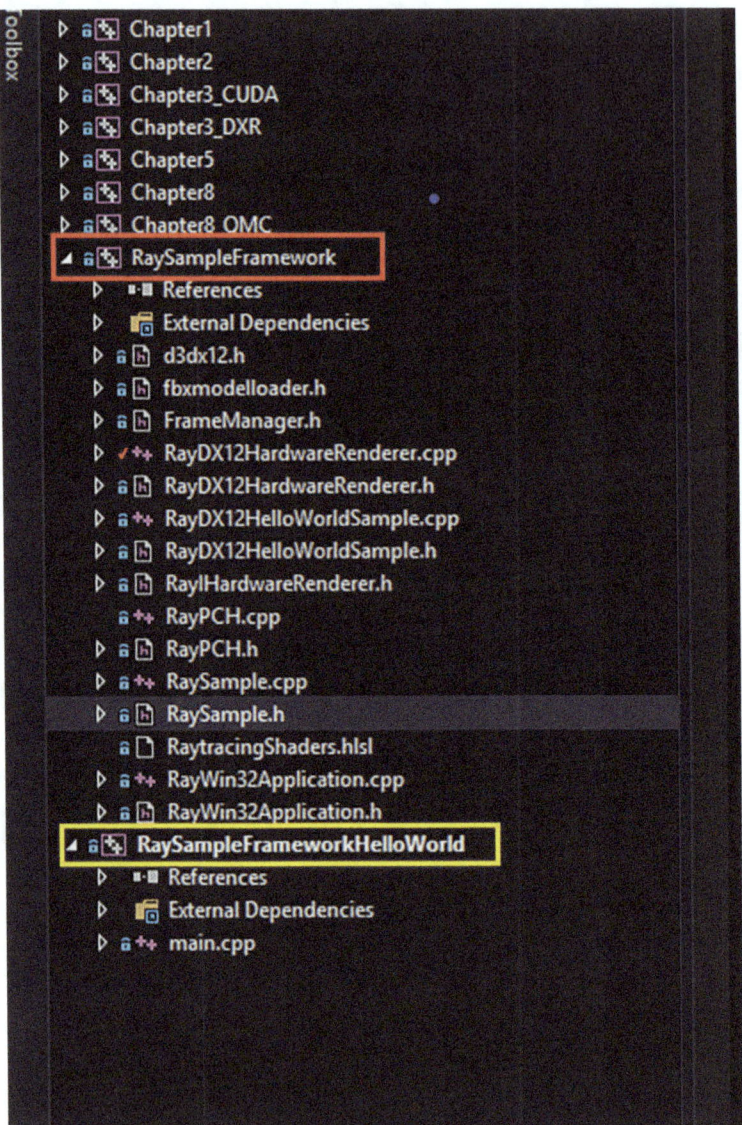

Figure 9-1. *The collection of projects of the book (including the RaySampleFramework and a sample created with it named RaySampleFrameworkHelloWorld)*

Any sample that we create will basically link itself (statically) to the `RaySampleFramework`. In fact, the framework is a project that, once compiled, will produce a static `.lib` library file. The name of this library is `RaySampleFramework.lib`.

244

CHAPTER 9   DIRECTX 12 AND REAL-TIME RAY TRACING IN DXR

To get access to each project properties in our VS2022 solution, we need to right-click the project name (Figure 9-2 shows this visually).

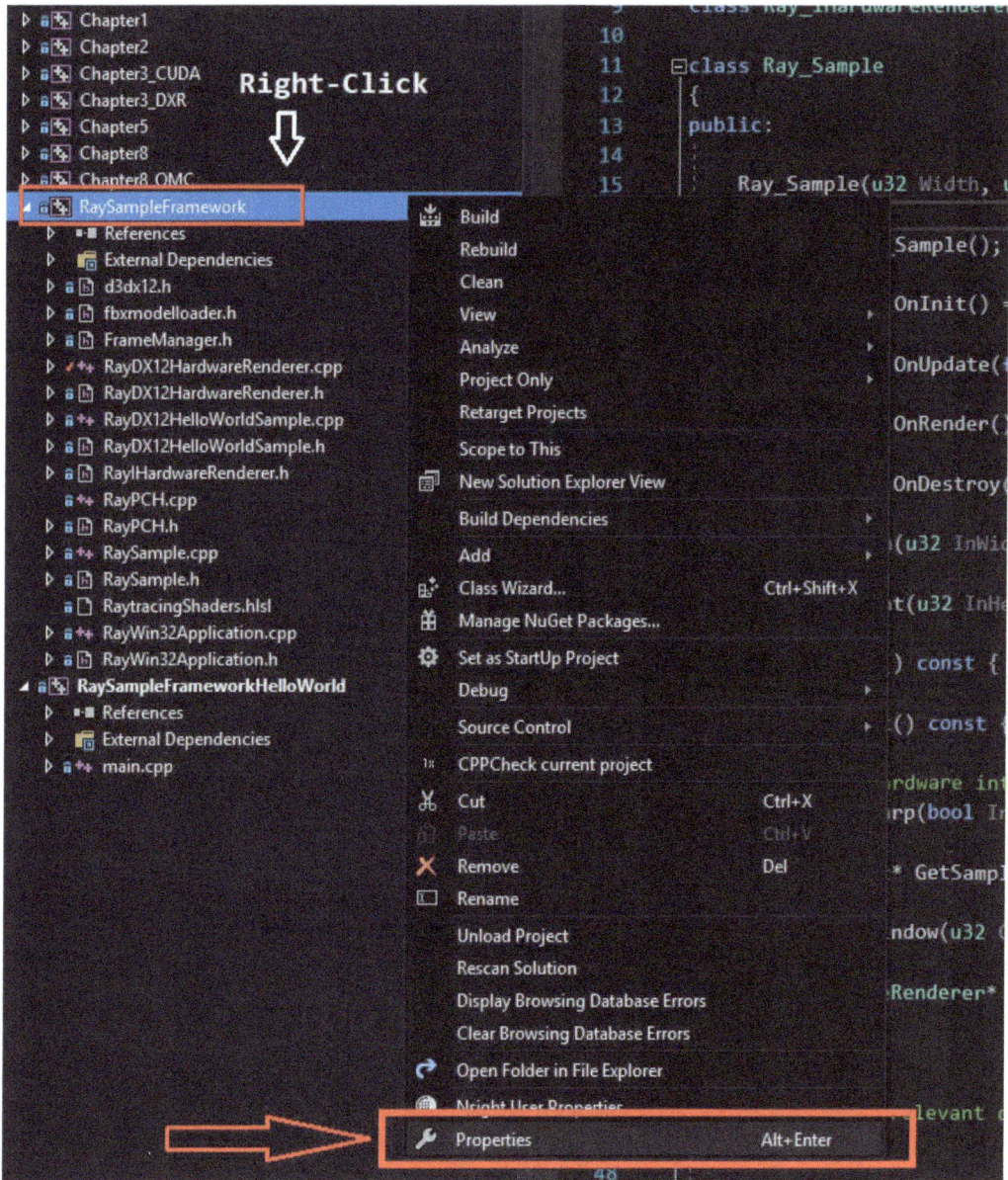

Figure 9-2. *Contextual menu will open up once we right-click the project name of our interest*

CHAPTER 9   DIRECTX 12 AND REAL-TIME RAY TRACING IN DXR

The relevant steps are as follows:

- Right-click the project name.
- Select Properties from the contextual menu.
- You will be presented with a window with a caption that has the following:

  <YourProjectName> Property Pages

Figure 9-3 shows how the framework VS2022 property pages look (the black box indicates the configuration type).

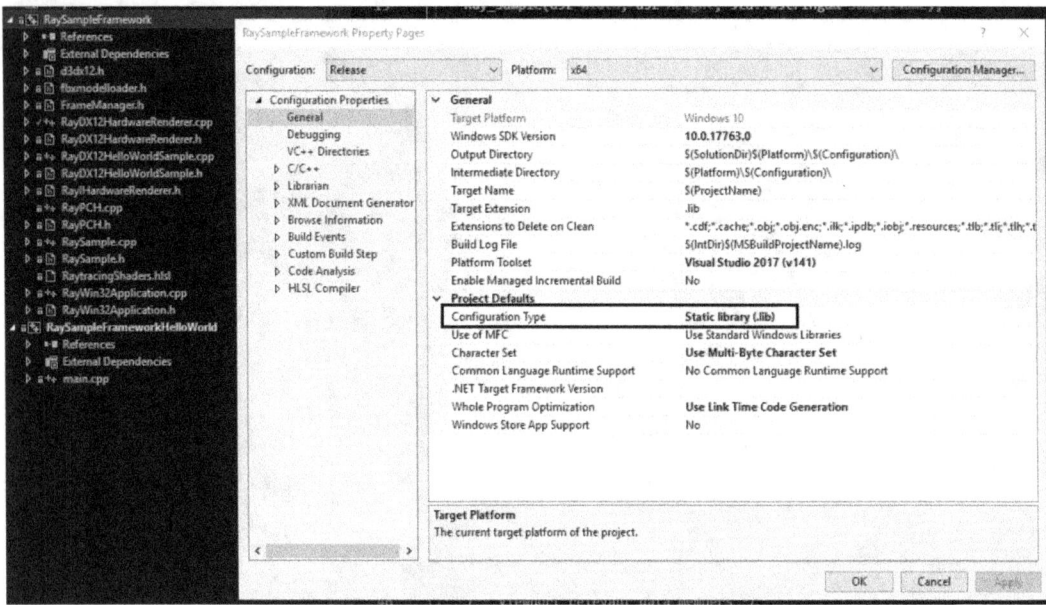

Figure 9-3. *Our RaySampleFramework project will produce a static library .lib file*

`RaySampleFrameworkHelloWorld` is a sample project that has been derived from and that links to the `RaySampleFramework`. This sample project will include `RaySampleFramework.lib` and all the D3D12 relevant library files.

Those files will be specified under the property pages: Linker ➤ Input ➤ Additional Dependencies. Figure 9-4 shows exactly what library files are added in the additional dependencies field to better clarify how the framework, and the samples we derive, are interrelated.

CHAPTER 9   DIRECTX 12 AND REAL-TIME RAY TRACING IN DXR

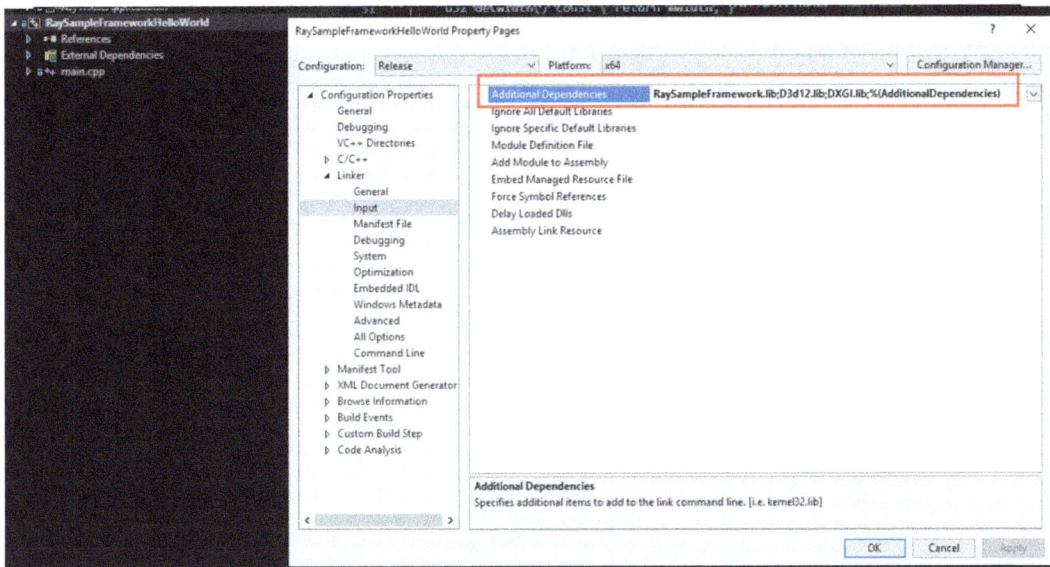

Figure 9-4. *The additional dependencies under the Librarian section of the property pages include all the relevant *.lib files*

As you can see in the additional dependencies, there are also the D3D12 lib files (i.e., D3D12.lib, DXGI.lib).

So basically, any sample that is derived from our framework will have those dependencies:

- RaySampleFramework.lib

- D3D12.lib

- DXGI.lib

We will describe the structure of our framework in much more detail in the next section. However, before diving into the framework structure, we will introduce some fundamental concepts related to D3D12 programming. There is one topic related to CPU/GPU synchronization that in D3D12 must be handled explicitly by the programmer.

DirectX 12 Boilerplate Initialization Code

Let's start by discussing the required steps to get DirectX 12 (DX12) up and running. I have to promise that the code provided here is part of the samples that come with this book and it doesn't have to be considered by any means production ready. However, you

247

are encouraged to try to run the samples, modify the code, and so on. It is important to always keep the official Microsoft DX12 documentation as a side reference for all the API functions/objects while experimenting with the code.

So, the main steps are outlined in Figure 9-5.

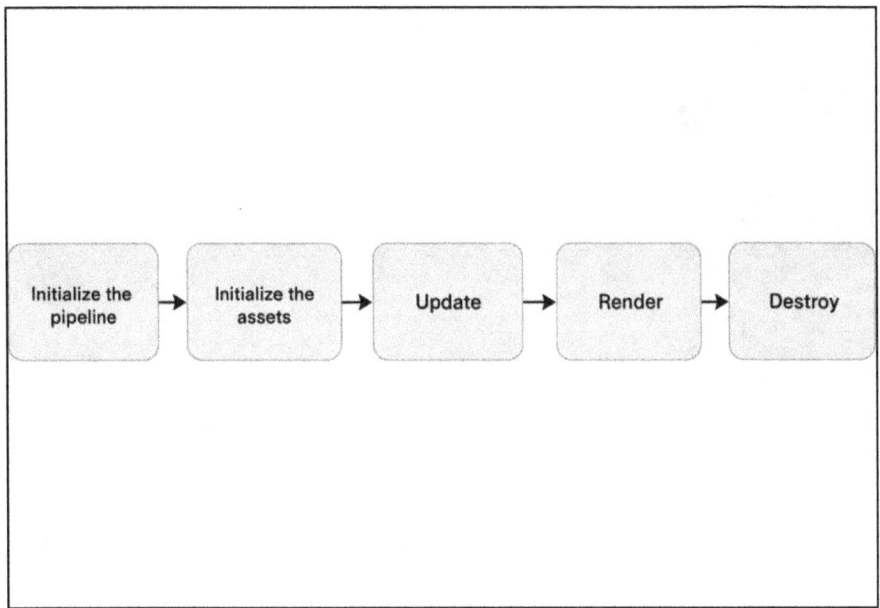

Figure 9-5. *Main steps to initialize boilerplate code*

We took inspiration from the Microsoft documentation in naming each initialization step of Figure 9-5. We could have just named them differently, but it doesn't harm anyone to keep the naming conventions closer to the Microsoft one.

Moreover, it helps that ou know the Microsoft way of naming things in code. It is important because DX12 is a very verbose API and following the naming convention up front will help you find your way in the DX12 verbosity. So, starting from the topmost box of the diagram, we can spot the first step, i.e., initializing the pipeline.

This step is composed of several other substeps that aim to initialize the minimum DX12 infrastructure for a typical application. We will go through each the five steps of Figure 9-5 by giving them a dedicated subsection in the reminder of this main section.

Initializing the Pipeline

The main substeps to initialize the basic infrastructure for DX12 are summarized in Figure 9-6 (follow the arrows to get a feel of the initialization flow).

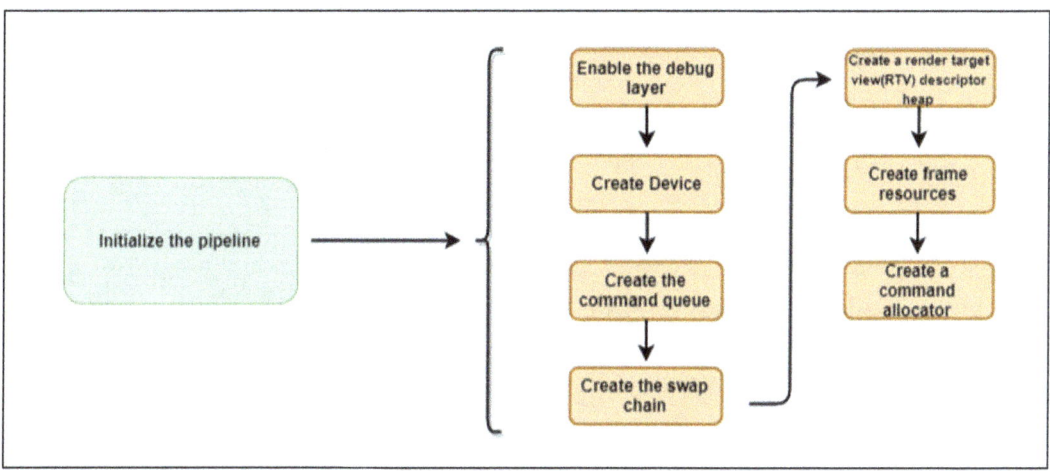

Figure 9-6. *DX12 initialization flow is showed. Follow the arrows from left to right and top to bottom*

By referring to the box on the left of Figure 9-6, we can follow the arrow and get an expanded view of the main initialization substeps.

By following the arrows, we will describe each step and its relevant code. The first step we encounter is to enable the debug layer.

This step will be present only in the debug build of our sample. If we compile in release mode, that step will eventually get ignored. The DX12 code for that step is shown in the following code snippet:

```
#if defined(_DEBUG)
    ComPtr<ID3D12Debug> DebugInterface;
    ThrowIfFailed( D3D12GetDebugInterface(IID_PPV_ARGS(&DebugInterface)) );
    DebugInterface->EnableDebugLayer();
#endif
```

We declare a ID3D12Debug object, which represents the DX12 debug interface. Next, we make a call to get a pointer to the actual underlying interface:

```
D3D12GetDebugInterface(IID_PPV_ARGS(&DebugInterface))
```

CHAPTER 9   DIRECTX 12 AND REAL-TIME RAY TRACING IN DXR

After we've got a pointer to the required interface, we can enable the debug layer like this:

`DebugInterface->EnableDebugLayer();`

Notice that during the whole process the code is embedded in a C preprocessor block.

```
#if defined(_DEBUG)
// code to include in compilation build goes here
#endif
```

This is necessary because we want to compile/include that code there only if we compile our application in debug mode.

Including this step in our debug builds is important because we can take advantage of the verbose debug output. By having a verbose output, we can spot any DX12-specific issue more quickly. We will find any debug message related to DX12 in the Visual Studio output window located below the dev environment.

Following the arrow in Figure 9-6, we have the Direct3D 12 (D3D12) device creation step. The device represents a virtual graphics adapter, and it is normally used to create fences, command lists, heaps, pipeline state objects, etc.

The D3D12 interface for our device is ID3D12Device5, and the number appended at the end represents the latest version of this device interface.

Before creating a virtual device, we need to first create a so-called adapter, which, in this case, represents a physical graphics adapter. Once we've selected the correct physical graphics adapter, we can create the actual virtual graphics adapter.

The code to enumerate the available adapters is shown here, and it makes use of DirectX Graphics Infrastructure (DXGI):

```
ComPtr<IDXGIAdapter4> Ray_DX12HardwareRenderer::GetAdapter(bool InUseWarp)
{
    ComPtr<IDXGIFactory4> DXGIFactory;
    u32 CreateFactoryFlags = 0;
#if defined(_DEBUG)
    CreateFactoryFlags = DXGI_CREATE_FACTORY_DEBUG;
#endif
    ThrowIfFailed(CreateDXGIFactory2(CreateFactoryFlags,
    IID_PPV_ARGS(&DXGIFactory)));
```

CHAPTER 9 DIRECTX 12 AND REAL-TIME RAY TRACING IN DXR

```
    ComPtr<IDXGIAdapter1> DXGIAdapter1;
    ComPtr<IDXGIAdapter4> DXGIAdapter4;
    if (InUseWarp)
    {
        ThrowIfFailed(DXGIFactory->EnumWarpAdapter(IID_PPV_
        ARGS(&DXGIAdapter1)));
        ThrowIfFailed(DXGIAdapter1.As(&DXGIAdapter4));
    }
    else
    {
       SIZE_T MaxDedicatedVideoMemory = 0;
       for (UINT i = 0; DXGIFactory->EnumAdapters1(i, &DXGIAdapter1) !=
       DXGI_ERROR_NOT_FOUND; ++i)
       {
           DXGI_ADAPTER_DESC1 dxgiAdapterDesc1;
           DXGIAdapter1->GetDesc1(&dxgiAdapterDesc1);
           if ((dxgiAdapterDesc1.Flags & DXGI_ADAPTER_FLAG_SOFTWARE) == 0
             && SUCCEEDED(D3D12CreateDevice(DXGIAdapter1.Get(),D3D_FEATURE_
               LEVEL_11_0, __uuidof(ID3D12Device),
             nullptr)) && dxgiAdapterDesc1.DedicatedVideoMemory >
             MaxDedicatedVideoMemory)
               {
                   MaxDedicatedVideoMemory = dxgiAdapterDesc1.
                   DedicatedVideoMemory;
                   ThrowIfFailed(DXGIAdapter1.As(&DXGIAdapter4));
               }
       }
    }

    return DXGIAdapter4;
}
```

CHAPTER 9   DIRECTX 12 AND REAL-TIME RAY TRACING IN DXR

We first declare a DXGI factory object of version 4, and then we query for its interface, specifying the factory creation flag in debug mode if we are building in debug and otherwise 0:

```
ComPtr<IDXGIFactory4> DXGIFactory;
u32 CreateFactoryFlags = 0;
#if defined(_DEBUG)
    CreateFactoryFlags = DXGI_CREATE_FACTORY_DEBUG;
#endif
```

Then we should be ready to create the DXGI factory object by making a call to CreateDXGIFactory2 passing the create factory flags as the first parameter and a pointer to the actual DXGI factory interface.

```
ThrowIfFailed(CreateDXGIFactory2(CreateFactoryFlags,IID_PPV_ARGS(&DXGIFactory)));
```

After this call, we should be left with a valid pointer to a DXGI factory interface in our DXGIFactory object.

Then we can actually use our factory object to enumerate adapters, get all the available resolutions supported by our adapter, and query for the available adapter memory.

The second part of our previous code snippet does exactly this by first checking whether we are asking for a Windows Advanced Rasterization Platform (WARP) adapter or not:

```
ComPtr<IDXGIAdapter1> DXGIAdapter1;
ComPtr<IDXGIAdapter4> DXGIAdapter4;
if (InUseWarp)
{
    ThrowIfFailed(DXGIFactory->EnumWarpAdapter(IID_PPV_ARGS(&DXGIAdapter1)));
    ThrowIfFailed(DXGIAdapter1.As(&DXGIAdapter4));
}
```

The WARP adapter is a software rasterizer fully DX12 compliant, and it is normally useful when we need to test, or implement, features that are not directly supported by the underlying graphics hardware.

We retrieve our WARP adapter by making a call to the factory method `EnumWarpAdapter`, and we are done. The method will return a valid pointer to a DXGI adapter 1. Then we will convert it to a DXGI adapter version 4, and we return a pointer to it from the function.

If we don't intend to use a WARP adapter, then we will start by enumerating all the available adapters. In this case, we will make a call to the factory method `EnumAdapters1` for each adapter. We will try to create a D3D11 device to see if we succeed (we make a call to `D3D12CreateDevice`) for each enumerated adapter. If we succeed, then it means we've found a D3D12-compliant adapter with the maximum available memory. Finally, when the loop ends, we should have a valid D3D11-compliant graphics adapter with the maximum available memory on-board. We query for a D3D11-compliant adapter to guarantee that at least the minimum D3D11 support is present.

The second part of the code snippet does implement the enumeration loop we've just mentioned:

```
else
{
    SIZE_T MaxDedicatedVideoMemory = 0;
    for (UINT i = 0; DXGIFactory->EnumAdapters1(i, &DXGIAdapter1) !=
    DXGI_ERROR_NOT_FOUND; ++i)
    {
     DXGI_ADAPTER_DESC1 dxgiAdapterDesc1;
     DXGIAdapter1->GetDesc1(&dxgiAdapterDesc1);
     if ((dxgiAdapterDesc1.Flags & DXGI_ADAPTER_FLAG_SOFTWARE) == 0 &&
         SUCCEEDED(D3D12CreateDevice(DXGIAdapter1.Get(),D3D_FEATURE_
         LEVEL_11_0, __uuidof(ID3D12Device),nullptr)) &&
         dxgiAdapterDesc1.DedicatedVideoMemory >
         MaxDedicatedVideoMemory )
        {
            MaxDedicatedVideoMemory = dxgiAdapterDesc1.
            DedicatedVideoMemory;
            ThrowIfFailed(DXGIAdapter1.As(&DXGIAdapter4));
        }
    }
}
return DXGIAdapter4;
}
```

CHAPTER 9   DIRECTX 12 AND REAL-TIME RAY TRACING IN DXR

Finally, when we are done, we return from the adapter enumeration function, returning the found adapter DXGIAdapter4.

Having the adapter, we are now ready to create the virtual device. Let's remind us that the interface that we want to create now is of type ID3D12Device5. The number 5 at the end of the interface object name represents the version. We've chosen version 5 because it's the one that has the support for DirectX ray tracing (DXR) objects creation.

The code for the device creation is shown here. Notice we pass the adapter in order to create the device:

```
ComPtr<ID3D12Device5>
Ray_DX12HardwareRenderer::CreateDevice(ComPtr<IDXGIAdapter4> InAdapter)
{
    ComPtr<ID3D12Device5> d3d12Device5;
    ThrowIfFailed(D3D12CreateDevice(InAdapter.Get(),D3D_FEATURE_LEVEL_12_1,
    IID_PPV_ARGS(&d3d12Device5)));
    D3D12_FEATURE_DATA_D3D12_OPTIONS5 d3d12Caps = {};
ThrowIfFailed(d3d12Device5->CheckFeatureSupport(D3D12_FEATURE_D3D12_
OPTIONS5, &d3d12Caps,sizeof(d3d12Caps));
    if (d3d12Caps.RaytracingTier < D3D12_RAYTRACING_TIER_1_0)
    {
        OutputDebugString("Device or Driver does not support ray
        tracing!");
        throw std::exception();
    }
#if defined(_DEBUG)
    ComPtr<ID3D12InfoQueue> pInfoQueue;
    if (SUCCEEDED(d3d12Device5.As(&pInfoQueue)))
    {
        pInfoQueue->SetBreakOnSeverity(D3D12_MESSAGE_SEVERITY_
        CORRUPTION,TRUE);
        pInfoQueue->SetBreakOnSeverity(D3D12_MESSAGE_SEVERITY_ERROR, TRUE);
        pInfoQueue->SetBreakOnSeverity(D3D12_MESSAGE_SEVERITY_
          WARNING,TRUE);
```

```
            D3D12_MESSAGE_SEVERITY Severities[] =
            {
                D3D12_MESSAGE_SEVERITY_INFO
            };
            // Suppress individual messages by their ID
            D3D12_MESSAGE_ID DenyIds[] =
            {
                D3D12_MESSAGE_ID_CLEARRENDERTARGETVIEW_MISMATCHINGCLEARVALUE,
                D3D12_MESSAGE_ID_MAP_INVALID_NULLRANGE,
                D3D12_MESSAGE_ID_UNMAP_INVALID_NULLRANGE,
            };
            D3D12_INFO_QUEUE_FILTER NewFilter = {};
            NewFilter.DenyList.NumSeverities = _countof(Severities);
            NewFilter.DenyList.pSeverityList = Severities;
            NewFilter.DenyList.NumIDs = _countof(DenyIds);
            NewFilter.DenyList.pIDList = DenyIds;
            ThrowIfFailed(pInfoQueue->PushStorageFilter(&NewFilter));
        }
#endif
    return d3d12Device5;
}
```

The first step in the method is the creation of the device:

```
//Ray tracing capable device creation
ComPtr<ID3D12Device5> d3d12Device5;
ThrowIfFailed(D3D12CreateDevice(InAdapter.Get(), D3D_FEATURE_
LEVEL_12_1,IID_PPV_ARGS(&d3d12Device5)));
```

We create a device that targets features for DX12.1, including shader model 5.0. That means we want to support all the DX12.1 features, and by creating a version 5 of the device we want the support for hardware ray tracing as well. This will allow us to create DXR objects, pipeline state objects, command lists, and so on.

CHAPTER 9   DIRECTX 12 AND REAL-TIME RAY TRACING IN DXR

If everything goes well, we should be safely going the next step. We actually check for ray tracing support with the following code:

```
ThrowIfFailed(d3d12Device5->CheckFeatureSupport(D3D12_FEATURE_D3D12_
OPTIONS5, &d3d12Caps, sizeof(d3d12Caps)));
if (d3d12Caps.RaytracingTier < D3D12_RAYTRACING_TIER_1_0)
{
    OutputDebugString("Device or Driver does not support ray tracing!");
    throw std::exception();
}
```

We query for D3D12_FEATURE_D3D12_OPTIONS5, and then we check that we support at least ray tracing tier 1.0. If not, we output an error message, and we throw an exception. We need to be sure to have it supported, before creating any DXR-specific object/state.

We then have the usual debug code block that gets compiled in, only if we are building in debug mode. In this block, we check if we can temporarily convert our device into an ID3D12InfoQueue object.

Then, if we succeed, we set the severity levels represented by the fact that we want to break if we get errors, warning, or corruption-related issues.

The part of the code that is configuring this debug behavior is in the following code block:

```
#if defined(_DEBUG)
ComPtr<ID3D12InfoQueue> pInfoQueue;
if (SUCCEEDED(d3d12Device5.As(&pInfoQueue)))
{
pInfoQueue->SetBreakOnSeverity(D3D12_MESSAGE_SEVERITY_CORRUPTION, TRUE);
pInfoQueue->SetBreakOnSeverity(D3D12_MESSAGE_SEVERITY_ERROR, TRUE);
pInfoQueue->SetBreakOnSeverity(D3D12_MESSAGE_SEVERITY_WARNING, TRUE);
```

Then we want to also ignore irrelevant messages. We achieve this with the next part that follows from the previous code block:

CHAPTER 9   DIRECTX 12 AND REAL-TIME RAY TRACING IN DXR

```
D3D12_MESSAGE_SEVERITY Severities[] =
{
D3D12_MESSAGE_SEVERITY_INFO
};
// Suppress individual messages by their ID
D3D12_MESSAGE_ID DenyIds[] = {
D3D12_MESSAGE_ID_CLEARRENDERTARGETVIEW_MISMATCHINGCLEARVALUE,
D3D12_MESSAGE_ID_MAP_INVALID_NULLRANGE,
D3D12_MESSAGE_ID_UNMAP_INVALID_NULLRANGE,
};
D3D12_INFO_QUEUE_FILTER NewFilter = {};
NewFilter.DenyList.NumSeverities = _countof(Severities);
NewFilter.DenyList.pSeverityList = Severities;
NewFilter.DenyList.NumIDs = _countof(DenyIds);
NewFilter.DenyList.pIDList = DenyIds;
ThrowIfFailed(pInfoQueue->PushStorageFilter(&NewFilter));
}
#endif
return d3d12Device5;
}
```

in the last code block, we create an info queue filter struct descriptor. We fill this struct with the filters we've just created, and we pass the descriptor as a parameter to the function `PushStorageFilter`, called from our `pInfoQueue` object.

Finally, we can return an instance of our `d3d12Device5`. This is our virtual device. With the device ready, we can start creating any DX12 object we need. The next in the list (please always refer to Figure 9-6) is the command queue (or command buffer). We need a command queue to execute any issued command on the GPU.

The command queue creation is pretty straightforward and is represented by this line of code:

```
mD3DCommandQueue = CreateCommandQueue(mD3DDevice,D3D12_COMMAND_LIST_TYPE_
DIRECT);
```

CHAPTER 9   DIRECTX 12 AND REAL-TIME RAY TRACING IN DXR

The first parameter is our device mD3DDevice followed by the type of command queue we want to create. In this case, we create a queue that can accept command lists of type Direct. The types of queues are listed here:

- Direct (D3D12_COMMAND_LIST_TYPE_DIRECT)
- Bundle (D3D12_COMMAND_LIST_TYPE_BUNDLE)
- Compute (D3D12_COMMAND_LIST_TYPE_COMPUTE)
- Copy (D3D12_COMMAND_LIST_TYPE_COPY)
- Video Decode (D3D12_COMMAND_LIST_TYPE_VIDEO_DECODE)
- Video Process (D3D12_COMMAND_LIST_TYPE_VIDEO_PROCESS)

You can check the Microsoft documentation for further information and examples. We use the Direct type because it is enough for what we want to do, i.e., issuing draw commands and dispatch rays!

We don't have other specific needs; therefore, it is suited perfectly to what we want to achieve rendering-wise.

The next section will focus on the swap chain creation. There are quite a lot of flags to set before creating a swap chain.

Your First Rendering Window and the Swap-Chain

Following the arrow in Figure 9-6 next in the list is the swap-chain creation. We've separated the swap-chain creation and put the code in a separate method.

Take a look at the following code:

```
ComPtr<IDXGISwapChain4> Ray_DX12HardwareRenderer::CreateSwapChain(HWND
InhWnd
, ComPtr<ID3D12CommandQueue> InCommandQueue
, u32 InWidth
, u32 InHeight
, u32 InBufferCount)
{
ComPtr<IDXGISwapChain4> dxgiSwapChain4;
ComPtr<IDXGIFactory4> dxgiFactory4;
UINT CreateFactoryFlags = 0;
```

```
#if defined(_DEBUG)
CreateFactoryFlags = DXGI_CREATE_FACTORY_DEBUG;
#endif
ThrowIfFailed(CreateDXGIFactory2(CreateFactoryFlags,
IID_PPV_ARGS(&dxgiFactory4)));
mBackBufferFormat = DXGI_FORMAT_R8G8B8A8_UNORM;
DXGI_SWAP_CHAIN_DESC1 SwapChainDesc = {};
SwapChainDesc.Width = InWidth;
SwapChainDesc.Height = InHeight;
SwapChainDesc.Format = mBackBufferFormat; //If we want to let the hw
perform gamma correction for us we should use _SRGB format instead
SwapChainDesc.Stereo = FALSE;
SwapChainDesc.SampleDesc = { 1, 0 };
SwapChainDesc.BufferUsage = DXGI_USAGE_RENDER_TARGET_OUTPUT;
SwapChainDesc.BufferCount = InBufferCount;
SwapChainDesc.Scaling = DXGI_SCALING_STRETCH;
SwapChainDesc.SwapEffect = DXGI_SWAP_EFFECT_FLIP_DISCARD;
SwapChainDesc.AlphaMode = DXGI_ALPHA_MODE_UNSPECIFIED;
```

First, as we did when we created the IDXGIAdapter, we re-create the IDXGIFactory4 again. Enable the debug mode for the factory creation and use it later to create the actual swap-chain, as shown in the following snippet:

```
// It is recommended to always allow tearing if tearing support is
available.
IsTearingSupported = CheckTearingSupport();
SwapChainDesc.Flags = IsTearingSupported ? DXGI_SWAP_CHAIN_FLAG_ALLOW_
TEARING : 0;

//Create Swapchain
ComPtr<IDXGISwapChain1> swapChain1;

ThrowIfFailed(dxgiFactory4->CreateSwapChainForHwnd(InCommandQueue.Get(),
                                                   InhWnd,
                                                   &SwapChainDesc,
                                                   nullptr,
                                                   nullptr,
                                                   &swapChain1));
```

```
    // Disable the Alt+Enter fullscreen toggle feature. Switching to
    fullscreen
    // will be handled manually.
    ThrowIfFailed(dxgiFactory4->MakeWindowAssociation(InhWnd,DXGI_MWA_NO_
    ALT_ENTER));
    ThrowIfFailed(swapChain1.As(&dxgiSwapChain4));
    //Get the index of the current swapchain backmbuffer
    mBackBufferIndex = dxgiSwapChain4->GetCurrentBackBufferIndex();
    return dxgiSwapChain4;
}
```

In the second part of the swap-chain creation code, we check if we have support for tearing. If yes, we set the flag to our swap-chain by filling the flags field:

```
SwapChainDesc.Flags = IsTearingSupported ? DXGI_SWAP_CHAIN_FLAG_ALLOW_
TEARING : 0
```

Then we pass the DXGI_SWAP_CHAIN_DESC1 we've just filled to the CreateSwapChainForHwnd function along with the window handle InHwnd. We should, however, spend some words on the DXGI_SWAP_CHAIN_DESC1. The purpose of the struct is to describe the swap-chain to the GPU, such that when it comes the time to create it, the creation function will return a swap-chain with characteristics we've just asked.

Again, the main purpose of this chapter is to provide ready-to-use code to make experiment and not to provide a full API reference. You can refer to the official Microsoft documentation for more information about anything we present throughout this chapter.

The fields that are relevant to us in relation with our swap-chain struct are as follows:

- **SwapChainDesc.Width**: The width of the buffers managed by the swap-chain.

- **SwapChainDesc.Height**: The height of the buffers managed by the swap-chain.

- **SwapChainDesc.Format**: The pixel format for the swap-chain buffers.

- **SwapChainDesc.Stereo = FALSE**: Whether we want support for stereo rendering or not (in our case we set it to FALSE).

- **SwapChainDesc.SampleDesc = { 1, 0 }**: This field is used to enable or disable multisample antialiasing (MSAA). In our case, we set 1 for the Count field of the SampleDesc struct and 0 for the Quality field of the same struct, meaning we don't want MSAAed buffers.

- **SwapChainDesc.BufferUsage**: This flag will describe how the resource surface is used and the CPU access options for the backbuffer in our case we set to DXGI_USAGE_RENDER_TARGET_OUTPUT.

- **SwapChainDesc.BufferCount**: The number of buffers this swap-chain will manage (the minimum is two buffers but, in our case, we've specified three buffers such that we can disable vsync and support variable refresh rate displays without incurring in the tearing problem). The tearing problem is present when we disable vsync and we have just two buffers in our swap-chain.

- **SwapChainDesc.Scaling**: This flag is set to decide what resize behavior to use when the size of the backbuffer doesn't match the one of the target output (in our case we've chosen DXGI_SCALING_STRETCH behavior).

- **SwapChainDesc.SwapEffect**: This flag represents the presentation model to adopt during the presentation of the surface and how its content should be handled (in our case we've set DXGI_SWAP_EFFECT_FLIP_DISCARD, meaning we discard the contents of the backbuffer after the presentation, and we left the driver to decide the most efficient presentation technique for the swap-chain).

- **SwapChainDesc.AlphaMode**: This flag identifies the transparency behavior of the swap-chain backbuffer (in our case we've specified DXGI_ALPHA_MODE_UNSPECIFIED, meaning that the transparency behaviour is not specified).

The next function we call will have the effect of disabling full-screen transition with the Alt+Enter accelerator key. We disable it because we want to be able to control the full-screen transition manually by ourselves. Take a look the following code:

```
ThrowIfFailed(dxgiFactory4->MakeWindowAssociation(InhWnd,DXGI_MWA_NO_ALT_ENTER));
```

Finally, we get the index of the current swap-chain backbuffer:

`mBackBufferIndex = dxgiSwapChain4->GetCurrentBackBufferIndex();`

We return the created swap-chain interface pointer:

`return dxgiSwapChain4;`

This is pretty much everything related to the swap-chain creation. With a back buffer index and a swap-chain, we are now ready to create the frame resources and the command list we'll use to record GPU commands. The frame resources creation step is a bit more involved in that it requires additional concepts to be introduced to the reader.

Because DX12 has been designed to give more control to the developer when it comes to resource management, the memory must be explicitly handled by hand. This means that every time we create a resource, we have to also decide how that same resource will be placed in memory. This will also mean that more code is needed when it comes to DX12 compared to DX11, and with great power comes great responsibilities.

Moreover, we will see that when we record commands in our command lists, we will have to synchronize the CPU with the GPU. It happens that while we submit commands, the GPU could still have work in flight, and, therefore, we have to be sure that the GPU has actually finished executing them before we submit further work.

Finally, these are the key points in relation to what we've just mentioned:

- DX12 resources memory management is a key concept to understand.
- CPU-GPU synchronization is also a central part of how a GPU and a CPU interact with each other.

Failing in managing one or the other previous bullet points will open ourselves a world of pain!

Understanding the Frame Resources Creation

Resource creation in DX12 gives us the challenge of choosing the best way to place resources in GPU memory. In this subsection, we will show how we create the resources that we use to handle our rendered frame. But there is more to know besides how we specifically create them and manage them in our application.

CHAPTER 9   DIRECTX 12 AND REAL-TIME RAY TRACING IN DXR

There isn't one "right" way to manage GPU resources, but, rather, there is the right way for a given application domain. This is to say that one game engine will favor one strategy versus another and vice versa based on its needs. However, it is detrimental to know how they are created and stored in memory to be able to take the best decision and strategy given the problem domain.

We will explain how many different types of resources we have and how they are stored in GPU memory. Moreover, you will see also how we can reference them from the CPU.

In DX12 everything that can be bound to the pipeline is a resource or, more precisely, an ID3D12Resource.

When we talk about resources, we most often think about them as resource views. The way we have to access and manage the binding of resources is through the use of descriptors, descriptor tables, descriptor heaps, and root signatures.

There are nine types of resource views:

- **Resources visible to shaders** (i.e., they can be bound to shader registers through the so-called *root signature*)

  - Constant buffer view (CBV)

  - Unordered access view (UAV)

  - Shader resource view (SRV)

  - Samplers

- **Resources that are not visible to shaders** (i.e., they are normally bound to the graphics pipeline with a specific command list call)

  - Render target view (RTV):

    - Command list

      call: ID3D12GraphicsCommandList::OMSetRenderTargets

  - Depth stencil view (DSV)

    - Command list call:

      ID3D12GraphicsCommandList::OMSetRenderTargets

263

- Index buffer view (IBV)
    - Command list call:

        ID3D12GraphicsCommandList::IASetIndexBuffer
- Vertex Buffer view (VBV)
    - Command list call:

        ID3D12GraphicsCommandList::IASetVertexBuffer
- Stream output view (SOV)
    - Command list call:

        ID3D12GraphicsCommandList::SOSetTargets

These resources are described to the GPU with descriptors. A descriptor is an actual C++ struct defined by the DX12 API that we have to fill with valid data to describe our resource.

CBVs, UAVs, and SRVs descriptors can share the same heap space, while all the other types of descriptors will be stored in their own descriptor heap.

The size of CBV, UAV, and SRV descriptors, in particular, can be 32 or 64 bytes depending on the underlying hardware.

Let's take a look at some examples of resource creation. In particular, we will show how to create a heap descriptor to store the descriptors for the render target views (RTVs) of our swap-chain render targets:

```
D3D12_DESCRIPTOR_HEAP_DESC Desc = {};
Desc.NumDescriptors = kMAX_BACK_BUFFER_COUNT;
Desc.Type = D3D12_DESCRIPTOR_HEAP_TYPE_RTV;
ThrowIfFailed(mD3DDevice->CreateDescriptorHeap(&Desc,IID_PPV_
ARGS(&mRTVDescriptorHeap)));
```

First, we declare and initialize our descriptor heap. Then we fill the following fields:

```
Desc.NumDescriptors = kMAX_BACK_BUFFER_COUNT
```

In this case, we are interested in storing render target views (RTVs) descriptor in our heap, which is why we have the flag D3D12_DESCRIPTOR_HEAP_TYPE_RTV.

CHAPTER 9 DIRECTX 12 AND REAL-TIME RAY TRACING IN DXR

The step consists of creating the actual descriptor heap by invoking this:

```
mD3DDevice->CreateDescriptorHeap(&Desc,IID_PPV_ARGS(&mRTVDescriptorHeap))
```

We pass the desc structure and the address of a pointer (i.e., a pointer to pointer) that will be filled with a valid RTV descriptor heap address.

The last step for our swap-chain RTV creation is the one that actually creates the RTVs and places them in each one of the heap slots:

```
CD3DX12_CPU_DESCRIPTOR_HANDLE
RTVHandle(mRTVDescriptorHeap->GetCPUDescriptorHandleForHeapStart());
for (int i = 0; i < kMAX_BACK_BUFFER_COUNT; ++i)
{
    ComPtr<ID3D12Resource> backBuffer;
    ThrowIfFailed(mSwapChain->GetBuffer(i, IID_PPV_ARGS(&backBuffer)));
    mD3DDevice->CreateRenderTargetView(backBuffer.Get(), nullptr,
    RTVHandle);
    mRenderTargets[i] = backBuffer;
    RTVHandle.Offset(mRTVDescriptorSize);
}
```

The first function this code calls is the GetCPUDescriptorHandleForHeapStart() method, which will return the address to the beginning of the heap. The idea is to use it as a base address from which we can retrieve all the other handles (pointers) to the other heap blocks. However, in DX12 we will not have the possibility to access pointers straightaway, but we need to use handles. The handles mechanism protects us from erroneously dereferencing pointers that might not be valid.

Then we perform a loop for each of our backbuffer by getting a pointer to our backbuffer resource from the swap-chain by invoking the method GetBuffer. The first parameter is the index to the i-th buffer, and the second is the address of a pointer that we will use as a reference.

Then given the descriptor handle RTVHandle and the backbuffer pointer, we create the actual association between the descriptor and the actual backbuffer ID3D12Resource.

Finally, we cache our backbuffer pointer to the current array index mRenderTargets[i].

CHAPTER 9   DIRECTX 12 AND REAL-TIME RAY TRACING IN DXR

Then we advance to the next heap block by calling the function `Offset` (last line in the loop body) on the `RTVHandle`. We advance exactly by `mRTVDescriptorSize` (i.e., the size of one descriptor).

That's everything we need to do to create our RTVs heap descriptor and resources.

Remember that there is a difference between a descriptor and a resource, and they don't have to be confused. A resource is the actual memory that holds the actual data, while a descriptor is a description to the GPU of that resource.

To recap, we have three ways around resource memory management and binding. We've listed them here:

- Descriptors
- Descriptor heaps
- Descriptor tables
- Root signatures

We will dedicate a subsection to briefly describe all the previous descriptors, heaps, tables, and root signatures. However, what we are interested in now is to explain the last steps that will conclude the so-called pipeline initialization process, as depicted in Figure 9-6.

We are left with two additional steps:

- Command allocators creation
- Command list creation

A command list doesn't have to be confused with a command queue. A command queue will execute one or more command lists. A command list or a command buffer is, instead, employed to record commands to be executed by the GPU on a queue.

So, for the command allocator, we need to create as many commands allocator as are the total number of swap-chain backbuffers (in our case three).

Take a look at the following code snippet for the command allocator creation:

```
ComPtr<ID3D12CommandAllocator>
Ray_DX12HardwareRenderer::CreateCommandAllocator( ComPtr<ID3D12Device2>
InDevice, D3D12_COMMAND_LIST_TYPE InType )
```

```
{
    ComPtr<ID3D12CommandAllocator> CommandAllocator;
    ThrowIfFailed( InDevice->CreateCommandAllocator(InType,IID_PPV_
    ARGS(&CommandAllocator)) );
    return CommandAllocator;
}
```

In the previous code, we will create a command allocator for a given type of command list. We wrapped that code in a function called CreateCommandAllocator, which is defined in our class Ray_DX12HardwareRenderer.

```
for (int i = 0; i < kMAX_BACK_BUFFER_COUNT; ++i)
{
    mD3DCommandAllocator[i] = CreateCommandAllocator(mD3DDevice,D3D12_
    COMMAND_LIST_TYPE_DIRECT);
}
```

In the previous code snippet for each buffer in the swap-chain, we create a command allocator. A command allocator is where a command list stores the actual commands. We need a command allocator for each backbuffer, because we might have commands recorded in each of three potential buffered frames.

The command list creation is pretty straightforward, as you can see in the following code:

```
ComPtr<ID3D12GraphicsCommandList4>
Ray_DX12HardwareRenderer::CreateCommandList( ComPtr<ID3D12Device2> InDevice
                                            , ComPtr<ID3D12CommandAllocator>
                                            InCommandAllocator
                                            , D3D12_COMMAND_LIST_
                                            TYPE InType)
{
    ComPtr<ID3D12GraphicsCommandList4> CommandList;
    ThrowIfFailed(InDevice->CreateCommandList(0, InType,
    InCommandAllocator.Get(), nullptr, IID_PPV_ARGS(&CommandList)));
    //Before to reset a command list, we must close it because it is created
    in recording state.
```

```
    ThrowIfFailed(CommandList->Close());
    return CommandList;
}
```

We create a command list version 4 (`ID3D12GraphicsCommandList4`), because this is the version that supports recording for ray tracing commands as well. To create a command list, we pass a command allocator and an address to a command list pointer.

Then we make a call to a D3D12 function called `CreateCommandList` to create the actual command list. We finally close the command list, because when it's first created, it's in recording state. We don't need for the command list to record any command at the moment of its creation.

```
mD3DCommandList =
CreateCommandList(mD3DDevice,mD3DCommandAllocator[mBackBufferIndex],D3D12_
COMMAND_LIST_TYPE_DIRECT);
```

As we did for the command allocator creation part, even for the command list creation we've created a method in our framework that wraps the actual D3D12 command list code creation. As a side note, it would be better to refactor the code and make a separate interface for the command list type. This will help if we want to support different graphics API interfaces.

Our `CreateCommandList` will take the D3D12 device, the current command allocator given the backbuffer index, and the type of list we want to create (i.e., `D3D12_COMMAND_LIST_TYPE_DIRECT`). It will return a valid command list stored in `mD3DCommandList` data member.

The pipeline creation process concludes with the command list creation. You can actually check again in Figure 9-6 as a refresher for the steps.

As we mentioned, we have one more subsection left. We will concentrate on descriptor heaps, descriptor tables, and root signatures.

Understanding DX12 Descriptors Management and Root Signatures

When it comes to descriptors, we have to think about a C/C++ struct that has, as the main scope, to describe a GPU resource to the GPU itself. However, we need to have a way to store a collection of descriptors, and that is what exactly heaps are.

CHAPTER 9   DIRECTX 12 AND REAL-TIME RAY TRACING IN DXR

Descriptor heaps are collections of descriptors. A descriptor can be 32 or 64 bytes in size, and that size is hardware dependent. Therefore, we should always query explicitly for the descriptor size.

The descriptor heap is represented in Figure 9-7.

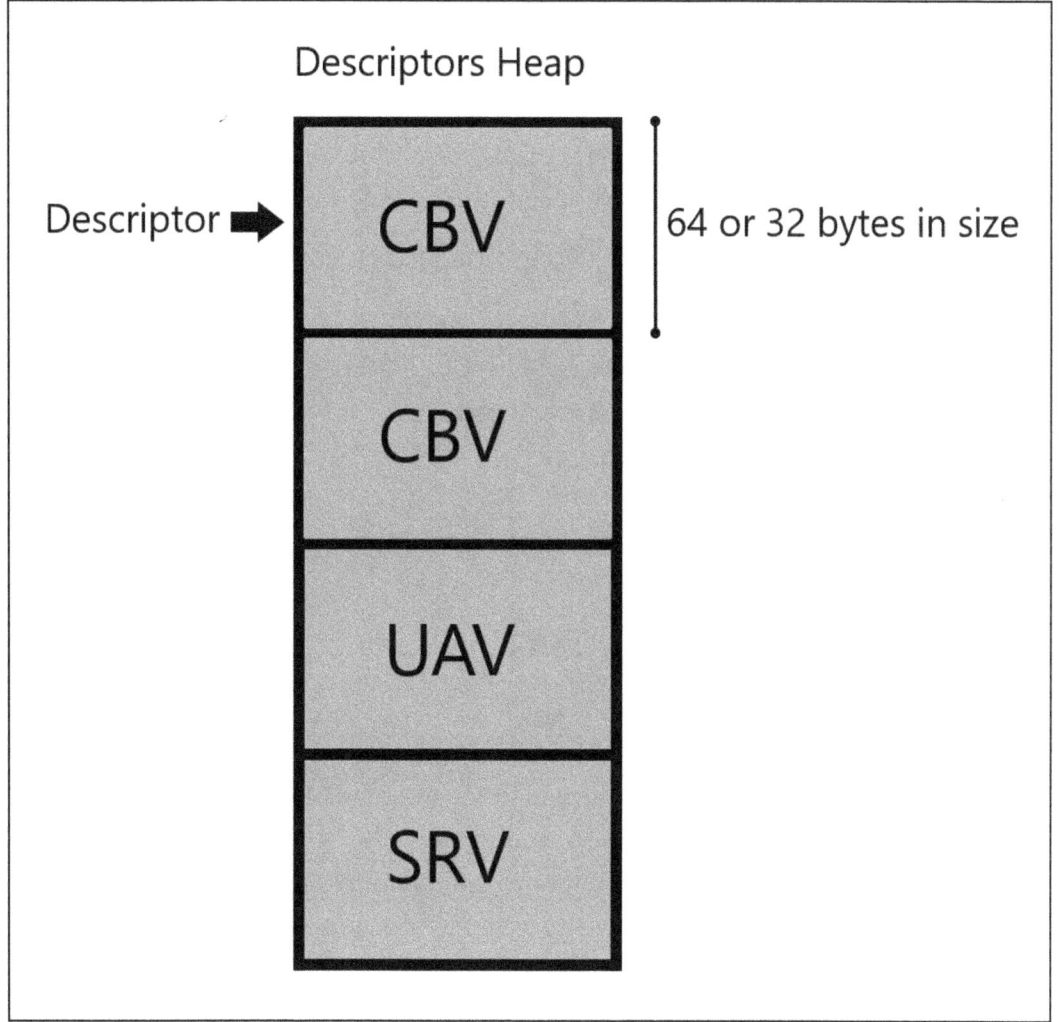

Figure 9-7. *Descriptor heap containing four descriptors: 2 CBV, 1 UAV, and 1 SRV*

Now let's see how we can declare in real code the descriptor heap depicted in Figure 9-7.

As you can see, we first declare the descriptor heap, initializing with zero (initializing with zero a D3D12 struct will have the effect to give default values to each struct field):

```
D3D12_DESCRIPTOR_HEAP_DESC DescriptorHeapDesc = {};
```

Then for the most important field, this is where we specify which type of descriptors will end up in our heap (in our case we ask for a heap for CBV, SRV, and UAV):

```
DescriptorHeapDesc.Type = D3D12_DESCRIPTOR_HEAP_TYPE_CBV_SRV_UAV;
```

Then we want to specify if we want for the descriptors to be visible to the shaders. We need to have them visible; therefore, we specify this necessity like in the following code:

```
DescriptorHeapDesc.Flags = D3D12_DESCRIPTOR_HEAP_FLAG_SHADER_VISIBLE;
```

We set the last field to zero. This field will identify the adapter to which the descriptor applies in the context of multiple adapters. Since we are working with just one adapter, we set it to zero, which means single-adapter operations.

```
DescriptorHeapDesc.NodeMask = 0;
```

Finally, we are ready to create our descriptor heap by making a call to a specific device method:

```
mD3DDevice->CreateDescriptorHeap(&DescriptorHeapDesc,IID_PPV_
ARGS(&mCBVSRVDescriptorHeap));
```

We pass the struct we've just filled in as the first parameter, and we get a pointer back from the second parameter. The second parameter is of type `ID3D12DescriptorHeap` and is declared as a data member in our framework class.

So, we end up having a valid descriptor heap pointer referenced by our `mCBVSRVDescriptorHeap` variable.

So, the same process applies the other types of descriptors, i.e., RTVs, DSVs, SOVs, and samplers. The only difference is that they will have to be in their own descriptor heap. So, for example, if we want to create a heap to store four RTVs, we will have the same field filled as in the previous code with the exception of the type field.

Take a look at the following code:

```
D3D12_DESCRIPTOR_HEAP_DESC Desc = {};
Desc.NumDescriptors = 4;
Desc.Type = D3D12_DESCRIPTOR_HEAP_TYPE_RTV;
```

```
Desc.NodeMask = 0;
ThrowIfFailed(mD3DDevice->CreateDescriptorHeap(&Desc,IID_PPV_
ARGS(&mRTVDescriptorHeap)));
```

The only difference is the type of descriptor heap we are going to create; in fact, the type field is specifying heap type RTV.

Have a look the following code:

```
Desc.Type = D3D12_DESCRIPTOR_HEAP_TYPE_RTV;
```

We ask for a total of four RTVs to be stored in our descriptor heap. The fact that the number of descriptors is the same for the RTV as one of the CBV/UAV/SRV ones is just coincidence. We can create as many descriptors as we want by still keeping the total number within the hardware limits of course.

We could give an example for DSV and samplers, but they would be pretty much identical to the previous one. The only exception would be in type field. For samplers we would have this:

```
Desc.Type = D3D12_DESCRIPTOR_HEAP_TYPE_SAMPLER;
```

We would have this for DSVs:

```
Desc.Type = D3D12_DESCRIPTOR_HEAP_TYPE_DSV;
```

That is pretty much everything for descriptor heap creation.

There is one exception, though, that we haven't talked about, and that is related to IBVs and VBVs (index buffer views and vertex buffer views). In fact, they don't have specific heap types and, therefore, are passed directly to API methods.

In our samples we are not drawing meshes by using the standard rasterization pipeline, because we want to mainly illustrate the new ray tracing DXR API. In fact, as we will see, the vertex buffer and index buffer will be passed to the acceleration structure creation routines and not used to create the actual VBVs and IBVs.

Now that we know how to create a descriptor heap for any type of resource, we want to understand how we can allocate a resource to the memory heap ID3D12Heap.

Memory heap *and* ***descriptor heap*** *are two different types of memory. They play different roles. The first is a subportion of GPU memory where we place a resource. The second one is a portion of GPU memory where we place descriptors. The descriptors represent views to the GPU resources stored in one or more resource heaps.*

Let's see how many allocation strategies we can use in D3D12 to allocate GPU resources.

Understanding GPU Resources Allocation Strategies in D3D12

First of all, GPU resources are allocated in a so-called memory heap. The type in D3D12 that represents this type of heap is ID3D12Heap (not to be confused with ID3D12DescriptorHeap).

There are three allocation methods for GPU resources:

- **Committed resources**: Both the resource and an implicit heap are created at the same time. The size of the created heap is big enough to fit the resource. A committed resource is created by calling the ID3D12Device::CreateCommittedResource method.

- **Placed resources**: This type of allocation strategy will give more responsability to the programmer. To create this type of resource, there are two steps:

  - Create a heap of type ID3D12Heap by calling ID3D12Device::CreateHeap.

  - Create the actual resource providing an offset inside the heap created previously by calling ID3D12Device::CreatedReservedResource.

- **Reserved resources**: We can create reserved resources without specifying a heap. The resources that we create can be bigger than a given heap. The idea is that we can map a subportion of our big resource to a given heap. The process to create a reserved resource involves a call to ID3D12Device::CreateReservedResource. To map a subportion of a resource to a given heap, we need to call ID3D12Device::UpdateTileMappings.

A use case for the third type of allocation strategy (i.e., reserved resources) can be, for example, the allocation of a big terrain heightmap texture as a GPU resource and the progressive mapping of subportions of it as the camera moves in the terrain world.

However, in most cases, the first allocation strategy is generally used. If we need to create texture resources, constant buffers, or statically sized resource (i.e., the resource size doesn't change), committed resources are the way to go. Moreover, we can create larger resources in an upload heap if we need to upload dynamic resources like vertex buffer or index buffer.

Take a look at the following code to see an example of how we create a committed resource and the corresponding descriptor:

```
const u32 CBufferSize = (sizeof(SceneConstants) +
(D3D12_CONSTANT_BUFFER_DATA_PLACEMENT_ALIGNMENT - 1)) &
~(D3D12_CONSTANT_BUFFER_DATA_PLACEMENT_ALIGNMENT - 1); // must be a
multiple 256 bytes

ThrowIfFailed( mD3DDevice->CreateCommittedResource(
&CD3DX12_HEAP_PROPERTIES(D3D12_HEAP_TYPE_UPLOAD),
                    D3D12_HEAP_FLAG_NONE,
                    &CD3DX12_RESOURCE_DESC::Buffer(CBufferSize),
                    D3D12_RESOURCE_STATE_GENERIC_READ,
                    nullptr,
                    IID_PPV_ARGS(&mSceneConstantsCB)) );
CD3DX12_RANGE readRange(0, 0);
ThrowIfFailed(mSceneConstantsCB->Map(0, &readRange,reinterpret_
cast<void**(&mScenConstantsCB_DataPtr)));

D3D12_CONSTANT_BUFFER_VIEW_DESC CBVDesc = {};
CBVDesc.SizeInBytes = CBufferSize;
CBVDesc.BufferLocation = mSceneConstantsCB->GetGPUVirtualAddress();

auto DescriptorHeapCpuBase = mCBVSRVDescriptorHeap->GetCPUDescriptorHandleForHeapStart();
auto CBufferCPUHandle = CD3DX12_CPU_DESCRIPTOR_
HANDLE(DescriptorHeapCpuBase);
CBufferCPUHandle.Offset(mDescriptorSize);
mD3DDevice->CreateConstantBufferView(&CBVDesc, CBufferCPUHandle);
```

In the previous code, we created a constant buffer (CB) in a heap of type upload. This means we'd like to update the CB every frame and copy a bunch of data into it (e.g., think about a CB data that changes per draw). To this purpose, we actually map the memory of the CB resource `ID3D12Resource::Map` to get a CPU-side pointer that we can use to reference the CB memory. In this way, anytime we need to upload our data, we can perform a memcpy of our data on that pointer (it will be our destination pointer).

Then we create a descriptor view struct `D3D12_CONSTANT_BUFFER_VIEW_DESC` and we fill it, by specifying the constant buffer size CBufferSize and the GPU virtual address of the just created resource by calling `ID3D12Resource::GetGPUVirtualAddress` on the resource itself. Then we get our CPU heap base descriptor handle, which is basically a handle to reference the start of our descriptor heap. Then we create a handle to place our CBV descriptor, and we offset the handle in order to place it in the correct place in our descriptor heap. In the end, we call `ID3D12Device::CreateConstantBufferView` by providing the CBV desc struct and the CB handle. With this last step, we actually create the descriptor associated with the CB resource, specifying which slot in the descriptor the heap will end up being in.

When we create constant buffer resources, we must align their size to a multiple of 256 bytes. This is what the first line of code in our previous code block is doing.

The alignment to a power of two size is achieved in general with the following code:

```
size_t RoundedUpSize = (SomeDataSize + Aligment - 1) & ~(Alignment - 1)
```

The previous line of code is actually performing a round-up of the value SomeDataSize to the next multiple of alignment. Some hardware platforms require you to have some of their data structures to be aligned to some value. Most of the time the alignment is a power of two, which is convenient because we can round up (or down depending on what we need to achieve) with the previous line of code.

If aligment is not a power of two, then the previous code will not work.

Now that we mentioned the three main types of resource allocation schemes, we are ready to explain how we can actually pass parameters to shaders.

To specify which parameters a shader will access, we need to create a so-called root signature. The root signature is defined to be a binding convention that we define up front. Pretty much all the mapping and the shader type parameter definition will happen here.

Understanding Root Signature

We can think about a root signature like an API function signature where we define a comma-separated list of parameters. These parameters will represent the function arguments. Every entry in the root signature is a root parameter while the actual values set and changed at runtime are called *root arguments*.

The root signature can contain three types of parameters:

- *Root constants* (constants inlined in the root arguments): They cost zero levels of indirection

- *Root descriptors* (descriptors inlined in the root arguments): They cost one level of indirection.

- *Descriptor tables* (pointers to a range of descriptors in the descriptor heap): They cost two levels of indirection.

It appears to be obvious that the less levels of indirections, the better in terms of how fast we get to read the resource. However, we have to keep in mind that the maximum memory footprint for a root signature is 64 DWORDs. Let's remember that 1 DWORD is equal to 32 bits (or 4 bytes). So, we have to be careful to not go past that limit and, in general, keep the root signature as small as possible for performance reasons.

Keeping the root signature small means to favor descriptor tables versus root constants and root descriptors (remember that they are inlined/embedded in the root signature; therefore, they eat up root signature space).

In general, how we define the size of the root signature is always application dependent. The parameters should be sorted based on different criteria, such as the following:

- Frequency of updates, for example

- The need for low access latency

The DX12 types that are important for the root signature creation are:

- CD3DX12_ROOT_PARAMETER1 (it actually represents a root signature parameter)

- CD3DX12_DESCRIPTOR_RANGE1 (used particularly when we need to define a range for a descriptor table)

CHAPTER 9 DIRECTX 12 AND REAL-TIME RAY TRACING IN DXR

Therefore, if we need to create a root signature with four parameters and one descriptor table, we would do something like this in code:

```
CD3DX12_ROOT_PARAMETER1 RootParameters[4];
CD3DX12_DESCRIPTOR_RANGE1 DescRange;
DescRange.Init(D3D12_DESCRIPTOR_RANGE_SRV,2,0); // t0-t1
RootParameters[0].InitAsConstants(2,0); // 2 constants at b0
RootParameters[1].InitAsConstantBufferView(0,5,D3D12_ROOT_DESCRIPTOR_FLAG_
DATA_STATIC); // CBV at b5
RootParameters[2].InitAsDescriptorTable(1,&DescRange);
RootParameters[3].InitAsConstants(4,1); // 4 constants at b1
```

In the previous code, we initialize space for a descriptor table and a total of four parameters for our root signature. Then this is what happens:

```
DescRange.Init(D3D12_DESCRIPTOR_RANGE_SRV,2,0);
```

We create a range for our descriptor table for a SRV that is mapping to exactly two shader registers, t0-t1.

```
RootParameters[0].InitAsConstants(2,0); // 2 constants at b0
```

Then we create the first root signature parameter by creating two 32-bit root constants at shader register b0:

```
RootParameters[1].InitAsConstantBufferView(0,5,D3D12_ROOT_DESCRIPTOR_FLAG_
DATA_STATIC); // CBV at b5
```

We create a constant buffer view type of parameter starting at shader register b5 and register space 0, as you can tell from the first two parameters. Then we specify a flag in the third parameter that is data static. The documentation doesn't say much about this flag except that, if specified, the driver will be able to do special optimizations:

```
RootParameters[2].InitAsDescriptorTable(1,&DescRange);
```

We then create one descriptor table type of a parameter by passing our previously defined desc range and specifying just one descriptor range in the first argument of the InitAsDescriptorTable function:

```
RootParameters[3].InitAsConstants(4,1); // 4 constants at b1
```

As we did for the first root parameter, we create four 32-bit constants at shader register b1.

This is one example of root signature creation. We will see that, when DXR comes into play, we will have two types of root signatures:

- Global root signatures (parameters are bound directly from the command list)
- Local root signatures (parameters are pulled out from the shader table)

This distinction has been introduced to differentiate between parameters that are pulled out from the shader table and parameters that are bound directly from the command list.

Moreover, this was the only way in which parameters could be bound before DXR. We know about two root signature versions:

- D3D_ROOT_SIGNATURE_VERSION_1_0: This is the first version that was introduced when the DX12 API was released.
- D3D_ROOT_SIGNATURE_VERSION_1_1: This is the second version that was released as it allows for the option for drivers to make optimizations by knowing that some descriptors or the memory they point to. It's static for some period of time.

To be sure to target root signature version 1.1, you need to install the Windows 10 Anniversary Update SDK. Do it if you haven't already done so. The chance to let the driver optimize where possible is always very convenient.

For more examples of root signature creation, the Microsoft documentation related to the DX12 programming guide is quite complete. It's possible to find different scenarios for root signature creation there. We can find examples of any combination of constant root parameters/constant root descriptor and descriptor tables.

In the example code that comes with this chapter, we create a global and a local root signature. They will be used to set parameters for our ray tracing shaders (remember we need a local and a global root signature if we are working with the DXR API).

CHAPTER 9   DIRECTX 12 AND REAL-TIME RAY TRACING IN DXR

We handle the local and global root signature creation in the following function. The first part of the function is devoted to the creation of the global root signature. Take a look at the following code:

```
void Ray_DX12HardwareRenderer::CreateRootSignatures()
{
   D3D12_FEATURE_DATA_ROOT_SIGNATURE featureData = {};

   featureData.HighestVersion = D3D_ROOT_SIGNATURE_VERSION_1_1;

   if(FAILED(mD3DDevice->CheckFeatureSupport( D3D12_FEATURE_ROOT_SIGNATURE
                                            , &featureData
                                            , sizeof(featureData))) )
   {
      featureData.HighestVersion = D3D_ROOT_SIGNATURE_VERSION_1_0;
   }

   // Global Root Signature
   // This is a root signature that is shared across all raytracing shaders
   invoked during a DispatchRays() call.
   {
     CD3DX12_DESCRIPTOR_RANGE1 DescriptorRangeUAV;
     CD3DX12_DESCRIPTOR_RANGE1 DescriptorRangeCBV;

     // We want to define a bounding convention for descriptor that fall in
     the range of UAV types.
     DescriptorRangeUAV.Init(D3D12_DESCRIPTOR_RANGE_TYPE_UAV, 1, 0);
     CD3DX12_ROOT_PARAMETER1 RootParameters[GlobalRootSignatureParams::Co
     unt] = {};

     // UAV used to store ray tracing results (color buffer that will be
     used by the ray tracer to store the color)
     RootParameters[GlobalRootSignatureParams::OutputViewSlot].
     InitAsDescriptorTable(1, &DescriptorRangeUAV);

     // Scene Constant buffer
     DescriptorRangeCBV.Init(D3D12_DESCRIPTOR_RANGE_TYPE_CBV, 1, 1,
     0,D3D12_DESCRIPTOR_RANGE_FLAG_DATA_STATIC);
```

```
    RootParameters[GlobalRootSignatureParams::SceneConstantBuffer].
    InitAsDescriptorTable(1, &DescriptorRangeCBV);

    //Parameter mapping for the Top Level Acceleration structurepassed for
    ray tracing

    RootParameters[GlobalRootSignatureParams::AccelerationStructureSlot].
    InitAsShaderResourceView(0);
    CD3DX12_VERSIONED_ROOT_SIGNATURE_DESC GlobalRootSignatureDesc(ARRAYSIZE
    (RootParameters), RootParameters);

    SerializeAndCreateRaytracingRootSignature(GlobalRootSignatureDesc,
                                              &mRaytracingGlobalRootSignature
                                              ,featureData.HighestVersion);

    NAME_D3D12_OBJECT(mRaytracingGlobalRootSignature);
}
```

the function continues with the creation of the local root signature:

```
// Local Root Signature
// This is a root signature that enables a shader to have unique arguments
that come from shader tables.
  {
    CD3DX12_ROOT_PARAMETER
    RootParameters[LocalRootSignatureParams::Count];
    RootParameters[LocalRootSignatureParams::ViewportConstantSlot].
    InitAsConstants(SizeOfInU    int32(mRayGenCB), 0, 0);
    CD3DX12_VERSIONED_ROOT_SIGNATURE_DESC LocalRootSignatureDesc(ARRAYSIZE(
    RootParameters), RootParameters);
    // D3D12_ROOT_SIGNATURE_FLAG_LOCAL_ROOT_SIGNATURE - Denies the domain
    shader access to the root sig    nature
    // TODO: Check how this flag is related to ray tracing pipeline
    LocalRootSignatureDesc.Desc_1_1.Flags = D3D12_ROOT_SIGNATURE_FLAG_
    LOCAL_ROOT_SIGNATURE;
    SerializeAndCreateRaytracingRootSignature(LocalRootSignatureDesc,
                                              &mRaytracingLocalRootSignature,
                                              featureData.HighestVersion);
```

CHAPTER 9   DIRECTX 12 AND REAL-TIME RAY TRACING IN DXR

```
    NAME_D3D12_OBJECT(mRaytracingLocalRootSignature);
  }
}
```

Now let's try to understand what's happening in the previous code block. We will describe every step to better clarify the role of each parameter defined in the two root signatures.

The beginning of the function `CreateRootSignatures()` will be devoted to check what the highest root signature version supported is:

```
D3D12_FEATURE_DATA_ROOT_SIGNATURE featureData = {};
featureData.HighestVersion = D3D_ROOT_SIGNATURE_VERSION_1_1;
if(FAILED(mD3DDevice->CheckFeatureSupport(D3D12_FEATURE_ROOT_SIGNATURE,&featureData,sizeof(featureData))))
{
    featureData.HighestVersion = D3D_ROOT_SIGNATURE_VERSION_1_0;
}
```

`D3D_ROOT_SIGNATURE_VERSION_1_1` is the highest version the sample supports. If `CheckFeatureSupport` succeeds, the `HighestVersion` returned will not be greater than this. If our check fails, then we will fall back to `D3D_ROOT_SIGNATURE_VERSION_1_0`.

Then we proceed with global root signature creation. Take a look at the following code snippet:

```
CD3DX12_DESCRIPTOR_RANGE1 DescriptorRangeUAV;
CD3DX12_DESCRIPTOR_RANGE1 DescriptorRangeCBV;

// We want to define a bounding convention for descriptor that fall in the range of UAV types.
DescriptorRangeUAV.Init(D3D12_DESCRIPTOR_RANGE_TYPE_UAV, 1, 0);
CD3DX12_ROOT_PARAMETER1 RootParameters[GlobalRootSignatureParams::Count] = {};

// UAV used to store ray tracing results (color buffer that will be used by the ray tracer to store the color)
RootParameters[GlobalRootSignatureParams::OutputViewSlot].
InitAsDescriptorTable(1, &DescriptorRangeUAV);
```

CHAPTER 9 DIRECTX 12 AND REAL-TIME RAY TRACING IN DXR

```
DescriptorRangeCBV.Init(D3D12_DESCRIPTOR_RANGE_TYPE_CBV, 1, 1,0,D3D12_
DESCRIPTOR_RANGE_FLAG_DATA_STATIC);
RootParameters[GlobalRootSignatureParams::SceneConstantBuffer].InitAsDescri
ptorTable(1,&DescriptorRangeCB);
```

The global root signature is shared across our ray tracing shaders. In this specific case, we prepare to create two descriptor tables, specifically for UAV and CBV. For the descriptor range related to the UAV buffer, we specify exactly 1 descriptor and 0 for the base shader register (the register space is defaulting to 0). Then we've defined exactly GlobalRootSignatureParams::Count number of root paramters of type CD3DX12_ROOT_PARAMETER1. We create the UAV parameter as a descriptor table, and the root parameter in this case is indexed by GlobalRootSignatureParams::OutputViewSlot.

The scene constant buffer is created next. We first create the descriptor table asking for one descriptor starting at shader register 1 and shader register space to be 0. Finally, we ask for this descriptor to be static by specifying the flag D3D12_DESCRIPTOR_RANGE_FLAG_DATA_STATIC. Then we create the actual descriptor table for our scene constant buffer by making a call to InitAsDescriptorTable, specifying one descriptor and passing the address to the range variable.

GlobalRootSignatureParams is a namespace containing a value enum type defined just for clarity. It is not necessary per se, but it helps in clarifying the role of each global root signature parameter. Look at the following code snippet to better understand how it is defined:

```
// Handy way to the define global root parameters slot mapping
namespace GlobalRootSignatureParams
{
    enum Value
    {
        OutputViewSlot = 0, // UAV slot
        AccelerationStructureSlot, // Acceleration structure slot
        SceneConstantBuffer, // Scene Constant buffer
        Count // Total number of global signature in use
    };
}
```

CHAPTER 9   DIRECTX 12 AND REAL-TIME RAY TRACING IN DXR

This definition is located in `ShaderParameters.h`, which is part of the framework that comes with this book.

We can see, in Figure 9-8, a representation of what a root signature is to a shader.

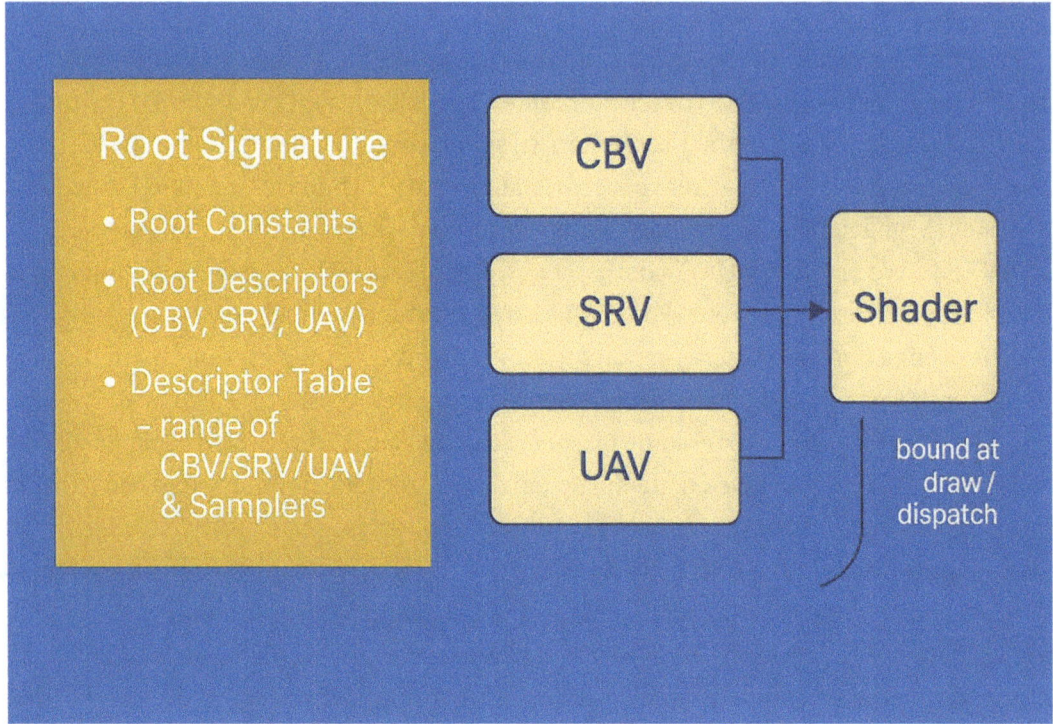

Figure 9-8. Root signature conceptual representation

Then there is one more bit to explain, and that is the synchronization of the CPU with the GPU during command list execution

The next section will go through this process by explaining how the whole process works. In this context, fence objects and operating system events are key concepts to understand how to achieve CPUGPU synchronization.

Understanding CPU-GPU Synchronization and Command Lists

When we want to execute "work" on the GPU, we need to first populate a command list with commands and then execute it on a command queue. By that moment on, your work/commands will be in flight on the GPU for execution. These commands can be any

CHAPTER 9   DIRECTX 12 AND REAL-TIME RAY TRACING IN DXR

among draw-call, compute dispatch, copy resource commands, and dispatch of rays if we are ray tracing our scene.

When the GPU is executing commands, we have to wait for that work to finish before we move to the next frame. This kind of synchronization is achieved by the use of a fence object, a fence value, and an operating system event.

The D3D12 fence object is ID3D12Fence. The fence value is a 64-bit integer value that gets incremented any time we step to the next frame, and the event is a classic win32 event.

We can achieve this kind of synchronization in two ways. The first is the simple one, but it is also not the way to go. The second one is the preferred way among the two.

For the first approach we do something like this (pseudocode):

- CommandQueue->ExecuteCommandLists(...)
- SwapChain->Present(...)
- WaitForGPUToFinish()

The synchronization magic happens inside the function WaitForGPUToFinish(). The code looks like the following:

```
void WaitForGPUToFinish()
{
    FenceValueToBeReached = FenceValue;
    CommandQueue->Signal(FenceObject,FenceValueToBeReached);
    ++FenceValue;
    if(FenceObject->GetCompletedValue() < FenceValueToBeReached)
    {
        FenceObject->SetValueOnCompletion(FenceValueToBeReached,FenceEvent);
        WaitForSingleObject(FenceEvent,INFINITE);
    }
    mFrameIndex = mSwapChain->GetCurrentBackBufferIndex();
}
```

Before we describe the previous code block, we have to highlight a few things. When the fence object is first created, in this case its initial value is set to 0, and the FenceValue counter will start from 1. This is because when we issue commands to the command list, we have to put ourselves in a scenario where the initial fence value is always smaller than the one to be reached. This will make sense out of the if statement in the WaitForGPUToFinish() function.

Let's take a look at Figure 9-9 for a better explanation.

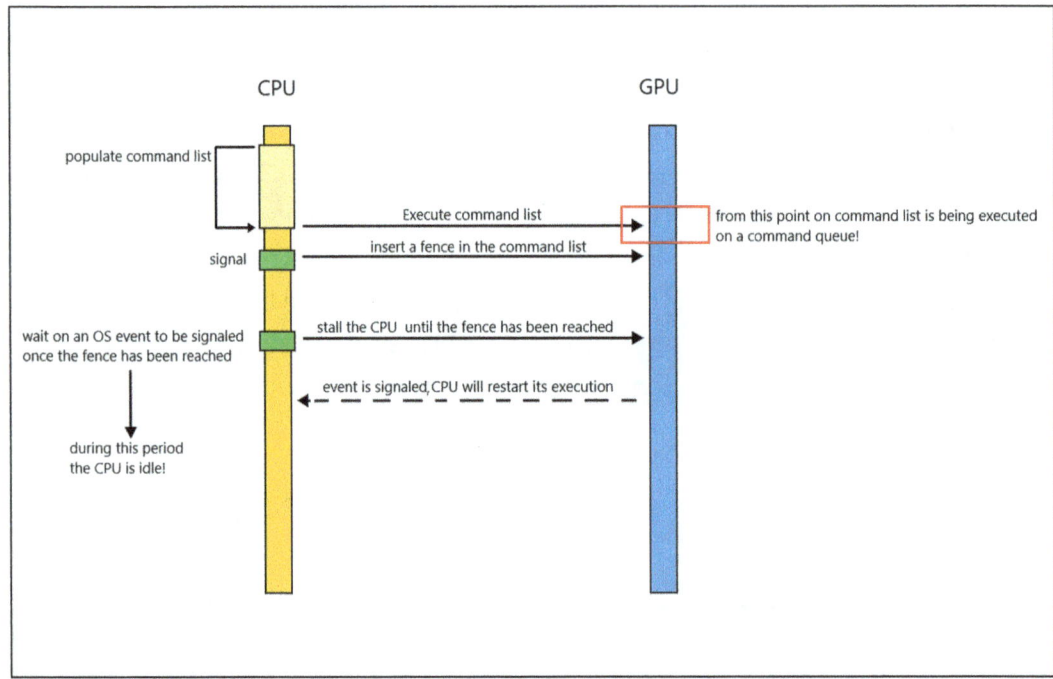

Figure 9-9. *CPU-GPU synchronization where we stall the CPU until the GPU has reached the fence*

As you can tell from Figure 9-9, we stall the CPU thread before the work in flight on the GPU is not completed (signaling the command queue on the GPU). See the solid arrow that calls `Signal(<frame index>)`.

We wait for the previous frame to complete before proceeding by calling `WaitForGPUToFinish(<frame index>)`.

Then, when the fence value is reached, the GPU signals back the CPU thread (dashed arrow in Figure 9-9), and we can proceed to the next frame.

Despite this method works well, it is not the best in practice. Stalling the CPU to wait for GPU work to finish is not good for parallelism and for better GPU utilization.

The second approach will solve this. In this case, we don't stall the CPU because we create two command allocators and two fence values. We use the two fence values to track the progression of each list of commands related to each command allocator.

When it's time to move to the next frame, we track the fence value of the previous frame to be sure it's been reached.

We do so by comparing the previous frame fence value against the current frame value, if that value is greater or equal than the current frame one (normally it's equal), then we don't stall the CPU, and we can proceed to the next frame. Most of the time the previous frame work is usually completed, and therefore, in many cases we end up moving to the next frame without blocking at all.

In other words, in most cases, we don't block, but if there is a chance that the GPU did not finish to render the previous frame, then, and only then, we block the CPU to let the GPU to catch up.

The difference between the first method compared to the second method is that, in the second case, we track the advancement of two or more frames simultaneously. In the first case we don't, because we just wait on one fence value all the time before moving to the next frame.

The key to implement the second better synchronization strategy for two or more frames swap-chain is to have the following:

- *Two or more command allocators*

- *Two or more fence values*

We stall the CPU only if the GPU didn't finish executing the previous frame commands. So, in many cases we don't block at all, and the CPU stall is very limited to the previously mentioned case.

The idea is to queue up one more frame instead of always waiting for the previous one to finish.

Let's take a look at the following code:

```
void MoveToNextFrame()
{
    // Schedule a Signal command in the queue.
    const u64 CurrentFenceValue = mFenceValues[mFrameIndex];
    mCommandQueue->Signal(mFence.Get(), CurrentFenceValue);
    // Update the frame index.
    mFrameIndex = mSwapChain->GetCurrentBackBufferIndex();
    // If the next frame is not ready to be rendered yet, wait until it
    is ready.
```

```
    if (mFence->GetCompletedValue() < mFenceValues[mFrameIndex])
    {
        ThrowIfFailed(mFence->SetEventOnCompletion(mFenceValues[
        mFrameIndex],mFenceEvent));
        WaitForSingleObjectEx(mFenceEvent, INFINITE, FALSE);
    }
    // Set the fence value for the next frame.
    m_fenceValues[mFrameIndex] = CurrentFenceValue + 1;
}
```

We signal the queue with the current fence value, get the frame index for the next backbuffer, and finally check whether the current frame has been rendered. Basically, we check whether the current frame fence value is greater than or equal to the next frame one. If yes, we won't block, and we will be ready to render the next frame. This mechanism allows us to skip the CPU blocking step.

Take a look at Figure 9-10 to better understand what the second approach is about.

CHAPTER 9 DIRECTX 12 AND REAL-TIME RAY TRACING IN DXR

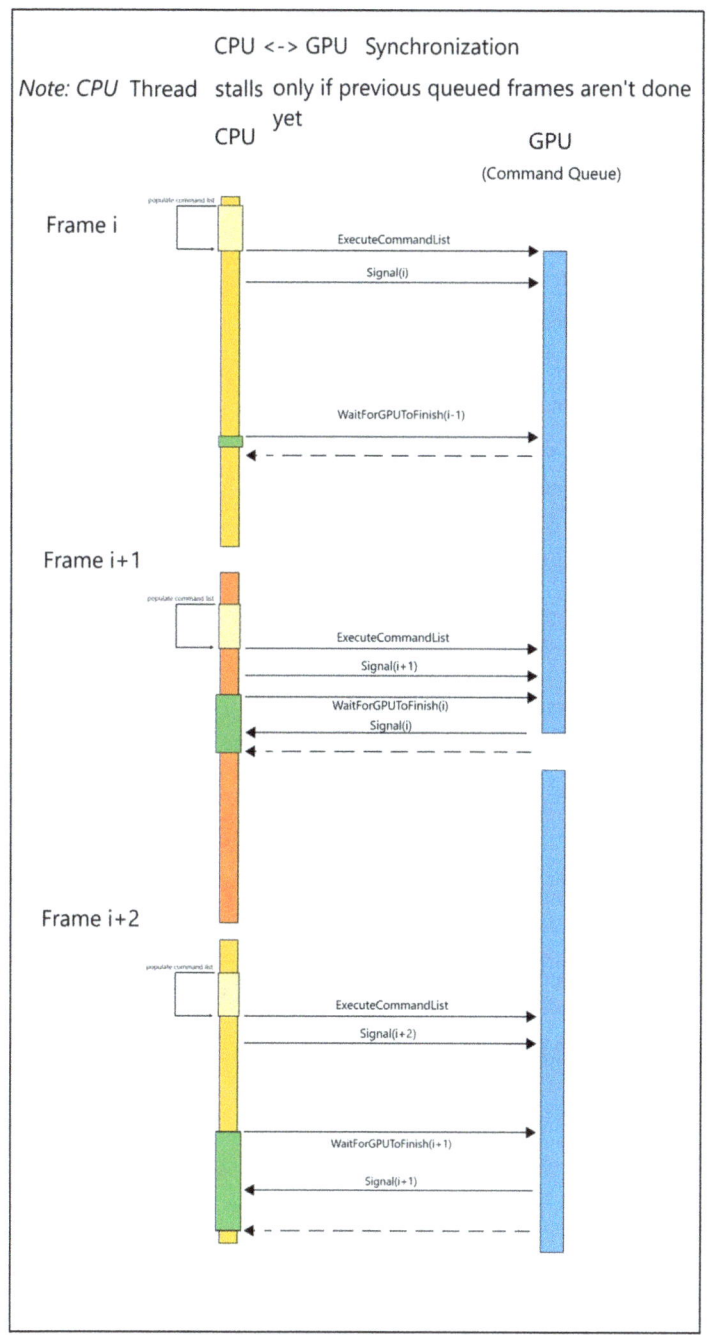

Figure 9-10. *CPU-GPU synchronization where we let one or more frames queue up, avoiding to stall the CPU all the times (this is the preferred way)*

Chapter 9 DirectX 12 and Real-Time Ray Tracing in DXR

As you can see in Figure 9-10, stalling the CPU will prevent us from reaching maximum parallelization. The second approach outlined in Figure 9-10 will let us queue one or more frames, but in this case, we stall only if the currently executed frame(s) did not reach the fence, and, therefore, we wouldn't be able to move to process the next frame.

We now have covered the basic steps to prepare the application for the DXR initialization part. For the remainder of this chapter, we will concentrate on describing the steps needed to create the acceleration structures, the shader tables, and the link between the local root signature with the shader table and the shader themselves. Remember that the parameters defined by the local root signature allow a shader to have unique parameters coming from the shader table. This makes a lot sense, because as the global root signature will define global parameters (i.e., parameters that don't change on a per-shader/object basis), the local root signature will define, instead, parameters that are unique to a given shader.

Then we will describe the structure of the `RaySampleFramework` that comes along with the code of this book.

Finally, we will close the chapter with our first ray-traced scene. To render the scene, we will simply employ the Whitted ray tracing approach. This will be the first ray traced scene shaded in DXR.

Without anything further to say, let's jump to the next section and see how to initialize the DXR part.

DirectX Ray Tracing (DXR) New Structures and Shader Stages

It's time to go deep into DXR API and structures. The first thing we will show is, after we've loaded the actual mesh data in the form of index and vertex buffer, how to build the acceleration structures out of it. Moreover, we will provide a refresher concerning the new shader stages being introduced in DXR. We've already talked about them very briefly in Chapter 3; now we will put them to good use!

There are few structures that are relevant to this process, and they are represented by the following:

- D3D12_RAYTRACING_GEOMETRY_DESC
- D3D12_BUILD_RAYTRACING_ACCELERATION_STRUCTURE_INPUTS

CHAPTER 9   DIRECTX 12 AND REAL-TIME RAY TRACING IN DXR

- D3D12_RAYTRACING_ACCELERATION_STRUCTURE_PREBUILD_INFO
- D3D12_RAYTRACING_ACCELERATION_STRUCTURE_BUILD_FLAGS
- D3D12_BUILD_RAYTRACING_ACCELERATION_STRUCTURE_DESC

These structures will allow us to grab the geometry data and create the TLAS and BLAS acceleration structures. These structures represent the hierarchical tree structures that will be employed to accelerate ray tracing intersection tests.

The first thing we have to do is to let the DXR API to know where our actual mesh data is coming from. To reach our goal, we need to describe the API for each mesh we want to trace against.

The data structure descriptor we need to fill is represented by D3D12_RAYTRACING_GEOMETRY_DESC. What we have to do is shown in the following code snippet (let's assume we've loaded a bounce of meshes from disk and that we now have index and vertex buffer available):

```
// NOTE: This code snippet is taken from BuildAccelerationStructures()
function present in RaySampleFramework
std::vector<D3D12_RAYTRACING_GEOMETRY_DESC> GeometryDescs;
for (auto& RPacket : mRenderList)
{
    bool Use32BitIndices = (RPacket.mVertexCount >= 65536);
    D3D12_RAYTRACING_GEOMETRY_DESC GeometryDesc = {};
    GeometryDesc.Type = D3D12_RAYTRACING_GEOMETRY_TYPE_TRIANGLES;
    GeometryDesc.Triangles.IndexBuffer =
    RPacket.mIB->GetGPUVirtualAddress();
    GeometryDesc.Triangles.IndexCount = RPacket.mIndexCount;
    GeometryDesc.Triangles.IndexFormat = Use32BitIndices ?
    DXGI_FORMAT_R32_UINT : DXGI_FORMAT_R16_UINT;
    GeometryDesc.Triangles.VertexBuffer.StartAddress =
    RPacket.mVB->GetGPUVirtualAddress();
    GeometryDesc.Triangles.VertexCount = RPacket.mVertexCount;
    GeometryDesc.Triangles.VertexFormat = DXGI_FORMAT_R32G32B32_FLOAT;
    GeometryDesc.Triangles.VertexBuffer.StrideInBytes = sizeof(MyVertex);
    GeometryDesc.Triangles.Transform3x4 = 0;
    GeometryDesc.Flags = D3D12_RAYTRACING_GEOMETRY_FLAG_OPAQUE;
```

```
    // Store the geometry desc for this mesh
    GeometryDescs.push_back(GeometryDesc);
}
```

In the previous code snippet, we are assuming that the geometry we are tracing against is all opaque. Knowing up front that some of the geometry will be opaque can enable important ray processing optimizations. The reason is simple: when rays encounter opaque geometry, any hit shader will not be executed whether it is present or not.

We inform the API that the geometry we are processing is opaque by setting this flag:

```
GeometryDesc.Flags = D3D12_RAYTRACING_GEOMETRY_FLAG_OPAQUE
```

Then we fill all the other fields of the struct with the index buffer and vertex buffer pointers, the vertex format, and so on. We repeat this process for each mesh (or in our case a render packet).

Let's make it clearer with an example.

Suppose we want to build a bottom-level acceleration structure (BLAS) for a mesh consisting of a single cube. The cube is made up of 12 triangles (36 indices) and 8 unique vertices.

When the framework processes the corresponding RenderPacket, the geometry description is filled as follows:

```
RenderPacket CubePacket;
CubePacket.mVB           = CreateVertexBufferForCube();   // contains 8
                                                          vertices
CubePacket.mIB           = CreateIndexBufferForCube();    // contains
                                                          36 indices
CubePacket.mVertexCount = 8;
CubePacket.mIndexCount  = 36;

// Inside BuildAccelerationStructures():
D3D12_RAYTRACING_GEOMETRY_DESC CubeGeom = {};
CubeGeom.Type                          = D3D12_RAYTRACING_GEOMETRY_TYPE_
                                         TRIANGLES;
CubeGeom.Triangles.IndexBuffer         = CubePacket.mIB-
                                         >GetGPUVirtualAddress();
CubeGeom.Triangles.IndexCount          = 36;
```

```
CubeGeom.Triangles.IndexFormat          = DXGI_FORMAT_R16_UINT;
                                        // 36 < 65536
CubeGeom.Triangles.VertexBuffer.StartAddress = CubePacket.mVB-
                                        >GetGPUVirtualAddress();
CubeGeom.Triangles.VertexCount          = 8;
CubeGeom.Triangles.VertexFormat         = DXGI_FORMAT_R32G32B32_FLOAT;
CubeGeom.Triangles.VertexBuffer.StrideInBytes = sizeof(MyVertex);
CubeGeom.Triangles.Transform3x4         = 0;
CubeGeom.Flags                          = D3D12_RAYTRACING_GEOMETRY_
                                          FLAG_OPAQUE;

GeometryDescs.push_back(CubeGeom);
```

In this example:

- The index format is chosen as DXGI_FORMAT_R16_UINT because the cube has fewer than 65,536 vertices.

- The vertex format is fixed to three 32-bit floats (DXGI_FORMAT_R32G32B32_FLOAT).

- Both index and vertex buffer GPU addresses are passed directly from the packet.

By repeating this procedure for each mesh in the scene, the GeometryDescs vector ends up containing one description per object, ready to be consumed by the BLAS builder.

We define a render packet to be the minimal set of data needed to render a mesh. It's a small and cache-friendly piece of data. It is defined like so:

```
struct RenderPacket
{
  RenderPacket() = default;
  // convenient name alias for verbose microsoft WRL ComPtr object
  template<typename T>
  using ComPtr = Microsoft::WRL::ComPtr<T>;
  /** Vertex Buffer */
  ComPtr<ID3D12Resource> mVB;
  /** Index Buffer */
```

```
    ComPtr<ID3D12Resource> mIB;
    /** Vertex Count */
    u32 mVertexCount;
    /** Index Count */
    u32 mIndexCount;
};
```

The size of the previous struct is 24 bytes, and it is indeed aligned to 8 bytes (remember we are compiling to target 64 bits platform; therefore, pointers will be represented using 8 bytes). Considering that we will normally have an array of those render packets, it is a fundamental requirement for this struct to be as small as possible. This will allow us to make good use of our CPU caches, by ensuring that as many render packet structs as possible will fit in the CPU cache lines. Let's remind to ourselves that L1 CPU data caches have a 64-byte-wide cache line. Once we've created our geometry description struct, we store it in our vector:

```
// Store the geometry desc for this mesh
GeometryDescs.push_back(GeometryDesc);
```

We will end up having an array of geometry desc structs for each mesh. The geometry type is of course represented by triangular meshes. Therefore, we specify this:

```
GeometryDesc.Type = D3D12_RAYTRACING_GEOMETRY_TYPE_TRIANGLES;
```

The geometry `descs` array will be then passed down to the acceleration data structure's building step.

Then we have two sections in this same descriptor where we actually fill vertex and index buffer related data. For the index buffer, we have these lines of code:

```
GeometryDesc.Triangles.IndexBuffer = RPacket.mIB->GetGPUVirtualAddress();
GeometryDesc.Triangles.IndexCount = RPacket.mIndexCount;
GeometryDesc.Triangles.IndexFormat = Use32BitIndices ? DXGI_FORMAT_R32_UINT
 : DXGI_FORMAT_R16_UINT;
```

We pass the pointer to the actual D3D12 index buffer resource, and then we specify the number of indices and finally what format they need to have (either 32 or 16 bits). The vertex buffer is also pretty straightforward. Take a look at the following lines:

```
GeometryDesc.Triangles.VertexBuffer.StartAddress = RPacket.mVB-
>GetGPUVirtualAddress();
GeometryDesc.Triangles.VertexCount = RPacket.mVertexCount;
GeometryDesc.Triangles.VertexFormat = DXGI_FORMAT_R32G32B32_FLOAT;
GeometryDesc.Triangles.VertexBuffer.StrideInBytes = sizeof(MyVertex)
```

In the first line, again, we pass the pointer of the actual D3D12 vertex buffer resource, then the vertex count, then the vertex format, and, finally, the vertex stride in bytes that is needed where the next vertex starts in memory.

There is also a field to which we can assign a transformation matrix to be used to transform vertices during acceleration structure construction (the vertex buffer will not be affected but just the resulted constructed acceleration structure containing the given geometry will). In our case, we do not need to perform any transformation on vertices, and we therefore set that field to zero.

Take a look at the following code:

```
GeometryDesc.Triangles.Transform3x4 = 0;
```

After this first look at how we can describe the geometry to the GPU through the DXR API, we are ready to go straight to the other missing steps. These steps are related to knowing what shader stages we have at our disposal and how to load these shaders to bind them to the new DXR ray tracing pipeline.

The next subsection will be a refresher on shader stages, and then it will explain how to load them, get the shader bytecode, and pass it to the shader table and the ray tracing pipeline state object.

Understanding the New Shader Stages and Shader Loading

The new shader stages as we've already mentioned in Chapter 3 are represented by the following ones:

- Ray generation shader
- Closest-hit shader

CHAPTER 9 DIRECTX 12 AND REAL-TIME RAY TRACING IN DXR

- Miss shader
- Any-hit shader
- Intersection shader

The ray generation shader will kick the ray casting process. Here, primary rays will be traced typically from the world space camera position into the scene. We will not redescribe these shader stages again and their purpose. If you need a more detailed description other than this refresher, refer to Chapter 3.

We will show how to compile a shader from a file. Let's assume we want to load and compile a shader from file. Let's look at some code now:

```
ComPtr<ID3DBlob> VertexShader;
ComPtr<ID3DBlob> PixelShader;
#if defined(_DEBUG)
UINT CompileFlags = D3DCOMPILE_DEBUG | D3DCOMPILE_SKIP_OPTIMIZATION;
#else
UINT CompileFlags = 0;
#endif
D3DCompileFromFile(L"SomePathOnYourDisk/shaders.hlsl", nullptr,
nullptr,"VSMain", "vs_5_0",CompileFlags, 0, &VertexShader, nullptr);
D3DCompileFromFile(L"SomePathOnYourDisk/shaders.hlsl", nullptr,
nullptr,"PSMain", "ps_5_0", CompileFlags, 0, &PixelShader, nullptr));
```

In the previous code, we have a file with the HLSL shader source code in it. Then we load and compile the shader that we are interested in by specifying the shader entry point (e.g., VSMain), the shader model (vs_5_0), the compilation flags, and the address in which the shader bytecode will end up being.

As for the compile flags, if we are compiling in debug mode, we want to skip the shader optimization D3DCOMPILE_SKIP_OPTIMIZATION and state that we want to compile in debug mode: D3DCOMPILE_DEBUG. We combine these two flags by actually creating a bitmask that is stored in the integer variable CompileFlags.

Compiling in debug is useful when we want to debug the shader code and have the symbols available to step through the code after we've made graphics capture with a profiler.

As you can tell from the previous code snippet, what we are doing is loading a vertex shader and a pixel shader. Both the shader entry points are in the same file (i.e., shaders.hlsl).

The content of the *.hlsl file will look like this (the syntax is in HLSL):

```
struct PSInput
{
    float4 position : SV_POSITION;
    float4 color : COLOR;
};

PSInput VSMain(float4 position : POSITION, float4 color : COLOR)
{
    PSInput result;
    result.position = position;
    result.color = color;
    return result;
}

float4 PSMain(PSInput input) : SV_TARGET
{
    return input.color;
}
```

We can clearly see the entry points of the vertex shader and the pixel shader. The same rule applies if we try to load ray tracing shaders. These shaders will have their own entry points too, and the only thing we have to do to load and compile their bytecode is to specify their entry point as an argument to the D3DCompileFromFile function.

> *To be able to use the D3D compiler API, we need to include the header file D3Dcompiler.h and specify d3dcompiler.lib in the additional dependencies section in the Linker options under the Visual Studio project properties.*

So, if we have a ray generation shader, we would basically do the same thing we did in the case of pixel and vertex shader loading. Suppose we have a ray generation shader like the following one in the HLSL file; it's named raytracingshaders.hlsl.

```
[shader("raygeneration")]
void CastRays()
{
    TraceRay(...)
}

[shader("closesthit")]
void RayCastClosestHit(inout RayPayload payload, in
IntersectionAttributes attr)
{
}

[shader("miss")]
void RayCastMiss(inout RayPayload payload)
{
}
```

Then if we want to load it by calling D3DCompileFromFile, we would pass the entry point of the ray generation shader or the one of the closest-hit shaders or the miss shader (i.e., CastRays or RayCastClosestHit or RayCastMiss), the correct shader model and the usual compilation flags.

Take a look at the following code for a better explanation of what we've just said:

```
ComPtr<ID3DBlob> RayGenerationShader;
#if defined(_DEBUG)
    UINT CompileFlags = D3DCOMPILE_DEBUG | D3DCOMPILE_SKIP_OPTIMIZATION;
#else
    UINT CompileFlags = 0;
#endif
D3DCompileFromFile(L"SomePathOnYourDisk/raytracingshaders.hlsl",
                   nullptr,
                   nullptr,
                   "CastRays",
                   "vs_5_0",
                   CompileFlags,
                   0,
                   &RayGenerationShader,
                   nullptr);
```

CHAPTER 9 DIRECTX 12 AND REAL-TIME RAY TRACING IN DXR

In this case, we are compiling and loading the bytecode for the ray generation shader. The pointer to ID3DBlob will hold the so-called "blob" of memory where the actual bytecode is stored.

DirectX Ray Tracing (DXR) API Initialization Code

In this section, we will go through the two main parts of the whole DXR preparation for ray tracing: the creation of a ray tracing pipeline state object (RTPSO) and the shader table creation.

This is where we pass root arguments for our shaders and the shader entry point bytecode pointers. We will actually have a table for each shader category:

- Ray generation shader table
- Miss shader table
- Hit group shader table

These are the table from where each shader will pick its root arguments and descriptors. Remember that the root arguments were described by the local root signature definition.

Create Ray Tracing Pipeline State Object

This function constructs the ray tracing pipeline state object (PSO), which is the central object used by DirectX Raytracing to define how rays are traced through the scene. The PSO bundles together all shaders, root signatures, and configuration parameters into a single immutable object.

Let's take a look at the following code:

```
void Ray_DX12HardwareRenderer::CreateRaytracingPipelineStateObject()
{
    CD3D12_STATE_OBJECT_DESC RaytracingPipeline{ D3D12_STATE_OBJECT_TYPE_
    RAYTRACING_PIPELINE };

    // DXIL library
    // This contains the shaders and their entrypoints for the
       state object.
```

CHAPTER 9 DIRECTX 12 AND REAL-TIME RAY TRACING IN DXR

```
// Since shaders are not considered a subobject, they need to be passed
in via DXIL library subobjects.
auto Lib = RaytracingPipeline.CreateSubobject<CD3D12_DXIL_LIBRARY_
SUBOBJECT>();
D3D12_SHADER_BYTECODE Libdxil = CD3DX12_SHADER_BYTECODE((void
*)gRaytracingShaders, ARRAYSIZE(gRaytracingShaders)); // <-
bytecode pointer
Lib->SetDXILLibrary(&Libdxil);

// Define which shader exports to surface from the library.
// If no shader exports are defined for a DXIL library subobject, all
shaders will be surfaced.
// In this sample, this could be omitted for convenience since the
sample uses all shaders in the library.
{
    Lib->DefineExport(gRaygenShaderName);
    Lib->DefineExport(gClosestHitShaderName);
    Lib->DefineExport(gMissShaderName);
}

// Triangle hit group
// A hit group specifies closest hit, any hit and intersection shaders
to be executed when a ray intersects the geometry's triangle/AABB.
// In this sample, we only use triangle geometry with a closest hit
shader, so others are not set.
auto HitGroup = RaytracingPipeline.CreateSubobject<CD3D12_HIT_GROUP_
SUBOBJECT>();
HitGroup->SetClosestHitShaderImport(gClosestHitShaderName);
HitGroup->SetHitGroupExport(gHitGroupName);
HitGroup->SetHitGroupType(D3D12_HIT_GROUP_TYPE_TRIANGLES);

// Shader config
// Defines the maximum sizes in bytes for the ray payload and attribute
structure.
auto ShaderConfig = RaytracingPipeline.CreateSubobject<CD3D12_
RAYTRACING_SHADER_CONFIG_SUBOBJECT>();
```

```
u32 PayloadSize = 4 * sizeof(float) + sizeof(u32);   // float3 color,
float t, uint depth;
u32 AttributeSize = 2 * sizeof(float); // float2 barycentrics
ShaderConfig->Config(PayloadSize, AttributeSize);

// Local root signature and shader association
// Miss shader in this sample is not using a local root signature and
thus one is not associated with it.
{
    auto LocalRootSignatureSubObj = RaytracingPipeline.
    CreateSubobject<CD3D12_LOCAL_ROOT_SIGNATURE_SUBOBJECT>();
    LocalRootSignatureSubObj->SetRootSignature(mRaytracingLocalRootSign
    ature.Get());

    // Shader association
    auto RootSignatureAssociationSubObj = RaytracingPipeline.
    CreateSubobject<CD3D12_SUBOBJECT_TO_EXPORTS_ASSOCIATION_
    SUBOBJECT>();
    RootSignatureAssociationSubObj->SetSubobjectToAssociate(*LocalRootS
    ignatureSubObj);
    RootSignatureAssociationSubObj->AddExport(gRaygenShaderName);
    RootSignatureAssociationSubObj->AddExport(gClosestHitShaderName);
}

// Global root signature
// This is a root signature that is shared across all raytracing
shaders invoked during a DispatchRays() call.
auto GlobalRootSignature = RaytracingPipeline.CreateSubobject<CD3D12_
GLOBAL_ROOT_SIGNATURE_SUBOBJECT>();
GlobalRootSignature->SetRootSignature(mRaytracingGlobalRootSignatu
re.Get());

// Pipeline config
// Defines the maximum TraceRay() recursion depth.
auto PipelineConfigSubObj = RaytracingPipeline.CreateSubobject<CD3D12_
RAYTRACING_PIPELINE_CONFIG_SUBOBJECT>();
```

```
// PERFOMANCE TIP: Set max recursion depth as low as needed
// as drivers may apply optimization strategies for low
recursion depths.
u32 MaxRecursionDepth = 1; // ~ primary rays only.
PipelineConfigSubObj->Config(MaxRecursionDepth);

// Create a ray tracing pipeline state object (PSO) for the DXR
pipeline
ThrowIfFailed(mD3DDevice->CreateStateObject(RaytracingPipeline, IID_
PPV_ARGS(&mDXRStateObject)), L"Couldn't create DirectX Raytracing state
object.\n");
}
```

This is the process:

1. **DXIL library:** The compiled shader bytecode (gRaytracingShaders) is loaded and registered. From this library, the relevant entry points are surfaced: the ray generation shader, the closest hit shader, and the miss shader.

2. **Hit group:** A hit group describes how intersections with geometry are handled. In this example, only triangle geometry is used, so the hit group consists of a closest hit shader only (no any-hit or custom intersection shaders).

3. **Shader config:** The maximum sizes for the **ray payload** (data carried along with the ray, such as color, hit distance, recursion depth) and the **intersection attributes** (barycentric coordinates in this case) are defined. This ensures the runtime knows how much memory to allocate per ray.

4. **Local root signature association:** A local root signature, which allows passing resources specific to certain shaders, is associated with the ray generation and closest hit shaders. The miss shader does not require a local root signature in this sample.

5. **Global root signature:** A global root signature, shared across all shaders in the ray tracing pipeline, is defined. This typically includes scene-wide resources such as acceleration structures, output UAVs, or constant buffers.

6. **Pipeline config:** The maximum recursion depth for ray tracing is set. In this case, it is restricted to 1, which means only primary rays are traced. Limiting recursion depth helps performance, as drivers can optimize for shallow ray stacks.

7. **Create the PSO:** Finally, all these subobjects are combined and passed to CreateStateObject, producing the actual ray tracing PSO (mDXRStateObject) that will be bound and used during rendering.

In summary, this function prepares the blueprint of the ray tracing stage: which shaders to run, how they are grouped, how data flows between them, and how deep rays can recurse. Without this state object, no ray tracing work can be dispatched.

Create Shader Table

We create a shader table for each type of shader that needs one. In our case, we have three types of shaders: one ray generation shader, one miss-shader and a closest-hit shader. So, there are three shader table in total.

When we create a shader table, we first create a shader table record, and we then add it to the table. See Figure 9-11.

CHAPTER 9   DIRECTX 12 AND REAL-TIME RAY TRACING IN DXR

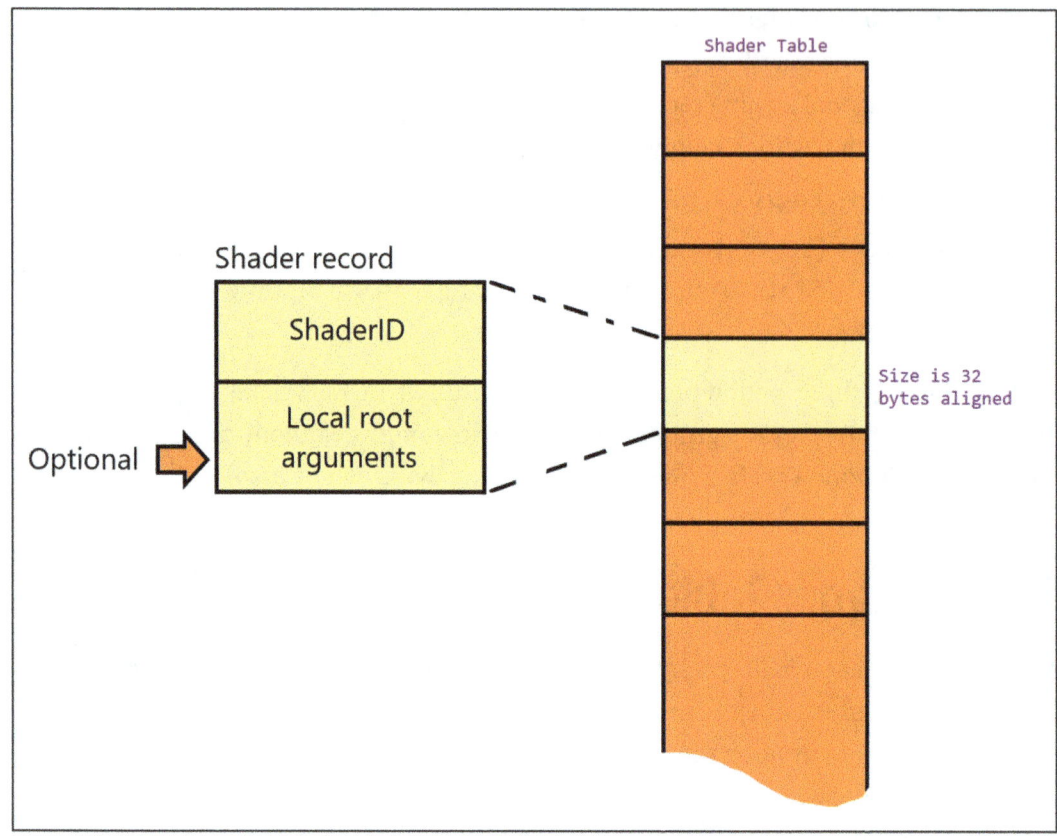

Figure 9-11. *Shader record (left) is stored in the shader table (right)*

As we can see in Figure 9-11 for each record, we have a shader identifier and optional local root arguments. The size of a shader record must align to 32 bytes. This alignment is guaranteed by the shader table class itself, so when it's time to allocate and store one table record, it makes sure that the size is aligned to 32 bytes boundary.

This code snippet shows the `BuildShaderTables()` method body. Here the shader tables are created.

```
// Build shader tables, which define shaders and their local root
arguments.
void Ray_DX12HardwareRenderer::BuildShaderTables()
{
    auto Device = mD3DDevice.Get();
```

```cpp
// Pointers to shader ids
void* RayGenShaderIdentifier = nullptr;
void* MissShaderIdentifier = nullptr;
void* HitGroupShaderIdentifier = nullptr;

// Convenient lamda function to get the shader identifiers
auto GetShaderIdentifiers = [&](auto* stateObjectProperties)
{
    RayGenShaderIdentifier = stateObjectProperties->GetShaderIdentifier
        (gRaygenShaderName);
    MissShaderIdentifier = stateObjectProperties->GetShaderIdentifier(g
        MissShaderName);
    HitGroupShaderIdentifier = stateObjectProperties->GetShaderIdentifi
        er(gHitGroupName);
};

// Get shader identifiers.
size_t ShaderIdentifierSize;

// state object properties prototype
ComPtr<ID3D12StateObjectProperties> StateObjectProperties;

// DXR state object interpreted as State object prototype
ThrowIfFailed(mDXRStateObject.As(&StateObjectProperties));

GetShaderIdentifiers(StateObjectProperties.Get());

// Shader id size must be 32 bytes aligned
ShaderIdentifierSize = D3D12_SHADER_IDENTIFIER_SIZE_IN_BYTES;

// Ray gen shader table
{
    struct SRootArguments
    {
        // Constant buffer for the ray generation shader
        RayGenCB cb;
    } RootArguments;
```

CHAPTER 9   DIRECTX 12 AND REAL-TIME RAY TRACING IN DXR

```
        RootArguments.cb = mRayGenCB;

        // How many records we want in the ray gen shader table
        u32 NumShaderRecords = 1;

        // What is the size of one record
        usize ShaderRecordSize = ShaderIdentifierSize +
        sizeof(RootArguments);

        ShaderTable RayGenShaderTable(Device, NumShaderRecords,
        ShaderRecordSize, L"RayGenShaderTable");

        // Add the newly created shader to the table (it will actually copy
        // the record in the D3D12 upload buffer resource)
        RayGenShaderTable.push_back(ShaderRecord(RayGenShaderIdentifier,
        ShaderIdentifierSize, &RootArguments, sizeof(RootArguments)));

        // Done, let's get our actual shader table D3D12 resource
        mRayGenShaderTable = RayGenShaderTable.GetResource();
    }

    // Miss shader table
    {
        u32 NumShaderRecords = 1;
        usize shaderRecordSize = ShaderIdentifierSize;
        ShaderTable missShaderTable(Device, NumShaderRecords,
        shaderRecordSize, L"MissShaderTable");
        missShaderTable.push_back(ShaderRecord(MissShaderIdentifier,
        ShaderIdentifierSize));
        mMissShaderTable = missShaderTable.GetResource();
    }

    // Hit group shader table
    {
        u32 NumShaderRecords = (u32)mRayTracingRenderPacket.
        mLocalToFlatVBIBGeometryData.size();
        usize shaderRecordSize = ALIGN32(ShaderIdentifierSize +
        kLocalRootSize);
```

CHAPTER 9   DIRECTX 12 AND REAL-TIME RAY TRACING IN DXR

```
    ShaderTable HitGroupShaderTable(Device, NumShaderRecords,
    shaderRecordSize, L"HitGroupShaderTable");
    for (auto& sm : mRayTracingRenderPacket.
    mLocalToFlatVBIBGeometryData)
    {
        HitGroupShaderTable.push_back(ShaderRecord(HitGroupShader
        Identifier, ShaderIdentifierSize, &sm,sizeof(Geometry
        OffsetData)));
    }
    mHitGroupShaderTable = HitGroupShaderTable.GetResource();
  }
}
```

In the previous code snippet, we retrieve the identifier for each shader type by querying the state object properties object by the mean of the method GetShaderIdentifier(). The object properties variable is of type ID3D12StateObjectPropertiesPrototype and is retrieved by casting the DXR state object (see the .As method in the previous snippet).

Each shader identifier (ShaderID in Figure 9-11) will then be used to construct a shader record by calling the constructor of the ShaderRecord class. As we've already pointed out, each shader record contains a shader identifier and optional root arguments.

It turns out that in our specific case we are passing a constant buffer containing the viewport size (i.e., RayGenCB) to be available for use in the ray gen shader table.

The code continues by constructing the shader record for the other two types of shaders: miss and closest-hit shader. The code for each shade record is pretty straightforward. First a shader record is constructed, and then it's added to the relative table as outlined here:

```
// Miss shader table
{
    u32 NumShaderRecords = 1;
    usize shaderRecordSize = ShaderIdentifierSize;
    ShaderTable missShaderTable(Device, NumShaderRecords,
    shaderRecordSize, L"MissShaderTable");
    missShaderTable.push_back(ShaderRecord(MissShaderIdentifier,
    ShaderIdentifierSize));
```

```
            mMissShaderTable = missShaderTable.GetResource();
        }
        // Hit group shader table
        {
            u32 NumShaderRecords = (u32)mRayTracingRenderPacket.
            mLocalToFlatVBIBGeometryData.size();
            usize shaderRecordSize = ALIGN32(ShaderIdentifierSize +
            kLocalRootSize);
            ShaderTable HitGroupShaderTable(Device, NumShaderRecords,
            shaderRecordSize, L"HitGroupShaderTable");
            for (auto& sm : mRayTracingRenderPacket.
            mLocalToFlatVBIBGeometryData)
            {
                HitGroupShaderTable.push_back(ShaderRecord(HitGroupShader
                    Identifier, ShaderIdentifierSize, &sm,sizeof(Geometry
                    OffsetData)));
            }
            mHitGroupShaderTable = HitGroupShaderTable.GetResource();
        }
```

Hit-Group Shader Table Construction

This block builds the hit-group section of the Shader Binding Table (SBT). Each entry (record) corresponds to one submesh and carries the data the closest-hit shader needs to translate local mesh indices into the global/flat vertex and index buffers used by the scene.

- **Record count**

    NumShaderRecords equals the number of submeshes:

    mRayTracingRenderPacket.
    mLocalToFlatVBIBGeometryData.size().

- **Record layout**

    Each record stores the following:

    - The hit-group shader identifier (ShaderIdentifierSize bytes)

- The local root arguments, here a GeometryOffsetData struct (kLocalRootSize bytes) that encodes the per-submesh index/vertex offsets and material ID.

  The record size is aligned to 32 bytes:

  ALIGN32(ShaderIdentifierSize + kLocalRootSize)

- **Population**

  For every `GeometryOffsetData sm`, a `ShaderRecord` is pushed with the following:

  - `HitGroupShaderIdentifier` (binds this record to the closest-hit program)
  - The bytes of `sm` (passed as the local root so the shader can map local indices ➤ flat VB/IB).

- **Resulting GPU resource**

  The constructed table is finalized, and its underlying resource is stored in `mHitGroupShaderTable` for use during `DispatchRays`.

During Whitted ray tracing (discussed later in this chapter), the closest-hit shader uses the per-record GeometryOffsetData to locate the correct slice of the flat VB/IB for the intersected submesh, ensuring materials and geometry are fetched consistently across the entire scene.

After we've compiled the shaders, created the relative shader tables, and created all the geometry descs and the acceleration structures, we are ready to trace rays into the scene.

At this point, we will not go through the description of every single function in the framework. Instead, you are encouraged to carefully examine the code directly. This is a valuable exercise, as it builds familiarity with both the structure of the framework and the DirectX Raytracing API itself. The provided code has been written with clarity in mind and is thoroughly commented, making it suitable for self-study. By reading and reasoning through the implementation details, you will reinforce the concepts discussed so far and develop the habit of learning from well-documented codebases—an essential skill for graphics programming.

CHAPTER 9   DIRECTX 12 AND REAL-TIME RAY TRACING IN DXR

To gain a deeper understanding of the architecture and design of the framework, the following section will examine its structure in detail. We will explore how the different components interact, why certain design choices were made, and how they support flexibility and extensibility in rendering applications.

Understanding RaySampleFramework Structure

What follows is a description of how the accompanying sample framework—which we will refer to as the `RaySampleFramework`—is structured. This framework provides the foundation for building graphics samples in a consistent and reusable way. At its core, it separates application logic from the underlying graphics API by introducing an abstract rendering interface and a well-defined sample lifecycle.

In the next pages, we will walk through the major building blocks of the framework: the application driver, the abstract `Ray_Sample` base class, the renderer interface, concrete rendering backends, and the lightweight data structures that feed the rendering pipeline.

To make this easier to grasp, Figure 9-12 illustrates how these pieces fit together. It highlights the relationships between the sample layer, the rendering interface, the DirectX 12 implementation, and the supporting geometry structures. Take a moment to study Figure 9-12 before diving into the detailed explanations—it will serve as a map for the architecture we are about to discuss.

> *Within this framework, the* `RaySampleFramework` *used throughout the book includes a dedicated FBX model loader class, making it possible to bring real-world 3D assets directly into the examples. This allows you to experiment with Whitted-style ray tracing not just on simple primitives but also on imported FBX models, bridging the gap between theory and practical rendering. Take a look at the code and see how it is used.*

Figure 9-12 shows the architecture of our sample framework through a class diagram.

CHAPTER 9   DIRECTX 12 AND REAL-TIME RAY TRACING IN DXR

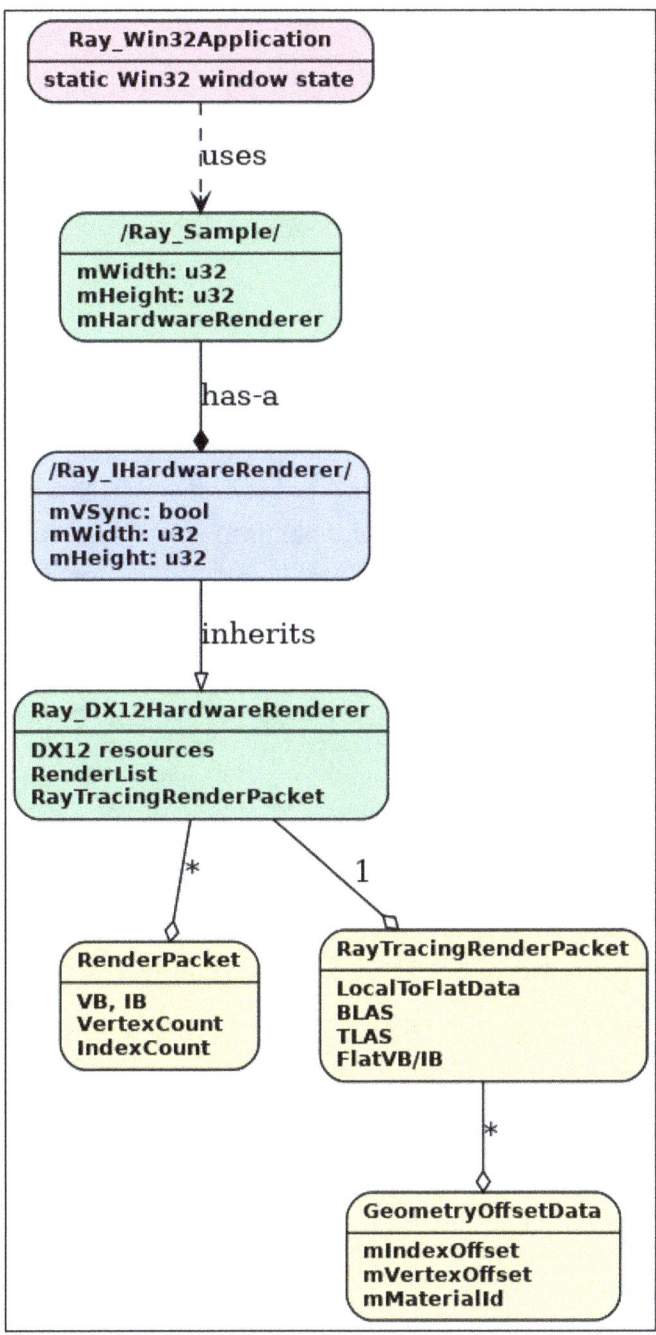

Figure 9-12. *A class diagram showing the architecture of RaySampleFramework*

CHAPTER 9   DIRECTX 12 AND REAL-TIME RAY TRACING IN DXR

Diagram Description

The class diagram illustrates the architecture of a DirectX 12–based rendering framework with support for ray tracing. It highlights the relationships between the core rendering interface, its DirectX 12 implementation, the application sample layer, the Win32 host application, and several supporting data structures.

- **Ray_IHardwareRenderer:**
  - An abstract interface that defines the common rendering operations (Init, Destroy, Resize, BeginFrame, Render, EndFrame) as well as VSync management.
  - It encapsulates basic viewport state (mWidth, mHeight, mVSync) and serves as the base class for platform-specific renderers.
  - Shown in pastel indigo to distinguish it as an interface.
- **Ray_DX12HardwareRenderer:**
  - A concrete subclass of Ray_IHardwareRenderer that implements rendering using DirectX 12 and DXR
  - Manages DirectX device objects, command queues, swap chains, root signatures, and ray tracing pipeline state
  - **Aggregates**:
    - A collection of RenderPacket objects for rasterized geometry
    - A single RayTracingRenderPacket representing the acceleration structures and flat buffers needed for ray tracing
  - Shown in pastel green to denote a core implementation class
- **Ray_Sample:**
  - An abstract sample application class that manages dimensions and rendering state
  - Holds a composition relationship with Ray_IHardwareRenderer via a unique_ptr, enabling flexible selection of the underlying graphics API (DX12, Vulkan, etc.)

- Provides lifecycle hooks (OnInit, OnUpdate, OnRender, OnDestroy) for concrete samples
- Shown in pastel green but italicized to indicate abstraction

- **Ray_Win32Application**

  - A utility class responsible for creating and managing the Windows application window, handling messages, toggling fullscreen, and launching a Ray_Sample.
  - Maintains a static pointer to the active sample.
  - Connected with a dashed dependency arrow labeled uses to indicate that it orchestrates the sample's execution but does not own it.
  - Shown in pastel pink as an application-level utility.

- **Supporting data structures:**

  - **GeometryOffsetData**: Encodes index/vertex offsets and material IDs for submeshes, enabling mapping between local and global buffers.
  - **RenderPacket**: Bundles vertex/index buffers and their counts for rasterized rendering.
  - **RayTracingRenderPacket**: Encapsulates ray tracing state including BLAS, TLAS, and flat geometry buffers. Contains a vector of GeometryOffsetData objects.
  - All are shown in pastel yellow to represent lightweight struct-like components.

- **Relationships:**

  - **Inheritance**: Ray_DX12HardwareRenderer → Ray_IHardwareRenderer
  - **Composition/Aggregation**:
    - Ray_Sample → Ray_IHardwareRenderer (owns via unique_ptr)
    - Ray_DX12HardwareRenderer → RenderPacket (0..*)

- Ray_DX12HardwareRenderer → RayTracingRenderPacket (1)
- RayTracingRenderPacket → GeometryOffsetData (0..*)
- **Dependency**: Ray_Win32Application → Ray_Sample (*uses/manages*)

Creating a Ray_Sample and Why the Abstract Renderer Matters

This section shows how to implement a concrete sample built on the framework you provided and explains why an abstract renderer interface (Ray_IHardwareRenderer) is a long-term win for portability, testability, and iteration speed.

What a Ray_Sample Is

Ray_Sample is the application layer that owns a renderer (via std::unique_ptr<Ray_IHardwareRenderer>), manages window size/aspect ratio, and exposes four lifecycle hooks:

- OnInit(): Create resources and initialize the renderer
- OnUpdate(delta): Per-frame simulation/camera/UI
- OnRender(): Issue draw/raytrace calls through the renderer
- OnDestroy(): Free resources in a safe order

You never talk to DX12 (or Vulkan) directly from the sample; you call the renderer interface. That keeps the sample focused on *what* to render, not *how*.

A Minimal Concrete Sample

The following is a compact "Hello Triangle (or Rays)" sample that uses the interface only. Swap the concrete renderer (DX12, Vulkan…) without changing the sample code:

```
// MyFirstSample.h
#pragma once
#include "RaySample.h"               // your abstract base
#include "RayIHardwareRenderer.h"    // the interface
```

CHAPTER 9   DIRECTX 12 AND REAL-TIME RAY TRACING IN DXR

```cpp
class MyFirstSample final : public Ray_Sample
{
public:
    MyFirstSample(u32 w, u32 h)
        : Ray_Sample(w, h, L"My First Sample") {}

    void OnInit() override;
    void OnUpdate(float dt) override;
    void OnRender() override;
    void OnDestroy() override;

private:
    float mTime = 0.0f;
    float mClear[4] = { 0.08f, 0.10f, 0.12f, 1.0f };
};
```

And in your header file you will implement the interface functionality:

```cpp
// MyFirstSample.cpp
#include "MyFirstSample.h"
#include "RayDX12HardwareRenderer.h"   // concrete backend (can be swapped)

void MyFirstSample::OnInit()
{
    // Choose a backend at runtime (DX12 here, but Vulkan/Metal could
    be used).
    mHardwareRenderer = std::make_unique<Ray_DX12HardwareRenderer>();

    // Initialize the renderer using the window handle managed by Ray_
    Win32Application.
    HWND hwnd = Ray_Win32Application::GetWindowHandle();
    mHardwareRenderer->Init(GetWidth(), GetHeight(), hwnd,
    /*UseWarp=*/false);

    // Sample-level assets go here: load meshes, build AS, PSO, etc.
}
```

CHAPTER 9   DIRECTX 12 AND REAL-TIME RAY TRACING IN DXR

```cpp
void MyFirstSample::OnUpdate(float dt)
{
    mTime += dt;

    // Update uniforms, camera, animation...
    // (Keep this API-agnostic: write to your own CPU-side structs.)
}

void MyFirstSample::OnRender()
{
    // Frame lifecycle is identical across backends.
    mHardwareRenderer->BeginFrame(mClear);
    // Issue draw/trace through your renderer; you might publish a thin scene API:
    //   - Submit render packets (raster)
    //   - Dispatch rays (DXR path)
    mHardwareRenderer->Render();
    mHardwareRenderer->EndFrame();
}

void MyFirstSample::OnDestroy()
{
    // Release GPU resources via the backend.
    if (mHardwareRenderer) mHardwareRenderer->Destroy();
}
```

Integrating with the Win32 Driver

The Ray_Win32Application runner already exposes a Run() method that takes a Ray_Sample*. All you need is a tiny entry point:

```cpp
// main.cpp
#include "MyFirstSample.h"
#include "RayWin32Application.h"
```

CHAPTER 9   DIRECTX 12 AND REAL-TIME RAY TRACING IN DXR

```
int WINAPI wWinMain(HINSTANCE hInst, HINSTANCE, PWSTR, int nCmdShow)
{
    MyFirstSample sample(1280, 720);
    return Ray_Win32Application::Run(&sample, hInst, nCmdShow);
}
```

The Win32 layer owns the message pump and calls your sample's lifecycle functions. The sample owns the renderer and talks to it exclusively through the interface.

Picking a Backend (3D Graphics API) (Compile Time or Runtime)

You can decide the backend in several ways:

- Compile-time switch

    ```
    #if defined(USE_DX12)
        mHardwareRenderer = std::make_unique<Ray_
        DX12HardwareRenderer>();
    #elif defined(USE_VULKAN)
        mHardwareRenderer = std::make_unique<Ray_
        VulkanHardwareRenderer>();
    #endif
    ```

- Run-time factory

    ```
    std::unique_ptr<Ray_IHardwareRenderer>
    CreateRenderer(std::wstring api)
    {
        if (api == L"dx12")   return std::make_unique<Ray_
        DX12HardwareRenderer>();
        if (api == L"vulkan") return std::make_unique<Ray_
        VulkanHardwareRenderer>();
        // ... add Metal, GL, etc.
        throw std::runtime_error("Unknown renderer API");
    }
    ```

    The rest of the sample is unchanged.

Why an Abstract Renderer Interface Is the Right Design

Separation of concerns:

- The Sample logic (camera, animation, scene composition) is independent of the GPU API ceremony (devices, heaps, barriers, swap chains).
- You can focus on features without churn every time you tweak low-level details.

Portability and longevity:

- Port to Vulkan/Metal/Console by implementing Ray_IHardwareRenderer once.
- Existing samples continue to work; no changes in game or editor code.

Testability:

- Provide a Null/Headless renderer that validates draw lists or shader table contents without a GPU (perfect for CI).
- Inject a Mock renderer to unit-test frame sequencing (BeginFrame/Render/EndFrame) and resource lifetime.

Performance experiments without lock-in:

- Try different backends or feature levels (e.g., DX12 WARP on laptops, Vulkan on Linux) with the same sample.
- A/B test ray tracing pipelines or raster fallbacks by swapping implementations.

Cleaner error handling and diagnostics:

- Centralize GPU synchronization, device loss handling, and debug markers in one place.
- Consistent frame lifecycle simplifies profiling and captures across APIs.

Team workflow:

- Engine/backend engineers iterate on the renderer; content/feature engineers build samples and tools.
- Clear ownership reduces merge conflicts and cognitive load.

Drop this into a new sample, hook it up to `Ray_Win32Application::Run`, *and you have a clean, API-agnostic starting point that scales from raster to ray tracing and from DX12 to future backends with minimal code churn.*

The `RaySampleFramework` establishes a clear and reusable structure for developing rendering samples. By separating the abstract renderer interface from its concrete implementations, the framework makes it possible to explore different graphics APIs without rewriting sample code. This separation of concerns not only improves maintainability but also creates a consistent environment in which new techniques can be demonstrated and compared.

The class diagram presented earlier should now serve as a reference point for understanding how the application layer, the rendering interface, and the supporting data structures interact. With this foundation in place, subsequent sections can focus on the details of implementing specific rendering features, confident that the underlying framework provides a stable and extensible base.

Let's Ray Trace: Whitted Ray Tracing in DXR

Whitted-style ray tracing, introduced by Turner Whitted in 1980, is the classical formulation of recursive ray tracing that many modern techniques evolved from. At its core, it simulates how light interacts with surfaces using three key effects:

- **Local Illumination**

  For every visible point on a surface, lighting is computed using direct contributions from light sources (e.g., diffuse and specular shading).

- **Reflection**

  If a surface is reflective, a new ray is spawned in the mirror-reflection direction to gather secondary light contributions.

- **Refraction (Transmission)**

    Transparent or refractive materials generate rays that pass through the object, bending according to Snell's law.

- **Shadow Rays**

    To determine the visibility of light sources, shadow rays are cast from the surface point toward each light. If they hit something before reaching the light, that light's contribution is blocked.

Figure 9-13 shows the classic and simple Whitted-style ray traced scene.

Figure 9-13. Whitted ray traced scene. We can see reflections, refractions, shadows, and diffuse direct lighting

This recursive process continues until a termination condition (like max recursion depth or negligible contribution) is met. The result is a physically inspired but relatively simple rendering of reflections, refractions, and shadows.

Whitted ray tracing *is limited to computing direct illumination, specifically handling diffuse and specular reflection from direct light sources, but it does not account for the indirect light transport that contributes to global illumination. In contrast,* path tracing *builds on the full rendering equation, tracing many possible light paths as they bounce throughout the scene. This makes path tracing a more complete approach, as it naturally incorporates indirect lighting effects such as color bleeding, soft shadows, and caustics, thereby offering a better solution to the global illumination problem.*

DirectX Raytracing

DirectX raytracing (DXR) provides hardware-accelerated support for ray tracing in real-time graphics. A Whitted-style ray tracer can be expressed directly in DXR through the following:

- **Ray generation shaders**: Where primary rays (camera rays) are spawned into the scene
- **Closest hit shaders**: Where shading happens, including spawning reflection and refraction rays in Whitted-style recursion
- **Any-hit and miss shaders**: Allowing early ray termination or background color/environment sampling
- **Acceleration structures**: Enabling fast BVH traversal in hardware

In DXR, the recursion of Whitted-style ray tracing maps naturally to recursive calls to `TraceRay()` inside hit shaders. Each reflective or refractive event results in another ray traversal through the acceleration structure, while shadow rays can be launched as secondary "visibility tests."

The first step is to cast primary rays through the ray generation shader. Here we compute the world space ray direction with the following steps:

- Compute NDC.
- Transform NDC to viewspace.
- Transform the viewspace ray dir rd to world space.

- Construct the ray thorugh the HLSL intrinsic RayDesc (a predefined HLSL struct that represents a ray):
  - **ro:** The ray origin (i.e., the camera position)
  - **rd:** The ray direction in world space
- Construct RadiancePayload (i.e., a struct that will carry the radiance/color contribution throughout the whole ray tracing process). We already explained what a payload is in a previous chapter, in this case we will use it to accumulate radiance at every bounce.
- Start tracing ray by calling the HLSL intrinsic TraceRay().

```
[shader("raygeneration")]
void RayGen()
{
    uint2 pix = DispatchRaysIndex().xy;
    uint2 dim = DispatchRaysDimensions().xy;

    float2 uv = (float2(pix) + 0.5) / float2(dim);
    float2 ndc = uv * 2.0 - 1.0;

    // Reconstruct view ray
    float4 nearP = mul(invProj, float4(ndc, 0, 1));
    nearP /= nearP.w;
    float4 farP  = mul(invProj, float4(ndc, 1, 1));
    farP  /= farP.w;

    float3 ro = mul(invView, float4(0,0,0,1)).xyz;
    float3 rd = normalize( mul(invView, float4(normalize(farP.xyz - nearP.xyz),0)).xyz );

    RadiancePayload p;
    p.color = 0;
    p.t     = 1e9;
    p.depth = 0;

    RayDesc ray;
    ray.Origin = ro;
    ray.Direction = rd;
```

```
    ray.TMin = 0.001;
    ray.TMax = 1e38;

    TraceRay(SceneBVH, RAY_FLAG_NONE, /*InstanceMask*/ 0xFF,
            /*HitGroupIndex*/ 0, /*HitGroupCount*/ 1, /*MissIndex*/ 0,
            ray, p);

    Output[pix] = float4(p.color, 1);
}
```

Here is the code for the **closest hit shader**:

- Compute normal.

- Fetch material.

- Branch on type.

- Spawn reflection/refraction or shadow rays (call TraceRay() recursively).

```
float3 FresnelSchlick(float cosTheta, float3 F0)
{
    return F0 + (1.0 - F0) * pow(1.0 - cosTheta, 5.0);
}

bool TraceShadowRay(float3 origin, float3 lightDir, float maxDist)
{
    ShadowPayload sp; sp.visible = true;

    RayDesc sray;
    sray.Origin = origin + lightDir * 0.001;
    sray.Direction = lightDir;
    sray.TMin = 0.0;
    sray.TMax = maxDist - 0.002;

    TraceRay(SceneBVH, RAY_FLAG_ACCEPT_FIRST_HIT_AND_END_SEARCH | RAY_FLAG_
    SKIP_CLOSEST_HIT_SHADER,
            0xFF, /*hitGroup*/1, /*num*/1, /*miss*/1, sray, sp); // use
            Shadow miss/hit
    return sp.visible;
}
```

CHAPTER 9   DIRECTX 12 AND REAL-TIME RAY TRACING IN DXR

```hlsl
[shader("closesthit")]
void ClosestHit(inout RadiancePayload p, in HitAttrib attrib)
{
    // Geometry
    uint prim = PrimitiveIndex();

    uint idx = mIndexOffset + prim*3;
    uint i0 = Indices[idx+0] + mVertexOffset;
    uint i1 = Indices[idx+1] + mVertexOffset;
    uint i2 = Indices[idx+2] + mVertexOffset;

    float3 p0 = Vertices[i0].pos;
    float3 p1 = Vertices[i1].pos;
    float3 p2 = Vertices[i2].pos;

    float2 b = attrib.bary;
    float3 pos = b.x * p1 + b.y * p2 + (1 - b.x - b.y) * p0;
    float3 Ng  = normalize(cross(p1 - p0, p2 - p0));
    float3 N   = faceforward(Ng, -WorldRayDirection(), Ng);
    float3 V   = -normalize(WorldRayDirection());

    // Material (assume per-instance or via custom index—simplified here)
    Material m = Materials[InstanceID()];

    // Single directional light
    float3 Ldir = normalize(float3(0.5, 0.9, 0.1));
    float3 Lo = 0;

    // Diffuse term + shadow
    float NdotL = saturate(dot(N, Ldir));
    if (NdotL > 0)
    {
        bool lit = TraceShadowRay(pos + N * 0.001, Ldir, /*maxDist*/ 1e30);
        if (lit) Lo += m.albedo * NdotL;
    }
```

CHAPTER 9 DIRECTX 12 AND REAL-TIME RAY TRACING IN DXR

```
// Reflection / Refraction (Whitted)
if (p.depth < maxDepth)
{
    if (m.type == 1) // mirror
    {
        float3 R = reflect(-V, N);
        RadiancePayload rp; rp.color=0; rp.t=1e9; rp.depth =
        p.depth + 1;

        RayDesc rray; rray.Origin = pos + R * 0.002; rray.Direction =
        R; rray.TMin=0; rray.TMax=1e38;
        TraceRay(SceneBVH, RAY_FLAG_NONE, 0xFF, 0, 1, 0, rray, rp);

        // Schlick Fresnel around F0 from albedo as tint
        float3 F = FresnelSchlick(saturate(dot(N, V)), m.albedo);
        Lo += F * rp.color;
    }
    else if (m.type == 2) // glass (ior)
    {
        float eta = dot(N, V) > 0 ? 1.0 / m.ior : m.ior;
        float3 Nn = dot(N, V) > 0 ? N : -N;
        float cosi = saturate(dot(Nn, V));
        float k = 1.0 - eta*eta*(1.0 - cosi*cosi);

        float3 F0 = float3(pow((m.ior - 1)/(m.ior + 1), 2.0));
        float3 F  = FresnelSchlick(cosi, F0);

        // Reflection ray
        float3 R = reflect(-V, Nn);
        RadiancePayload refl; refl.color=0; refl.t=1e9; refl.depth=
        p.depth+1;
        RayDesc r; r.Origin=pos + R*0.002; r.Direction=R; r.TMin=0;
        r.TMax=1e38;
        TraceRay(SceneBVH, RAY_FLAG_NONE, 0xFF, 0, 1, 0, r, refl);
```

CHAPTER 9   DIRECTX 12 AND REAL-TIME RAY TRACING IN DXR

```
            float3 Tcol = 0;
            if (k > 0.0) // refraction valid
            {
                float3 Tdir = refract(-V, Nn, eta);
                RadiancePayload refr; refr.color=0; refr.t=1e9;
                refr.depth=p.depth+1;
                RayDesc t; t.Origin=pos + Tdir*0.002; t.Direction=Tdir;
                t.TMin=0; t.TMax=1e38;
                TraceRay(SceneBVH, RAY_FLAG_NONE, 0xFF, 0, 1, 0, t, refr);
                Tcol = refr.color;
            }
            Lo += F * refl.color + (1.0 - F) * Tcol;
        }
    }
    // Combine
    p.color = Lo;
    p.t = RayTCurrent();
}
```

If we miss the geometry, then the miss shader will be invoked:

```
// Here we can generate a simple sky gradient or sample a cubemap
[shader("miss")]
void RayCastingMiss(inout RadiancePayload payload)
{
    float3 dir = WorldRayDirection();
    float t = 0.5 * (dir.y + 1.0);
    payload.color = lerp(float3(1, 1, 1), float3(0.1, 0.7, 1.0), t);
    // simple sky gradient
}
```

In the previous code, we return a simple sky gradient for simplicity, but that could also have been looked up from an environment cube map.

Proposed Geometry Organization (Whitted Ray Tracing)

Whitted tracing needs fast primary hits and then material lookups for direct lighting plus perfect specular reflection/refraction (no diffuse GI). A simple and efficient layout does the following:

Acceleration structures

- **TLAS**: One instance per object/mesh with its transform.
- **BLAS**: One per unique mesh. Build once; reuse via TLAS instances.

Buffers (global, shared across all meshes)

- VertexBuffer:

  ```
  struct Vertex
  {
      float3 pos;
      float3 nrm;
      float2 uv;
      float4 tan;
  }
  ```

    - If memory is tight: compress normals/tangents to 10:10:10:2 or snorm16.

- IndexBuffer: 16-bit where possible; 32-bit otherwise.
- MaterialBuffer: array of compact material records (base color factor/texture indices, metalness/roughness, IOR, flags).
- InstanceBuffer (optional): per-instance data (material table base, texture set base, offsets).
- **Textures**: bindless array(s); materials reference them by index.

Per-instance constants (root constants/SBT local)

- mVertexOffset, mIndexOffset (as in your snippet).
- materialBaseIndex or a geometryMaterialIndex for single-material submeshes.
- Optional: lightmap/light set IDs.

SBT (Shader Binding Table)

- Hit group record per (geometry, material-shader) pair. For Whitted, you can keep a single closest-hit and miss, passing material/offsets via local root params to avoid SBT bloat.

Closest-hit responsibilities (Whitted)

1. Fetch triangle indices and attributes (as shown).
2. Interpolate shading attrs (normal/uv/tangent; build TBN if needed).
3. Read material from MaterialBuffer (via geometryMaterialIndex).
4. **Direct lighting only**:
   - Loop over lights; for each, evaluate BRDF * N·L.
   - Cast **shadow rays** (any-hit) to test visibility.
5. **Specular**:
   - If reflective/refractive, spawn one reflection/transmission ray (optionally with recursion limit or attenuation).
6. Return radiance; no diffuse path bounces (i.e., no indirect GI).

The following code where the relevant geometry offsets are coming from, the ray tracing acceleration structure SceneTLAS and the structured buffers holding the vertex and index data for a given mesh/object:

```
// Local root (per instance / geometry) parameters
cbuffer GeometryOffsets : register(b0) {
    uint mVertexOffset;   // first vertex of this mesh in the global
                          Vertices buffer
    uint mIndexOffset;    // first index  of this mesh in the global
                          Indices  buffer
    uint geometryMaterialIndex;
};

// Attributes provided by the triangle hit
struct Attributes { float2 bary; };
```

```
// Vertex format (example)
struct Vertex {
    float3 pos;
    float3 nrm;
    float2 uv;
    // float4 tan; // optional
};

// SRVs (as you defined)
RaytracingAccelerationStructure SceneTLAS       : register(t0);
StructuredBuffer<Vertex>        Vertices        : register(t1, space0);
StructuredBuffer<uint>          Indices         : register(t2, space0);
```

Why This Layout Works Well for Whitted

This works because:

- Global buffers + per-instance offsets keep memory contiguous and cache-friendly.

- Minimal SBT permutations; materials are data-driven.

- Shadow rays and specular rays don't need extra attributes beyond those fetched once.

The accompanying code is well-commented and cross-referenced with the text, enabling readers to connect each concept to its implementation and context. Please note: the code is continually refactored, so specific implementations may shift slightly, but the overall structure remains consistent.

In summary, Whitted ray tracing was the first practical algorithm to unify reflection, refraction, and hard shadows in a single framework. While limited to mirror-like surfaces and point-light shadows, it set the foundation for modern ray tracing techniques. Today's path tracers extend these ideas with stochastic sampling for diffuse interreflection, soft shadows, and global illumination, but the Whitted model remains an essential stepping stone—both historically and pedagogically—for understanding how rays can simulate light transport in a physically intuitive way.

CHAPTER 9   DIRECTX 12 AND REAL-TIME RAY TRACING IN DXR

Summary

In this chapter, we covered the essential building blocks required to set up and use DirectX 12 with DirectX Raytracing (DXR). We began with the practical steps of configuring Visual Studio, initializing DirectX 12, and creating a rendering window and swap chain. From there, we examined the new structures and shader stages introduced by DXR and looked closely at the API initialization sequence needed to enable ray tracing features.

We also introduced the `RaySampleFramework`, a lightweight but extensible framework designed to abstract rendering logic from low-level API details. By studying its class diagram and implementation, we saw how the framework provides a clean separation between sample logic, the abstract renderer interface, and the concrete DirectX 12 backend. With this structure in place, we then demonstrated its use in practice by building a Whitted-style ray tracer, showing how rays can be dispatched and shaded in a modern DXR pipeline.

Taken together, this chapter gave you both the practical knowledge to initialize DX12 and DXR and the architectural insight to extend the framework for your own experiments.

In the next and final chapter, we will step outside of DirectX and explore path tracing in CUDA. This will allow us to compare different approaches to ray tracing, highlight the flexibility of GPU programming, and see how concepts carry across APIs.

Questions

Based on the knowledge that you gained in this chapter, it is your turn to answer some questions:

- What are the key steps required to set up a DirectX 12 project under Visual Studio 2022?
- Why is boilerplate initialization code important, and what does it typically include?
- What role does the swap chain play in a rendering application?
- How is triple buffering (or multiple back buffers) related to swap chain configuration?

CHAPTER 9 DIRECTX 12 AND REAL-TIME RAY TRACING IN DXR

- What are the main shader stages used in DirectX Raytracing (ray generation, hit groups, miss), and what is the responsibility of each?
- Why do we need acceleration structures (BLAS and TLAS), and how do they differ?
- Which subobjects must be created and combined to build a DXR pipeline state object (PSO)?
- What does the recursion depth parameter control, and why is it important for performance?
- Why does the framework define an abstract renderer interface (Ray_IHardwareRenderer)?
- How does Ray_Sample manage the rendering lifecycle, and why is this abstraction useful for supporting different backends (e.g., DX12, Vulkan)?
- What is the main difference between Whitted-style ray tracing and path tracing?
- How does the Whitted tracer in this chapter make use of the DXR pipeline?

Further Reading

The following are a few resources that you can use to expand the horizon of your knowledge on this chapter:

- https://docs.microsoft.com/en-us/windows/win32/direct3d12/directx-12-programming-guide
- https://www.scratchapixel.com/lessons/3d-basic-rendering/ray-tracing-overview/light-transport-ray-tracing-whitted.html

CHAPTER 10

Path Tracing: Global Illumination

Rendering light convincingly is half science, half art. After learning the foundations in earlier chapters, you're now ready to step into the deep end—where mathematics, probability, and GPU horsepower converge to produce images that flirt with photorealism. This chapter explores the modern toolkit for physically based global illumination, showing you how today's film and game engines trace, tame, and turbocharge light.

We begin with path tracing, the gold-standard Monte Carlo method that models every bounce of light to capture soft shadows, caustics, and subtle color bleeding. You'll learn how to extend a basic tracer with tone mapping and gamma correction, preserving delicate highlights while ensuring your final pixels look right on real displays. Next, we peel back the curtain on hybrid rendering pipelines—workflows that fuse blister-fast rasterization with targeted ray-tracing passes to balance quality and performance.

Because brute-force sampling is rarely practical, the chapter dives into Monte Carlo importance sampling and the art of choosing an effective probability-density function (PDF). You'll see how correct PDFs slash noise and converge images faster and how Russian-Roulette path termination keeps your estimator unbiased while cutting wasted rays. We close with a pragmatic look at performance tools and best practices, giving you profiling tactics and GPU hints that let ambitious ideas survive real-time budgets.

By the end of this chapter, you'll not only understand why these techniques matter but have the conceptual and practical know-how to weave them into your own renderer—pushing pixels that both look and run like a modern masterpiece.

The following topics will be covered in this chapter:

- Path tracing: global illumination
- Adding tone mapping and gamma correction to your ray tracer

- Hybrid rendering pipelines
- Adding Monte Carlo importance sampling to your path tracer
- Choosing the right PDF
- Russian roulette and unbiased rendering
- Performance tools and best practices

Technical Requirements

The following tools will be required before we get started:

- Visual Studio 2022 Community (Visual Studio 2015 is the minimum supported dev environment and includes the D3D12 graphics debugging tools)
- Windows 10 RS5 update
- Windows 10 SDK
- CUDA Toolkit 13.0.1

Minimum hardware requirements:

- GeForce GTX 1060

Path Tracing: Global Illumination

Path tracing is a Monte Carlo method for simulating global illumination in rendering, capturing both direct and indirect lighting by tracing the paths of many light rays as they interact with surfaces. Unlike direct illumination models, path tracing can realistically simulate complex lighting phenomena like color bleeding, caustics, and soft shadows. Each ray may bounce multiple times, reflecting or refracting based on material properties, accumulating light energy until it reaches a light source or terminates. Although computationally expensive, path tracing forms the foundation of photorealistic rendering and is used in modern offline renderers and real-time engines (e.g. Unreal Engine 5).

In this chapter, we will use snippet from our CUDA Path Tracer to better support the introduction of the various subjects.

CHAPTER 10   PATH TRACING: GLOBAL ILLUMINATION

Let's take a look at the following code snippet for a C-Like implementation for the main loop of a path tracer:

```
//----------------------------------------------------------------------
// render()  -- high-level driver
//----------------------------------------------------------------------
void render(Image* img, int W, int H, int SPP, int MaxBounces)
{
    for (int y = 0; y < H; ++y)                      // image rows
    {
        for (int x = 0; x < W; ++x)                  // image columns
        {
            Vec3 pixelColor = {0,0,0};

            // ----- multiple stochastic samples per pixel -----
            for (int s = 0; s < SPP; ++s)
            {
                Ray   ray  = GeneratePrimaryRay(x, y); // jitter inside pixel
                Vec3 throughput = {1,1,1};             // path weight
                Vec3 radiance   = {0,0,0};

                // ----- walk one light path -----
                for (int bounc = 0; bounc < MaxBounces; ++bounc)
                {
                    Hit hit = IntersectScene(ray);

                    // miss → environment light
                    if (!hit.hit)
                    {
                        radiance += throughput * SkyColor(ray.dir);
                        break;
                    }

                    // direct emission from the hit surface (if any)
                    radiance += throughput * Emission(hit);

                    // sample the material's BRDF
```

```
            Vec3  wi;         // new direction
            float pdf;        // probability of the sample
            Vec3  f = SampleBRDF(hit, -ray.dir, &wi, &pdf);

            if (pdf == 0.0f || IsBlack(f))
                break;        // path ends if no contribution

            // update path weight:  f · cosθ / pdf
            throughput *= f * AbsDot(hit.normal, wi) / pdf;

            // Russian-roulette termination (after a few bounces)
            if (bounc >= 3)
            {
                float p = MaxComponent(throughput);
                if (Random() > p) break;
                throughput /= p;              // keep unbiased
            }

            // spawn next ray
            ray.origin = hit.pos + EPS * wi;   // offset to avoid
            self-hit
            ray.dir    = wi;
        } // end single path
        pixelColor += radiance;
    } // end samples

    // average samples and write to frame-buffer
    img->set(x, y, pixelColor / float(SPP));
        }
    }
}
```

The previous code shows a basic path tracer, but it contains all the important pieces of information that we need to start understanding. We will dissect the previous code and describe the relevant parts to give you a high-level understanding. Then we will show how our CUDA path tracer will implement it.

The path tracing process starts by looping through the grid of pixels that represents the image plane. The pixel color is black at the beginning, because we will accumulate the radiance at that pixel during the tracing process:

```
for (int y = 0; y < H; ++y)                    // image rows
{
    for (int x = 0; x < W; ++x)                // image columns
    {
        Vec3 pixelColor = {0,0,0};
```

First, we'll start shooting primary rays. Primary rays are the ones that start from the camera and go straight into the scene. They will be responsible for the first hit.

This extracted code snippet shows where and when, in the path tracing function, we start shooting primary rays:

```
Ray ray = GeneratePrimaryRay(x, y); // jitter inside pixel
```

As you can see, the previous function is placed inside the loop that takes care of looping through the samples of a given pixel. So, the first thing to keep in mind and, also the first step, is to decide how many samples for each pixel we want start with. The number of samples will help us in raising the quality of the rendered image. Once we decide how many samples per pixel to use, we apply jittering to each one. This prevents visible artifacts that could arise from purely regular sampling patterns. Instead of sampling pixels in a fixed grid, we perturb sample positions slightly so that the noise becomes stochastic (grain-like) rather than structured. This process, known as *stochastic sampling*, is fundamental to Monte Carlo path tracing. In practice, we may use pure random jittering or more advanced schemes such as stratified or low-discrepancy sequences to improve convergence. Refer to Chapter 8 for an in-depth explanation of the different sampling strategies.

We know that the light bounces in the environment. The number of bounces defines what we call the *light path*.

This process is shown in the following snippet:

```
// ----- walk one light path -----
for (int bounc = 0; bounc < MaxBounces; ++bounc)
{
    Hit hit = IntersectScene(ray);
```

```
            // miss → environment light
            if (!hit.hit)
            {
                radiance += throughput * SkyColor(ray.dir);
                break;
            }

            // direct emission from the hit surface (if any)
            radiance += throughput * Emission(hit);

            // sample the material's BRDF
            Vec3   wi;          // new direction
            float  pdf;         // probability of the sample
            Vec3   f = SampleBRDF(hit, -ray.dir, &wi, &pdf);

            if (pdf == 0.0f || IsBlack(f))
                break;          // path ends if no contribution

            // update path weight:   f · cosθ / pdf
            throughput *= f * AbsDot(hit.normal, wi) / pdf;

// Russian-roulette termination (after a few bounces)
            if (bounc >= 3)
            {
                float p = MaxComponent(throughput);
                if (Random() > p) break;
                throughput /= p;                // keep unbiased
            }

            // spawn next ray
            ray.origin = hit.pos + EPS * wi;    // offset to avoid self-hit
            ray.dir    = wi;
        } // end single path
```

We literally "walk" on the light path. Here is a breakdown of the relevant parts:

`Hit hit = IntersectScene(ray)`

CHAPTER 10   PATH TRACING: GLOBAL ILLUMINATION

We determine whether there is an intersection/hit of a given ray with the scene. If not, we sample the scene radiance (e.g., the sky color/procedural sky color function, an environment map) and terminate the path:

```
// miss → environment light
            if (!hit.hit)
            {
                radiance += throughput * SkyColor(ray.dir);
                break;
            }
```

If we have a hit, instead, we compute the material response of the object:

```
            // direct emission from the hit surface (if any)
            radiance += throughput * Emission(hit);

            // sample the material's BRDF
            Vec3  wi;       // new direction
            float pdf;      // probability of the sample
            Vec3  f = SampleBRDF(hit, -ray.dir, &wi, &pdf);

            if (pdf == 0.0f || IsBlack(f))
                break;      // path ends if no contribution

            // update path weight:  f · cosθ / pdf
            throughput *= f * AbsDot(hit.normal, wi) / pdf;
```

By looking at the previous snippet, we can highlight the following steps:

- Compute the emission of the object (is it an emissive object like for example a light or a very hot/warm object?). If the emission is zero, then the object does not belong to any of the previous categories. It's either a cold or an ambient temperature object.

- We sample the material BRDF. That will determine how the material will appear at our eyes. The BRDF encodes the surface's visual properties (diffuse, glossy, specular, etc.). By sampling it, we generate the next bounce direction(s) of the path.

- If we don't have any contribution, we end the path.

- Otherwise, we apply importance sampling: instead of sampling directions uniformly, we draw them according to a probability distribution (PDF) proportional to the BRDF (and cosine). When computing the contribution, we divide by this probability density to keep the estimator unbiased. This way, more samples are concentrated in the directions that matter most for the material's appearance, which greatly reduces variance. Refer to Chapter 8 for a detailed discussion of importance sampling.

The next step is to avoid infinite recursion/iterations. We can achieve this through the so-called Russian roulette. Basically, at each iteration, we randomly terminate the path with some probability *p*. We will discuss briefly Russian Roulette later in this chapter.

Then we will spawn the next ray:

- ***wi***: New ray direction coming from the BRDF sampling.

- ***EPS***: A huge number to ensure that the ray will travel far "enough" in the scene such that the ray can reach any object in the scene without being prematurely clipped.

- ***hit*.pos**: We will restart tracing from the hit point.

```
// spawn next ray
ray.origin = hit.pos + EPS * wi;// offset to avoid self-hit
ray.dir    = wi;
```

Finally, we compute the pixel's radiance estimate by averaging over all samples. This is done by summing the contributions from each sample path and dividing by the number of samples per pixel. The resulting color is then stored in the framebuffer, which accumulates the final image.

```
// average samples and write to frame-buffer
img->set(x, y, pixelColor / float(SPP));
```

CHAPTER 10   PATH TRACING: GLOBAL ILLUMINATION

Path Tracing in CUDA

In this section, we will go through the main parts of our CUDA path tracer. This path tracer implementation is meant to be not real time. It's an actual offline renderer.

The minor implementation details won't be discussed and can be found in the source code. Once you understand the main concepts, it's just a matter of re-connecting the dots.

Oftentimes, when it comes to details, this saying stands:

It's like a finger pointing to the moon: don't concentrate on the finger, or you will miss all that heavenly glory!

Or we could even think about the opposite:

The devil is in the details!

Both sayings have their own pros and cons. However, while all the implementation details matter when it comes to write a program, if we haven't understood the big picture, then you might lose yourself in the details and find the "devil." It's just a call to strike a balance between both visions.

So, having said that, let's start by analyzing the Path Tracer CUDA kernel:

```
//the keyword __global__ instructs the CUDA compiler that this function is
the entry point of our kernel
__global__ void RenderScene(Scene* scene,const u32 InScreenWidth,const u32
InScreenHeight, float* ColorBuffer)
{
    u32 x = blockIdx.x*blockDim.x + threadIdx.x;
    u32 y = blockIdx.y*blockDim.y + threadIdx.y;

    float Aspect = static_cast<float>(InScreenWidth) / static_
    cast<float>(InScreenHeight);
    //Create a camera
    Camera camera(make_float3(55, 52,300),30.f,Aspect,make_float3(50,20,1));

    // Final Radiance
    float3 HDRRadiance = make_float3(0,0,0);
    float3 FinalRadiance = make_float3(0,0,0);

    u32 Seed0 = x;
```

CHAPTER 10   PATH TRACING: GLOBAL ILLUMINATION

```
    u32 Seed1 = y;

    const float InvSPP = 1.0f / ((float)kSPP);

    float FocalLength = camera.GetFocalLength();
    float ApertureSize = camera.GetApertureSize();

#pragma unroll
    for (u32 i=0;i<kSPP; ++i)
    {
        // We distribute the samples/rays accross the pixel surface
        float cx = GetRandom(&Seed0, &Seed1);
        float cy = GetRandom(&Seed0, &Seed1);

        //Compute the world space ray direction
        float3 WSDir = normalize(camera.GetWorldSpaceRayDir(((float)x) +
        cx, ((float)y) + cy, InScreenWidth, InScreenHeight));

        //Construct a ray in world space that originates from the camera
        Ray WSRay(camera.GetCameraEye(), WSDir);

        // Create a ray with the origin shifted according to camera
        Aperture and Focal Length
        Ray DOFRay = GetDOFRay(WSRay, ApertureSize, FocalLength, &Seed0,
        &Seed1);

        // Trace a ray into the scene
        HDRRadiance += TraceRay(scene,DOFRay,&Seed0,&Seed1, camera.
        GetCameraEye());
    }

    HDRRadiance *= InvSPP;

    // Tone map and apply gamma correction (we use a simple reinhard
       tonemapping operator)
    float Exposure = 1.0f;
    FinalRadiance = TonemapAndApplyGamma(HDRRadiance*Exposure);
```

```
//We access the linear ColorBuffer storing each color component
separately (we could have a float3   color buffer for a more compact/
cleaner solution)
int offset = (x + (InScreenHeight - 1 - y)  * InScreenWidth) * 3;

//Store the results of your computations
ColorBuffer[offset] = FinalRadiance.x;
ColorBuffer[offset + 1] = FinalRadiance.y;
ColorBuffer[offset + 2] = FinalRadiance.z;
}
```

Let's analyze the previous function.

First, we compute the x,y coordinate of the pixel. This is possible because the CUDA programming environment will provide us with the necessary intrinsics (or system values if we want to look at them using the Microsoft HLSL shading language naming convention).

These intrinsics are represented by the following:

- blockIdx.x/blockIdx.y: The x,y coordinate of the block of threads

- blockDim.x/blockDim.y: The number of threads along x,y axis

- threadIdx.x/threadIdx.y: The x,y coordinate of the thread inside a block of threads

```
u32 x = blockIdx.x*blockDim.x + threadIdx.x;
u32 y = blockIdx.y*blockDim.y + threadIdx.y;
```

So, as you can see, the most important part here is represented by the fact that CUDA is executing a kernel for each pixel in parallel. This is a gigantic leap with respect to the naïve double C/C++ loop. Everything is executed in parallel by the GPU for us. This is absolutely wonderful and will allow us to generate images like Figure 10-1 (generated with our CUDA path tracer).

CHAPTER 10 PATH TRACING: GLOBAL ILLUMINATION

Figure 10-1. *The classic Cornel box rendered with our CUDA Path Tracer. The light source here is of type squared. Notice how the caustics and the overall illumination are affected by the shape of the light source*

CHAPTER 10   PATH TRACING: GLOBAL ILLUMINATION

See also Figure 10-2.

Figure 10-2. *Here we have an emissive sphere that acts like a light source. Notice how the lighting here is more diffuse with respect to the squared one*

Now we have the for loop that manages the number of samples/rays per pixel:

```
for (u32 i=0;i<kSPP; ++i)
{
    // We distribute the samples/rays accross the pixel surface
    float cx = GetRandom(&Seed0, &Seed1);
```

CHAPTER 10   PATH TRACING: GLOBAL ILLUMINATION

```
float cy = GetRandom(&Seed0, &Seed1);

//Compute the world space ray direction
float3 WSDir = normalize(camera.GetWorldSpaceRayDir(((float)x) + cx,
((float)y) + cy, InScreenWidth, InScreenHeight));

//Construct a ray in world space that originates from the camera
Ray WSRay(camera.GetCameraEye(), WSDir);

// Create a ray with the origin shifted according to camera Aperture
and Focal Length
Ray DOFRay = GetDOFRay(WSRay, ApertureSize, FocalLength, &Seed0,
&Seed1);

// Trace a ray into the scene
HDRRadiance += TraceRay(scene,DOFRay,&Seed0,&Seed1, camera.GetCameraEye());
}
```

As you can see, we apply stochastic sampling (jittering). In our path tracer snippet, the jittering process is more explicit and clearer.

In our case, we are using a purely pseudorandom sequence (not ideal as we discussed previously) but still giving decent results and quality when it comes to rendering accuracy. You can tell this by looking at Figure 10-1 and Figure 10-2.

Indeed, a picture is worth a thousand words!

Here is the relevant snippet:

```
// We distribute the samples/rays accross the pixel surface
float cx = GetRandom(&Seed0, &Seed1);
float cy = GetRandom(&Seed0, &Seed1);
```

Then we construct the world space direction of our ray applying jittering to it (see cx,cy computed earlier):

```
//Compute the world space ray direction
float3 WSDir = normalize(camera.GetWorldSpaceRayDir(((float)x) + cx,
((float)y) + cy, InScreenWidth, InScreenHeight));
```

We are ready to construct the ray and start the ray/path tracing process. The following snippet is doing exactly that:

```
//Construct a ray in world space that originates from the camera
Ray WSRay(camera.GetCameraEye(), WSDir);

// Create a ray with the origin shifted according to camera Aperture
and Focal Length
Ray DOFRay = GetDOFRay(WSRay, ApertureSize, FocalLength, &Seed0,
&Seed1);

// Trace a ray into the scene
HDRRadiance += TraceRay(scene,DOFRay,&Seed0,&Seed1, camera.GetCameraEye());
```

In the previous snippet, we are deliberately ignoring the depth of field (DOF) part. We discussed DOF in a previous chapter, so refer to that chapter for a detailed discussion and relevant code.

The *TraceRay()* function is at the heart of our path tracer. Here, we manage the total number of light bounces while evaluating the BRDF, applying the PDF to implement importance sampling and Russian Roulette to prevent virtually infinite light bounces. In this way, we obtain unbiased results while reducing the expected number of bounces. Russian roulette ensures efficiency without introducing bias, since surviving paths are properly weighted by the inverse of their survival probability.

```
__device__ float3 TraceRay(Scene* scene,const Ray& ray,u32* Seed0,u32*
Seed1,float3 CameraPos)
{
    // Final accumulated radiance
    float3 AccuColor = make_float3(0, 0, 0);

    // Color that is collected at each bounce
    // Incoming radiance
    float3 Li = make_float3(1.0f,1.0f,1.0f);

    Ray LocalRay = ray;

    // Let's start bounching our ray
    for (u32 bounce=0;bounce<BOUNCES;++bounce)
    {
        HitData OutHitData;
        if ( !scene->ClosestHit(LocalRay, OutHitData) )
        {
```

```cpp
        // if there is no intersection we return background color
        return make_float3(0.0f);
    }

    // get the object that was hit by its id
    auto Obj = scene->GetObjectById(OutHitData.mId);
    //return Obj.mColor + Obj.mEmissive;

    if (Obj.mEmissive.x > 0.0001 && Obj.mEmissive.y > 0.0001 && Obj.mEmissive.z > 0.0001)
    {
        AccuColor = Li * Obj.mEmissive;
        break;
    }

    // we have an intersection
    float3 HitPos = LocalRay.PositionAtT(OutHitData.t);
    float3 Normal = normalize(HitPos - Obj.mCenter);

    // Facing normal
    bool Entering = dot(Normal, LocalRay.mDirection) < 0.0f;
    float3 N = Entering ? Normal : -Normal;

    float3 ReflectedDir = make_float3(0.0f);
    float  cosTheta     = 0.0f;
    float  pdf          = 1.0f;
    float3 BRDF         = make_float3(1.0f);
    switch (Obj.mReflType)
    {
        case eRT_Diff:
        {
            //Ready to compute diffuse brdf
            float r1 = GetRandom(Seed0, Seed1);
            float r2 = GetRandom(Seed0, Seed1);

            float r = sqrt(r2);
            float theta = 2.0f * M_PI * r1;

            float x = r * cos(theta);
```

CHAPTER 10 PATH TRACING: GLOBAL ILLUMINATION

```
    float z = r * sin(theta);

    // Scattered dir across the hemisphere local space
    //float3 ScatteredDir = CosineSampleHemisphere(r1, r2);

    // we need to create a basis to rotate and orient our
       scattered dir
    float3 w = N;
    float3 u = normalize(cross(abs(N.x) > 0.1f ? make_float3(0,
    1, 0) : make_float3(1, 0, 0), N));
    float3 v = cross(w, u);
    ReflectedDir = normalize(u * x + w * sqrt(1 - r2) + v * z);

    // Diffuse BRDF
    BRDF = (Obj.mColor / M_PI);

    cosTheta = dot(ReflectedDir,N);

    pdf = (cosTheta / M_PI);

    LocalRay.mOrigin = HitPos + N * 0.05f;
}
break;
case eRT_Spec: //Perfect specular
{
    ReflectedDir = reflect(LocalRay.mDirection, N);

    cosTheta = dot(ReflectedDir, N);

    // Specular BRDF
    BRDF = (Obj.mColor / cosTheta);

    // Pdf
    pdf = 1.0f;

    LocalRay.mOrigin = HitPos + N * 0.05f;
}
break;
default: //Refraction
{
```

```
                float p = GetRandom(Seed0, Seed1);

                ReflectedDir = Refract(LocalRay.mDirection,N,1.517f,p);

                cosTheta = dot(ReflectedDir, N);

                // Specular BRDF
                BRDF = (Obj.mColor   / cosTheta);

                // Pdf
                pdf = 1.f;

                auto NRefr = Entering ? -Normal : Normal;
                LocalRay.mOrigin = HitPos + NRefr * 0.05f;
            }
            break;
    };

    // Construct the new ray ready for the next bounch
    LocalRay.mDirection = ReflectedDir;

    // Accumulate any emissive contribution (typically coming from a
    light source)
    AccuColor = Li * Obj.mEmissive;

    // pick the reflectivity of the object at each bounch
    Li = Li * BRDF * cosTheta / pdf;

    //Russian Roulette
    if (bounce > 5)
    {
        float p = max(max(Li.x,Li.y),Li.z);
        if (GetRandom(Seed0, Seed1) > p)
        {
            break;
        }
        Li = Li * (1.f / (p + 0.0001f));
    }
}
```

```
    // Return the final hdr radiance
    return AccuColor;
}
```

Every part of this function is thoroughly commented, and you can refer to the source code provided with this book for a more detailed view of each implementation. I will not go into low-level details here, since we have already discussed the big picture in the previous section. If you've understood the earlier concepts, you'll be able to reconnect the dots as you read. In fact, reading the code itself is an excellent exercise: it helps you get used to the implementation by moving back and forth between the book and the source.

However, I will briefly refer to relevant parts of this function in the following paragraphs to keep the learning process streamlined.

Should you encounter any errors, bugs, or improvements, feel free to reach out to me.

Add Tone Mapping and Gamma Correction to Your Ray Tracer

Raw radiance values from path tracing can exceed the displayable range and lack perceptual linearity. Tone mapping compresses this high dynamic range (HDR) to low dynamic range (LDR) to display images properly on standard monitors. Common tone mapping operators include Reinhard, filmic, and ACES, each offering trade-offs in dynamic range compression and color fidelity. Gamma correction is also essential—linear RGB must be converted to a gamma-encoded space (typically sRGB) for accurate display. Without this step, images appear overly dark or washed out. Together, tone mapping and gamma correction ensure rendered images look both realistic and visually consistent across devices.

> *We will not go too much in detail on tone mapping theory because it goes beyond the scope of this book. There are many different tone mapping operators out there, and entire books have been written on the subject.*

CHAPTER 10   PATH TRACING: GLOBAL ILLUMINATION

Take a look at the straight C-like implementation of tone mapping in the following code snippet:

```
// Simple Reinhard global tone-mapper
Vec3 ToneMapReinhard(Vec3 c) {
    return c / (1.0f + c);
}

// Standard γ-correction (e.g. γ = 2.2 for sRGB)
Vec3 GammaCorrect(Vec3 c, float gamma) {
    float inv = 1.0f / gamma;
    return { powf(c.x, inv), powf(c.y, inv), powf(c.z, inv) };
}

// ----- inside the pixel write-out step -----
Vec3 mapped     = ToneMapReinhard(pixelColor / float(SPP));
// average + tone map
Vec3 finalColor = GammaCorrect(mapped, 2.2f);
// convert to display space
img->set(x, y, finalColor);
```

A comparable implementation can be found in our CUDA path tracer, included with the book's source code. The core computations remain unchanged, and the differences are limited to minor implementation details (primarily syntactic sugar).

As you can see, the functions in the previous code snippet make it all clear. From top to bottom:

- The tone mapper function (in this case we've chosen Reinhard tone mapping operator)
- The gamma correction function (to account for the gamma of the monitor)
- Apply them to the color in order to map it from HDR to LDR and correct it with the gamma

We use tone mapping because real-world lighting spans 10 to 12 orders of magnitude, while monitors, projectors, and print can reproduce only about two to three. Without a mapping step, the brightest parts of a physically based render would clip to white, and the darkest would collapse to black, erasing detail and destroying the scene's intended mood. Tone mapping does the following:

- **Compresses HDR into displayable range:** It preserves highlights and shadow detail instead of hard-clipping.

- **Mimics human perception:** Our eyes adapt locally; good operators roll off highlights and boost mids to match that response.

- **Provides artistic control:** Exposure keys, shoulder strength, and contrast curves let you steer the final "look."

- **Prepares the image for subsequent transforms:** Gamma-correction, color-grading, and compression all assume an LDR signal.

- **Ensures cross-device consistency:** The same mapped image will reproduce predictably on SDR monitors, VR headsets, and print.

In short, tone mapping bridges the physics of global-illumination output and the limitations of real-world displays, letting viewers see the richness your renderer actually computes.

When we talk about tone mapping, we just refer to the process of mapping the High Dynamic Range (HDR) input radiance (scene color) to Low Dynamic Range (LDR) output radiance.

These are only just a few of the tone mapping operators we know:

- **Reinhard 2002 (Simple):** Also, the one we will use in our path tracer. Refer to Figure 10-3.

- **Reinhard 2005.** Photographic, "key" and "white" parameters.

- **Hable/Uncharted 2**. A filmic tone mapper designed to mimic cinema stock; soft shoulder, gentle toe. Good color reproduction when paired with sRGB.

We will employ Reinhard 2002. Figure 10-3 shows Reinhard tone mapping curve.

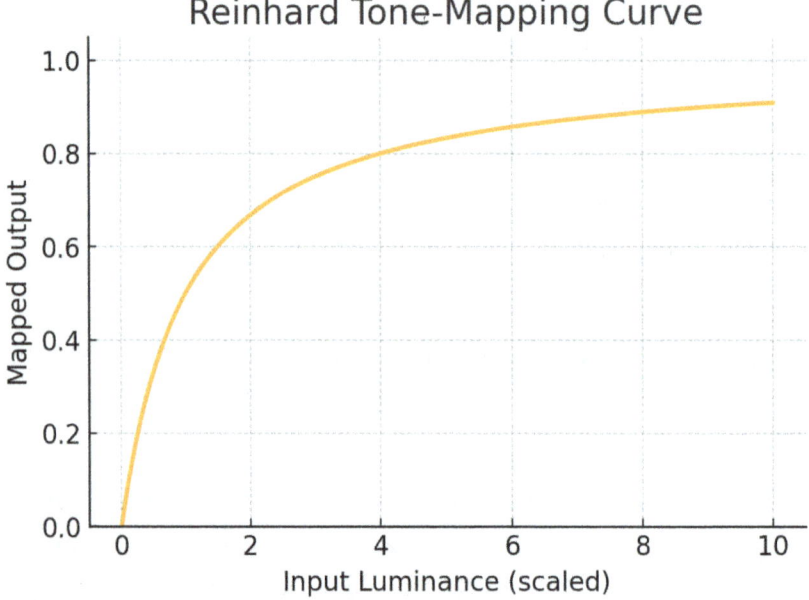

Figure 10-3. This is the Reinhard Tone Mapping curve. As you can see, the higher dynamic range luminance (on the x-axis) is mapped into [0,1] lower dynamic range one to fit the displayable range

Tone-mapping operators are the practical mathematical functions that perform the compression from HDR to displayable LDR range. They decide how to:

- **Scale exposure:** *Choose a scene-wide or local brightness anchor.*

- **Compress highlights:** *Apply a curve (e.g., Reinhard, Filmic, ACES) that rolls off bright values smoothly instead of clipping.*

- **Preserve midtones and contrast:** *Keep important details and color relationships readable.*

- **Prepare the signal for output.** *Leave the image in an LDR space ready for gamma correction or further creative grading.*

In short, once you recognize the need to map HDR to LDR, a tone-mapping operator is the mathematical recipe that shapes that mapping, balancing physical accuracy with aesthetic intent.

Hybrid Rendering Pipelines

Hybrid rendering combines rasterization and ray tracing to balance performance and realism. While rasterization excels at speed and is widely supported on hardware, it struggles with complex light interactions like reflections and global illumination. Ray tracing handles these well but is slower. Hybrid pipelines might use rasterization for primary visibility and basic shading and uses ray tracing for effects like shadows, ambient occlusion, or reflections. Real-time engines like Unreal Engine and Unity increasingly adopt hybrid approaches, leveraging hardware acceleration (e.g., DXR or Vulkan RT) to achieve high-fidelity visuals without sacrificing frame rate.

Figure 10-4 shows a chart of a typical hybrid rendering pipeline breakdown.

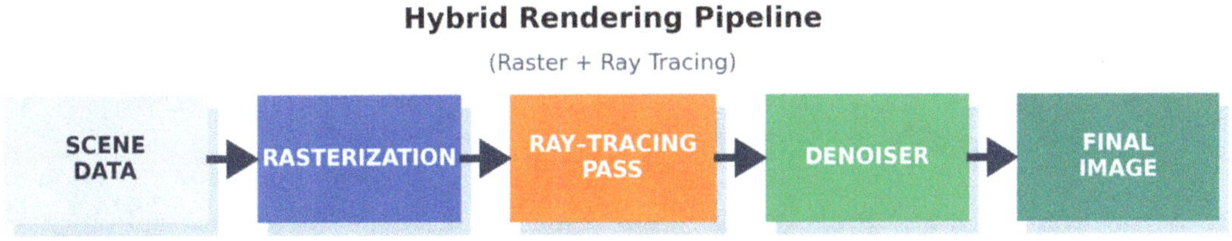

Figure 10-4. Hybrid rendering pipeline chart showing the main stages of a modern future-proof rendering engine

The ray tracing pass (i.e., the orange box in Figure 10-4) can be implemented using hardware-accelerated ray tracing (HWRT) via APIs such as DirectX Raytracing (DXR) or Vulkan RT, as we have already discussed. However, many 3D engines—most notably Unreal Engine 5—also implement custom *software-based* solutions to handle global illumination more efficiently. For example, Unreal Engine 5 introduces Lumen, a system that primarily relies on software techniques but can also leverage hardware ray tracing in a hybrid fashion to improve accuracy or performance in specific cases.

This approach is generally more portable than relying exclusively on HWRT, since it can scale across a wider variety of systems, including those without dedicated ray tracing hardware.

> *The rationale is historical as well: when HWRT-capable GPUs first reached the market, the computational power available was not yet sufficient to support full real-time path tracing. Hybrid or software-driven GI solutions offered a practical bridge, combining partial HWRT acceleration with optimized software techniques to deliver real-time results.*

Adding Monte Carlo Importance Sampling to Your Path Tracer

Monte Carlo integration is central to path tracing, but naive uniform sampling can result in noisy renders due to high variance. Importance sampling improves convergence by biasing samples toward directions or areas that contribute to more light. For instance, sampling the Bidirectional Reflectance Distribution Function (BRDF) directly, or focusing more samples toward light sources, increases efficiency. When done properly, importance sampling reduces noise significantly for the same number of samples per pixel. Implementing multiple importance sampling (MIS) further combines strategies (e.g., BRDF and light sampling) with a weighting scheme to balance their strengths.

The relevant code snippet that account for this is shown here:

```
// pick the reflectivity of the object at each bounch
      Li = Li * BRDF * cosTheta / pdf;
```

As you can see, we multiply by the cosine term and divide by the sampling PDF, yielding $f \cos \theta / pdf$. Using a cosine-weighted PDF concentrates samples in the most important directions while keeping the estimator unbiased.

> *The importance sampling is exactly in the cosine-weighted sampling of the diffuse branch and in the * cosTheta/pdf weighting of the throughput.*

Choosing the Right PDF

The effectiveness of importance sampling depends on using an appropriate PDF. In rendering, the PDF determines how likely a ray is to be sampled in a given direction. Matching the PDF to the shape of the BRDF or light distribution is key to reducing variance. For instance, glossy materials benefit from PDFs that concentrate rays around the specular lobe, while diffuse surfaces may perform well with cosine-weighted sampling. Inaccurate PDFs lead to poor sampling efficiency and visible noise. When combining sampling strategies, such as in Multiple Importance Sampling (MIS), accurate PDFs for each method must be maintained and evaluated consistently to preserve unbiased rendering. In practice, one chooses the PDF that best approximates the BRDF–cosine product: cosine-weighted sampling for diffuse surfaces, lobe-shaped PDFs for glossy surfaces, delta directions for perfect specular, and light-proportional sampling for direct illumination. MIS then blends these strategies to achieve robust results across all cases.

The PDF should ideally be proportional to the integrand you're trying to estimate. In rendering, that integrand is:

$$f(\omega_i, \omega_o) L_i(\omega_o) \cos \theta$$

where:

- f = BRDF
- L_i = Incoming radiance
- $cos\theta$ = Geometry term

Since we usually don't know L_i in advance, we approximate by matching the BRDF shape or light distribution:

1. **Diffuse surfaces**
   - The integrand contains $cos\theta$.
   - A cosine-weighted hemisphere PDF matches this well.

2. **Glossy surfaces**
   - Energy is concentrated around the mirror direction.
   - Use a Phong lobe or GGX distribution (matching the BRDF's highlight shape).

3. **Specular/mirror/refraction**
   - These are delta functions.
   - PDF is treated as 1 for the chosen deterministic direction.

4. **Direct lighting**
   - When sampling light sources, use a PDF proportional to light area/intensity so bright/small lights are more likely to be hit.

5. **MIS combination**
   - Use both BRDF sampling and light sampling, and combine with MIS weighting (balance or power heuristic).

Russian Roulette and Unbiased Rendering

To keep rendering unbiased but reduce the computational load of infinite bounces, Russian roulette is used as a probabilistic termination strategy. After a few bounces, each ray has a chance to be terminated based on a survival probability—typically proportional to its energy contribution. When a ray survives, its weight is adjusted (divided by the survival probability) to maintain an unbiased estimate. This technique helps manage performance while avoiding artifacts from hard cutoff thresholds, ensuring that brighter paths are more likely to continue while dimmer, less significant ones are terminated early.

Russian roulette:

- **Goal:** Prevent infinite recursion (paths bouncing forever) while *keeping the estimator unbiased.*

- **How:**
    - At each bounce, you randomly terminate the path with some probability *p*.
    - If the path survives, you scale the contribution by *1 /p*.
    - This preserves the expectation but shortens average path length.

- **Effect:** It reduces wasted computation from very long, low-energy paths.

Performance Tools and Best Practices

Efficient path tracing is not only about mathematical correctness but also about making the implementation scalable on modern hardware. Profiling is the first step: tools like NVIDIA NSight Compute, NSight Systems, or even CUDA's built-in profiling APIs allow developers to pinpoint performance bottlenecks. Intel VTune is useful on CPU, but for CUDA code, Nsight provides deeper insights into warp execution, memory throughput, and kernel occupancy. Within an engine, built-in profilers help tie GPU timings back to rendering features, making it easier to understand which parts of the path tracer consume the most frame time.

The following are key CUDA-focused best practices:

- **Acceleration structures**: A well-built BVH is essential. On GPUs, *wide BVHs* (e.g., BVH4, BVH8) can increase SIMD efficiency by testing multiple child nodes in parallel. CUDA kernels should minimize recursion (since it's expensive) and prefer iterative BVH traversal with explicit stacks.

- **Parallelism and occupancy**: Each ray path is naturally parallelizable, but efficient CUDA code requires good warp utilization. Avoid divergent branches within a warp (e.g., handling diffuse, glossy, and refractive cases in a single kernel may reduce efficiency). Profile warp divergence with Nsight and consider separating kernels or restructuring code when divergence dominates.

- **Memory bandwidth and cache coherency**: Align data structures to 32- or 64-byte boundaries for coalesced memory access. Store rays, hits, and materials in structure-of-arrays (SoA) layout rather than array-of-structures (AoS), since this better matches GPU memory access patterns. Keep frequently used data (e.g., BRDF parameters) in shared memory or registers if possible.

- **Adaptive sampling**: On CUDA, adaptive sampling can be implemented with per-pixel counters stored in global memory. To avoid contention, use atomic operations sparingly and favor persistent thread blocks that work until all pixels converge below a noise threshold.

- **Denoising**: AI-based denoisers like OptiX Denoiser integrate directly with CUDA workloads and can dramatically reduce required samples per pixel (spp). Classical wavelet-based denoisers are also viable but less hardware-accelerated. Always profile the denoiser too, as in some cases it may dominate GPU time if the render kernel is highly optimized.

- **Kernel fusion vs. modularity**: Fewer, larger kernels reduce memory traffic between stages but can increase register pressure. Nsight helps you find the sweet spot by showing occupancy and register usage.

- **Asynchronous execution**: Overlap ray generation, shading, and denoising with CUDA streams to hide memory transfer costs and fully exploit the GPU's compute pipelines.

Summary

In Chapter 10 we reinforced the book's logical arc from theory to implementation by showing how each modern rendering technique slots into a working engine—and by walking you through our compact CUDA path tracer, which serves as a concrete, line-by-line example of how a minimalist global-illumination core is wired together on today's GPUs. You first extended that CUDA tracer to calculate full global illumination, witnessing how every bounce deepens realism. You then compressed the resulting HDR radiance into display-ready color with tone-mapping curves and gamma correction, completing the HDR-to-LDR pipeline introduced earlier. Building on your rasterization skills, we integrated hybrid pipelines that interleave raster passes with targeted ray-tracing calls, exactly as our CUDA sample hands off data between compute kernels. To reduce noise without wasting time, you added Monte-Carlo importance sampling and learned to pick probability-density functions tailored to each BRDF or light, all demonstrated inside the same codebase. Russian-roulette termination rounded out your statistical toolkit, keeping estimates unbiased while trimming kernel runtimes. Finally, you profiled the CUDA tracer with GPU timers and cache-friendly layouts, turning abstract best practices into measurable speed-ups. Together these sections remind you not only *what* you learned—global illumination, tone mapping, hybrid workflows, variance reduction, and performance hygiene—but *how* each idea manifests in a fully functioning CUDA renderer.

Questions

Based on the knowledge that you gained in this chapter, it is your turn to answer some questions:

- How would you go if you wanted to change the code to use another tone mapping operator?
- What are the advantages in implementing a path tracer in CUDA?

- How would you speed up the ray tracing process?
- What's the meaning of unbiased rendering?
- Try to integrate a better sampling strategy in the provided CUDA path tracer.
- Try to implement BVH in the provided path tracer to speed up intersection tests.
- Try adding mesh rendering not just analytical shapes like spheres, for example.

Further Reading

The following are a few links that you can use to expand the horizon of your knowledge on this chapter:

- "High Dynamic Range Imaging: Acquisition, Display, and Image-Based Lighting" (May 2010 edition)
- "Physically Based Rendering, fourth edition: From Theory to Implementation" (March 2023 edition)

Index

A

AAA games, 26
Abstract renderer, 312, 316, 317
Acceleration structures, 357
Accuracy, 182–185
Ada lovelace architecture, 24
Adaptive sampling, 357
Adaptive supersampling, 97–101
Albedo, 199
Aliasing
    sampling strategy, 88, 89
    supersampling, 89–94
Allocation strategy, 273–275
ALU, *see* Arithmetic logic unit (ALU)
Analytic solution, 151–156
Any-hit shaders, 32, 33, 117, 118, 294, 319
AoS, *see* Array-of-structures (AoS)
Aperture, 128
Aperture size, 103
Arbitrary image dimensions, 46
Arithmetic logic unit (ALU), 6
Array-of-structures (AoS), 357
Asynchronous execution, 358

B

Barycentric coordinates, 169–177
Basic lighting
    definition, 128–131
    illumination equation, 130
    rendering equation, 131
    school pixel shader, 133
    specular contributions, 131
    specular reflection, 133–136
Bidirectional reflectance distribution function (BRDF), 54, 131, 196, 198, 354
Bidirectional scattering distribution function (BSDF), 197, 238
Big picture, 26
Blackwell architecture, 25
BLAS, *see* Bottom-level acceleration structure (BLAS)
Blinn-Phong model, 4
blockDim, 18
blockIdx, 18
Boilerplate initialization code
    DX12 verbosity, 248
    Microsoft DX12 documentation, 248
    pipeline, 249–258
Bottom-level acceleration structure (BLAS), 53, 75, 80–84, 290
Bounding volume hierarchy (BVH), 76
    ray–triangle, 84
    traversal, 79
    tree data, 78
    tree structure, 85
BRDF, *see* Bidirectional reflectance distribution function (BRDF)
BSDF, *see* Bidirectional scattering distribution function (BSDF)
BVH, *see* Bounding volume hierarchy (BVH)

INDEX

C

Camera frustum, 126
Camera model, 56–59
    math symbols, 124
    pin-hole, 126
    ray tracing (RT), 125–129
CB, *see* Constant buffer (CB)
CBV, *see* Constant buffer view (CBV)
C-Cache, *see* Constants cache (C-Cache)
CDF, *see* Cumulative distribution function (CDF)
Central processing unit (CPU), 2, 7, 10
    analogy, 9
    CPU-GPU synchronization, 282–288
    vs. graphics processing unit (GPU), 8–12
    host, 43
Chemical emulsion, 125
Chronological order, 42
C++ interface, 186–188
C++ library, 222
C-Like implementation, 333
C-like pseudocode, 164, 165
C-like struct, 98
Closest-hit shader, 32, 34, 294, 296, 305, 306
Code block, 105
Code snippets, 53, 54, 102, 106, 253
Color buffer, 16, 17
Command allocator, 266
Command queue creation, 257
Committed resources, 272
Compute units (CUDA) cores, 37, 39, 48, 66, 120
    code snippet, 44, 90
    directX ray tracing (DXR), 73
    hardware, 73
    implementation, 28, 53
    kernel implementation, 55
    program, 55
    ray casting, 64–67
    version, 93
Concrete renderer, 312–314
Conditional branch divergence, 20, 22
Confidential computing support, 25
Constant buffer (CB), 274
Constant buffer view (CBV), 82, 263, 264
Constants cache (C-Cache), 47, 48
Containment test, 164, 165
C preprocessor block, 250
CPU, *see* Central processing unit (CPU)
CreateCommandList, 268
CreateDXGIFactory2, 252
CreateRootSignatures(), 280
CUDA, *see* Compute units (CUDA) cores
Cumulative distribution function (CDF), 224
Cutting-edge technology, 75

D, E

Data cache, 78
Data structure descriptor, 289–294
D3D12, *see* Direct3D 12 (D3D12)
D3DCompileFromFile function, 295
Degree of parallelization, 22
Denoising, 357
Depth of field (DOF), 103–109
Depth stencil view (DSV), 263, 270, 271
Descriptors, 268–272
DirectCompute, 101
Direct3D 12 (D3D12), 241–243, 250
    function, 268
    GPU resources allocation, 272–274
    programming, 247
    vertex, 293

Direct radiance, 195
Direct specular reflection, 134
DirectX 12 (DX12)
    boilerplate initialization code, 247–249
    descriptors management, 268–272
    frame resources creation, 262–268
    setup under Visual Studio 2022, 242–247
    swap-chain creation, 258–262
    technical requirements, 242
DirectX Graphics Infrastructure (DXGI), 250–252
DirectX ray tracing (DXR), 53, 67–70, 241, 353
    API, 79
    API initialization code, 297
    code, 6, 16, 75
    multi-hit ray tracing, 115–120
    new shader stages, 293–297
    ray tracing (RT), 319–324
    shader stages, 288–293
    structures, 288–293
    supersampling, 95–98
Dispatch unit, 41
DOF, *see* Depth of field (DOF)
DOFRay, 94
DSV, *see* Depth stencil view (DSV)
DXGI, *see* DirectX Graphics Infrastructure (DXGI)
DXGIAdapter4, 254
DXR, *see* DirectX ray tracing (DXR)

F

Fermi architecture, 7
Fermi Streaming multiprocessors (SMs), 40
Fixed-point numbers, 182

Floating-point precision, 182–185
Focal length, 103
Focal plane distance, 128
Frame resources creation, 262–268
Fresnel law, 137–139

G

Gamma correction, 349–352
GeForce 256 GPU, 3, 4
Geometric solution, 155–159
Geometry shader, 6
GetDOFRay, 106–108
GetShaderIdentifier(), 305
GI, *see* Global illumination (GI)
GitHub code repository, 127, 128
Global illumination (GI), 191
Global root signatures, 277
Glossy BRDF, 198, 200
Glossy specular surfaces, 136
GPU, *see* Graphics processing unit (GPU)
GradientInterp, 93
Graphics processing unit (GPU), 67, 72, 247, 257, 262
    anatomy of, 13–21
    and central processing unit (CPU), 8–12
    CPU-GPU synchronization, 282–288
    CUDA core, 8, 9
    with descriptors, 264
    evolution 101, 3–8
    memory, 262
    resource, 268
    resources allocation strategies, 272–274
    streaming multiprocessors (SMs), 38
    technical requirements, 2
    turing, 76–78
Grid of pixels, 13–15

INDEX

H

Hardware-accelerated ray tracing (HWRT), 353
Hardware execution, 20–22
HDR, *see* High dynamic range (HDR)
Helmholtz reciprocity, 197
High dynamic range (HDR), 349, 351
Hit-count buffer, 119
HitData object, 63
Hit-group shader table, 306–308
Hit-or-miss Monte Carlo (MC) integration, 203–208
Hit-record, 115, 117
Hit-record buffer, 119
Hopper architecture, 24, 25
HWRT, *see* Hardware-accelerated ray tracing (HWRT)
Hybrid rendering pipelines, 353, 354

I

IBV, *see* Index buffer view (IBV)
I-Cache, *see* Instruction cache (I-Cache)
Image plane, 126
Importance sampling, 218, 220–224
Incoming-reflected radiance, 230
Index buffer view (IBV), 264, 271
Index of refraction (IOR), 124, 137–139
Indirect radiance, 195
Instruction cache (I-Cache), 48
Instruction execution, 8
Intel VTune, 356
Intersection shader, 31, 33, 294, 300
Inverse transform sampling, 218, 219
IOR, *see* Index of refraction (IOR)

J

Jittered sampling, 231

K

KD-Tree, 67
kEpsilon, 184
Kernel, 16–20
    fusion, 357
    hardware execution, 20–22

L

Lightmass, 195
Light path, 335–338
Light propagation, 191
Linear combination, 177
Linear memory access patterns, 15
Local root signatures, 277
Low dynamic range (LDR), 349, 351

M

MacOS/iOS development, 6
Math symbols, 124
Memories, 11, 12
Memory bandwidth, 357
Memory hierarchy, 44–46
Memory sharing, 9
Mental model, 32
Microsoft documentation, 248
MIS, *see* Multiple importance sampling (MIS)
Miss shader, 32, 33, 53, 72, 294, 296, 297, 300, 319
Möller-Trumbore algorithm, 177–182

INDEX

Monte Carlo (MC) integration, 191, 201
    hit-or-miss, 203–208
    sample mean approach, 208–218
Motion blur, 110–115
MSAA, *see* Multisample antialiasing (MSAA)
Multi-hit ray tracing, 115–120
Multiple importance sampling (MIS), 354, 355
Multisample antialiasing (MSAA), 261

N

New shader stages, 293–297
NVIDIA architectures, 83
NVLink Switch System, 9, 25, 42

O

Octrees, 67
On-chip memory, 42

P

Parallelism, 357
Parametric-mathematical form, 128
Pascal architecture, 22
Path tracing
    code snippet, 333–339
    CUDA, 339–349
    Monte Carlo integration, 354
    Monte Carlo method, 332
    performance tools, 356–358
PDF, *see* Probability-density function (PDF); Probability distribution function (PDF)
Perfect mirror reflection, 135
Photorealism, 331
pInfoQueue object, 257

Pin-hole camera model, 125, 126
Pipeline state object (PSO), 297–301
Placed resources, 272
Primary rays, 54
Probability-density function (PDF), 331, 355, 358
Probability distribution function (PDF), 216, 220, 221
Proposed geometry organization, 325–328
Pseudocode, 98, 100
Pseudorandom sequence, 344
PSO, *see* Pipeline state object (PSO)
PushStorageFilter, 257
Pythagorean theorem, 158

Q

QMC, *see* Quasi-Monte Carlo (QMC)
Quasi-Monte Carlo (QMC), 191, 233–237

R

Raster-based techniques, 29
Rasterization, 2, 28, 115
Ray casting, 64–67
RayCastingShader, 95
RayDesc, 95
Ray generation shader, 31, 32, 294
Ray payload, 300
Ray-plane intersection, 159–161
Ray-primitive intersection techniques
    analytic solution, 150–156
    barycentric coordinates, 169–177
    containment test, 164, 165
    geometric solution, 155–159
    ray-quad, 161–164
    ray-triangle intersection, 165–169
Ray-quad intersection, 161–164

INDEX

Ray_Sample, 312
RaySampleFramework, 243
    abstract renderer, 312, 316, 317
    backend, 315, 316
    building blocks, 308
    class diagram, 310
    concrete renderer, 312–314
    diagram description, 310–312
    DirectX 12 implementation, 308
    Win32 driver, 314, 315
RaySampleFrameworkHelloWorld, 246
Ray-sphere intersection, 60–64
Ray tracing (RT), 1, 18
    basic lighting, 128–130
    camera model, 125–129
    compute-based *vs.* directX ray tracing (DXR), 72, 73
    in computing, 54–56
    core, 78–80
    definition, 59, 60
    depth of field (DOF), 103–109
    directX ray tracing (DXR), 319–324
    in hardware, 6, 22
    motion blur, 110–115
    pipeline, 30–34
    pipeline state object (PSO), 297–301
    primary rays, 54
    real-time core, 26–28
    sampling strategies, 88, 89
    stochastic, 101–103
    technical requirements, 88
    terminology, 124
    whitted-style ray tracing, 317–319
Ray tracing pipeline state object (RTPSO), 297
Ray-triangle intersection, 165–169
Real-time graphics, 83

Real-time ray tracing, 28–30, 76
Refraction, 137–139
Rendering equations, 131
    bidirectional reflectance distribution function (BRDF) types, 198–201
    estimation, 228
    expression, 196, 197
    illumination equation, 194, 195
    red box, 195
    reflected radiance, 193
    solution, 201–203
    stratified sampling, 230–232
    technical requirements, 192
    unit hemisphere, 194
    variance, 219, 220
Render target view (RTV), 263–265, 271
Reserved resources, 272
Resource memory management, 266
Root arguments, 275
Root signatures, 263, 266
    coding, 280–283
    DX12 types, 275
    DXR, 277
    parameters, 275
Rotational symmetry, 197
RT, *see* Ray tracing (RT)
RTPSO, *see* Ray tracing pipeline state object (RTPSO)
RTV, *see* Render target view (RTV)
Russian Roulette, 356

S

Sample mean approach, 208–218
SBT, *see* Shader binding table (SBT)
Scene depth perception, 108
Screen space reflections (SSR), 29
SER, *see* Shader execution reordering (SER)

Shader binding table (SBT), 80, 306–308
Shader execution reordering (SER), 24
Shader loading, 293–297
ShaderParameters.h, 282
Shader resource view (SRV), 263, 264, 270
Shader stages, 288–293
Shader table, 301–306
Shader table record, 81
Shadow mapping, 29
Shared memory, 41–47, 78
Shoot shadow rays, 54
SMs, *see* Streaming multiprocessors (SMs)
Snell's law, 140–144
SOV, *see* Stream output view (SOV)
Spatial aliasing, 88
Spatial data structure, 67
Specular BRDF, 199, 200
Specular Phong reflection, 123, 132, 135
Specular reflection, 123, 133–136
sphere class, 64
Sphere struct, 111
SRV, *see* Shader resource view (SRV)
SSR, *see* Screen space reflections (SSR)
Stochastic convergence, 210
Stochastic ray tracing, 101–103
Stochastic sampling, 335
Stratified sampling techniques, 191, 230–232
Streaming multiprocessors (SMs), 6, 8
    components, 38, 39
    configurability, 39
    Fermi, 39
    global device memory, 43
    graphics processing unit (GPU), 38
    memory hierarchy, 44–46
    multiprocessors, 43
    shared memory, 41–47
    technical requirements, 37
    Visual Studio, 38

Stream output view (SOV), 264, 270
Supersampling, 89–94
    adaptive, 97–101
    in directX ray tracing (DXR), 95–98
Swap-chain creation, 258–262

T

Temporal aliasing, 89
Tensor cores, 77
Tensor Memory Accelerator (TMA), 24
threaIdx, 17
3D engines, 133
3D models, 3
TIR, *see* Total internal reflection (TIR)
TLAS, *see* Top-level acceleration structures (TLAS)
TMA, *see* Tensor Memory Accelerator (TMA)
Tone mapping, 349–352
Top-level acceleration structures (TLAS), 53, 68, 72, 74, 80–83
Total internal reflection (TIR), 143–147
TraceRay, 96
TraceRay() function, 71, 72, 345
Transformation matrix, 293
Transformer engine, 24
Transforms and lighting (T&L), 3
Transmission direction, 141
Transparent objects, 115–120

U

UAV, *see* Unordered access view (UAV)
UE4, *see* Unreal Engine 4 (UE4)
Unordered access view (UAV), 82, 83, 97, 263, 264, 270, 271, 300
Unreal Engine 4 (UE4), 195

V

Variance reduction, 218
VBV, *see* Vertex Buffer view (VBV)
Vertex Buffer view (VBV), 264, 271
Visual Studio, 38
Visual Studio 2022 (VS2022), 242–247
Vulkan, 6

W, X, Y

WARP, *see* Windows Advanced Rasterization Platform (WARP)

Warps, 8
Warp scheduler, 38, 41
Wavefronts, 13
Whitted-style ray tracing, 317–319, 327
Windows Advanced Rasterization Platform (WARP), 252, 253
Win32 driver, 314, 315
Workload division, 9

Z

Z-buffer, 1

GPSR Compliance
The European Union's (EU) General Product Safety Regulation (GPSR) is a set of rules that requires consumer products to be safe and our obligations to ensure this.

If you have any concerns about our products, you can contact us on

ProductSafety@springernature.com

In case Publisher is established outside the EU, the EU authorized representative is:

Springer Nature Customer Service Center GmbH
Europaplatz 3
69115 Heidelberg, Germany

www.ingramcontent.com/pod-product-compliance
Lightning Source LLC
LaVergne TN
LVHW081346060526
838201LV00050B/1726